OLYMPIC CITIES: 2012
AND THE REMAKING OF LONDON

Olympic Cities: 2012 and the Remaking of London

Edited by

GAVIN POYNTER
University of East London, UK

and

IAIN MACRURY
University of East London, UK

ASHGATE

Published by
Ashgate Publishing Limited
Wey Court East
Union Road
Farnham
Surrey GU9 7PT
England

Ashgate Publishing Company
Suite 420
101 Cherry Street
Burlington, VT 05401-4405
USA

www.ashgate.com

British Library Cataloguing in Publication Data
Olympic cities : 2012 and the remaking of London. --
  (Design and the built environment series)
  1. Olympic host city selection--2012. 2. Olympic host city
  selection--History. 3. Olympics--Environmental aspects--
  England--London. 4. Olympics--Social aspects--England--
  London. 5. Urban renewal--England--London--Case studies.
  6. East End (London, England)--Economic policy. 7. East End
  (London, England)--Social policy.
  I. Series II. Poynter, Gavin, 1949- III. MacRury, Iain.
  796.4'8-dc22

Library of Congress Cataloging-in-Publication Data
Poynter, Gavin, 1949-
  Olympic cities: 2012 and the remaking of London / by Gavin Poynter and Iain MacRury.
       p. cm. -- (Design and the built environment)
  Includes bibliographical references and index.
  ISBN 978-0-7546-7100-8
  1. Olympic Games (30th : 2012 : London, England) 2. City planning--England--London. 3. Urban renewal--England--London. 4. Olympics--History--Case studies. 5. East End (London, England)--Buildings, structures, etc. 6. East End (London, England)--Environmental conditions. I. MacRury, Iain. II. Title.
  GV7222012 .P69 2009
  796.48--dc22

                                                                    2009008826
ISBN 978-0-7546-7100-8
Reprinted 2010

Mixed Sources
Product group from well-managed
forests and other controlled sources
www.fsc.org Cert no. SA-COC-1565
© 1996 Forest Stewardship Council

Printed and bound in Great Britain by
MPG Books Group, UK

Contents

PART 1: THE MODERN GAMES AND SOCIAL CHANGE

1   Sport, Spectacle and Society: Understanding the Olympics   3
     Michael Rustin
     The author examines the multi-faceted nature of the Olympic Games
     as an emergent type of 'globalised' institution, operating in both
     an international market-place, and an intergovernmental space of
     cooperation, competition, negotiations, and rules.

2   The Evolution of the Olympic and Paralympic Games
     1948–2012   23
     Gavin Poynter
     The author provides a framework for examining the motivations of the
     cities that have recently hosted the Games; identifying three types of
     approaches – the 'Commercial', 'Dynamic' and 'Catalytic'. The chapter
     situates these mega event approaches within the wider process of urban
     development and renewal in the twenty-first century.

3   Branding the Games: Commercialism and the Olympic City   43
     Iain MacRury
     The author explains and assesses the Olympic brand as a vehicle for
     commercial sponsorship and how a 'good' Olympics depend upon the
     sensitive and ongoing management of balances between cost, commerce
     and cultural value.

4   Olympic-driven Urban Development   73
     Dean Baim
     The author examines how the modern Olympic Games (1896 to
     2004) have evolved over time to include a widening agenda of themes
     associated with urban development.

PART 2: OLYMPIC CITIES

PART 4: OLYMPIC LEGACIES

List of Figures and Tables

Figures

Tables

List of Contributors

The Editors

Iain MacRury is Director of London East Research Institute and Principal Lecturer in Cultural Studies and Creative Industries, School of Social Sciences, Media and Cultural Studies, University of East London.

Gavin Poynter is Chair, London East Research Institute and Professor of Social Sciences, School of Social Sciences, Media and Cultural Studies, University of East London.

Other Contributors

Dean Baim is Professor of Economics and Finance, Seaver College, Pepperdine University and Visiting Research Scholar, Humanistics Olympics Studies Center, Remnin University, China.

Penny Bernstock is Senior Lecturer in Social Policy, School of Social Sciences, Media and Cultural Studies, and a member of the Management Board of London East Research Institute, University of East London.

Andrew Blake is Professor and Associate Dean of the School of Social Sciences, Media and Cultural Studies and a member of the Management Board of London East Research Institute, University of East London.

Ferran Brunet is Professor of Economics in the Faculty of Economics and member of the Center for Olympic Studies, Universitat Autonoma de Barcelona.

Andrew Calcutt is convenor of the MA in Journalism and Society, School of Social Sciences, Media and Cultural Studies, Editor of *Rising East* and member of the London East Research Institute Management Board, University of East London.

Richard Cashman is Adjunct Professor and Director of the Australian Center for Olympic Studies, University of Technology, Sydney.

Allan Edwards is a Senior Lecturer at Griffith University on the Gold Coast, Australia and co-author of *Qualitative Research in Sport Management*, Butterworth-Heinemann 2009.

Keith Gilbert is Director of the Centre for Disabilities, Sport and Health in the School of Health and Biosciences at the University of East London. He is author of a number of books and papers on Olympic and Paralympic issues, and co-editor of *The Paralympic Games: Empowerment or Side Show*, Meyer & Meyer 2009.

Kevin Hylton is Senior Lecturer in Sport and Education Development, Carnegie Faculty of Sport and Education, Leeds Metropolitan University.

Nigel D. Morpeth is Senior Lecturer in Tourism and Management, Leslie Silver International Faculty, Leeds Metropolitan University.

Roy Panagiotopoulou, is Associate Professor, Department of Communication and Mass Media, University of Athens.

Emma Roberts is a Consultant with WM Enterprise, an economic development and regeneration consultancy.

Michael Rustin is Professor of Sociology, School of Social Sciences, Media and Cultural Studies at the University of East London, a Visiting Professor at the Tavistock and Portman NHS Trust and member of the Management Board of London East Research Institute.

Otto J. Schantz is Dean of the Institute of Sport Sciences at the University of Koblenz-Landau, Germany. He is author of a number of books and papers on Olympic and Paralympic issues, and co-editor of *The Paralympic Games: Empowerment or Side Show*, Meyer & Meyer 2009.

Paul Toyne is Head of Sustainability, Bovis Lend Lease.

Hyunsun Yoon is Lecturer in Media Studies in the School of Social Sciences, Media and Cultural Studies, University of East London.

Zuo Xinwen is a member of the Olympic Project Office of the Beijing Development and Reform Commission.

Preface

Iain MacRury and Gavin Poynter

The Olympic and Paralympic Games is the most important global event in the international sporting calendar. Entering the competition to host the event is not a decision to be taken lightly. Indeed, the bid to stage the Games is in itself a public declaration about the identity and aspirations of the city, and the nation, in which it occurs. What the spectator assigns to memory may vary from images of a black power salute or a terrorist incident to an unexpected victory or a great race. The enduring nature of the image of the event itself is but one dimension of the Games. The pre- and post-event phases create different kinds of dramas. The scale and cost of the contemporary Games demands its organisers to deliver a variety of non-sporting outcomes or legacies for the host city and nation.

Legacy has multiple dimensions, tangible and intangible, that can only be explained and effectively analysed by reference to the social, economic and cultural conditions of that time. Our book examines these conditions, digging beneath the image and the immediacy of the event. It is less about the sociology of sport and more about the sociology of the city; how a sporting mega event captures a moment in time and enhances our understanding of cities and contemporary social, cultural and economic change.

To date, many studies of Olympic cities have served instrumental purposes, seeking to evaluate the specific impact of the Games on a city or nation's economy. Relatively few have attempted to move beyond the cost/benefit format that typifies such work; those that do have focused upon economic, cultural, anthropological and sociological interpretations of the event and a few have examined the history of the Olympic movement, breaking with the sanitised version of the International Olympic Committee (IOC).[1] This book draws upon a range of interdisciplinary approaches, including case studies from recent host cities, in order to identify the common and distinctive characteristics of the social changes that hosting the event have illuminated and catalysed. In this sense, the Games are a vehicle for a comparative study of cities and their approaches to urban development and renewal. There is though another dimension. The Games take place in a city but their coverage is global. By hosting the Games, a city is seeking to affirm or secure a new status as a 'global city'.

---

1   Examples of wider ranging academic studies include Senn (1999) and Guttman (1992).

Over recent years, particularly with the advent of the problematical concept of globalisation,[2] the city has become an important focus of study for diverse academic disciplines – cultural theorists, anthropologists, environmentalists, sociologists and economists amongst them. Rapid urbanisation and industrialisation in less developed nations has been marked by the emergence of global cities in the developed and developing world. The global city is characterised as playing an increasingly significant role in the economies of 'western' and 'emerging' states. As manufacturing industries shift between different developing nations and regions – carrying with them the often exploitative labour practices and smokestack industries of earlier western industrialisation - the global city in the advanced nation, it is argued, provides a focus for the emergence of new, clean knowledge-based service industries. The city brings proximity so that knowledge may be shared; creates districts in which the clustering of industry-specific expertise takes place and offers the advanced communications infrastructure required to support innovation (Castells 1997; 2006). The global city, and those that seek such status, appear in the twenty-first century to be the key to providing the platform for international economic success. This contemporary 'good press' for the city stands in sharp contrast to the 1970s and 1980s when, in the advanced nations, the city was widely seen to be the harbinger of social decay, falling populations and economic depression (Parkinson and Boddy 2004: 1). A study of recent Olympic cities is, therefore, multi-layered. It must capture the narratives associated with the specific host city and relate these to the changing perception of the city as a source of economic and cultural dynamism rather than as a symbol of social decline and decay.

This book addresses the complex multi-layered approach required to analyse Olympic Cities by dividing into four sections. The chapters contained in Part 1 address the broader themes arising from the Olympics as the major mega event of the twenty and twenty-first centuries. The chapters present an overview of the Games and their role as catalyst of urban development and social change. The philosophy underpinning 'Olympism' is examined with a critical eye. The end of industrialism in advanced societies may also herald the end of those values associated with modernity and the Enlightenment, values that strongly informed the thinking of the founder of the modern Olympic Games, Pierre de Coubertin. For de Coubertin, the Games represented a popular celebration of science, reason, progress and the striving for perfection. The Olympic Movement symbolised a universal spirit that rose above the specific interests of nations. In the twentieth century such aspirations were thwarted by the competing interests of the world's dominant nations; with the Games used to contest the dominance of a particular ideological outlook – Fascism against

---

2   Problematic in the sense that as Hirst and Thompson (1996) argued the concept of 'globalisation' encompasses 'a wide variety of views'. For a discussion of the concept in relation to mega events, see Roche (2000), especially chs 7 and 8.

Democracy in 1936 and Democracy against Communism over the decades of the Cold War. By contrast, in the twenty-first century, Olympism faces different kinds of challenges not least 'from within', its conversion from a material form of global Event to a reified form as 'a brand'.

Part 2 provides insights into the cities that have been hosts to the Olympic and Paralympic Games in the period 1988 to 2008; a period of 20 years during which five Games (at the time of going to press) have taken place. Seoul (1988) represented the last Olympics to take place during the Cold War whilst, arguably, Barcelona (1992) represents the opening of a new, post cold war phase when cities began to utilise the Games as a major catalyst of urban regeneration and renewal, a process that flowed from the uneven transition toward the post-industrial service-based economy experienced by all advanced industrial nations. Whilst Atlanta's (1996) hosting of the Games borrowed much from the approach of Los Angeles (1984); Sydney (2000) and Athens (2004) may be seen as being more in the image of Barcelona. The scale of investment in the city for the Beijing (2008) Games dwarfs those of other cities and is symbolic of China's announcement of its entry onto the world stage as a key economic and political power likely to challenge US global supremacy in future decades. The developmental trajectory of the cities is sketched in each chapter, touching upon the pre-event phase and concluding with comments about the legacy of the Games.

Part 3 focuses upon London (2012), and offers some detailed insights into the intentions and consequences of hosting the Games for the city from the perspective of being within the 'pre-event' phase. During the writing of this book, many significant developments have taken place concerning London's preparations, especially in relation to the cost of the Games and the domestic and international impact of public concerns over human rights in China and the UK's role in assuming responsibility from Beijing for continuing the spirit and festivals of Olympism in the period leading up to 2012. Contributions to Part 3 attempt to address issues and concerns that are likely to retain their resonance and topicality throughout the years to 2012, and possibly beyond. Several dimensions of London's experience are examined with authors, in particular, focusing upon the potential for realising the ambitious socio-economic and cultural regeneration of East London, the main location of the Olympic Park.

East London is a relatively deprived region of the city where traditional manufacturing industries and an extensive docklands area experienced closure and de-industrialisation in the 1970s and 1980s. Regeneration has occurred in specific spaces and places over the past twenty five years. This process of decline and renewal has been matched by the fluidity of the area's population, with movement inwards and outwards creating a uniquely multinational and multi-ethnic population. East London experiences a heady mix of social inclusion and exclusion and poverty and wealth. It was these conditions that the London Olympic bid was designed to address – an ambitious programme of urban renewal backed by both central government and the City's Mayor.

The chapters in Part 3 focus upon several of the dimensions of renewal and regeneration in East London; the real and imagined opportunities and challenges facing the local population, enterprises and the city, local and national governments.

Part 4 draws some conclusions about Olympic Cities and their legacies – cultural, social, economic and environmental – comparing recent experiences of hosting the Games and providing some reflections upon the role of mega events in catalysing urban development. The authors reflect, in particular, on the use of such events to promote what might be called 'good city building' – dynamic economies, social inclusion and connectedness and a high quality of living. Olympic cities experience an acceleration of infrastructural and social renewal at a pace that is more rapid than 'normal' development. The Games places stringent demands upon planners, developers and builders to meet pressing construction deadlines; the resulting transformations can accentuate existing social divisions or serve to reduce them through the opportunities presented by the creation of improved transport infrastructure, extensive housing developments, the adoption of 'green' agendas and the creation of new employment opportunities.

Alongside this 'hard' legacy there is also an intangible or 'soft' legacy for the host city, reflected in estimations of its enhanced or diminished international status and esteem and its desirability as a place to visit, live and work. Hosting the Games presents opportunities for the political, social and business elites of the city to re-present globally and domestically an official version of nationhood and nationalism, to legitimate in the popular imagination a particular set of social and cultural values that may otherwise have found little resonance with the population of the host nation (Roche 2000: 9). Such outcomes are particularly relevant to host cities in the twenty-first century, a period when all the old certainties of the social formations of industrialism seem to have disappeared. Evaluating these outcomes is a complex affair. In part 4, the authors explore the relationships between hard and soft legacies and how these impact upon the long term, post-event, development of the Olympic city.

References

Castells, M. (1997) *The Rise of the Network Society*, Oxford: Blackwell.

Guttman, A. (1992) *The Olympics: A History of the Modern Games*, Chicago: University of Illinois.

Hirst, P. and Thompson, G. (1996) *Globalisation in Question*, London: Polity

Parkinson, M. and Boddy, M. (eds) (2004) *City Matters, Competitiveness, Cohesion and City Governance*, Bristol: The Policy Press.

Roche, M. (2000) *Mega-Events and Modernity*, London: Routledge.

Senn, A. (1999) *Power, Politics and the Olympic Games*, Champaign, IL: Human Kinetics.

Acknowledgements

This book is a companion to *London's Turning – the Making of Thames Gateway* edited by our colleagues, Professor Philip Cohen and Professor Michael Rustin. Both publications examine major development projects that are re-shaping the communities, cultures and economy of East London. The books could not have been produced without the seminars, events, conferences and discussions organised over recent years by London East Research Institute (LERI) and attended by many local people and participants from throughout the UK and across the globe.

We wish to thank all the staff in UEL who have contributed to the activities of London East over the recent past and those who have presented at our events and made the writing of this book possible. Very warm thanks are due to our contributors for providing their chapters, often to tight schedules and in the midst of doing many other things.

We would, in particular, like to thank Karina Berzins for the creation of illustrations to accompany Chapter 12; Emma Roberts for all her efforts in supporting the early stages of this book project in her role as research administrator at LERI and Aygen Kurt, Jo Sherman and Linda Talbot for tireless efforts behind the scenes in helping LERI to develop as a research institute. Many colleagues, outside UEL, have influenced our thinking on Olympic Cities and London 2012, including Paul Brickell, Richard Derecki and Norman Turner, and it has been a real pleasure to meet and discuss with many Olympics scholars from different parts of the world, including the staff at the Olympic Studies Institute, UAB Barcelona and Lamartine Da Costa, Tony Mangan, John McAloon and Bruce Kidd. As the London 2012 project unfolds, we look forward to developing our collaborative research with these and many other colleagues across the world. Lastly, our deepest thanks go to our families and friends for their support throughout the process of the creation of 'Olympic Cities'.

Iain MacRury and Gavin Poynter
June 2008.

PART 1
The Modern Games
and Social Change

Chapter 1

Sport, Spectacle and Society: Understanding the Olympics

Michael Rustin

What are the Olympic Games? Obviously, they are the world's leading festival of sports. The International Olympic Committee, the legal owner of 'the Olympic Games', likes to refer to the Olympic Movement as the collective social embodiment of the sporting ideals to which it is committed. It traces these ideals and this commitment all the way back to the Olympic Games of ancient Greece, which were revived in 1896 after a 1,500 year lapse of time by the visionary Pierre de Coubertin. Coubertin[1] provided the philosophy for this new movement. Paragraph Two of the Fundamental Charter of the Olympic Games includes his formulation:

> Olympism is a philosophy of life, exalting and combining in a balanced whole the quality of body, will and mind. Blending sport with culture and education, Olympism seeks to create a way of life based on the joy found in effort, the educational value of good example and respect for universal fundamental ethical principles. (http://www.olympic.org/uk/organisation/missions/charter_uk.asp)

Consistent with this proclaimed commitment to moral and aesthetic values, the modern Olympic Games are framed by ceremonies. These include the worldwide procession of the Olympic Flame, carried by athletes and notables for hundreds of miles in many countries, the choreographed opening and closing Ceremonies, attended by thousands and viewed by billions on television worldwide, and the medal presentations to the successful contestants in every field of sport represented in the Games, with their national anthems and flags. All this gives the Games an aura, an aspect of the sacred in the broadest sense of that term.

It thus seems a triumph in its own right to be the host city and nation for the Games, when the four-yearly prize is awarded. The competition to welcome the Olympics to one's country seems an opportunity to contribute

---

1   There is a considerable literature about Coubertin and the development of Olympism (see, for example, Loland 1995). His writings are available as de Coubertin (2000).

to, and share in, something of honour and value, to be a distinction for the hosts, and a source of pride for its citizens. This is perceived to be the case for the London Olympics of 2012. It is expected that the nation, city, and even the East London region of the city, as places, and countless enterprises, organisations and individuals, will share in the aura and bounty which the Games is to bring.

However, the controversies surrounding the processing of the Olympic Flame for the Beijing Olympics of 2008 have already reminded us that the Olympic Games are about more than Games. The Chinese government, like most governments who host the Olympics, hope that the Games will show off their country and, in this case, their capital, to great advantage. Major architectural developments and urban improvements have been undertaken to provide a worthy showcase for the Games, and to place its host country and city in the forefront of modernity. Yet while the Chinese government pursues this agenda, Tibetans and their sympathisers follow a different one. 'Does a nation which is deficient in its respect for human rights have a moral entitlement to hold the Games?' was the question they choose to put to the world. They took the opportunity posed by the display of the Olympic Torch through many of the world's cities, over a period of several months, to assert their cause. The immense global visibility of the Olympics, now the essence of its commanding position as a world spectacle, was thus also turned into a resource for protest, which transformed what was originally envisaged as a 'showing of the Olympic flame' in many local and at most national contexts, into a political demonstration, which gathered participants worldwide as each phase of the display of the Torch was shown on television. Nothing could have more clearly demonstrated that the Olympics Games is an event with dimensions wider than those of sport.

Remarks made by the International Olympic Committee about the risks to the 'Olympic Brand' incurred by these scenes of protest revealed the commercial aspects of the Games, as the conflict between the Chinese government and its Tibetan and Tibetan-sympathising opponents revealed its political dimensions. It was indeed surprising to see the term 'brand', whose origin lies in marketing but which has now become an almost universal signifier of reputation, used without embarrassment about an event whose essence was once defined as being above considerations of commerce.

In reality, the 'Olympic Movement' and its proprietary International Olympic Committee is an institution of a very particular and modern kind, committed to its own advancement, as are most worldly and even many spiritual institutions. The Olympics are difficult to characterise, compared with many more familiar types of entity. The Olympic Games are 'stateless', though they depend always on finding a territorial location within nations, and on the support of Local Olympic Committees, sporting associations, and governments, in many nations. It is not a profit-making corporation operating in a straightforward commercial market, even though it is highly dependent on transactions with the corporate world, and generates and spends vast sums of money during its four-yearly cycle of Games. Nor is it a governmental organisation, though it depends on the support and involvement of governments, without whose commitment and investments no significant Games would take place.

The Olympic Games belongs to an emergent type of 'globalised' institution, operating in both an international market-place, and an intergovernmental space of cooperation, competition, negotiations, and rules. It also occupies an important cultural and even moral space, as a celebration of a sphere of values, now recognised and cultivated across the world. One can hardly give an account of contemporary popular culture without recognising the great importance in it of competitive sport. This involves as its primary activity the cultivation and development of many kind of physical and bodily prowess, strength, speed, and grace. Thus the Olympics exists in the sphere of markets, of states, and of culture, occupying, with other comparable entities, an increasingly large space in these hybrid worlds.

Sport and Contemporary Culture

Any adequate description of popular culture now has to take account of the leading role of competitive sport within it. In earlier days when the term culture was mostly used to refer what to we now call 'high culture', it was usual to think of sport as belonging to a different and indeed lower sphere of life. But the redefinition of culture which has taken place in the last fifty years, intellectually informed by anthropological ideas of culture as an inclusive description of a way of life,[2] and by a democratic rejection of cultural hierarchy, has changed all that. In so far as what we term the culture of a society is now taken to include all its forms of expressive and symbolic behaviour, its scope is much broader. Culture, in Raymond Williams' phrase, has become ordinary (Williams 1958). It includes not only its high literature, music, art and drama, but also its popular literature, music, and its mass media. And not only these explicitly artistic forms of expression, but also, for example, the forms of design, cuisine, fashion, and the patterns of everyday speech prevailing in a society and its sub-cultures. This is because it can be seen that all these social activities are recognisably patterned and shaped in every society in relation to its prevailing ideas of the beautiful and the ugly, the normal and the deviant, the refined and the vulgar, or whatever particular normative antitheses hold sway in a given social order. When Delia Smith in her television cookery lessons shows her audience how they can make attractive dishes which nevertheless allow them to take 'short-cuts' or to 'cheat' by the standards of haute cuisine,

---

2   In Britain, the work of Richard Hoggart (1957) and Raymond Williams (1961) were influential in bringing about this democratic change of definitions.

she positions her programme in a definite cultural niche, one which seeks to make reasonable quality achievable within everyday limits of time and skill. It is clear that in any such broader conception of culture, sport has a central place.

Sport involves as its primary activity the cultivation and development of many kinds of physical and bodily prowess, strength, speed, and grace. To acknowledge that sport has an important place in many cultures is to reject the devaluation and denigration of the bodily and the physical, compared with the mental and the spiritual, which was a long-standing aspect of both Christian and Enlightenment cultures.[3] When the Olympic Movement sought in the 1890s to identity itself with the original Olympic Games of ancient Greece, it was proposing the revival of norms and values which had been largely forgotten in the intervening eras. (The physical cults of the Roman period, with the central place that they gave to armed combat to the death, were regarded with greater ambivalence, because of Christian notions of the sacredness of human life, and the fact that Christians had at one time been prime victims in the Roman arena.)[4] And while the traditions of sports since the Greeks give a central place to competition, which is as central to the Olympic Games as it ever was, the idea of the cultivation of the body and its capabilities and aesthetic properties is broader than this. Dance and keep-fit have developed as broadly-based activities, parallel to those of sports themselves, in part expressing a reaction by women against the idea that physical activity and culture has to be competitive for there to be any point in it.

The great sociologist Norbert Elias (1939/1978) and his disciples developed an argument which gave a place to sport as part of the 'civilising process' which has taken place in western societies since the Middle Ages. Elias argued that the inhibition and cultural regulation of bodily impulses and appetites – the development of rules governing the bodily functions of eating and drinking, spitting, defecation, physical violence, sexual behaviour – had been a central feature of the emergence of 'civilised' social forms,[5] which depended on the normal observance of complex and usually hierarchically ordered social

---

3   Thomas Dixon's *From Passions to Emotions* (2003) gives an account of the negative view of the passions taken by St Augustine and St Thomas Aquinas from the first tradition, and by Descartes at the start of the second.

4   The revival of the 'Olympic ideal', in the 1890's, coincided with the beginnings of modern archaeological investigations of the ancient world, and shared some of the same implicit preferences for ancient over Christian values as were expressed in the philosophy of Nietzsche.

5   Iain MacRury has pointed out to me that the curbing of spitting is indeed now a preoccupation of the organisers of the Beijing Olympic Games, in pursuit of a 'more civilised lifestyle'. See http://en.beijing2008.cn/news/olympiccities/beijing/n214259657.shtml.

norms.[6] In this context, Elias and Dunning (1986) at the University of Leicester were able to show that sport had become an essential element in the 'civilising' process of inhibition and sublimation. In competitive sports, violence, aggression, competition and conflict were given a modulated and regulated form. (This is also incidentally true of homoerotic attraction and desire, both in the bonding of teams, and in the love and admiration of sporting heroes, which find a tacit place in sports.) It is a commonplace now that it is better that nationalistic antagonisms should be played out in international sporting championships than on the battlefield. The violent passions aroused both on the field of competition, but, more strikingly, among thousands of sports fans and followers, shows how powerful the sentiments of antagonism which are given expression in sporting competitions can be.[7] Sport can sometimes be a focus of symbolic social integration and conflict-resolution, as the celebration in France of the triumph of its multi-ethnic football team in the 1998 World Cup showed.

These analyses enable us to see sports, the Olympics included, as occupying a key place in the expressive life of societies and the different groups of which they are made up. Sports encode social values and social differences, and become prisms through which some of the central preoccupations, both aesthetic and moral, of a society, can be perceived. The role of professional boxing as context for the assertion of identity by black citizens of the United States is a famous example. At a recent stage of this development, Muhammad Ali's prowess, articulacy, and persona were hard to imagine outside the context of the contemporary challenge by black social movements to white hegemony which Ali's career both reflected and contributed to.[8] The game of cricket has been and continues to be (with the current challenge of the Twenty20 competition

---

6   As Zigmunt Bauman (1979) pointed out when *The Civilising Process* was translated into English in 1978, nearly 40 years after its first publication in German, Elias had shown how the thesis of Freud's *Civilisation and its Discontents* (1929) concerning the necessary repression and sublimation of instinctual impulses could be made the basis of an interpretation of the social history of modernity.

7   Franklin Foer's book, *How Soccer Rules the World* (2004) gives an illuminating account of the relations between societal violence and the followings of football, including contexts such as those of the Balkans at the time of the break-up of Yugoslavia, when gang leaders on the football terraces morphed into paramilitary thugs and warlords. Foer describes the extreme and often racialised antagonisms which pervade many football followings, and are expressed in routine chants and songs, though this dimension is usually censored out of mass media coverage of matches.

8   Particularly impressive about Ali was his own understanding of what was at stake in his public role, thus his explicit change of name and thus social identity, from Cassius Clay to Muhammad Ali, his identification with the Black Muslims, his refusal to fight in Vietnam, and his capacity to run rings round journalists and interviewers as well as opposing boxers. The Black Power salute given by the US athletes Tommie Smith and John Carlos on their victory podium at the Mexico Olympics in 1968 was a

in India to the established values of the game[9]) an intense representation of the cultural conflicts arising from the British Empire and its ending, in which antagonisms to the former dominant British power have been enacted in their different ways by Australians, West Indians, Pakistanis and Indians, to name the most obvious, each with their different histories and moments of heightened conflict. Several fine books have chronicled this development, among the most sociologically perceptive being those by C.L.R. James (1963), Ashis Nandy (1989) and Mike Marqusee (2005).

Thus more than exceptional talent at a particular sport is symbolised and celebrated in the success of champions. Leading sportspersons become emblems of, what is deemed to be, admirable in human life, offering models for emulation which seem more accessible to audiences than most other forms of achievement. And this emblematic function is highly variable, in relation to the norms and ideals of a particular place and time. Bobby Charlton, George Best and David Beckham seem to belong to different cultural generations (even though Charlton and Best were near contemporaries in age) in terms of the qualities and talents for which they were each admired – Beckham having been admired as much for his role as a style-icon, and for his celebrity life and marriage, as for his talents and achievements as a footballer.

Mega Sporting Events and the Olympics

The Olympics shares its place at the pinnacle of international sporting events with many other global competitions and festivals – for example the World Athletic Championships, the Football and Rugby World Cups, and the Formula One Motor Racing Championship, to name only the largest of these. We can add to these the Continent-wide competitions in many sports – the European Football Championship, or the Five-Nations and Tri-Nations tournaments in Rugby Union – and the immense number of international competitions of different kinds – test matches between competing cricket nations, League and Cup competitions between leading city football clubs, and the great City Marathons. These latter are perhaps the most democratic of all these major events, since unlike others these allow ordinary citizens to run in (ostensibly)

---

memorable moment from the same era in which politics and the Olympics came into dramatic juxtaposition.

9   A key difference lies in the symbolic significance of time in the contrasting new and old versions of the game. In Twenty20 cricket, 40 overs are allotted to an entire match, which can thus, like a baseball game, be completed in an evening. In a test match, 450 overs may be bowled, and a match allotted a duration of five six-hour days, with lunch and tea intervals added. This was a game designed for players and spectators with time to spare, and often played in a leisurely and elegant style to match. It was, that is to say, initially conceived as a game meant for gentlemen.

the same races as the leading performers, weakening the boundary between competitor and spectator as no other great sporting event does.

Maurice Roche (2000) in his pioneering book, has linked the Olympics and other international sporting events to a larger phenomenon, that of the Mega-Event, Expo, or Festival whose emergence with the Great Exhibition of 1851 and the many similar and subsequent Expos significantly preceded the Olympics. These events have a long ancestry in the great trade fairs of early modern Europe. Always such events were occasions for symbolic as well as actual exchange – making artifacts or commodities known so that they could become elements in future trade, as well as selling them there and then. Modern Expos like the Festival of Britain of 1951, or the Brussels Exhibition of 1958, or the Seville Expo of 1992 were symbolic showcases, opportunities for virtual tourism in both time and space which could be accomplished through exhibition pavilions and their displays, at a single location. Expos became identified with the expression and advocacy of modernity itself, in their architectural forms and in the technologies they exhibited. The function and significance of these international shows has diminished as it has become possible for more people to travel widely, and for television and the media to disseminate images and representations more effectively than by gathering displays in one place.

But whereas multi-purpose international expos may have declined relatively in their global significance, by contrast the great sporting events have grown. Indeed they have become a significant mode of production and consumption in their own right, generating significant investments and expenditures, and large flows of people, commodities, and of images and information.[10] This is

---

10   What has happened is that international expos and festivals have specialised by function. Trade exhibitions (Motor or Boat Shows, Book Fairs etc.) are a major sub-industry. Leading cultural festivals like Edinburgh and Bayreuth continue to thrive, and almost every city seeks to create some event of its own of this 'festival' character. There is a more carnivalesque tradition, an expressive alternative to high cultural forms, now in Britain, exemplified by Glastonbury and the Notting Hill Carnival. Even the political gatherings of statesman can accrue some symbolic value to a city. The G7 economic summit held in Naples in 1994 is credited with providing the opportunity for its mayor at the time, Antonio Bassolino to achieve a major improvement programme in its city centre, and for changing the image of the city (for a time at least) as a tourist destination. And summit meetings of political leaders have also been occasions for massive protest demonstrations, against globalisation itself, as at the Seattle WTO conference in 1999, and at the G8 meeting in Seattle in 2002. Theme parks, with their focus on children, families and young people, occupy yet another niche in this varied market. These are the descendants of travelling funfairs, but need permanent locations because of their expensive technical and thematic installations. (It thus becomes more feasible for the customers to travel to the largest fairs, than for the fairs to travel to the customers.) The Disneyland parks became the market leaders here, being able to make new use of the existing asset of Disney film icons. Incidentally, the change of

clearly one global business in which the British are keen to occupy a prominent part, perhaps in consequence of their retreat or defeat in many others. Success in bidding for the 2012 Olympics has been followed by Prime Minister Gordon Brown announcing his support for a European Football Cup bid for 2018, and soon after that, in November, came the announcement of Glasgow's success in bidding for the Commonwealth Games in 2014.

The Olympic Games has vastly expanded, as a global enterprise, as a consequence of the development of electronic media of communication, especially television, of travel affordable by millions, and of the emergence of national and international markets which make it commercially advantageous to attach the images of commodities – soft drinks like Coca Cola, Nike sports shoes and clothing – to sports like Formula One or football – and to iconic sportspersons. The commercial sponsorship of the Olympics, and its diffusion through commercial contracts with mass media organisations, has become one of its central foundations, as important as its backing by states. As tourism, global media, and mass consumption of commodities of all kinds have grown, so events like the Olympics have become major engines for their propagation and exploitation. This nexus of commercial and media activity has created a new context of motivation for individual sportspersons and their entourages of trainers and advisers, since it is now possible through international sporting success for a very few individuals to join the ranks of the super-rich and famous, as almost never happened even 25 years ago. Sport has become a central instance of the new global phenomenon described by Robert Franks (Franks and Cook 1995) as the economic law of 'winner takes all'. This means that the mass-visibility through the media of those deemed to be the best has amplified their potential rewards by multiples over those competitors who do not achieve this global visibility, and whose recognition and thus economic opportunities are confined to more localised, sectoral or niche markets.

As one would only expect, it is organisations as well as individuals who have taken advantage of this new market situation. The great football clubs – Real Madrid, Barcelona, Juventus, A.C. Milan, Manchester United, Chelsea and Arsenal – have been protagonists in this economic reorganisation of sport. Football has led the way in the transformation of sports enterprises from being at best medium-scale businesses, organised in rather primitive ways by successful businessmen in a city or region who sought public recognition, into

---

aesthetic from the displayed raw mechanical power of previous top sites like New York's Coney Island (developed in the 1920s when suburban rail connections to New York were established) to the later themed and styled 'experiences' of Disneyland and Disneyworld signifies a shift from industrial age to post-industrial iconography, parallel to that between the exposed machinery of the motor-bike to the panelled form of the motor scooter. International sports festivals are now only the largest of what has become a vast genre of international shows and gatherings of different kinds. It has become 'a Society of Spectacle' (Debord 1967) in many senses.

listed public companies or as the private property of international capitalists like Roman Abramovich or the American owners of Liverpool and Manchester United. Cricket is following this pattern, with the challenge of the Twenty20 competition in India to the national and international organisations which hitherto controlled the game.[11] Often this more 'rational' and 'professional' form of development leads to conflict with established elites whose authority is threatened by these developments. The economic law of 'winner takes all' operates at this institutional as well as individual level, since the globally successful organisations (which may still be called clubs or teams but which are in substance corporations and brands) can achieve followings through the global media which the less successful can only dream of.[12] The splitting-off of the Premier League from the Football League in 1992 was a crucial early step in this development.

It would be somewhat naïve simply to lament here the 'contamination' by multi-nation business of a sphere of sporting values which was previously pure and uncorrupted. Sports have never existed in isolation from the societies in which they took place. They have always been intermeshed with significant interests in every society in which they have been practised. Sports are usually, among other things, symbolic representations of aspects of ways of life which societies and groups wish to celebrate, and through which they may wish to assert their identities against others. What is new in the contemporary situation is not that social forces 'external' to sport are influencing this hitherto autonomous sphere of life, but that the forces and interests now in play are so distinctively market-oriented in their character, as the corporate institutions of capitalism have become so much more powerful relative to others.

For example, the Olympics of ancient Greece were celebrating and cultivating, in part, martial as well as what we might think of as innately sporting virtues. The javelin, after all, is in its origin and essence, a spear, used in war. The gladiators in imperial Rome were playing out the endemic cruelties and heroisms of a society whose lifeblood came from military conquest. The tournaments of medieval courts were testing grounds for another kind of martial prowess, particular to a nobility who alone in that society fought on

---

11   However, at a recent meeting of the British Psychoanalytical Society's Applied Section, former England captains Mike Brearley and Mike Atherton said that they believed the Twenty20 competition would benefit the game, and would generate renewed interest in its traditional versions, especially if the latter became once again accessible on terrestrial TV. Cricket was recognised by the International Olympic Committee in 2007, but will regrettably not be included in the 2012 Olympics, even as a 'demonstration sport'. Instead, the Olympic archery competition will be staged at Lords Cricket Ground. http://content-uk.cricinfo.com/magazine/content/story/326855.html.

12   Not only have gate receipts fallen for English football clubs in the lower divisions, but it is now reported that spectator support for most Premiership clubs with the exception of the top five or so has been declining too.

horseback. Sports in these epochs were more closely tied to the inculcation of warlike capacities and habits of mind than they have subsequently become. The pro-sports muscular culture of the English public schools since their development in the nineteenth century was however conceived as character formation for future military officers and imperial civil servants.

We have earlier discussed the influence on different sports of class cultures and the social ambitions associated with them. Boxing has been noteworthy for the possibilities it has given for underprivileged citizens to achieve recognition, success and triumph over representatives of more established groups. This has been the case for different immigrant groups in the United States – Americans of Italian descent such as Rocky Marciano and the great line of Afro-American fighters from Joe Louis onwards. The Peacock Gym, in Canary Wharf in East London, is a continuing shrine to the fighting achievements of working class East Enders.[13] In his classic *Beyond a Boundary*, the Trinidadian Marxist C.L.R. James (1963) described the symbolic appropriation of the quintessentially English and upper-class game of cricket, by black West Indians, who showed themselves able to play the colonising white man's game better than its inventors, and on their territory too. Soccer was for long a context in which working class men could achieve a measure of fame, dignity and success within their community. But until the 1960s when the maximum wage for footballers in Britain was abolished, players were able to earn little more than skilled artisans even if they were attracting tens of thousands of spectators and followers. Horse racing in England has long been celebrated as a cultural space which uniquely brought together, or at least into some proximity, members of the aristocracy who find in the bloodlines of horses a symbolic counterpart to their own veneration of breeding and bloodstock, and pleasure-loving members of the proletariat who could find in a day at the races, a flutter, and perhaps the rare opportunity to rub shoulders with the toffs. 'Derby Day' is the traditional epitome of this symbolic joining together of opposites on a shared field.

So there has never been a 'pure' world of sports, only sports differentially shaped by specific communities. Some sports have found their symbolic space within circumscribed social spheres, allowing or inviting little border-crossing. Polo or grouse shooting are examples. In some sports, such as cricket in England, there was an awkward coexistence between different classes playing the same game, enshrined in the distinction between amateurs and professionals, celebrated, if that is the word, from 1806 until 1963 in the annual match at Lords between Gentlemen and Players. Rugby still has two codes, Rugby Union played (in England) by the middle class and Rugby League by the working class in the north, though this boundary too has become more permeable in recent years, and the idea of a merger between the two codes is now discussed. The variant class structures of the peripheral

---

13   I am indebted to Bruce Jerram for pointing this out to me.

nations of the British Isles, compared with the south of England in particular, were also expressed through participation in sports, Rugby Union being more democratic in Wales, and golf in Scotland, than its counterparts in the Home Counties.

Thus there is a lot to understand from differences between sports, and changes in them from one epoch and generation to another. But this should not be thought of in terms of a decline from a past 'golden age', which only seems luminous from the point of view of a world of hierarchy and deference. The days in England when various annual matches between Eton and Harrow Schools, or between teams from Oxford and Cambridge universities, were peaks in the annual sporting year, no doubt had their appeal, but few now see this as a lost paradise. The annual Oxford and Cambridge Boat Race does however survive as a national spectacle, thanks to television, though like other elite achievements a rowing Blue has now become a step in a career as a virtually professional oarsman for many crew members, both British and foreign.

'The Olympic Movement', in this context, is remarkable for its adaptability to changing circumstances and opportunities, as subsequent chapters in this book on the Olympic Games of recent years show. But the Olympic Movement has its own specificities in this respect. It is an umbrella for many different sports, each of them with its own national and international federations. Only athletics, what is sometimes called track and field, has a fully global appeal, many of the other sports represented being pulled along by the interest which track and field events bring to the Games as a whole.

The fact that the Olympics is a display case for many different sports, many of them weak in their global appeal and following, gives it a distinctive institutional character. It is much more than the sum of its parts. One might describe it as a holding company whose brand is much more powerful than that of its component members.[14] This makes the Olympics particularly dependent on its relations with states and governments, with the global corporations who provide sponsorship, and with the national and international media organisations who provide most of its audiences and thus ultimately its funding streams.

Because the leaders of the Olympic Committee are dependent on national governments to provide host cities for the four-yearly Games, the Olympics was always liable to be influenced by political pressures, and by the climate of international relations at any given time. Thus there was the role of the Nazis in seeking to shape the climate of 1936 Berlin Games; the conflicts surrounding the Moscow Olympics at the height of the Cold War (which some

---

14   Compare this situation with that of soccer in Europe, in which many fans would prefer to watch and support their multinational club sides than their own national team. However the European and World Cups do retain their drawing power, in spite of this.

nations including the United States boycotted) and the successful adoption
of the Olympics by Barcelona as a symbol of a rising city and quasi-nation
(Catalonia) within newly democratic Spain, now a member of the European
Union. The narrative of negotiation between the Olympic Movement and
its agencies, and the governments and societies among whom it has to find
partners, is always specific to each case. The question posed for political
economy and sociology of the Olympic Games is how to describe and explain
differences of these kinds.

Recent decades have seen a longer-term development in the nature of
the Games which reflects an increase in the power of markets over that of
states, as a general fact of life. 'Globalisation' has been described in many
different ways, some of them obscuring more than revealing its realities, but
undoubtedly one of its essential concomitants has been the increasing sway of
markets over the powers of states in the world. One of the leading theorists
of globalisation, Manuel Castells (1998), has argued that the weakening of
nation-states, and the larger and more rapid flow of finance, commodities,
people and information across their boundaries has made it possible for new
kinds of trans-national agency to come into being, and to become major
sources of power in the modern world. In the new 'network society', as Castells
has called it, such agencies, operating in spaces between the jurisdiction of
national governments, have multiplied. Multinational corporations like the
major sponsors of the Olympic Games, Non-Governmental Organisations
(NGOs) like Amnesty International or Médecins Sans Frontières, and criminal
organisations or mafia trafficking in drugs or illegal migrants, are three such
organisational types. Another consists of entities such as FIFA, Formula
One Motor Racing, or the International Olympic Committee. In the world
of global sports, such entities can be more formally representative in their
structures (international sporting federations normally represent their national
associations in some constitutional way), or they can be more commercial.
Although the rules of Formula One are set and maintained by a federation
of a kind, much power seems to reside in the owner of the event's name or
'brand', Bernie Ecclestone, who is able to 'franchise' Formula One races to
tracks based in different nations, for commercial advantage both to the sport
and to himself as its dominant figure.[15] The Olympics, by contrast, though
now heavily enmeshed with many kinds of global business, is committed by its
traditions, and by its wish to preserve its status as embodiment of the intrinsic
values of sport, to maintaining some distance from the commercial. This is
expressed in its insistence on decorum and restraint in the 'commercialisation'
of the Games, via advertising and sponsorship. It is held to be acceptable
and indeed necessary, to draw incomes from many markets, and to permit

---

15   The controversy which in early 2008 surrounded the reputation of the president
of the FIA (Federation Internationale de l'Automobile) gave another illustration of
the broader societal force fields within which these international sports are located.

the promotion of products of many kinds, but this is meant to be in a way which does not overshadow or vulgarise the Olympic idea. Thus one Games which was deemed to have been excessively 'commercial' in temper, Atlanta in 1996, is widely regarded as a negative example, providing lessons of what has to be avoided in future. This, of course, requires the International Olympic Committee to ensure that governments are strongly committed to the Games, providing alternatives in their support and in funding to what would otherwise be the excessive domination by the market place.

So here is the 'globalisation' of major sports, such that they have come to operate in an international market which connects tourism, commercial, sponsorship, media coverage and governmental support in great concentrations of resources and capital. Such a system also changes the balance of powers within sports of the different classes who are engaged in them. In the era when sports were mainly a pursuit of the young generation of leisured classes, rewards were primarily rendered in terms of honour and status, and perhaps access to privileged positions, not material reward. The 'amateur' tradition, and the proscription of 'professional sportsmen' from participating in the Games, preserved a monopoly of access by the leisured classes to the celebrity that came from achievement in sports. To allow sports to become a means by which individuals could earn high material rewards threatened an established status order, and was at first resisted. One remembers the uneasy compromises in some sports, such as cricket, where professionals were allowed to compete, and earn modest incomes, but at first only under the governance and captaincy of amateurs.

But as sports became an element of a more consumption-driven culture, and especially when media coverage vastly enlarged the numbers of people who could watch, and thus increased the flows of funding into them, social relations within major sports changed. Where earnings from sporting success had been limited, both by the small pool of available resources, and from the limits to access and reward imposed by the 'amateur' code, in the new era of commercialised mass sport, earnings for the most successful became virtually limitless. The value of the most outstanding performers to their teams, owners, and even sponsoring nations, became extraordinary, and they and their agents are now able to exact the full market price for their talents.

As success became achievable on a larger scale, through international competition supported by global media coverage, so the returns for success to teams were also vastly increased. The consequence was a throughgoing 'professionalisation' of every aspect of top-level sporting activity, including recruitment, training, marketing, public relations, the exploitation of associated property, etc. Indeed, in England several of the most successful football clubs have become companies listed on the Stock Exchange, one kind of corporate enterprise. Another aspect of this phenomenon as we have said is the exceptional rewards now won by the most talented and successful, compared with other performers who reach a reputable professional standard.

This concentration of the highest rewards at the very top arises from the global extension of markets and thus of the flows of resources that are attracted and extracted by the market leaders. Global communication and distribution gives rise to new economies of scale, such that the investment in the brand of a football team or individual footballer (Manchester United or David Beckham) can be recouped through a much larger and wider consumption of its various 'products' (many of which are spin-offs, virtual or symbolic connections) than was the case when 'distribution' was confined to more local or even national markets. This phenomenon leads to exceptionally unequal reward structures in many cultural fields, including fiction (even children's fiction, in the case of Harry Potter), rock music, and architecture. The institution of prizes in fields of art makes them similar to competitive sports in that 'victory' in a context, or relative success, comes to be valued as a measure of quality in itself. The publicity accorded to comparative viewing or sales figures – 'best-sellers' of various kinds – has a similar effect, encouraging people to purchase and admire products for no better reason than that large numbers of other people do so.

Exceptionally high rewards given to those at the very top are growing across the board in marketised societies. They are not confined to spheres of activity in which leading products, or leading personalities, can be sold to global audiences and thus attract additional income streams. It seems unlikely that there is a genuine market in most chief executive positions in the private sector, and certainly not the public sector, yet the gap between the rewards of those occupying top positions in virtually all fields relative to the average of their employees has grown by multiples. The change may be assigned to culture and ideology as much as to any tangible link between such rewards and performance. Those in a position to make decisions about relative remuneration come to share a belief that it is necessary to keep up with high earnings or differentials elsewhere. Members of these elite groups also use their power to set top-level rewards to look after their collective interests.

Sports, and other branches of the entertainment industry, are now one of the most visible manifestations of this 'winner-take-all' phenomenon. They thus contribute significantly to the legitimation of the equation of competitive success with enormous wealth. One of the functions of sport is indeed to offer societies ideals of achievement for public emulation. Thus the equation of a sportsperson's success by reference to the fortune they earn and the life-style they become able to afford, has an influence beyond sport. It seems surprising that the level and breadth of support of people for professional sport has remained undiminished by the ascent of the top echelon of its stars into a world of exceptional wealth and the celebrity that tends to go with it. But, as with the highly-visible life-style of Hollywood film stars of an earlier era, this extravagant success and exotic lifestyle seems to lead not to disenchantment with formerly relatively 'ordinary' and familiar heroes, but rather to give a new reason for admiring them. In societies where opportunities for great upward mobility are indeed highly limited, sporting heroes offer images of possibility for everyone, illusory as these may be. Such vicarious identification upholds the legitimacy of this unequal state of affairs. The negative feelings and ambivalence that are bound also to be part of the picture also find full expression within the modern cultures of sport – indeed in all spheres of highly visible success – in the sudden withdrawal of sympathy for disgraced heroes, or those who fail to meet the excessive expectations placed on them. Managers of the English football team may be paid an inordinate amount of money, but they are quickly caricatured as 'turnips' or as monsters of greed if they fail.

One of the unfortunate aspects of a culture in which the position of winner in the largest competition available is the only things that matters, is that it takes value away from more mundane achievements, and the enjoyment of a sport for its own sake. Where positions in league tables, or in the Formula One driver's championship, or in golf's Orders of Merit (whose measure is indeed prize-money earned) count for most, the meaning of particular events is lessened. There is, as they say, 'nothing to play for'. Even more diminished in the public mind are the performances that take place at lower levels or in lesser leagues. Thus television audiences for top national and international sporting events become ever larger, while participation in sport stagnates, and the population of television-viewers grows obese.

It is an indication of how protean and adaptable the institution and culture of the Olympic Games has been that it has been able to adapt so easily and seamlessly to this new, globalised, market environment. The abandonment of the rule that only amateurs could compete was accepted as self-evidently inevitable by the Olympic movement, even though the integrity of the value of Olympic sport had previously been held to depend on its being uncontaminated by money. A new order of status and power, founded on competitive success and monetary reward, has replaced the aristocratic order which formerly dominated the Olympics in particular. In reality of course this was always an order of inculcated culture and aspiration, as well as of inherited privilege. Team sports were believed to be significant educators in virtues desirable for those destined to exercise authority. These were leadership (and followership), cooperation with peers, acceptance of codes of rules which opponents (and inferiors) might then be induced to follow by example, modesty in success (in order not to provoke resentment from the defeated), dignity in defeat. Given the decline of a social order founded on explicit signs of social difference and hierarchy (dress, accent, tastes) it is unsurprising that such sporting codes are no longer what they were, and that more emphasis is now given to the achievements of exceptional individual performers. The new order is one of sporting meritocracy, in which in popular sports the successful can achieve high rewards. Although the Olympic tradition holds that the important thing is not winning but taking part (this is one of de Coubertin's best-remembered aphorisms) the adaptability of the Olympic brand is such that it has been well able to adapt to the success-oriented culture of modern market society.

Of course, no-one should imagine that this situation necessarily destroys the aura, magic or integrity of sports themselves, though the pervasive problems of drugs in modern sport shows how much potential for such corruption there is. When sportspersons, or commentators say, as they frequently do, it is not the prize that matters, it is the competition, and the thrill of winning itself, that is the principal pleasure, this may be at least part of the truth. After all, if the performers were not able to perform according to the specific virtues and codes of their sport, no-one would be interested in them, and the rewards, which depend on the public's enthusiasm, would disappear. The fact that a 'Corinthian' athlete competed in part for wider honour – success in a sport was an asset whose aura would often transfer to wider social spheres – did not mean that he was not dedicated to the values of his sport.[16] Nor does the fact that a top level footballer may earn millions of pounds in a month mean that he may not live and breathe the specific 'habitus'[17] of football. Our argument is that the 'sporting' values do not come unconnected with other values and interests drawn from their wider social connections. .If we want to understand sport in society, and the Olympics in particular, we have to attend to and map the specific nature of these engagements.

Britain and the Olympics

Once one understands the role of the Olympics as a hybrid entity in the globalised social order, in part commercial, in part governmental, and in part value-oriented, there is no surprise in the importance that Britain's government attaches to hosting it. The Games has become an emblem of desirable forms of partnership between state and market, and is a powerful symbol of the need for 'competitiveness' and adaptation to 'globalisation' which are central elements of New Labour's agenda, but also of other British political parties in this 'post-ideological' which is to say pro-market era. And what could be a better engine of prosperity for a nation like Great Britain, committed since its de-industrialisation to living on intangible earnings ('thin air', as one New Labour advocate, Charlie Leadbetter (1999) described it) than an Olympic Games which looks like a virtual tropical storm of commercial and prestige-

---

16   It was only a few months back since the former Liberal Democrat leader Menzies Campbell was able to (modestly) display as one creditable element of his cv his youthful success as an Olympic sprinter. More commonly, successful rugby players find corporate posts on the strength of their fame, and many leading sportspersons find employment in the administration, promotion and reporting of sport, as a frequent reward.

17   Bourdieu's (1984) influential discussion of the role of symbolic cultures as competitive markers of social position and hierarchy has considerable relevance to the understanding of sport, as one such cultural field.

generating activity bringing a deluge of benefits to the recipients of its four-yearly landfall.

The Olympic Games, and major sporting competitions like it, not only constitute a field in which individual success can be celebrated,[18] but are also a field for competition between nations. The fact that international sporting success advances a nation's reputation in the world also explains the enthusiasm of politicians for it. The commitment of Tony Blair and the British government to winning the 2012 Olympics against the competition of Spain and, in particular, Chirac's France, was not a distraction from national foreign policy, but one of its strategic instruments.

The London Olympics of 2012

The Olympics today, as we have said, is a chameleon-like phenomenon, changing its appearance in response to the demands of its particular environments. The bid for the London Games was shaped in response to judgements about what the international Olympic Committee, the voting nations, and British public opinion, would most readily respond to. As one might expect in the present era, a mixed economy of governmental and corporate support, sensitivity to 'legacy effects' and a 'Green' regard for the environment, were crucial elements in the bid. The potential benefits from the Olympic legacy, and anxiety about how such a large expenditure of money for such a short period of time could conceivably be justified, gave force to the idea that the Games should be located not merely in London (already the richest city in the United Kingdom) but more specifically in East London, which has long been the most deprived area of the city. Thus the Games was given its justification in terms of urban regeneration. It proved possible rhetorically to link the essentially multi-ethnic and multi-national character of the Games, and the multi-ethnic character of London and East London, though quite how this mixed local population, and the mass of short-term visitors are going to interact in any tangible way is hardly clear.[19] Here was a potential Games, it was argued, with a physical

---

18   Although one says individual success, this is is now dependent on well-funded systems of recruitment, training, support, whether these are organised by single-minded governments, as in the bad old days of the Eastern Bloc, or more often nowadays by mixed-economy systems to which governments, sports federations, American universities and commercial sponsors all contribute.

19   Each Olympic Games is preceded by a four-year-long Olympic Cultural Festival, although little or nothing has so far been said about the plans for this in Britain between 2008–2012. Such a Festival could provide an opportunity to make something of the international and multi-ethnic attributes of London and East London, by means of cultural events linked to the Games which could bring together, literally and virtually, participants in many world cities. Four years is a more feasible time-scale for developing connections and capacities than a three week time-span in

presence of ethnically mixed young people to match, in which the cosmopolitan
and also demographic youthfulness of the East London population would
resonate with the culture of the Games themselves. [20]

Various awkward questions are avoided in this rhetoric. The concentration
of the Games in a three-week time-span, and the spatial location of most of it
within a very small area, undermines the idea that the Games will be an engine
of urban regeneration on anything but the most local scale. Winning the bid
for the Games certainly brings advantages in terms of prestige for the host
nation and city. Both Britain's national government and the London Mayor
are in no doubt that this has been a great success for them. But it remains much
less clear who the actual beneficiaries of this event will be. It seems certain
that returns will accrue to East London as a geographical entity, both in terms
of much needed investment, employment, and in a new visibility. But benefit
to Newham or East London as *places* is not necessarily the same as benefit
to their existing *inhabitants*. Many employment opportunities will be taken
by incomers from outside the area, rising house prices and gentrification will
displace some existing residents, and local businesses will be driven out by new
construction and by rising rents. Regional economic regeneration always has
these complicated distributive effects. Even so, East London seems likely to see
the greatest benefit from the Games. Another beneficiary may be the broader
London economy, through new investment as well as visitor flow and income,
though this has implications for the balance of investment, wealth and income
across the nation as a whole, in which London is already greatly advantaged.
The opportunity cost of concentrating development in one region is that
there are less resources for development elsewhere. And furthermore, given
the soaring costs of the infrastructure being built for the Games, who can be
certain that there will in the end be any net economic benefit for Britain at all?

What seems certain is that there will be a discrepancy between those who in
reality will gain most from the Games, and those whom the bid for the Games
emphasised as its most important beneficiaries. One is reminded of Stuart
Hall's (2003) observations about the functions of 'spin' under New Labour
governments. Its function and necessity, he wrote, was to justify a political
programme which had been largely constructed to meet the needs of global
capitalism, to a following which was still largely working-class, and which was
offered little direct benefit from the programme. The London Olympics seems

---

which participants and spectators alike will parachute in and out of East London. It
seems likely however that there will be few resources left to promote this Festival, given
the larger anticipated overspends on the Olympic facilities themselves.

20   This brilliant presentation to the IOC was widely said afterwards to have
clinched London's success, over its nearest rival, Paris. Seldom referred to is the
possibility that the narrow deciding vote was crucially but silently influenced by a
strong American influence, brought to bear in favour of Blair and in particular against
Chirac, in the light of the bitter preceding conflicts over the war in Iraq.

to have many attributes of this kind, and one may therefore expect that its putative benefits will be heavily 'spun' for all who may listen, for the four years to come.

References

Bauman, Z. (1979) 'The Phenomenon of Norbert Elias', *Sociology* 13(1): 117–25.

Bourdieu, P. (1984) *Distinction: A Social Critique of the Judgement of Taste*, London: Routledge and Kegan Paul.

Castells, M. (1998) *The Information Age Economy Society and Culture*, Vols 1, 2 and 3, Oxford: Blackwell.

Debord, G. (1967) *The Society of the Spectacle*, New York: Zone Books.

de Coubertin, P. (2000) *Olympism: Selected Writings*, Lausanne: International Olympic Committee.

Dixon, T. (2003) *From Passions to Emotions*, Cambridge: Cambridge University Press.

Elias, N. (1939/1978) *The Civilising Process*, Oxford: Blackwell.

Elias, N. and Dunning, E. (1986) *The Quest for Excitement: Sport and Leisure in the Civilising Process*, Oxford: Blackwell.

Foer, F. (2004) *How Soccer Explains the World*, New York: HarperCollins.

Franks, R.H. and Cook, P.J. (1995) *The Winner-Take-All Society*, New York: Free Press.

Freud, S. (1929) *Civilization and its Discontents*, The Standard Edition of the Complete Psychological Works of Sigmund Freud, Vol. XXI, London and New York: Hogarth Press.

Hall, S. (2003) 'New Labour's Double-Shuffle', *Soundings* 24: 10–24.

Hoggart, R. (1957) *The Uses of Literacy*, Harmondsworth: Penguin.

James, C.L.R.(1963) *Beyond a Boundary*, London: Hutchinson.

Leadbetter, C. (1999) *Living on Thin Air: the New Economy*, Harmondsworth: Penguin.

Loland, S. (1995) 'Coubertin's Ideology of Olympism from the Perspective of the History of Ideas', *Olympika. International Journal of Olympic Studies* 5: 49–78.

Marqusee, M. (2005) *Anyone but England: An Outsider Looks at English Cricket,* London: Aurum Press.

Nandy, A. (1989) *The Tao of Cricket: on Games of Destiny and the Destiny of Games*, New York: Penguin.

Roche, M.C. (2000) *Mega-Events and Modernity: Olympics and Expos in the Growth of Global Culture*, London: Routledge.

Williams, R. (1958) 'Culture is Ordinary', in Mackenzie N. (ed.) *Conviction*, London: McGibbon and Kee.

Williams, R. (1961) *The Long Revolution*, London: Chatto and Windus.

Chapter 2

The Evolution of the Olympic and Paralympic Games 1948–2012

Gavin Poynter

Introduction

The commercial potential of the Olympics as an international mega event in the post-1945 period was recognised in 1964 when the Tokyo Games was the first to be televised across the world. By the 1970s, the sale of television rights and sponsorship became a critical source of revenue as the event began to assume 'gigantic' proportions. Increased revenues also meant rising costs. The political economy of hosting the Olympic Games became an important affair. Technological advances and the expansion of the Olympic 'family', to include the newly independent post-colonial nations, facilitated the emergence of a truly global sporting event. The 1970s also appeared to prove that the event's rapid growth had outstripped the capacity of any one city to pay for it. So began a period in which hosting the Games was associated with different approaches to economic development and urban renewal.

This chapter provides a framework for examining the motivations of the cities that have recently hosted the Games. It divides into three parts. First, it briefly identifies the social and political changes that facilitated the emergence of a mega sporting event in the period since 1948. Second, it suggests that the cities that have been successful in their bids to host the Games in recent years may be categorised according to three approaches – the 'Commercial', 'Dynamic' and 'Catalytic'. Finally, the chapter situates these mega event approaches within the wider process of urban development and renewal in the twenty-first century.

The Olympics and Social Change 1948–2012

The International Olympic Committee (IOC) was established in 1894 by representatives from 15 nations. The committee was self-recruiting, drawn from the upper class social elites of each nation, with its members committed to 'Olympism' – a moral and philosophical outlook that drew inspiration from classical Greece, and which brought together cultural and sporting prowess in the form of the festival as an expression of human development and endeavour.

For de Coubertin, a founding member of the IOC and a leading figure in the creation of the modern Olympics in the late nineteenth century, the Games represented a celebration of science, reason, progress and the striving for perfection, a modernist perspective that sought to rise above the particular interests of nations.

More often, throughout the twentieth century, the Olympics provided an international stage for the expression of the competing ideological interests of the dominant nations. In the period before the Second World War, the expression of this contradiction between the moral aspirations of Olympism and the ideological outlook of nations that hosted the Games was revealed most starkly by the 1936 Olympics that took place in Berlin. The Games provided spectacular propaganda for Nazism and the International Olympic Committee was tarnished with the reputation as a willing collaborator. In particular, Hilary Brundage, then President of the American Olympic Association and later President of the IOC, was easily persuaded of Germany's suitability to host the Games (Roche 2000). The Second World War brought the defeat of fascism but lent little respite to the use of the Olympic Games as a mechanism for the expression of the competing ideologies and interests of the world's leading nations. The period 1948 to 1988 was dominated by the climate of the Cold War and the competing ideologies of democracy and communism. Since 1992, following the crumbling of the Soviet Union and its client states, the Olympic and Paralympic Games has assumed a different role in a post-ideological phase in which hosts have sought either to affirm or establish their status as global cities in a new kind of international economy.

When London last hosted the Olympic Games in 1948, the event took place to the backdrop of a nation and a continent that had been ravaged by war. The Games was labelled the 'Ration Book Olympics' (The National Archives 2004). Some competitor nations brought quantities of food with them – the Argentines a 100 tons of meat, Holland fruit and vegetables and Iceland frozen mutton. According to Dr Magnus Pyke of the UK's Ministry of Food (Catering Division) the USA's approach to food supply demonstrated a 'disregard for geography and expense'.[1] The British government guaranteed that all athletes would receive category A meal allowances; equivalent to the rations of heavy workers, such as miners and dockers, and would also receive 'two pints of milk per day and a half pound of chocolates and sweets per head per week'.[2] The Games participants were housed in Olympic Housing Centres – army barracks and government facilities – and the main venue was Wembley. The austere conditions for the competitors were not exactly matched by those experienced by IOC leaders who were welcomed to numerous receptions at, amongst others, Claridges, the Dorchester and Australia House. Cocktails at Buckingham Palace were the highlight of these social events. Three

---

1   www.nationalarchives.gov.uk, 'Ration Book Olympics', 12 August 2004.
2   Ibid.

competitors from each nation and IOC members, as the official IOC report recounted, met 'Their Majesties who, in a most democratic manner, conversed amicably with each guest' (IOC 1948). The 1948 Games were a success, with transport congestion eased by the construction of a new road and the highest number of nations and participants attending in the history of the event, though Germany and Japan were not invited.

The Games provided a glimpse into the longer term future of the event for several reasons. First, India and Pakistan participated for the first time as newly independent nations, commencing a process by which post-colonial states began to participate in increasing numbers over subsequent decades (Table 2.1). Second, satellite nations of the Soviet Union, such as Hungary attended, even though the Soviet Union itself did not participate, its non-participation anticipating the impact that the Cold War was to have on the Games in subsequent decades.

Third, the 1948 Games were transmitted to home TV sets for the first time. Though very few home sets existed in the UK in 1948, the transmission of the Games into the home represented the first major step toward the commercialisation of the event, a process that accelerated dramatically following the first global transmission of the Tokyo Games in 1964 (Table 2.2).

Lastly, London 1948 witnessed the event that was to lead to the setting up of the Paralympic Games. London provided the venue for sports events for World War Two veterans with spinal cord related injuries who were based at the UK's Stoke Mandeville hospital. The event was organised by Sir Ludwig Guttman and provided the inspiration for the Paralympics to commence alongside the Rome Olympic Games in 1960.

Informed by the IOC perspective, Preuss (Preuss 2004: 7) has provided a useful periodisation of the Games and, thereby, insights into the concept of its legacy. Period 1, 1896–1968, represents a phase when economic effects were poorly documented and were likely to be small for the host city because of the relatively modest scale of the Games. Period 2 (1969–1980) reflects a major time of change in the funding of the Games and their relative significance to host cities and nations. As television rights and sponsorship became very important, the 'gigantism' of the Games created opportunities and risks for the host city. While the opportunities arose from the new sources of commercial funding, the scale of the Games still demanded dependence upon federal, regional and city financial support for publicly funding Games – as the Munich Olympics of 1972 demonstrated and the financial failure of the city's public funding for the 1976 Montreal Olympics revealed.

The Moscow Olympics (1980) provided little detailed information on the economics of the event, so the third phase (1981–2003) commenced with the Los Angeles Games in 1984 when the city itself declined to underwrite any financial obligations and the private sector was able, as a result, to establish the event as a primarily commercial affair through the development of

Table 2.1   Participation and non-participation in the Olympic and Paralympic Games 1948–2004

Date	City	Number of participating nations	Non-participation by cause
1948	London	59	Aftermath WW2 – Germany, Japan, Soviet Union
1952	Helsinki	69	Soviet Union participates for first time
1956	Melbourne	72	Boycotts – Suez (Egypt, Lebanon and Iraq); invasion of Hungary (Netherlands, Spain, Switzerland
1960	Rome	83	None
1964	Tokyo	93	South Africa excluded apartheid
1968	Mexico City	112	'Black Power' protest – the US athletes banned from Games
1972	Munich	121	Palestinian attack on Olympic Village – Games halted 34 hours
1976	Montreal	92	22 African nations boycott New Zealand's participation (NZ refused to recognise ban on apartheid South Africa
1980	Moscow	80	US led 65 nation boycott of soviet union over invasion of Afghanistan
1984	Los Angeles	140	Retaliatory boycott by Soviet union and 13 other states
1988	Seoul	159	4 nations – N.Korea, Ethiopia, Cuba, Nicaragua – boycott host Korea
1992	Barcelona	169	Former Soviet and Yugoslav states appear for first time
1996	Atlanta	197	Terrorist bomb in vicinity of Olympic Park
2000	Sydney	199	None
2004	Athens	201	None

Source: IOC.

sponsorship rights. Subsequent events in this phase involved a mix of public/ private sector funding that tended to reinforce the commercialisation of the Games and generate, in some instances, financial corruption (Preuss 2004: 8). In keeping with this commercialisation, the Games also embraced the liberalisation of its amateur regulations for participants.

Table 2.2   Olympic Games broadcast revenue 1960–2008

Date	Olympic host city	Broadcast revenue in US$ (millions)
1960	Rome	1.178
1964	Tokyo	1.578
1968	Mexico City	9.750
1972	Munich	17.79
1976	Montreal	34.86
1980	Moscow	87.98
1984	Los Angeles	286.9
1988	Seoul	402.6
1992	Barcelona	636.0
1996	Atlanta	898.2
2000	Sydney	1,331.5
2004	Athens	1,494.0
2008	Beijing	1,706.0 (estimate as at March 2005)

Source: IOC, www.olympic.org June 2005, 'Revenue Generation and Distribution', p. 2.

The most recent phase, commencing in 2003, has witnessed a modification of the tendencies evident in the period of rapid commercialisation. The IOC developed a plan to protect the Olympics from over-commercialisation by establishing a core set of Olympic values including 'fair play, cultural exchange and ideals of equality, tradition, honour and excellence' (Preuss 2004: 8). To protect these values, the IOC identified corporate partners whose own brands are required to reflect these values and, along with such partners, the IOC requires legal protection of their values from the host cities. It is through this attempt to modify the commercial dimensions of the Games and to justify their rising costs, that 'legacy' has assumed a role as a central theme; increasingly informing the tenor of the bids for the Games taking place in the first decade or so of the twenty-first century. In the early 1990s, the IOC adopted environmental improvement as an important theme in the construction of bids to host the Games and in 2001 it introduced the Olympic Games Global Impact Study (OGGI) as a requirement for the host cities to undertake as an evaluative component of their legacy proposals. An OGGI Study will be completed for the first time following the Beijing Games (2008). The economic dimensions of the Games, and their influence on the development of IOC policy, may be conceptualised in a broader context, that of the role of mega events in the development and emergence of global cities.

Cities, Urban Development and Hosting the Games

As Peter Hall has argued, the emergence of great cities – those that have enjoyed periods of immense social creativity and innovation – has occurred through their relationship with one, or a combination of, the arts, culture, technology and commerce (see Hall 1998). In the twenty-first century a critic of contemporary urban development schemes might argue that city building has become more associated with sport and shopping; leisure activities that were once peripheral to the city's life have become its lifeblood. This trend has been reinforced by cities across the world using sporting events and other festivals to achieve a radical break from their present and past – using the events to catalyse processes of economic development and urban renewal. Such catalytic effects contain echoes of what Schumpeter referred to as a 'process of creative destruction'. (Schumpeter 1975) In the twenty-first century context of urban regeneration this often means shifting employment opportunities from declining production industries to the service economy, removing political and legal obstacles to rapid development and implanting or imposing development upon a locality rather than allowing it to organically change from within (see Raco 2004). In their defence, regeneration professionals would argue that such schemes focus primarily upon brownfield and derelict sites, areas of high unemployment and social deprivation, in short localities where urban decline has reached such a level that it is not possible to reverse such decline without major intervention from the outside.

The mega event facilitates this external intervention in several ways. It sets tight time limits on infrastructure development, creates new forms of financing investment through a combination of public/private funding and serves to legitimate this expenditure by appealing to the popular imagination. In this post ideological age, the sporting event, is increasingly used to mobilise public support for a programme of urban renewal and economic development in the twenty-first century that politicians and the social and business elites find difficult to justify using conventional, twentieth century political terms – a theme that MacRury explores in his chapter on the branding of the Games. This chapter contextualises this trend by providing a typology of approaches adopted by host cities over the past 20 years.

The Commercial Games

The Commercial approach to hosting the Olympic Games arose in the USA and was reflected most clearly by Los Angeles (1984) and Atlanta (1996). This American model addressed specific forms of urban decline and transition; processes that commenced in the 1960s and 1970s with the end of the so-called Golden Age of industrial expansion that followed the end of the Second World War. The underlying shift that cities faced has been well documented

– moving from urban economies based upon production industries to ones that are increasingly dependent upon services, especially financial services and new forms of consumption arising from rapid advances in technologies and the commodification of cultural and leisure activities. The post-industrial American city assumed a new identity that either embraced a little 'fantasy' of the Disney world or attributes of the 'informational city' in which congregated the offices of major finance houses and multinational companies (see Castells 1989).

The construction of the 'Fantasy City' focuses on visitor attractions, prestigious events and themed festivals. Their construction is primarily designed to conform to the images and expectations of the visitor rather than the practical needs of those living in them. Financing their development often generated local political and financial problems, in part because of the complex public/private financial arrangements upon which their development depends. The history of the development of event facilities and Convention Centres, illustrates how the construction of the Fantasy City often rested upon the dilution of the role of local government in planning processes and the removal of public scrutiny over the financing arrangements required to construct them. In this sense, consumption-based urban regeneration programmes were accompanied by a restructuring of local politics in order to accommodate the role of special purpose quasi-governmental agencies and the public-private partnerships that are required to create the financial framework for their implementation (Sanders 1992).

The Commercial model for hosting the Olympic Games arose from the experience of American cities and appeared to provide a solution to the problems posed by the experiences of Munich and Montreal for whom the cost of the Games weighed heavily upon the public purse. The Commercial approach may be characterised as driven by the private sector, circumventing local or city planning processes and laws; focused upon the re-branding of the city and the promotion of specific products and companies through their association with sport and, specifically Olympism; and directed to facilitating the expansion of a city's service economy. Such an approach appeared to address the IOC's concerns that arose as a result of the Montreal Games.

The financing of the Montreal Games rested with the Montreal Organising Committee of the Olympic Games (OCOG) and the city of Montreal. By the end of the event only 5 per cent of the funds required had been raised by the OCOG from private sources, the rest had to be met from the public sector. This resulted in interest on the debt to meet the cost of the Games being raised by municipal and provincial taxes. The final payment was completed in 2005–2006 (Preuss 2004: 15).

Agreement between the IOC and city leaders to locate the 1984 Games in Los Angeles took a considerable period of negotiation. A survey of local residents (1,200) had indicated strong support for hosting the event (70 per cent of those surveyed) but little enthusiasm for local taxes to be used to pay for it

(35 per cent voted in favour). City business leaders, led by Mayor Bradley, put together a private not-for-profit consortium to organise the Games – the Los Angeles Olympic Organising Committee (LAOOC). Their negotiations with the IOC provided the framework for the Games to take place on a commercial scale. Companies were licensed to sell Olympic products and all broadcast revenues, except one third of the TV rights that went to the IOC, were awarded to the private sector consortium of Games organisers to cover costs. Even the United States Olympic Committee escaped any financial responsibilities for the event. Little investment took place in the construction of new facilities and the US$ 683.9 million costs of the Games were more than matched by revenues, a surplus of $380.6 million being achieved that was distributed to US athletics associations (Preuss 2004: 16; LAOOC 1984).

The Los Angeles Games demonstrated the capacity of a business-centred approach to deliver an important intangible gain to a city, its branding as a global city, or as Keil (1998: 99) has argued, an effective 'testing ground for post-fordist innovation'. The city used the mega event, especially the opening and closing ceremonies, to project a little fantasy and advertise itself as a location for international investment, particularly in the new services sector, a sector that was extensively supported by immigrant labour. The city produced a successful Games, assisting the IOC to overcome the legacy of Montreal and provided a model for economic development policy making that eschewed the old federal-aid approach by championing entrepreneurialism. The longer term consequences of such an approach have been well documented in relation to the consequences for social cohesion and urban development, nonetheless, the 1984 Games demonstrated the capacity of influential city business interests to ally their objectives for commercial development to the bid to be an Olympic host city (Davis 1990).

The Atlanta (1996) Games had, outwardly, many of the same characteristics as the Los Angeles Games. The bid and the organisation of the Games was led by a private sector consortium drawn from the city's business community and a primary purpose was to project the city as an international convention centre and a southern US location for company headquarters. Unlike Los Angeles, the construction of new sports facilities was required and there was a more specific commitment to regeneration schemes; especially in relation to the development of the transport infrastructure and housing. The legacy of the Olympics was, however, mixed. Atlanta achieved its goal of securing the relocation of 18 major companies to the city following the completion of the Games and hosting the event was one of the key reasons for achieving the designation by the federal government as one of six 'federal empowerment zones'. On the other hand, the Olympics left a legacy of ill-will amongst particular neighbourhoods that lost housing and experienced severe dislocation arising from the urban developments that accompanied the event.

The difficulties in reconciling the social regeneration agenda with a business-centred approach to organising mega events was revealed by the experience of the Atlanta organisers. Despite this, the commercial model has remained a compelling approach to urban development over recent years, informing policy-making agendas for several cities that have sought to host major sporting events, including subsequent Olympic Games. At the core of the approach is the marketing of place and the branding of a city as a site for investment in, and venue for, consumption led economic development.

The Games as Catalyst of Regeneration

Whilst the Los Angeles model is primarily focused upon brand and business, several more recent host cities have adopted a broader agenda that has typically encompassed a greater 'space' – the city, region and, in the cases of Athens and Sydney, the nation – and a wider range of socio-economic objectives. Inevitably, this greater ambition has been matched by higher levels of infrastructure investment and the restoration of a mix of public and private sector funding to support the event and the infrastructure developments that surround it (Figure 2.1).

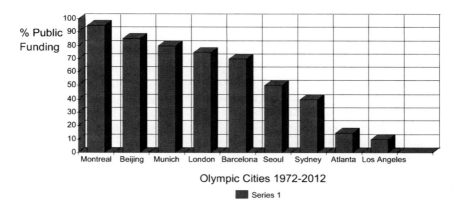

Figure 2.1   Public funding for staging the Olympic Games 1972–2012

The catalytic model has certain key characteristics. First, the commitment to public expenditure underpins an ambitious programme of commercial and social renewal. The emphasis is upon the event and its wider social, economic and cultural legacy. Second, it is focused upon facilitating a process of transformation that strengthens, in the 'western' context the service economy, and in the twenty-first century, the knowledge-based components of it. Finally, it sets out an important social policy agenda, aimed at enhancing social cohesion through achieving more than the 'trickle down' effect of the commercial, laissez faire model of city building.

Perhaps the most salient and successful example of this approach was Barcelona (1992); though, arguably, the success of Barcelona has been more widely recognised and accepted in the twenty-first century following the IOC's own conversion to a less commercially oriented Games following the experience of Atlanta where financial arrangements went 'close to the wire' and allegations of corruption flowed from the extensive commercialisation of the event (Preuss 2004: 13).

Historically, Barcelona's industrial and commercial base centred upon the docks and manufacturing industries; their decline caused the city and regional government of Catalunya to develop an urban regeneration plan that pre-dated the bid to host the Olympic Games in 1992. The implementation of the plan became a central goal in hosting the Games. The Games was a catalyst for urban renewal. Renewal took place in a wider context of Spain's entry to the European Community (1986) and the introduction of the European Union Single Market in 1992. These developments facilitated Barcelona's role in connecting the markets of northern Europe to the Iberian peninsula, enabling the city to become an attractive location for inward investment, especially by those companies engaged in the expanding European services sector. The investment made between 1986 and 1992 proved critical to Barcelona's subsequent economic success and has been followed by two further phases of development between 1992 and 2004 and 2004 to 2010.

The Olympics related investment phase focused upon coastal recovery, telecommunications and services, housing, office development, sports and cultural facilities and roads and transport. The second phase, 1992–2004, addressed the city environment, telecommunications and the continued improvement in transportation infrastructure through the opening of a high speed train service (AVE), the extension to the airport and the development of the regional train, tram and bus network. The current phase is centred upon further transport and environmental improvements and the creation of a high technology business park in the Poblenou district and the Forum 2004 – a flexible open space for cultural and creative activities. Each development has addressed omissions from previous phases and has sought to overcome negative effects of the preceding cycle of urban development. For example, the current period of regeneration is designed to more effectively distribute commercial, cultural and leisure activity across the city, reducing the overcrowding effect that arose with the successful regeneration of the city centre. In this sense, Barcelona's regeneration, as Brunet argues in his chapter, has proceeded through three phases, achieving a 'legacy momentum' that has outlived the immediate impact of hosting the 1992 event, and providing a 'model' that other host cities have attempted to follow.

The transformation of the city economy since 1986 has been led by growth in the services sector. Services accounted for 82 per cent of employment in 2006 (rising from approximately 40 per cent in 1986) compared to 67 per cent for Spain as a whole. The downturn in European regional economies in the early 1990s was significantly modified in Barcelona by the investment arising from hosting the 1992 Games. The city economy has specialised in the expansion of financial services, business services, real estate, health care, public administration and education. In the decade since 1995, the demand for space for tertiary activities has grown by 500,000 square metres per annum; the city and regional government has played a significant role in the development of investment and regeneration plans.

The Games represented a significant investment in infrastructure – over three times the sum spent upon the event itself. The cost of the Games was underwritten by national, regional and city governments, though investment was distributed across the public and private sectors (Spanish government 12 per cent, Catalunya Regional government 15 per cent, Barcelona 2 per cent, Spanish private companies 22 per cent, foreign private companies 11 per cent and Spanish public companies 14 per cent). The Games balance sheet was assisted by significant income from television rights (Los Angeles achieved $288 million, Barcelona $635 million) which contributed to an operating surplus of over $300 million. The example of the Barcelona Games provided the model for subsequent bids from cities that sought to use the event to catalyse the process of urban regeneration. The Sydney (2000), Athens (2004) and London (2012) bids followed this catalytic approach.

The Olympics in 2000 was designed by its organisers to promote Sydney as a 'global' city; enhance international tourism to New South Wales and Australia and attract service based industries from within the Asia/Pacific region. The Sydney Organising Committee of the Olympic Games had support from local, state and national governments. The Committee also carefully established local community relations, particularly with the Aboriginal people, who threatened to disrupt the Games with protests aimed at highlighting the Australian government's failure to recognise indigenous people's rights. New sporting facilities were constructed for the Games, including the main stadium and an aquatic centre (opened in 1994, one year after Sydney had been chosen as the venue for 2000). The main investment, however, was in telecommunications, including the Sydney Media Center and the city's transport system.

The promotion of Sydney was intimately linked to the promotion of Australia by the Australian Tourism Commission (ATC). The ATC established a sophisticated strategy for using the Games to, in effect, re-brand Australia as a young, vibrant country rather than a distant nation with lots of 'outback' (IOC 2001). The legacy of the Olympic Games for Sydney appears to be more mixed compared to Barcelona. Tourist visits to the city were up by 11 per cent in 2000 and £2.4 billion additional income from tourism was raised in 2001–2002 according to IOC and official government figures; convention business also increased by 34 per cent over the same period. Conversely, leading sports venues have remained underutilised since the Games ended. In 2001, the NSW government allocated $50 million to promote commercial development of the Olympics site, hoping eventually it would become self-supporting.

In its report to the New South Wales Parliament (2002) the Auditor General compared estimated and actual costs of the Games. Variances and their causes were identified. SOCOG had higher operating costs arising from underestimates of the costs of technology and ticketing arrangements. Slightly higher revenues were anticipated to cover these cost overruns. The late addition of some sports events accepted for the Games caused a cost rise though, on the other hand, income from the sale of the media village after the Games and a foreign exchange gain largely covered these costs. The Games cost was $4,788.2 million. It closed with a small deficit of $45 million. Secondary or infrastructural investment in Sydney cost approximately $2.6 billion with sports facilities, the Olympic village (later converted to housing) and transport development being the main expenditures. The Homebush 'brownfield' area on the outskirts of Sydney was extensively regenerated, though the overall catalytic effect of the Games was less than that achieved by Barcelona over the same post-event period of approximately seven years.

As Cashman argues in a later chapter, the legacy of the Sydney Olympic Games took time to define, proceeded through several stages and, arguably, became an important issue only after the event had taken place. In mitigation, however, the Sydney bid was formulated before the lessons of Barcelona could be learned and at an early phase in the IOC's deliberations on the importance of the catalytic role of the Games in delivering programmes of urban regeneration.

Athens and its region, Attica, sought to utilise the 2004 Games to achieve several goals. First, the city's infrastructure, particularly its transport systems, required major renewal and the city's environmental pollution required urgent attention. Second, the city was seeking to preserve and enhance its share of tourism which had decreased from 40 per cent of arrivals in Greece in 1980 to 16 per cent in the mid-1990s. Third, the city sought to increase the availability of industrial and commercial space, releasing an additional 1.1 million sq ft of space for event usage. Fourth, the Games provided a perceived opportunity to create significant numbers of new permanent and temporary jobs. Finally, Athens sought to achieve its re-branding as a European city of commerce and tourism, an important location for the location of economic activities in the eastern Mediterranean.

The relatively short period since 2004, suggests that the sustainability of the post-Games legacy is difficult to measure. Available evidence indicates that infrastructure and environment gains have been achieved. The underground rail network grew by a factor of 1.74, a new rail and bus network was created and 200 km of new and upgraded motorways were completed. Atmospheric pollution has correspondingly declined. The Attica region undertook four areas of urban renewal and development in Thessaloniki, Patrai, Volos and Herakleion. Infrastructure development was mainly funded by public authorities (about 95 per cent), while the private sector contributed to about 20 per cent of operational costs. Operating costs rose from an original budget of 611 $ million to $2.5 billion and Infrastructure costs rose by approximately 30 per cent over original cost estimates.

The effects of the Games on employment in Athens and the Attica region were significant in the pre-Games period. For example, in 1998 the country's labour force expanded from 4.5 million to 4.8 million employees, an increase of 7 per cent. In the Attica prefecture, the rise was from 1.59 million to 1.78 million, an expansion of 11.8 per cent. Equally, unemployment in Attica stood at 12 per cent in 1999 but fell between 2003 and 2005 to 9 per cent, one per cent lower than the national average for that period. The sectors most benefiting from an expansion in full-time employment were construction and hotels and restaurants.

Immediately following the Games, the positive employment effect moved into reverse. In the three months after the Games, September–November 2004, Greek industry lost 70,000 jobs, the majority in construction. The adverse effect of contraction in the construction industry is reflected in its overall importance to the Greek economy. Between 1997 and 2003, construction industry turnover rose from €6 billion to €13 billion; this represented 10 per cent of GDP in 2003. The sharp decline in the sector's fortunes following the completion of the Games had a significant impact on business confidence in the wider Greek economy in the months immediately following their completion. The catalytic impact of the Games upon the fortunes of Athens has been a mixed affair. Infrastructure and environmental improvements have occurred along with the creation of new organisational expertise in project management, as Panagiotopolou outlines in chapter nine, but these have to be balanced against the growing evidence of a weaker legacy in relation to employment and the progress of the wider Greek economy.

The catalytic role of London's bid, with its emphasis on non-sports related outcomes, is most readily captured in the prose of its most fervent advocate, Ken Livingstone, Mayor of London:

> The games have already unlocked billions in new transport investment right across London; they have made the massive regeneration project centred on Stratford and going south to the Thames deliverable when it was not before. This offers unparalleled new opportunities to some of the most deprived communities in the country, bringing with it 40,000 new homes and 50,000 new jobs.
>
> Cynics airily say that all this could have been done without the Olympics. It never would have been. The cardinal deception is the claim that the Olympic investment is for 16 days of sport, when it actually underpins the next 50 years of east London's future. (Livingstone 2007)

These values struck a cord with the IOC, in its post-commercialisation phase, and provided the foundation of London's successful bid. The achievement of 'a successful Games' has become closely associated with the effective construction, preparation and holding of the event and the attainment of a transformative legacy that impacts upon East London and the wider Thames Gateway urban regeneration project.

The ambitions set for London 2012 exceed those of other cities who have adopted 'the Games as catalyst' agenda even though, unlike Barcelona, they focus upon a specific part of the city – the East. East London has witnessed considerable change over the past twenty five years; change that has propelled parts of the region from a reliance upon traditional production industries clustered around the old docks to service industries, especially financial services, located in rejuvenated dock sites such as Canary Wharf. The transition has tended to sharpen the polarisation within the local economy and population, with vast wealth sitting uneasily alongside large pockets of social deprivation and poverty (Hamnett 2003: 241–4). It is precisely this divide that the 2012 Games is designed to address, bringing with it new affordable housing developments, employment for the less skilled and workless and environmental improvements to each of the five designated 'Olympic boroughs' – Greenwich, Hackney, Newham, Tower Hamlets and Waltham Forest.

The catalytic role of the Games has some distinctive characteristics in the London context. First, London already has the status of a global city that is underpinned by the international role of its financial services sector. This status may be reaffirmed by hosting the Games or tarnished by the experience. Second, recent flagship projects, such as the Dome, constructed for the millennium as a festival and leisure site, was a financial failure and the new national soccer stadium at Wembley was behind time and over budget; the failures associated with these projects have placed even greater pressures upon the 2012 organisers to deliver the Games on time and on budget in addition to delivering the ambitious legacy agenda. Lastly, London's economy already dominates the UK's regional economies in relation to its contribution to UK Gross Domestic Product (GDP), the Games may stimulate infrastructure developments and other improvements that reinforce this concentration of wealth creating activities within the city, serving only to shift its boundaries a few hectares eastwards. These specific features of the London Games brings into sharp relief what Roche has called the two dimensional nature of mega events (Roche 2000: 27). The Games simultaneously have global and localised dimensions; for London consolidation of its global role through the concentration of infrastructure, housing and retail investment in the city and its immediate surrounds may undermine the potential for achieving the localised and de-centred gains being sought in the wider Thames Gateway region. In this sense, the Games as catalyst of urban regeneration may initiate contradictory trends that require considerable qualities of governance to negotiate. These contradictions are explored in depth in Part 3 of this book.

The Dynamic Games

The emergence of the dynamic Games type is synonymous with the economic growth and development achieved in South and East Asia over the last three decades and reflects the desire of rapidly developing nations to secure international trade, inward investment and global recognition for their achievements. The dynamic model is characterised by societies that have achieved rapid GDP growth over a sustained period compared to their advanced 'western' counterparts and for whom hosting the Games symbolises global acknowledgement of their achievements and their acceptance as important contributors to the world economy. Such recognition may serve to challenge international perceptions of the recent history of the nation – in South Korea's case its military government and, in China, its widely criticised record of political and human rights. Domestic features of the dynamic model are reflected in processes of rapid urbanisation and the use of the mega event to support the development of a service sector that hitherto has been subordinate to the production industries that provided the initial catalyst for rapid economic growth.

Seoul (1988) and Beijing (2008) typify the dynamic model. For South Korea and China, staging the Olympics signifies entry as a major player in the world economy, into the (post) industrial world that contains 'global' centres. For both cities, local cultures and institutions combine with features of the 'fantasy' city to create a new and heady mix. Korea's successful bid for the 1988 Games represented, at the international level, its arrival as a developed industrial nation, a country that sought to play down the role of its military government and enhance its ties with North Korea and its strategic role in the south Asian region. Hosting the Olympics had, it seems, the desired effect, as Yoon suggests in chapter five. After the Seoul Games, for example, new airline links opened and the tourism industry expanded significantly with over half a million additional tourists visiting the country in the following decade.[3]

Equally, the Chinese government is seeking to use the Beijing Olympics as a vehicle for demonstrating the dynamism of Chinese economic development and as a means to legitimate its government's international standing by pursuing several non sport-related policies aimed at improving Beijing's environment and rapidly enhancing its housing and transport infrastructure. In relation to environmental matters, for example, it appears that such policies are having some effects (see Brajer and Mead 2003). Beijing (2008) is the shop window for a relatively dynamic national economy, with the Olympics providing a significant opportunity to attract inward investment and 'know-how' to expand the higher value added, high technology, sectors through partnerships

---

3   One estimate indicated that about 640,000 additional tourists visited South Korea in the 8–10 years following the hosting of the event. See Preuss (2004). See also this volume, Chapter 5

and alliances with western multinational companies as Brunet and Xinwen explain in their detailed analysis of the economic and social changes that have taken place in the city in the period leading up to the 2008 Games.

The Beijing bid was favourably received by the IOC (IOC 2001: 59–75). The bid focused upon plans for Sustainable Development (1998–2007) which included 20 key projects and the introduction of anti-pollution measures that incorporated the removal of old factories, the conversion of businesses from coal to gas and the planting of trees (IOC 2000: 62). The Olympic site, located to the north of the city centre, was projected to host 14 venues and the Olympic village and Beijing was to experience an expansion of its hotel and tourism sectors. The city's infrastructure plan included a significant improvement to transport, with a new international airport terminal to be built and extensive roadway construction to include the creation of 228 km of new roads (IOC 2001: 71). The Beijing cultural programme was designed to highlight the ancient civilisations of China and their contributions to contemporary Chinese development.

Secretary of the Beijing Municipal Communist Party of China, Liu Qi, provided a report to the 10th Municipal Conference in May 2007 on the progress of the city's economy and its preparation for the 2008 Games (*People's Daily Online* 2007). The report recorded the GDP growth rate in the city over the preceding five years as 12.5 per cent per annum and the projected growth rate of an average of 9 per cent for the period 2008–2012; with services accounting for 72 per cent of the local economy by 2012. The report emphasised the importance of the 'Green Games' initiatives aimed at improving environmental controls, including the completion of the dismantling of the city's Shougang steel works, and continued activities to cut exhaust emissions, particularly from the three million cars that were owned in the city. The speech also emphasised the importance of addressing social problems by improving public services and social security provision while also cutting out spitting, queue jumping and littering.

The Seoul and Beijing Games reflect the capacity of these nations to achieve a significant boost to their international standing, especially in the economic sphere. More specifically, in hosting the Games, for Seoul and Beijing, city-building has been propelled rapidly toward the consumer-oriented, service sector, thus emulating the configuration of the economies of other global cities. In this sense, the dynamic Games model accelerates a process of urban development in host cities that emulates the economic activities and work patterns of established global cities such as New York. This homogenisation process is tempered by the specific ways in which the national and city political and business leaders seek to re-present an official version of their cultural history. Interestingly, in the Beijing context, it may be argued that the nationalities that appeared for much of the twentieth century as forces that threatened national integration are presented through the festivals and events of the cultural Olympiad as ethnic groups that have come to symbolise China's long and distinguished history as an independent nation (see Bulag 2000).

Analysis of the interplay between the values and ideals of Olympism and the political and cultural development of dynamic cities and societies tends to emphasise the role that Olympic values may play in improving society, achieving individual rights, respecting cultural diversity and attaining sustainable, environmental development in the host nation. The Seoul Games may, according to some authors, have contributed to the democratisation process in South Korea and the Beijing Olympics may perform a similar role in relation to China. On the other hand, the Games represent an opportunity for political and business elites to re-present the city and nation's image, shifting external or international perceptions whilst not fundamentally shifting the locus of domestic power and wealth. As Calcutt suggests in his later chapter, Beijing's social and political elite may be using the Games as an opportunity to deploy the cultural in an attempt to reconstruct civil society in a form that is amenable to expansive urban social change Indeed, at the local level, it may be that the Games provides an opportunity to legitimate a process of social engineering in the city that does little to ameliorate the social inequalities of the host city's society.

The mega event facilitates a process of urban development that takes place from above, being 'state-centred' in its conception and execution but enacted under the 'cover' of the ideals of Olympism. While the commercial approach typically eschews explicitly egalitarian outcomes, the dynamic and catalytic models more closely aspire, at least in their rhetoric, to the ideals of Olympism; their success or otherwise in embracing such ideals is a theme examined throughout this book.

Conclusion: Mega Events and 'Good City Building'

To return to Peter Hall's argument that the emergence of great cities has occurred through their relationship with one, or a combination of, the arts, culture, technology and commerce; hosting a mega event is, perhaps, at best a signifier of one moment in that process of emergence. It is, however, a process or a journey in the twenty-first century that has not been clearly defined, nor the destination clearly identified. The good city of the twenty-first century will differ from those that went before. The global cities of earlier historic periods were great centres of trade and new forms of economic organisation. They contained considerable wealth and poverty; the majority living in squalid conditions. They were cities of some considerable size, for their age, and were 'creative cities … all places of great social and intellectual turbulence, not comfortable places at all' (Hall 1998: 286). These cities or 'cultural crucibles' included Venice, Florence, London, Vienna, Paris and Berlin and they arose in a pre-industrial age through which they could mature variously into centres of wealth creation and conspicuous consumption supported by empire, trade and more recently finance capitalism (Hall 1998: 288).

By comparison, the city of Hall's 'innovative milieu' relied less on cultural creativity and had a much greater appetite for technology and innovation – a defining feature of nineteenth and early twentieth century industrial cities such as Manchester, Glasgow, Detroit and in the latter part of the twentieth century, San Francisco and Tokyo-Kanagawa. Whether culturally creative or technically innovative in their origins, many cities experienced, especially in the twentieth century, a critical challenge to attain and sustain an urban order in what is an inherently disordered environment that presents challenges in securing clean water, sufficient food supplies, effective transport and sewage systems and adequate housing. Those that succeeded, according to Hall, seized a particular moment or conjuncture in their socio-economic development to bring together a 'particular political response' and a 'suitable cultural ambience'; at least for a period of time that enables them (Stockholm, Paris amongst others) to be referred to as the Essence of the Modernist city (Hall 1998: 938). For Hall, the twenty-first century presents all these challenges of sustainability and more in what some have called a post-modern world. The compression of time and space through the recent digital revolution presents a significantly new dimension to good city building, a dimension that arises as much from the virtual world as it does from the real; for the city that hosts the Olympics in the twenty-first century, the event is designed to hasten such progress and confirm its global status in a post-modern or post-ideological world.

The broadcasting of the Olympics across the world makes it simultaneously a global and local affair, 'a distinctive place connected to a shared global space'. (Short 2004) The aspirant to global status engages with a mega event that is designed to reveal the capacity of the city to hold a successful sporting festival and deliver a social agenda that chimes with the prevailing domestic and IOC discourse of good city building, a discourse that, especially in the London 2012 context, emphasises the therapeutic nature of sports participation and the prevailing social values of inclusion and multiculturalism; while also facilitating engagement with a new post-industrial service driven economic order. Such a vision may seek to reconcile contradictory trends – social integration and exclusion, economic creativity and destruction, cultural diversity and the assertion of national identity. This book examines how far recent Olympic Cities have achieved legacies that address these often conflicting paths of urban development.

References

Brajer, V. and Mead, R. (2003) 'Blue Skies in Beijing, Looking at the Olympic Effect', *Journal of Environment and Development* 12(2) June: 239–63.

Bulag, U. (2000) 'Alter/native Mongolian Identity', in Perry, E. and Selden, M. (eds) *Chinese Society*, 2nd edn, London: Routledge: 223–46

Castells, M. (1989) *The Informational City*, Oxford: Blackwell.

Davis, M. (1990) *City of Quartz*, New York: Vintage and Burbank.

Guttman, L. (1992) *The Olympics: A History of the Modern Games*, Chicago: University of Illinois.

Hall, P. (1998) *Cities in Civilisation*, London: Phoenix Giant.

Hamnett, C. (2003) *Unequal City*, Abingdon: Routledge.

International Olympic Committee (IOC) (1948) 'Notes on the 1948 Olympic Games in London', http://www.la84foundation.org/Olympic InformationCenter/OlympicReview/1948/BDCE11/BDCE11f.pdf.

International Olympic Committee (IOC) (2001) 'Observations from Past Olympic Communities: Executive Summary', http://www.olympic.org.

International Olympic Committee (IOC) (2008) 'Report of the IOC Evaluation Committee for the Games of the XXIX Olympiad', 3 April. Lausanne: IOC.

Keil, R. (1998) *Los Angeles, Globalisation, Urbanisation and Social Struggles*, New York: John Wiley and Sons.

Livingstone, K. (2007) 'We Must Defeat these Professional 2012 Cynics', *Guardian*, 9 March.

Los Angeles Olympic Organising Committee (LAOOC) (1984) 'Official Report of the XXIIIrd Olympiad', Los Angeles, http://www.aafla.com.

The National Archives (2004) 'Ration Book Olympics', 12 August, http://www.nationalarchives.gov.uk/news/stories/37.htm.

New South Wales Parliament Auditor-General (2002) 'Report to Parliament', Vol. 2, Sydney Organising Committee for the Olympic Games, http://www.audit.nsw.gov.au/publications/annual_report/2002/annrep02.htm.

People's Daily Online (2007) 'Beijing Secretary Vows to Make 2008 Olympics a Resounding Success', 17 May, http://english.people.com.cn/200705/17/eng20070517_375571.htm.

Preuss, H. (2004) *The Economics of Staging the Olympics*, Cheltenham: Edward Elgar.

Raco, M. (2004) 'The Social Legacy of the London Olympics', in Mean, M., Timms, C. and Vigor, A. (eds) *After the Goldrush*, London: DEMOS: 31–50.

Roche, M. (2000) *Mega-Events and Modernity*, London: Routledge.

Sanders, H. (1992) 'Building the Convention City: Politics, Finance and Public Investment in urban America', *Journal of Urban Affairs* 14(2): 135–60.

Schumpeter, J. (1975) *Capitalism, Socialism and Democracy*, New York: Harper.

Short, J. (2004) *Global Metropolitan, Globalising Cities in a Capitalist World*, London: Routledge.

Chapter 3

Branding the Games: Commercialism and the Olympic City

Iain MacRury

Branding the 'Good' Olympic Games

If all goes to plan[1] the London Olympic Games will close successfully on 11 September 2012.[2] Londoners, the International Olympic Committee (IOC), local, national and global TV audiences will express (variously) gratitude, pleasure and pride in a 'good Games' – or even 'the best Games ever'. The spectacular and moving events witnessed or reported on and off the sports field will be the culmination of considerable effort and investment – public, private, personal and institutional. Such an outcome will depend upon the successful management of tensions and contradictions within and between Olympic organisational bodies.[3] At some level and to some extent Olympism – as philosophy and practice – will have been tested and affirmed. Many Olympics-related questions and plans have already been hotly debated. No doubt further controversies will arise. Reflection on London 2012 will continue long after the Games are over. The Games' consequences and memories will be collated and contextualised globally and locally.

There are two areas which will certainly remain prominent in critique and analysis, before, during and after the event. The cost of the Games will continue to provoke criticism, counter-justifications, re-budgeting and muddle. Similarly, the assertively *commercial* 'feel' of the Olympic event-culture will attract ongoing attention. As the promotional register becomes yet more evident, notably in everyday advertising communications (via local and global media), attention will turn to the 2012 Games 'image' – to its 'brand' and the brands that circulate around the city and around the Olympic rings. The promotions associated culture of London 2012 will draw out questions

---

1   For instance, as outlined in DCMS (2008).

2   The dates for the London 2012 Games are 27 July–12 August and for the Paralympics 31 August–11 September.

3   Notably the IOC, the London Organising Committee for the Olympic Games (LOCOG), the Olympic Delivery Authority (ODA), the British Olympic Association (BOA) and the 200+ National Olympic Committees (NOCs) of other nations and various national and international sporting associations.

regarding the place and value of the Olympic 'brand' as an appropriate focus and vector for educational and social programmes; in health, sports participation, urban regeneration and the environment.

Some hint of the passion surrounding a 'promotional Olympics' emerged in 2007 with the launch of the London 2012 brand logo. Most critique was reserved for the logo itself. The logo, initially at least, was widely unpopular. Press and public indignation was aimed at LOCOG's chosen brand imagery[4] and at the £400,000 fee paid to brand consultants Wolff Olins. Critique of the logo as design object (i.e. as opposed to an analysis of the Olympic promotional system as a whole) deferred, displaced or replaced other anxieties and criticisms, e.g. that the hyper-commercialism of previous Games, notably Atlanta 1996, famously dubbed the 'Hamburger Games', might be repeated in London 2012.

The distinctive design of the London logo – unwieldy and garish as it is – has an uncorporate look which (apologists might argue), on reflection, signals some departure from the designer-slick image-making of past Games. If the multi-coloured and multi-changeable proto-chaotic London logo is anything to go by then some excesses of McDonaldisation[5] may be being curtailed (in LOCOG) in favour of more open ended approaches to the Games – at least

---

4   Journalists and other commentators took great pains to record the negative impact expressed by the public. *The Independent* canvassed global opinion: 'Cier Vianney, from Bayonne, in France, wrote yesterday: "This logo is one of the worst I have ever seen: and that's a point of view of a typographer." Jonathan Bradshaw, from Toronto, said the logo reminded him of "some sort of rejected logo of an early Nineties children's programme". Zoltan Banffy, from Budapest, said it was "very painful to look at". Amy Murphy, from Miami, called it "pathetic" and David Barnett in Dubai said it looked "like a failed soft-drinks label". Ryan Torres, from Massachusetts, called it "illegible, inelegant, and communicating absolutely none of the spirit, nobility, athleticism or beauty of the Olympics".'

One indicative serious criticism of the launch video was outlined in the *Daily Mail* (*Mail Online* 2007) which reported: 'Epilepsy Action said it had received reports of 22 people having fits while watching the video, with reports of others vomiting and having migraines.' In the House of Commons, 'Tory Philip Davies attacked the design as a "pathetic attempt to appear trendy" and called for it to be scrapped'. In a partially prophetic put down, government minister Alan Johnson dismissed the new logo with the observation that it looks 'like Boris Johnson's [famously chaotic] hair'. Following his election in 2008, Boris Johnson is now Mayor of London and currently central to planning for London 2012.

5   McDonalds, of course, are central to the imagery and funding of the Olympics, in London and elsewhere. McDonaldisation here refers to Ritzer's (2000) analysis of hyper rationalisation and commercial efficiencies – at the expense of the qualitative specificities of work and consumer experiences in contemporary institutional environments – and to the detriment of human engagement with culture and its objects.

at the level of the brand imagery. Even in relation to branding however, where appearances are seemingly all, the logo is not the main point.

Future criticism of Olympic marketing will focus more widely on qualitative aspects of the Games. The prominence and status of the Olympics, as the world premiere sporting mega-event, will invite evaluations of the *cultural* quality of the London Games. The Olympics will allow commentators of all kinds, in their various registers, to rehearse and record their sense of the meaning and value of a highly complex cultural-mega event experience. Prominent in the qualitative evaluation of the 'good' Olympics will be questions about the extent and nature of commercial elements in the 2012 'mix'. The delivery, experience and subsequent evaluation of a 'good' Olympics depend upon the sensitive and ongoing management of balances between the cost, commerce and cultural value. This chapter sets out some of the tensions that will inform judgements – of the 'good' Games in a "good" city. The aim is to consider one or two interdependences – notably between income and sponsorship – rather than to dwell too heavily on the extent to which these interdependencies form necessarily vicious or virtuous circles.

The Olympics and Commerce: Historical Contexts

Pavitt points out (2001: 48) that the modern Olympic movement emerged at the same time as a number of today's well known international brands. Pavitt cites BMW, ICI and HMV as examples of early modern proto-global brands that trace their history to a 'dramatic phase' of international commercial-institutional expansion between 1880 and 1925 (2001: 48). Kodak and Coca Cola might readily be added to the list. These brands might well owe some small portion of their historical international marketing successes to early-days Olympic affiliations. During this period some of the larger US advertising agencies were establishing quite extensive international networks to better service clients (e.g. General Motors) operating internationally. For instance, by the end of the 1930s US-based agency J. Walter Thompson had offices in over 30 countries. Historical accounts of Olympic marketing activities (Barney et al. 2004) suggest that despite this context (of potential global commercial operations) there were few large scale commercial collaborations directly supporting the modern Olympic movement and its events until the 1980s.

Indeed the IOC operated a *de jure* if not always *de facto* counter-narrative to commercial-centric visions of international sport. There was never quite an age of non-commercial innocence however (Toohey and Veal 2007: 279; Barney et al. 2004). Brand promotional commercialisation of the early and mid century Olympics (especially in the pre-television era) was largely a matter of opportunistic local sponsorships by entrepreneurial businesses. The powerful discourse of amateur sport that defined much in the meaning and operation of the Olympics until the 1980s appeared also to extend to an institution-wide anti-commercial stance in principle, and to only sporadic and opportunistic local arrangements in practice. Long-serving IOC president Avery Brundage (1952–1972) made it clear throughout his period of office that money and Olympic sport were, wherever possible, to be kept apart. Richard Pound points out in this connection that the IOC had 'lived hand to mouth for the first sixty or seventy years of its existence' (Pound 2004: 139) and that 'even as late as 1980 there was no concerted effort to develop private sector support for the games' (Pound 2004: 139).

The IOC (2008: 19) gives some indications of the extent of early commercial associations with Olympic Games. In 1896 companies including Kodak advertised during the Athens Games. In 1924 in Paris, advertising signs appeared for the first (and last) time within Olympic venues. At Amsterdam (1928) Coca Cola began its long running association with the Games. In the same year the IOC banned the appearance of advertising signage within Olympic venues – affirming a long-standing commitment to 'clean' Games spaces. As anthropologist Mary Douglas might put it (Douglas 1966/2005), the 'purity' of Olympic sport was defended against the 'danger' of commercial adulteration.

Berlin (1936) was a highly orchestrated 'promotional' or propagandist event. However, the IOC history does not record any commercial sponsorship as such – notwithstanding the prevalence and integration of Nazi imagery into the Olympic event. Notably 1936 witnessed the first 'live' Olympic broadcasts (Barney et al. 2004: 54–5). It was not until 1952 (Helsinki) that an International marketing programme of any kind was introduced, with companies gaining publicity in return for providing food for athletes – and flowers for medallists. In Rome (1960) a more extensive sponsor supplier programme was developed and in Tokyo (1964) over US$1m was generated via the new 'Olympia' cigarette brand. Two hundred and fifty companies made official marketing relationships with the Tokyo Games.

The 628 sponsors and suppliers to the 1976 Montreal Olympics contributed only US$7m for the OCOG. The event costs notoriously far outstripped OCOG incomes. This left Montreal with a serious debt. By the 1970s it had become clear that, as Tomlinson (2005: 180) puts it: 'The IOC was innocent and naïve in terms of the commercial exploitation of its product'. Significant sums were by this time being generated via television broadcasting rights deals. However the IOC largely resisted or ignored the potential for commercial sponsorship. The majority of income from TV and sponsorship was generated via US markets and corporations and disbursed via USCOG[6] – a state of affairs that undermined something of the 'global' character of the Olympic movement.

The large deficit after the 1976 Montreal Games was a watershed moment in the history of Olympic commercialism. The large municipal debt, estimated at US$2 billion, including interest, was finally paid off in 2006 and arose as

---

6   United States Committee for the Olympic Games.

a consequence of grandiose over-spending (especially on the stadium) and because the Canadian government refused to underwrite the city's mounting debt.[7] A contributory factor was the inadequacy of other income streams – inadequacy amplified by the national government's refusal to pick up the bill.

The events of 1976 are emblematic,[8] or perhaps symptomatic, of a broader dynamic in the financial management of large-scale sports, culture and entertainment events – 'industries' growing rapidly in the television age. The Montreal example, in amongst a good deal else[9], led to a crisis for the Olympic movement in the 1970s. Cities became reluctant to host Games (Poynter 2006; Preuss 2004) for fear of financial disaster. Naomi Klein (2000) gives a relevant summary of the broader socio-economic climate.

> In Canada under Brian Mulroney, in the US under Ronald Reagan and in Britain under Margaret Thatcher (and in many other parts of the world as well), corporate taxes were dramatically lowered, a move that eroded the tax base and gradually starved the public sector. As government spending dwindled, schools, museums and broadcasters were desperate to make up their budget shortfalls and thus ripe for partnerships with private corporations. It also didn't hurt that the political climate during this time ensured that there was almost no vocabulary to speak passionately about the non-commercialized public sphere. (Klein 2000: 30)

When, in 1982 the IOC established a Commission for New Sources of Finance, it was responding to this emerging worldwide socio-economic settlement. Adequate commercial exploitation of cultural assets became a compelling pre-condition for staging cultural events. Mega events, such as the Olympics, needed some quite deep-seated adjustments to survive in this new economic climate. The IOC took something of a leading role in the development of

---

7   The contexts of global financial turmoil – linked to the 1973 oil crisis – and local labour disputes were additional contributory problems to cost overruns.

8   Whitson notes that there are a number of checks in place against the likelihood of a Montreal style financial meltdown impacting the Olympic movement. 'The factors that produced the debts incurred by the Montreal Olympics are highly unlikely to be repeated. The political tensions that led to the Canadian government giving so little financial support to Montreal were a product of historically specific political circumstances (although one might compare Canada's response here to the generous support that Spain gave to Barcelona's Olympic infrastructure, Catalan nationalism notwithstanding). More generally, the revenues that Olympic cities now receive from television contracts have risen exponentially, almost guaranteeing that hosts can build the sports facilities required without going into debt. However, doing so still requires a readiness, on the part of local elites who may be ... consumed with place promotion ... to scale back 'signalling' ambitions to what they can afford' (Whitson 2004: 1220).

9   The 1970s and 1980s saw the Olympics plagued by serious boycotts, notably of the Moscow Games, by the USA and a number of other teams.

sponsorship-culture. As Klein notes: '... sponsorship went from being a rare occurrence (in the 1970s) to an exploding growth industry (by the mid eighties) picking up momentum in 1984 at the Los Angeles Olympics' (Klein 2000: 30–31).

During the 1980s the media-advertising-promotions-industry infrastructure was emerging in a way that encouraged the conception and establishment of large scale global marketing initiatives. McAllister (1997) points out:

> The year 1986 is known as 'The Big Bang' in the advertising industry. During this year, a series of major agencies merged, largely to facilitate global advertising efforts ... These mega agencies ... have become specialists in global advertising. Of the forty largest ad agencies in the US and Great Britain, only about one-third had departments specialising in global advertising in 1987; by 1992 only one agency of the forty did not have such a department. (McAllister 1997: 38)

The IOC was, by this time, more than willing to engage with global commerce.

Between Montreal and Los Angeles the Olympic 'funding' pendulum had swung from over-dependence (as it would today seem) on public funds (Montreal) towards (in LA) a large-scale 'privatisation' of the event and its associated cultural 'assets'. There were legitimate criticisms levelled at both 'business models', pointing to commercial excess at one end, and financial failure at the other. The IOC began to take steps to institute a more stable path binding Olympic 'goods', i.e. historic principles and the event-ethos, to public 'goods', i.e. managing costs and fulfilling event and regeneration potentials within the host city. In addition these were to be assertively linked to private 'goods', i.e. to commercial imperatives: consumer-advertising, brand building and other corporate agendas. It should not be assumed that private sponsorship has 'saved the day'. In Atlanta (1996) and LA (1984) less than 20 per cent of the Games funding came from state sources. However in Barcelona (1992), and as will be the case in London (2012), over 70 per cent of financial support is from public funds.

The practical and ethical dependence upon volunteers in the delivery of the Games is an indicative further complication of affairs. Within what might be referred to as the 'asset structure' of the Games (the blend of public, commercial, political and Olympic-institutional social, economic and cultural capital) there are significant contradictions to be grasped and managed. For example, the perceived tension between a sponsor who gives financial support in return for valuable corporate exposure, and volunteers who give freely of time, skills and commitment, in return for various, perhaps ill defined but powerful intangible 'rewards'. The volunteer is by definition willing to service the Olympic movement. But there is a question to be raised regarding the extent to which, however indirectly, his or her goodwill can be legitimately mobilised in the service of an event operating, in part, in the service of corporate commercial brands (and the profit motive).[10] Perhaps this is a logical rather than a practical contradiction. It is clear that recent Games have had few problems attracting volunteers. In London 2012 however such complexity will require considerable thought.

The TOPS Scheme: History and Operation

During the 1980s the IOC replaced a 'confusing commercial clutter' which 'acted to depress the values of sponsorships and to inhibit companies from venturing into the field at all' (Pound 2004: 144) with a highly lucrative marketing system. One journalist writing in *Adweek* after Barcelona (1992) observed that, as he saw it, 'the Olympics have transformed themselves from a nationalist sports festival to an international marketing event in just eight years' (Buchannan 1992: 20).

This radical response to the emerging necessity to more fully exploit the (global and local) income potential of the 'Olympic asset', during the presidency (1980–2001) of Juan Antonio Samaranch, and driven by marketing director Richard Pound (Pound 2004), depended upon the collaboration with commercial sponsorship and (global) advertising agencies. The IOC and the sponsorship industry contrived a partnership scheme to better enable corporate sponsors to develop marketing agreements with the Olympics – both within host cities and globally, across the numerous national Olympic committees. Given the large number of stakeholders (NOCs, the IOC, OCOGs, longstanding national sponsors, advertising and marketing agencies), and the complex international legal terrain being negotiated, it is perhaps unsurprising that the TOPS (The Olympic Partners) scheme took some years to institute (between 1982 and 1985). It was important to unify the Olympic marketing system under one (global) IOC banner, as opposed to having individual NOCs and OGOCs operating primarily local agreements – with reference to particular, selected national markets. This was in line with more widespread trends in commercial globalisation – facilitated by new technological and media networks.

There have been subsequent revisions and adaptations to TOPS, but it remains as it began: a mechanism to guarantee exclusive global and local sponsorship agreements from selected Olympic Partners (e.g. Visa, McDonalds, Coca Cola etc.) throughout renewable four-year licence periods (including one Winter and one Summer Games). TOP sponsors are permitted to use the Olympic logo and enter into other Olympic event related marketing activities across all national marketplaces. TOP sponsors become part of 'the Olympic

---

10   Further complexity emerges around the use of sponsors' corporate managers and other employees as 'volunteers'. This is discussed briefly, below.

family' and are required to adhere to certain promotional rules in respect of the Olympic 'brand'. The IOC gives guidance to sponsors encouraging them to promote and support Olympic ideals (staying however within partners' commercial promotional agenda's).

Sponsors pay for these exclusive rights (see Figure 3.1), rights which formally exclude competitors (within specified business or product sectors) from sponsoring the Games. For example, in the credit card sector, once Visa has signed its TOPs agreement for a particular "quadrennium", then the Visa brand owners possess and can deploy those rights to the exclusion of any similar corporations (e.g. American Express), who cannot join the scheme. The principles underpinning the partnerships are set out as follows by the IOC.

The aims of the TOPs scheme are:

- to contribute to the independent financial stability of the Olympic Movement;
- to generate continual and substantial support through sustained, long-term partnerships;
- to provide equitable revenue distribution throughout the Olympic Family;
- to ensure the financial and operational viability of the Olympic Games;
- to prohibit the uncontrolled commercialisation of the Olympic Games.

The sponsors must operate in line with the Olympic Charter. The IOC lists a number of rationales for the involvement of sponsors. In addition to the primary point of the scheme, i.e. that, 'Sponsorship provides valuable financial resources to the Olympic Family' (IOC 2008) There are a number of further motivations for collaboration:

- sponsors provide support for the staging of the Olympic Games and the operations of the Olympic Movement in the form of products, services, technology, expertise and staff deployment;
- sponsors provide direct support for the training and development of Olympic athletes and hopefuls around the world, as well as essential services for athletes participating in the Games;
- sponsors provide essential products and services for broadcasters, journalists, photographers and other media;
- sponsorship activation enhances the Olympic Games experience for spectators and provides the youth of the world with opportunities to experience the Olympic ideals at the global and local levels;
- sponsorship support contributes to the success of the educational, environmental, cultural and youth-oriented initiatives of the Olympic Movement;

- sponsors develop advertising and promotional activities that help to promote the Olympic ideals, heighten public awareness of the Olympic Games and increase support for the Olympic athletes (IOC 2008).

In financial and practical terms the TOPs scheme seems to have been a success. Certainly judged in terms of IOC income growth and other targets the scheme has performed well. Figure 3.1 shows the growth of the scheme in financial terms over a three yearly cycle since the first scheme commenced in 1985:.

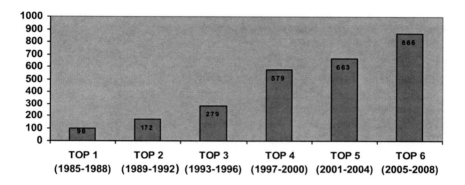

■ TOTAL REVENUE US$ million

Figure 3.1   Growth in TOP revenue 1985–2008

Figure 3.2 shows the allocation of income from the TOPs sponsors identifying the proportion given (in total) to the NOCs (which receive varying amounts of support) and the host cities (OCOGs). The allocations are made in part via Olympic Solidarity, an IOC sub-committee responsible for allocating funds (from TOPs and TV rights sales), via NOCs to the various national-local schemes, to the support of athletes and to sports development (Chappelet and Kubler-Mabbot 2008: 56–7).

The IOC outlines some basic principles governing the regulation of the TOPs scheme and its participants. The IOC aims:

- To ensure that no advertising or other commercial message in or near the Olympic venues is visible to the Olympic Games venue spectators or to the Olympic Games broadcast audience. No advertising or commercial messages are permitted in the Olympic stadia, on the person of venue spectators, or on the uniforms of the Olympic athletes, coaches, officials, or judges.

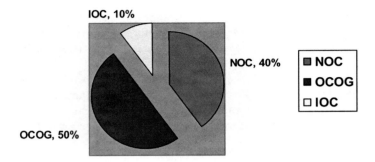

Figure 3.2   Overall proportional allocation of TOP income to beneficiary bodies

- To ensure a clean telecast by all Olympic Games broadcasters. Images of Olympic events are not allowed to be broadcast with any kind of commercial association.
- To control sponsorship programmes and the number of major corporate sponsorships…The TOP VI worldwide sponsorship programme…has twelve Partners, each with global category exclusivity.
- OCOG programmes are also designed to maximise support for the Games through the minimum number of partnerships.
- To control sponsorship programmes to ensure that partnerships are compatible with the Olympic ideals. The IOC does not accept commercial associations with tobacco products, alcoholic beverages (other than beer and wine), or other products that may conflict with or be considered inappropriate to the mission of the IOC or to the spirit of Olympism. (IOC 2008)

The benefits to sponsors accruing from affiliations are difficult to estimate (Miyazaki and Morgan 2001; Stipp 1998; Shani and Sandler 1992; Stipp and Schavione 1996). The Olympics offer a rich but unstable promotional and persuasive 'script' to consumers and marketers alike (Challip 2000). Crimmins and Horn (1996) examined various attitudinal data on US consumers in relation to Olympic sponsors:

> In studying the Olympics, we have found that about 60% of the US adult population say 'I try to buy a company's product if they support the Olympic Games.' And about 60% say 'I feel I am contributing to the Olympics by buying the brands of Olympic sponsors.' This gratitude exists before, during and after the games. A brand that creates an enduring link with the Olympics will enjoy the benefit of enduring consumer gratitude. (Crimmins and Horn 1996: 12)

However, such marketing success is not guaranteed. Consumers have no desire or need to be interested in who is sponsoring what. They often report ignorance and indifference regarding Olympic sponsorship deals, failing to identify Olympic sponsors, or mistaking non-sponsors promotional interventions for 'legitimate' Olympic marketing.

Marketers have pointed to the special global reach of the Olympics. For example Chinese beer makers, Tsingtao, named after the port city where the drink is brewed – and the host location for the Olympic sailing – hope to exploit the 2008 Games as an opportunity to promote their beer in global markets, especially the US (Matthews 2008). Martin Sorrel, Chairman of global advertising group WPP sees the Beijing Olympics as a central moment in the development of Chinese commerce – with the Games contributing to the development of local Chinese brands into significant global properties (Sorrell 2007, 2008). Visa brand managers point proudly to their long standing relationship with the Olympics and detail their commitment to a marketing approach which actively embed branding and other corporate activity within the Olympic Games – via athlete mentor schemes and other long term investments connected to their self styled marketing operation: 'Team Visa' (SportBusiness International 2007). The Visa approach is indicative of the incentive to bind corporate identities to the Olympic 'brand' as a means of re-defining or re-charcterising the ethos and public image of the enterprise.

Boltanski and Chiapello (2005) have observed that such re-characterisations of ethos have also been attached to various conceptions of the role, status and function of managers in contemporary corporations. People in management roles are described – and describe themselves and their activities – so that they 'become "team leaders", "catalysts", "visionaries", "coaches", "sources of inspiration" … [and even] … "business athletes"' (Boltanski and Chiapello 2005: 77–8). This was evident in Autumn 2005 when, following London's successful bid, *Spectra: The Journal of the Management Consultancies Association*, launched a special issue (2005) asking: 'Why Does Business *Love* Sport?' (italics in original). Wakerley (2005) discussed 'Exchanging the Office for the Olympics'; Adiba (2005) proposed 'Reaching Olympian Heights' and Phillipson (2005) considered 'Jumping on the Brandwagon'. This is perhaps an expression of a broader development identified by Omno Gruppe who points out that: 'sport [has] not only became part of cultural life, but furthermore a sportization of culture as a whole' has taken place (Gruppe 1990, cited DaCosta 2002: 112). The discourse of Olympic sport promises a hotline to a pervasive cultural sensibility. This is deemed highly valuable by corporate HR leaders, sponsors and advertisers.

Maintaining and Protecting the Olympic Brand

A good deal of the IOC agenda is assertively restrictive in relation to commercial-promotional agendas and practices. In some sense this simply secures the view that the IOC is behaving responsibly, as stewards of the intellectual and other properties within which the Olympics and Olympism – as global cultural assets – are enshrined. The IOC have worked hard (sometimes after the fact) to counter the kinds of flagrant over-commercialisation that characterised some aspects of, for example, the Atlanta (1996) 'Hamburger' Games.

However, there is clearly also a commercial motivation underpinning the principles outlined by the IOC in respect of TOPs. This is connected to the production, maintenance and credibility of the Olympic 'brand' as a commercial property. There are three constituencies for whom this 'brand'-credibility (in different ways) is a matter of considerable importance.

1. Citizens/and their governmental representatives: i.e. 'the public', who fund and support a good deal of Olympic activity (directly as 'consumers' but also via public support, financial underwriting and large subsides). The public are (also) at times the source and target for media-promotions. The public must, at some level, retain a sense of the credibility of the Olympic 'brand' as a values driven (educational) cultural asset. Otherwise the Olympics become, in some regard, (merely) one of a number of other (formally) comparable mega events (world championships, world cups, the Superbowl etc.). That is, spectacular sports events – but understood as largely disconnected from other socio-cultural values – and public policy agendas.
2. 'The Consumer': spectators and fans, and the targets of marketing commnications. Consumers must remain committed to the idea that the sporting spectacle is the point of the event. Attention is given to sponsors in passing, and as a consequence of their paid for support. If consumers/spectators feel that the 'tail' of commerce is wagging the Olympic-sports 'dog', then the credibility of both the event and of the associated sponsorship is diminished.[11] Likewise, as the IOC argue, if advertisers are associating themselves with the Olympic event without having however given approved IOC support, they are 'invading' and disrupting the consumers' experience and the event space – to the detriment of both.
3. Sponsors/sponsors' investors/shareholders: sponsors are formally committed to, and have a marketing interest in, the Olympic brand.

---

11   This dynamic is in operation in other areas of cultural entertainment. Donaton (2004) notes the convergence of commercial messages via placement of products in films, but also the wholesale adoption of events – which become the brand. This can turn consumers off.

They recognise that excessive or inappropriate exploitation of the Olympic event and its symbolic capital (by the IOC or by other sponsors and franchisees) is likely to diminish the value of their investment. It is the premium and 'special' nature of Olympic marketing affiliation that remains the IOC's USP in the work of persuading sponsors to sign up for TOPs and other sponsor relationships – and to keep the sponsors loyal. The Salt Lake City controversies in 2000 placed a good deal of pressure on the Olympic 'brand' values (Pound 2004) – as some sponsors' and others' trust in the principled operations of the IOC were diminished in the light of a corruption scandal (related to city bidding and inducements for IOC members).

The character of the Olympics 'brand' is important. It can serve (by its status as a socio-cultural 'good') to 'detoxify'[12] a sponsor brand in the face of consumers' boredom or cynicism in the face of yet more (run of the mill) marketing. The Olympics, notionally at least, offers a particular order of imagery, experience and value which is useful to advertisers seeking to transform their commodities into something that (seemingly) has a supra-marketing character.

It is perhaps for this reason (to maintain the auratic branding function of Olympic symbolic capital) that the IOC launched its 'celebrate humanity' brand building campaign in 2000. Celebrate humanity, as Maguire et al. (2008) propose, was partly an attempt to address anxieties over losing sponsors following the Salt Lake City corruption scandal. It was also a response to the media climate induced by the anti-globalisation movement and prominent anti-branding campaigns in that period. The IOC's campaign actively promoted the Olympics as a brand, and as a brand partner (Maguire et al. 2008) – hoping to re-produce the Olympics and Olympism as a sensitive and attuned vector for global or 'glocal' (commercial) relationships. This aim is affirmed in a campaign, which offered inspirational images around Olympic "brand propositions": hope, friendship and fair play for example.

The Olympic brand-building campaign marks a specific departure in terms of marketing practice on the part of the IOC. It included research into different regional and national 'markets' and feelings about the Olympic brand. Such information is helpful in persuading sponsors that the Olympic brand has 'reach', in the manner of a media channel, and 'currency', in the manner of a cultural icon. Both are key components of the Olympic brand value. This was not a matter of promoting this or that event or programme; nor was there a sponsors' brand leading the promotional strategy. Instead it was a matter of the IOC articulating, affirming and asserting its values (commercial

---

12   That is, remove the sense that it is an objectionable and over-marketed commodity and return the idea that, here, there is a credible cultural idea, product or relationship.

and cultural), in the language of branding, advertising and promotion. The motivations include aims:

1. to fulfil the IOC's longstanding commitment to promoting Olympic values world wide – here in an up to date manner using contemporary formats and technologies;
2. to maintain, develop, distinguish and defend the value of the Olympic brand to ensure the brand and its associated events could continue to serve sponsors as a suitable vector, or channel, for sponsorship and other promotional activities.

The second strategy is in line with a widening conception of what brands are, and what they do. Brands operate not just as clusters of values to pin to products and corporations, but as multidimensional channels touching multiple areas of life and culture.

Policing the Brand: Ambush Marketing

The IOC's, LOCOG's and NOC's dependence upon sponsors' belief in the integrity and distinctiveness of the Olympic brand has lead to a policy of stringent policing in relation to any infringements of the IOC's Olympic symbolic properties and rights, and, also to a detailed scrutiny of non-sponsors' activities in and around the Olympics. This latter is an attempt to offset non-sponsors' various attempts to draw valuable Olympic associations into their brand profile. To this end in advance of London 2012, LOCOG invites corporate (LOCOG 2007a, 2007b) and other institutions (charities and universities etc.) to 'respect our need to protect the value – both monetary and inspirational – of the London 2012 brand and of the Olympic and Paralympic Movements' (LOCOG 2007b). LOCOG set out guidelines[13] forbidding certain verbal and visual usage; this in defence of the Olympic brand. This misuse is now called 'ambush marketing'. LOCOG (2007b) defines it as follows:

---

13   For instance, for 2012 the following visual and verbal signs are regulated: the Olympic symbol, the Paralympic symbol, the London 2012 Olympic and Paralympic emblems; the words 'London 2012' and '2012', 'Olympic', 'Olympiad', 'Olympian' (and their plurals and things very similar to them – e.g. 'Olympix)'; the words 'Paralympic', 'Paralympiad', 'Paralympian' and their plurals and things very similar to them – e.g. 'Paralympix'; the Olympic motto – 'Citius Altius Fortius'/'Faster Higher Stronger'; the Paralympic motto – 'Spirit in Motion'; the Team GB logo; the Paralympics GB logo.; the British Olympic Association logo; the British Paralympic Association logo; London2012.com (and various derivatives).

... ambush marketing describes a business' attempts to attach itself to a major sports event without paying sponsorship fees. As a result, the business gains the benefits of being associated with the goodwill and public excitement around the event for free. This damages the investment of genuine sponsors, and risks the organiser's ability to fund the event.

This is by no means a new phenomenon. However, in the past, such infringements were policed in the name of *anti*-commercial values. Barney et al. (2004) cite instances of trademark protection (in the US) from the 1930s to the 1950s, especially with reference to the protracted conflict between IOC president Avery Brundage and Helm's Olympic bread (Barney et al. 2004; Tomlinson 2005: 180–81), at issue was not the value of the Olympic 'brand' but the 'purity' of the Olympic (amateur) ideal.

In Weymouth in 2007 a butcher was required to take down his Olympic sausages sign because it infringed IOC and LOCOG trademark rules. This seems like a trivial incident. In many ways it is. However the LOCOG response, i.e. that it had 'no discretion' in matters of rights protection indicates a rigorous commitment to brand value – in the commercial sense.

There have been far more serious instances of ambush marketing. Meenaghan (1994) cites Sandler and Shani (1989): 'In the 1988 Winter Olympics we observed Wendy's 'ambushing' McDonald's, American Express 'ambushing' Visa, Quality Inns 'ambushing' Hilton. Ambush marketing is a perennial issue. The *Financial Times* (Birchall 2008) reports that Nike, not an official Olympic 2008 sponsor, plans to launch a 'prominent' campaign during the Beijing Olympics – across all media. Nike is determined that it will not be affected by IOC and BOCOG efforts to police 'ambush' marketing[14]. Birchall reports further, indicating the complexity of image and rights issues:

> Efforts to control marketing by non-sponsors have become part of the modern Olympics. Beijing Olympic committee marketing officials have said local media would be advised against allowing advertising from non-Olympic sponsors. China Central TV and Li Ning, a local sportswear brand that is not an Olympic sponsor, have reportedly suspended a deal under which presenters and guests would have worn Li Ning's clothing in CCTV's studios during the games. (Birchall 2008: 5)

The policing of Olympic symbols and rights aims at preventing infringements of official sponsors' promotional investments, as well as curtailing promotional excess. There is a clear marketing rationale to such protections. There is a

---

14   Nike has a history of 'bad boy' ambush marketing (Klein 2000). This affirms its brand image as 'anti-institutional' and 'maverick' relative to competitors. At other times Nike have been in the fold, so that in Sydney (2000) Nike sponsored the Games (Pound 2004: 162)

further consequence however. As nef (the new economic foundation) (2008) point out: 'strict branding rules prevent local community organisations leveraging values from association with the Games' (nef 2008: 4). Given that the major sponsors of the Games are global brands there is a sense that – in it's promotional-symbolic dimension at least – 2012 will serve more often to signal global 'goods' as opposed to local ones.

A promotional tactic akin to "ambush marketing" is used not only by commercial competitors but also by political protestors. For instance there were anti-globalisation protests against the Olympic sponsors in Sydney – notably Nike and McDonalds (Lenskyj 2002: 207). Given the continuing mobilisation of branding and PR-style techniques[15] – facilitated by Internet and other new communications technologies – by political protestors and social movements, it is perhaps unsurprising that the Olympic brand and affiliates, can be 'ambushed' not by sponsors' competitors, but by political activists utilising the global prominence of the Olympics as a highly effective means to promote various agendas.

In recent months (in 2008) such activities have been focussed on the run up to the Beijing Games. Concerted campaigns highlighted human rights issues in Tibet (notably during the torch relay).[16] Another campaign, 'Dream for Darfur' picked up on the Beijing 2008 Olympic strap line 'One world, One dream' and urged people to target Olympic sponsors to lend active support in the alleviation of the famine and civil war in the Darfur region of Africa. The campaign web site describes its strategy:

> We are not calling for a boycott [of the Games]. But we are urging the Olympic corporate sponsors to join us in pressuring the International Olympic Committee (IOC) and China to, in turn, press Sudan to ensure that there is immediate protection for civilians and humanitarian workers on the ground in Darfur well before the Games begin. The Olympic corporate Partners, Sponsors, and Suppliers would prefer to say that this is not their problem. We believe that the more voices that are raised, the more hope there is for peace in Darfur. The Olympics belong to all of us, and in the face of genocide, anyone in a position of influence must try to act. (http://www.dreamfordarfur.org/index.php?option=com_content&task=view&id=33&Itemid=75)

A further'Dream for Darfur' campaign tactic has urged TV watchers to switch over during ad breaks to threaten TV rights and advertising revenue.

---

15   It might be more accurate to say that many new marketing techniques have borrowed from the 'informal' and ad hoc activities of new social movements – so that PR comes to resemble political agitation, just as political agitation comes to resemble PR.

16   However, Olympic online newspaper *Around the Rings* (18 April 2008) suggested that the protests over the Torch relay have had no effect on LOCOG's negotiations with potential sponsors.

Promoting the City

As numerous chapters in this book have suggested the Olympics can be understood as fulfilling a wide range of broadly 'promotional' briefs. Prominent, as discussed, is the highly visible advertising and marketing tie-in between the Games and corporate sponsors. However, other promotional agendas are perhaps equally central to the Olympic cycle – of bidding for the Games, planning and preparing for the event, hosting the event and developing and sustaining various legacies in the aftermath. Primarily these are related to the promotional activity of 'place-making'. Cities and nations demonstrably enter into various attempts, as the branding language has it, to 'reposition' themselves. This strategy is a response to an increasingly competitive global 'market'. Cities (and nations) aim to attract mobile capital, labour and tourism – as well as further mega events – as a means to develop, grow and assert themselves on the world stage. Both bidding for the Games (successfully or unsuccessfully) and in particular hosting the event, can signal to a global audience that this or that place (city, region, or nation) is in transition, increasingly ready to accommodate new businesses, new events and new ways of life. Burbank et al. (2001) argue that this entrepreneurial approach to city management in particular marks a shift in the modes and aims of municipal government. The Olympics can assist in promotional strategies towards:

- improving 'location factors' to bring in investors, new businesses (Preuss 2007);
- gaining attention from business and leisure tourists;
- signifying 'the good life' to tourists and potential inhabitants;
- reassurance against anxieties about 'unfamiliar' cites and nations or countries in political, economic or social transition.

In London there are significant sub-regions and locales which hope to benefit from the promotional aura of the 2012 Games. Olympic venues, such as the ExCeL Centre, will expect to accrue kudos from their Olympic partnership. Stratford, site of the main Olympic transport hub, will become more prominent 'on the map'. Local municipal boroughs (especially Newham, Tower Hamlets, Greenwich, Waltham Forest and Hackney) wish to boost their associations with the 2012 event – as 'host boroughs' and so enhance their 'brand image'. There is a tension, also, between an understanding, and projection, of 2012 as an *East* London event, as opposed to as a London-wide enterprise. One of the intended benefits of hosting 2012 is to be that London would affirm 'World city' status. The West End, the City of London and long-established tourist, retail and leisure locations[17] have a good deal of global 'cultural capital'

---

17 From The Bank of England to Soho and from The Tower of London to Buckingham Palace, the central royal parks and including Covent Garden, Oxford

already – with East London hoping that the Olympic experience will go some way in rebalancing (Greater) London's profile to better reflect the extended East End. The geographies of promotional activity around 2012 will feed the emergent sense, globally and locally, of post-Olympic London.

Retooling the City Ethos

As pointed out above Boltanski and Chiapello (2005) have observed the tendency to appropriate sporting and other metaphors in the reconception of management and other corporate practices. The sporting metaphors ('team', 'goals', 'business athletes' etc.) demarcate this or that 'new' business ethos as distinct from older, 'functional' or 'instrumental' descriptions of organisations and work patterns. In addition to the traditional processes of promotion and city-marketing the work of bidding for and delivering a Games allows numerous work-communities within the city to draw upon the Olympic ethos as an additional motivational script. This is often enacted in practical ways as corporate employees work as 'volunteers' in various functions. The intermingling of metaphors of current management-speak with Olympic Games discourses – i.e. discourses of the humanist ethical project and the sporting event – allows (at least in fantasy) for a reinvigoration and re-conception of service industry work – whether it be town planning, marketing, or other kinds of service provision (see e.g. Wakerley 2005; Adiba 2005; Smith and Westerbeek 2005).

The Olympic city promises (at the level of script and motivation) a (metaphoric) escape from instrumentalist managerialism (and its common languages) in favour of a more glamorous and revered ethos. Boltanski and Chiapello (2005) discuss the 'projective city'. One feature of this conception of an emergent working ethos is a focus on work as projects-based – activities bounded in time and linked by informal networks and connections – rather than by hierarchy or bureaucratic processes. This is a 'fit' and 'flexible' city. The drive (from government and business elites (Burbank et al. 2001) to become a host city is an expression of the urge to re-tool the city, to project a sense of the city as rehearsed in an ethos connected to the ultimate project (the Games) – and so, also for future projects. This serves a final promotional function: the Olympic city and its work force become associated and associates itself – reflexively and from outside – with the latest (motivational) discourses in (global) project management and delivery.

Street, Piccadilly, Kensington, The Strand and stretching towards Fulham, Chelsea and Richmond Park.

This Is and Is Not a Brand

> Olympism is a doctrine of the fraternity between the body and the soul.
> (Widely attributed to Pierre de Coubertin[18])

> For the thing we are looking for is not a human thing, nor is it an inhuman
> thing. It offers, rather, a continuous passage, a commerce, an interchange,
> between what humans inscribe in it and what it prescribes to humans. It
> translates the one into the other. This thing is the nonhuman version of the
> people.. What should it be called? Neither object nor subject. An instituted
> object, quasi object, quasi subject, a thing that possesses body and soul
> indissociably. (Latour 1996 cited Lury 2004: 148)

The operation of the Olympic brand has developed to play a significant
role in contemporary marketing and culture. Advertising and other media
agencies factor in an Olympic 'windfall' in those years when clients will
spend extra marketing budget on advertising around the Olympic festival and
corporate sponsors evidently pay a great deal to be involved. What is it, in
the contemporary moment, and as 2012 approaches, that makes the Olympic
brand such a compelling property? The Olympic 'brand', if that is the word,
seems to be both a powerful and a fragile property.

Sometimes, as we glimpse the famous and familiar five-ring symbol, or
see a medal placed around the neck of an athlete, perhaps one who has won
against the odds; or, as we intuit the long and lonely struggle (hitherto) of a
striving competitor (here and now) spontaneously joyful in simply taking part;
or, perhaps, as we grasp the cosmopolitan goodwill framed and ritualised in a
closing ceremony set against a host city backdrop, and remember or anticipate
the Olympic festival enlivening other fans and cities past and future; in these and
many other moments the 'Olympics' might affirm something of the 'good'.

In addition to the Games' snap-shot moments (and unlike many other
sporting events), the Olympics has a more explicit ethical commitment – to
a kind of humanism. Coubertin's philosophico-religious doctrine of 'the
fraternity between the body and the soul', draws upon, specifies, figures and re-
figures ancient and modern definitions of what it is to be human. The Olympics
(via 'Olympism' and the IOC), while being primarily a sports event, is also
a working discourse and a (global) movement actively defining, redefining,
and defending particular versions of personal and social 'good': prominently,
such values for example as 'fair play', 'taking part', 'commitment', 'joy' and
'effort', but also peace, community and social regeneration, developmental
sustainability and environmentalism.

The Olympics (as such) provides both an historic and contemporary
repository of imagery and ideals fit for the affirmation of 'good', this even

---

18   A sentiment widely echoed in de Coubertin's writings about Olympism.

in the light of scrutiny and analysis pointing up deficits, contradictions and infringements of explicit and implicit 'Olympic' ideals. The Games (as idea and event) opens and articulates spaces where (individually or collectively) we can ascribe, remember and build on a sense of values. Those experiencing the Games (directly or indirectly) can find, here or there, then or now, epitomes and epiphanies to capture or enact this or that otherwise abstract thought, relation or ideal. The Games invite and produce objectifications of 'the good' across numerous dimensions. Through its charters, in cities as they bid, plan and build, via media portrayals and *in situ*, Olympic Games provide unique 'arenas' to stage, experience and consider versions of the 'good'.

This 'inspirational' property is fundamental to Olympism. However, all of these features of the Olympics; the movement, its ideals, the moments and imageries of the Games, everything *good* about the Olympic 'good', produces also, and, increasingly, is produced *as*, a 'property'. This property is enshrined and embodied in athletes, in the Games, in the host cities and in Olympic paraphernalia of all kinds. It is a property which is ostensibly 'invaluable', but which is (therefore) also of great *commercial* value. The Olympic good can be – and is – transferred to 'goods' (cars, computers, financial services) and the Olympic 'values' can lend value – estimable and purchasable – to this or that brand. Thus, and incrementally, Olympian-human-cultural inspiration is (to a degree) reconfigured in the discourse of consumer motivation. In this transition, and in line with a long tradition of cultural criticism, (Williams 1980) there is a perceived (qualitative) diminution of human engagement – as, for instance, inspirational relationships between people are translated into aspirational relations to things (for sale).

In his (2004) analysis of commercial communication, entitled *Lovemarks: The Future Beyond Brands*, Saatchi and Saatchi CEO Kevin Roberts outlined his sense of some of the problems facing contemporary branding practitioners (and corporate bodies) charged with building and maintaining successful large-scale commercial communications strategies around logos, trademarks and advertising slogans. Brands, says Roberts (2004: 35), are 'running out of juice'. Roberts (from an advertising industry perspective[19]) outlines a number of reasons why branding, seen as such a powerful organisational principle for commercial and, increasingly also, 'non-commercial' activities[20] in the 1980s and 1990s, might require rethinking and reframing.[21]

---

19 Roberts's agency (Saatchi and Saatchi) held the 2004 Olympics campaign (Roberts 2004: 99).

20 It became widely intelligible and acceptable to talk about for instance universities, political parties and even religions (without irony) as 'brands' in the 1980s.

21 Roberts cites, for instance, the anti-brand lobby, the formulaic nature of contemporary brand management and communications design, new media and media clutter and customer apathy amongst the major problems for brand managers.

Roberts identifies a number of exceptional 'brands' and re-titles them as 'Lovemarks' in order to differentiate these, certain favoured exemplary iconic products and companies, against numerous ordinary run of the mill brands 'out there' in the cluttered environments of commercial communications. His list of cult brands – or rather 'Lovemarks' – includes some familiar and other less familiar 'brand' names; commercial and non-commercial icon. IPod, Lexus, Brahma beer, Olay, Guinness, Steinway, Doc Martens, the Statue of Liberty and the BBC are just some examples of 'Lovemarks'. He intimates (without any concerted attempt at providing evidence) the ways such 'brands' might enchant – 'beyond reason'. In sociological terms he finds a distinction between bureaucratic brands and charismatic 'Lovemarks' – those objects, activities and signs embedded in a space that describes neither (just) the market's arrays of reified objects and choices nor (only) the subjective space of desire, memory and affect (see Latour 1996).

The underlying point of Roberts's analysis[22] is that 'brands' (and the products – objects and events – they embody and in which they are embodied) succeed or fail in the extent to which they inspire passion and intimacy, and in the extent to which there is a degree of authentic engagement between the consumer and the activities, iconographies (and enacted values) of this or that corporate body. Brands which become formulaic, abstract and inauthentic fail. Such brands and associated products suffer 'commoditisation'. They become a mere 'thing', cast out and subjected entirely to the rational logics of the marketplace. They are forced (says Roberts) to resort to price-based competition and diminishing returns:

> One day you are sitting on a premium product, enjoying high margins and fighting off consumers. The next your product is being bottom-loaded on back shelves or dumped into 'specials' bins. (Roberts 2004: 29)

This is the brand managers' nightmare. The antidote to such a fate, for any and every brand, is to inspire passionate engagement – to become, no doubt with the help of Roberts's expensive team of advertising experts – a 'Lovemark'. The path to successful branding is (paradoxically) to be something more, or rather something *other* than a brand. If the 1990s were the decade for re-branding this, that and the other, then Roberts (alongside a number of other advocates for "new" marketing paradigms (Pine and Gilmore 1999; Gilmore and Pine 2007; Holt 2004)) is arguing for de-branding, or, as he puts it 'post-branding'.

Prominent on the list of 'brands/non-brands' which embody and inspire the passionate engagement characteristic of such post-brands or 'Lovemarks'

---

22   The book is in part analysis of contemporary communications problems, in part a kind of showcase for successful work undertaken by Saatchi and Saatchi (Roberts's agency) and in part perhaps a kind of 'pitch' aiming to attract the attention of potential future clients.

is the Olympics. Roberts points out that while the Olympics have become a 'marketing behemoth' they nevertheless 'hold tightly to the inspiration that sets them apart from other events'. He continues:

> The Olympic Spirit is characterized as Joy in Effort, Friendship and Fair Play, Dreams and Inspiration, and Hope. With sensational icons like the rings, the torch, the flame, and the medals as well as the sensual excitement of the opening events and competitions, the Intimacy of personal achievement, and the passion of thousand of athletes competing – the Olympics is a textbook Lovemark. (Roberts 2004: 99)

There are many ways in which the Olympics can be seen as a brand, and a powerful one.[23] However, and in a paradox that Roberts is alert to, the semiotic power and resonance of the Games, its nomenclatures, history, and its iconographies lie in the heritage of a movement whose distinction and mystique, such as it is, depends upon commitments to values formally and formerly understood to be 'outside' or at odds with commercial and marketing relationships. The IOC's 2004 Olympic Charter sets down some principles which are outlined as an appendix to the *IOC Olympic Marketing Fact-File 2008*.

> Olympism is a philosophy of life, exalting and combining in a balanced whole the qualities of body, will and mind. Blending sport with culture and education, Olympism seeks to create a way of life based on the joy found in effort, the educational value of good example and respect for universal fundamental ethical principles. The goal of Olympism is to place everywhere sport at the service of the harmonious development of man, with a view to encouraging the establishment of a peaceful society concerned with the preservation of human dignity. The Olympic Movement is the concerted, organised, universal permanent action, carried out under the supreme authority of the IOC, or all individuals and entities who are inspired by the values of Olympism. It covers the five continents. It reaches its peak with the bringing together of the world's athletes at the great sport festival, the Olympic Games. Its symbol is five interlaced rings. (IOC 2008: Appendix)

---

23   The Olympic five-ring symbol, as Chappelet and Kubler-Mabbott report (2008: 37) 'is said to be the best-known logo in the world, above that of Shell, the McDonalds golden arches, and the Mercedes star, and well ahead of the Red Cross or the United Nations'. The elision of distinctions between categories of organisation such as the UN, McDonalds and The Olympics within a notation that they are all 'brands' is important to note. Roberts (2004), the CEO of a global advertising agency, is willing after all to concede that thinking 'brand' can diminish the specificity and impetus of consumers' but also 'brand' strategists' recognition of the properties and activities in the marketplace and in consumer experiences.

These principles, this ethos, manifesto and constitution, have much in common with ideas that appear in branded statements. Perhaps what distinguishes Olympism and its institutions (if anything does) is a sense of a history, ancient and modern, and the knowledge, that unlike a car brand (think of Skoda) or a fashion label (e.g. Levis), the Olympics could not be so readily re-branded and remain, distinctively, Olympic. Unlike a product which is to an extent divisible from its cultural meanings (via revisions to marketing imagery), the symbolic power of the Olympics is indissociable from its ethos, history and institutions.

'Brand-speak' and the Olympics

This chapter has looked at some aspects of this paradoxical balance between Olympics as brand/non-brand, and outlines something of the ways that cities, sponsors and the IOC have attempted to both protect the Olympic 'mystique' and its values from commercial exploitation and to (concurrently) exploit heritage and 'mystique' for commercial gain – a 'mystique' embodied in intellectual and symbolic properties (logos, mascots, nomenclature and so forth), but also bound to the history and institutional structures of a cultural movement.

The terminology 'brand' here, above all, serves as a flag of convenience – since the irreducibility and relative complexity of the Olympics in its contexts is at issue – compared to a 'brand'. Such usage should be considered carefully on two counts. Lury (2004) warns in general that the term 'brand' used to account for corporations' economic activity can be a misleading shorthand implying 'a single thing' or 'a set of convergent processes' where there is none.

> To assume that the brand is a single thing would be to mistake the multiple and sometimes divergent layers of activity that have gone into producing the brand. (Lury 2004: 16)

This is perhaps particularly apposite in the context of discussing the Olympics 'brand' given the longstanding contestations over the extent to which such designations ('brand', 'branding' etc.) are adequate or accurate in describing and developing Olympic activities and values.

MacAloon[24] (2008) for instance reports ethnographic observations of the emergence of 'brand-speak' in the IOC's corridors of power. His detailed close observations enable him to provide a rich characterisation of the complexities underpinning notions of the Olympic brand – even within the IOC. MacAloon

---

24 MacAloon's analysis in this paper extends in more detail into a rich and important examination of the mobilisation of 'legacy' as a structuring term that has in some ways superceded 'brand and branding' in Olympic discourse.

suggests that 'the appearance of 'Olympic brand' conceptualisation and language' was by no means 'straightforward, unproblematic, and uncontested' (MacAloon 2008: 3). He goes on to point out that, on the contrary:

> To other IOC members, administrators, and interlocutors throughout the 'Olympic Family', this kind of [brand-] speech was taken to be offensive and it remains highly resented and resisted among such parties today. (MacAloon 2008: 3)

So the genealogy of 'brand' as a contested structuring concept is an important caveat. Nevertheless 'brand' certainly has currency, even hegemony, in current LOCOG and IOC documentation – and practice (IOC 2008; LOCOC 2007a, 2007b).

Lury's (2004) recognition of brands as necessarily multilayered and complex, and MacAloon's (2008) understanding of the fraught and contested genealogy of contemporary stratagems regarding the Olympic 'brand', in particular together, contextualise a contradiction which, in simple terms disentangles what, in practice, cannot be disentangled: i.e. the imbrications of Olympism by commerce, and the dependence of the commercial Olympic 'brand' upon the embedded history and culture of the Olympic movement and its institutions.

The risk that is only implicit in Roberts's (2004) celebration of the Olympics 'Lovemark' is that its symbolic, affective and institutional pre-eminence (for cities, athletes, fans, and sporting bodies) is provisional upon the careful and continuing maintenance of distinctions from other 'products', experience and entertainment commodities (Pine and Gilmore 1999; Wolf 1999). In this context, the maintenance of such distinctions is essential otherwise the Games becomes one of the herd – the numerous competing mega-event and sporting spectacles that are now characteristic of the increasingly competitive economies of entertainment, experience and cultural consumption – from the Superbowl, to the World Cup and other sporting and cultural mega-events.

Such potential 'brand' dedifferentiation and consequent over-commoditisation of the Games would be contingent upon a widespread and emergent sense that the values expressed and embodied in the Olympic charter, the Rings and via the actions and governance of host cites in their stewardship the Games and its legacies (i.e. London 2012), i.e. 'all individuals and entities [including sponsors] who are inspired by the values of Olympism', were (in fact) merely operationalising abstracted and instrumentalised bureaucratic 'brand values'. Contemporary consumers – if it is as 'consumers'[25] that we

---

25   The 'brand' paradigm invites the assumption that relations between people and institutions, objects, processes and events is necessarily in the manner of 'consumers'. This presumption is at odds with an older discourse of Olympism where the crowd engages as part of the spectacle. It is also at odds with participation in the Games by

are to relate to the Games – are highly alert to inauthentic pseudo-events and sloganeering (Gilmore and Pine 2007). The 2012 and other future Games may not be exempt from criticality – articulated by vociferous minorities and by apathetic majorities – aimed at various actual and perceived negligences in regard to the over-commercialisation of Olympic culture.

Savan (1994), in an article first published in 1988 just in the aftermath of the Seoul games, where the first TOPs scheme was in force makes the point with a telling irony:

> We Americans – heck, even Koreans – are tied in by cash, credit card, and consumption to the indomitable will of stadium studs. Today the Greek ideal of individualism has been pretty much reduced to choosing between Pepsi and Coke. If we don't run and dive with our heroes, we can at least drink and eat with them. Send the families, feel the heartbeat of America, add your two cents to history. It's just that this process makes family, heroism, and history taste like they come in Styrofoam containers. (Savan 1994: 93)

Conclusion

Klein's (2000) suggestion in regard to sponsorship schemes emerging in the 1980s, is relevant here.

> At first these arrangements seemed win-win: the cultural or educational institution in question received much-needed funds and the sponsoring corporation was compensated with some modest from of public acknowledgment and a tax break And, in fact, many of these ... public-private partnership arrangements are just that simple, successfully retaining a balance between the cultural event or institution's independence and the sponsor's desire for credit. (Klein 2000: 31)

There is however, and as Klein argues elsewhere, an issue of balance. The TOPs scheme has been a concerted attempt to balance the commercial development of the Olympic brand alongside and within the principles and parameters connected to its history as a global cultural and humanist movement. This balance no doubt shifts with, and within, broader trends governing the interplay of commerce and culture in the era of globalisation and consumer culture. In 2001, IOC marketing director Michael Payne's assessment was that:

---

volunteers, in the notion of citizens of host cities serving as 'hosts' to the games and not consumers of them. While 'consumer' is apt for the global TV audience (for games and advertising) it should not be the default category of all popular connections to the Olympic movement and its events.

> With the sheer size and complexity of today's Olympic Games, it has reached the point where if there were no sponsors, there would be no Games. (Michael Payne, cited DaCosta 2002: 108)

This seems like a somewhat partial assessment. Payne's economic logic might be flawless, but it is important not to underplay the relationships of interdependence –between a unique cultural property (The Olympics), governments, the public and a commercial system, at times desperate for credibility and trust, from jaded consumers.

The Olympic Games provide a widely recognised, intentional and ostensible signifier of a global good society. Embodied in the IOC, and practically applied in the complex process of city bids, Olympic congresses and, primarily in the Games themselves (Winter and Summer), Olympism seeks to transcend the places and controversies it touches and which touch upon it. It is the case that any such transcendence is an impossibility since Olympism also seeks to catalyse and crystallise positive transformations; regenerating cities, affirming values associated with fair play, environmental responsibility, health and well-being and so on. Lately, as we have seen, the Games have become closely associated with consumerist imperatives; binding inspiration to consumer motivations – in the service of brands and products.

As a result the Games and the Olympism becomes defined in dialogic controversies setting past ideals against current realities and future ambitions against real capacities. City by city and decade by decade the Olympics are constituted and reconstituted in the space of this dialogue. The dialogue between the Olympic movement and the commercial world requires a complex balancing act – only partially stabilised in the conception and development of an Olympic 'brand'. Reminiscent of some of the gymnastics performed during the games by young athletes, the IOC attempts a dynamic and spectacular balancing act. They strive to display their "brand", maintaining the prominence, integrity and significance of its symbolic and cultural presence – some times deploying spectacular and audacious manoeuvres – playing to win. At the same time they seemingly also have the means to resist submission to the gravity of commercial appropriation, and evoke the joy of the movement itself. Before, during and after 2012 spectators will watch critically on, partly in hope and partly in expectation, and wonder if the Olympian-marketing gymnasts will fall flat on their faces, or take a graceful bow and move on to the next event.

References

Adiba, P. (2005) 'Reaching Olympian Heights' in 'Perfect Match: Why Does Business *Love* Sport', special issue of *Spectra: The Journal of the Management Consultancies Association*, http://www.mca.org.uk/mca/pdf/spectra%20pdf.pdf: 18–19.

Barney, R.K., Wenn, S.R. and Martyn, S,G., (2004) *Selling the Five Rings : The International Olympic Committee and the Rise of Olympic Commercialism*, Salt Lake City: University of Utah Press.

Birchall, J. (2008) 'Nike Plans Olympic Ad Blitz', *Financial Times*, 1 July.

Boltanski, L. and Chiapello, E (2005) *The New Spirit of Capitalism*, London: Verso.

Buchanan, R. (1992) 'Higher, Faster, Farther', *Adweek*, 10 August, 20–21.

Burbank, M.J., Andranovich, G.D. and Heying, C.H. (2001) *Olympic Dreams: The Impact of Mega-Events on Local Politics*, Boulder, CO: Lynne Rienner.

Challip, L. (2000) 'Polysemy and Olympic Audiences: Lessons for Sports Marketing', Barcelona: Centre d'Estudis Olímpics UAB, http://olympicstudies.uab.es/pdf/wp097_eng.pdf>.

Chappelet, J. and Kubler-Mabbott, B. (2008) *The International Olympic Committee and the Olympic System*, London: Routledge.

Crimmins, J. and Horn, M. (1996) 'Sponsorship: From Management Ego Trip to Marketing Success', *Journal of Advertising Research* 36:11.

DaCosta, L. (2002) *Olympic Studies*, Rio de Janeiro: Gamma Filho Press.

Department for Culture, Media and Sport (DCMS) (2008) 'Before, During and After: Making the Most of the 2012 Games', 9 December. http://www.culture.gov.uk/reference_library/media_releases/5667.aspx/.

Donaton, S. (2004) *Madison and Vine: Why the Entertainment and Advertising Industries Must Converge to Survive*, New York: McGraw Hill.

Douglas, M. (1966/2005) *Purity and Danger*, London: Routledge.

Holt, D. (2004) *How Brands Become Icons: The Principles of Cultural Branding*, Cambridge, MA: Harvard University Press.

IOC (2008) *Olympic Marketing Fact File*, Lausanne: IOC.

Klein, N. (2000) *No Logo*, London: Flamingo.

Latour, B. (1996) 'On Interobjectivity', *Mind, Culture, and Activity: An International Journal* 3(4): 228–45.

Lenskyj, H.J. (2002) *The Best Olympics Ever? Social Impacts of Sydney 2000*, Albany, NY: State University of New York Press.

LOCOG (2007a) *Brand Protection: Businesses – What You Need to Know*, London: LOCOG.

LOCOG (2007b) *Brand Protection: Non-commercial Organisations – What You Need to Know*, London: LOCOG.

Lury, C. (2004) *Brands: The Logos of the Global Economy*, New York: Routledge.

MacAloon, J (2008) '"Legacy" and Managerial/Magical Discourse in Contemporary Olympic Affairs', paper presented at The International Journal of the History of Sport Conference *Olympic Legacies*, 29–30 March, St Antony's College, Oxford.

Maguire, J., Barnard, S., Butler, K. and Golding P. (2008) 'Celebrate Humanity or Consumers?: A Critical Evaluation of a Brand in Motion', paper presented at The International Journal of the History of Sport Conference *Olympic Legacies*, 29–30 March, St Antony's College, Oxford.

Mail Online (2007) 'Now Olympic logo is under fire for triggering migraines', June, http://www.dailymail.co.uk/news/article-460205/Now-Olympic-logo-triggering-migraines.html.

Matthews, V. (2008) 'Asian Challenger Brands in the US Beer Market', WARC Online, WARC.com, February.

McAllister, M.P. (1997) 'Sponsorship, Globalisation and the Summer Olympics', in Frith, K (ed.) *Undressing the Ad: Reading Culture in Advertising*, New York: Peter Lang.

Meenaghan, T. (1994) 'Point of View: Ambush Marketing: Immoral or Imaginative Practice?', *Journal of Advertising Research*, September/October: 77–88.

Miyazaki, A.D. and Morgan, A.G. (2001) 'Assessing Market Value of Event Sponsoring: Corporate Olympic Sponsorships', *Journal of Advertising Research* 41(9): 9–15.

nef (2008) 'Fool's Gold: How the 2012 Olympics is Selling East London Short, and a 10 Point Plan for a More Positive Local Legacy', http://www.new economics.org/gen/uploads/qdleej550fu2dr55vp3jhcin23042008185548. pdf.

Olins, W. (2003) *On Brand*, London: Thames and Hudson.

Paviit, J. (2001) 'In Goods We Trust?', in Pavitt, J. (ed.) *Brand.new*, London: Victoria and Albert Museum.

Phillipson, M. (2005) 'Jumping on the Brandwagon' in 'Perfect Match: Why Does Business *Love* Sport', special issue of *Spectra: The Journal of the Management Consultancies Association*, http://www.mca.org.uk/mca/pdf/spectra%20pdf.pdf: 13–15.

Pound, D. (2004) *Inside the Olympics*, London: Wiley

Poynter, G. (2006) 'From Beijing to Bow Bells: Measuring the Olympics Effect', London East Research Institute Working Paper in Urban Studies.

Preuss, H. (2004) *The Economics of Staging the Olympics*, Cheltenham: Edward Elgar.

Preuss, H. (2007) 'The Conceptualisation and Measurement of Mega Sport Event Legacies', *Journal of Sport and Tourism* 12(3–4), August–November: 207–27.

Roberts, K. (2004) *Lovemarks: The Future Beyond Brands*, London: Powerhouse.

Sandler, D.M. and Shani, D. (1993) 'Sponsorship and the Olympic Games: the Consumer Perspective', *Sport Marketing Quarterly* 2(3): 38–43.

Savan, L. (1994) *The Sponsored Life: Ads, TV and American Culture*, Philadelphia, PA: Temple University Press.

Shani, D. and Sandler, D. (1992) 'Sponsorship – An Empirical Investigation of Consumer Attitudes', presented at ESOMAR Sponsorship Research

Seminar, in conjunction with Sponsorship Europe '92, Monte Carlo, Monaco, 2–4 December.

Smith, A. and Westerbeek, H. (2005) 'Review: Leadership Lessons from Sport' in 'Perfect Match: Why Does Business *Love* Sport', special issue of *Spectra: The Journal of the Management Consultancies Association*, http:// www.mca.org.uk/mca/pdf/spectra%20pdf.pdf: 63–4.

Sorrell, M. (2008) 'The Power of Brands', *Admap*, China supplement, February.

Sorrell, M. (2007) 'Exciting Times', *Admap*, China Supplement, February.

Stipp, H. (1998) 'The Impact of Olympic Sponsorship on Corporate Image', *International Journal of Advertising* 17(1): 75–87.

Stipp, H. and Schiavone, N.P. (1996), 'Modeling the Impact of Olympic Sponsorship on Corporate Image', *Journal of Advertising Research* 36(4): 22–7.

Spectra (2005) 'Perfect Match: Why Does Business *Love* Sport', special issue of *Spectra: The Journal of the Management Consultancies Association*, http://www.mca.org.uk/mca/pdf/spectra%20pdf.pdf.

SportBusiness International (2007) 'Visa Europe – Team Visa: Torino 2006 Olympic and Paralympic Winter Games Leveraging Campaign', Sponsorship works 2007/www.sportbusiness.com.

Tomlinson, A. (2005) 'The Commercialization of the Olympics: Cities, Corporations, and the Olympic Commodity', in Young, K. and Wamsley, K. (eds) *The Global Olympics: Historical and Sociological Studies of the Modern Games. Research in the Sociology of Sport (3)*, London: JAI Press.

Toohey, K. and Veal, A.J. (2007) *The Olympic Games: A Social Science Perspective*, 2nd edn, Wallingford: Cabi.

Wakerley, M.J. (2005) 'Exchanging the Office for the Olympics', in 'Perfect Match: Why Does Business *Love* Sport', special issue of *Spectra: The Journal of the Management Consultancies Association*, http://www.mca. org.uk/mca/pdf/spectra%20pdf.pdf: 8–9.

Whitson, D. (2004) 'Bringing the World to Canada: The Periphery of the Centre', *Third World Quarterly* 25: 1215–32.

Wolf, M. (1999) *The Entertainment Economy: How Mega-Media Forces are Transforming Our Lives*, New York: Times Books, Random House.

Chapter 4
Olympic-driven Urban Development

Dean Baim

In 1896 the first Olympic Games of the modern era was held in Athens, Greece. Of the 311 athletes who competed, 230 were Greek nationals. When the Olympic Games returned to Athens 108 years later, they had evolved from a mostly national sporting event to an international sport spectacular that is watched by billions of people. In the 2004 Games 11,099 athletes from 202 countries competed.[1] As the popularity and magnitude of the Olympics have grown so has the interest in cities wishing to use the Olympics as a means to a changed urban environment and to raise global awareness of the city as a site for tourism and commerce.

Before analysing how the Olympic Games have been used over the years to alter the urban setting it is useful to categorise the areas of urban development that are typically affected by the Olympics in the most recent games. This chapter then observes how the Games have evolved over time to include an increasing number of these areas of urban development. This chapter analyses the impact of only the Summer Games. This is for two reasons. One is that the Summer Games are a much larger endeavour than the Winter Games, and as such have a greater opportunity to affect urban development. Second, the Winter Games are a newer series of Games and as such do not have the history that the Summer Games do.

Areas of Urban Change

Holger Preuss (2004: 91–2) identifies five sectors of a city that can be affected by the Olympic Games. They are:

- *Transportation*: the Olympic Games generate a classic peak-load problem for the host cities. If, as is hoped, a large number of out-of-town tourists visit the host city during the Olympics, there will be an increased demand on the city's public transit and roads. The city's international airport will see above normal traffic from athletes, officials, media, and fans. The city, wishing to make a good impression on its out-of-town guests, wants these additional traffic flows to be handled without

---

1 http://en.wikipedia.org/wiki/2004_Summer_Olympics.

delays, so it invests in expanded infrastructure of roads and public transportation options. The ability to handle the heavy transportation demands increases the likelihood that after the Games the city can compete successfully for private investment and conventions.

- *Telecommunication*: to handle the multinational media coverage afforded the Olympics the city's telecommunication system must be state-of-the-art. The city must have sufficient internet and mobile phone capacity to handle the extra demand, as well as the latest fibre optic networks and sufficient power systems to allow the Games to be broadcast globally. A strong telecommunication system makes the city more competitive for future business locations.
- *Sports venues*: the modern Olympic Games are an extension of the founder's theories of physical exercise as a basis of a balanced education and that organised international competition could serve to bring international unity. Two (of three) of Pierre de Coubertin's reasons for founding the Games had to do with the development of sports facilities and sites for training (Chalkley and Essex 1999).
- Many resources are devoted to the design and construction of the Olympic Stadium, which becomes one of the symbols of that city's Games. But most of the modern Games make significant expenditures on facilities for competitions that do not take place in the main venue. The longevity and post-Games contribution of these facilities varies with the host city depending upon the national culture and pre-Games planning (Baim 2004).
- *Housing*: where to accommodate more than 11,000 athletes securely is no minor issue. Athlete housing has become a more important and costly item with the increased concern for the athletes' security. An issue that arises is how the housing should be distributed at the conclusion of the Games. In many cities the housing is made available for the general public. In many cases the housing goes to the middle class and lower upper class. This has been criticised by those who believe the housing should be used for lower income groups. In some cases, the housing is donated to colleges and universities.
- *Urban culture*: the life-style of the city's citizens is often enriched through new or improved parks, and more facilities for leisure-time activity. There often is a heightened awareness of the national and city customs, sometimes through added museums and cultural shows. During the summer of the Games additional cultural activities are often made available.
- *Ecological Investment*: in the most recent Games, the host cities and the International Olympic Committee (IOC) have become increasingly sensitive to the ecological footprint imposed by the Games. This may be to offset the criticism lodged by ecological groups such as Greenpeace, but whatever the motivation, the Olympic Games have been used frequently

to mitigate existing ecological weaknesses as well as demonstrate new techniques designed to reduce the strain on the local and global eco-system. The IOC now requires bidding cities to respond to questions of how the city will address ecological issues. Preuss (2004) does not treat ecological investment as one of his five urban sectors affected by the Olympics. In face of the increased attention this is receiving both within the Olympic movement during the bidding process and outside the Olympic community, this is becoming a major development area.

Not completely separate from these areas of urban development, but occasionally a goal by itself, is the promotion of the city to the world as a center of leisure and/or commerce. This serves to promote the city for tourism, convention trade, and outside private investment.

Often the Olympics will accelerate the planning and implementation of the urban investments mentioned above. In this way, the mass transit project that normally would take decades to approve and implement is completed in a period of approximately seven years. This, of course, is a double edged sword. The good news is the city gets the benefit of the investment earlier than it otherwise would. The potential downside arises because the project may suffer from higher costs and more hurried planning.

The Evolution of the Olympic Games as an Agent for Urban Development

The very early modern Olympic Games were modest affairs that were generally held in association with international exhibitions such as a world's fair. The 1896 Games were cause to renovate the Panathenean Stadium with private funds. The Games of 1900 and 1904 were not enough of an event to stand on their own. The 1904 Games were originally given to Chicago, and would have been the first stand-alone Games, but the Chicago organisers experienced financial difficulties and the Games were moved to St Louis to complement the St Louis World's Fair (Chalkley and Essex 1999: 375). It was after the financial distress of Chicago that the IOC demanded financial guarantees from (mostly) government agencies to insure the Games would be held as planned. The 1908 Games were held in London in conjunction with the Franco-British Exhibition, but they were the first Games for which a facility was expressly built for the competitions.

Besides being the first stand-alone Games, the Stockholm Games of 1912 achieved a number of other firsts. It was the first to build a number of new sporting venues, not just a main stadium for the Olympics. The Stockholm Games were also the first where government involvement was used to finance the construction of facilities. During the planning stage, the main stadium evolved from a temporary stadium to a permanent one after the government permitted several lotteries to raise funds for a permanent venue. It also was the first stadium whose design expressed the culture of the Swedish people, a trait that continues to this day ((Chalkley and Essex 1999: 376).

The 1920 Olympics in Antwerp was the first Olympics driven by municipal boosters hoping to use the Games for their personal gain (Renson and den Hollander 1997). This perhaps was necessary since the International Olympic Committee was disoriented because of World War I and the 1920 Games were not awarded to Antwerp until April 1919, leaving the city less than 16 months to prepare for the event. If the Stockholm Games were the first to involve government intervention in the financing of the stadiums, the Antwerp Games were the first to promise government funding during the bidding process. According to the bid documentation, Antwerp agreed to build a new swimming facility and the city awarded the Games a grant of BF800,000. If at all, the nature of the urban development achieved prior to the Antwerp Games had been in the form of improved sports venues. The Antwerp Games were the first to start improving the transportation aspect when the city agreed to construct an access road to the Olympic stadium that was owned by the sporting society that was promoting the bid (Renson and den Hollander 1997: 76).

The Paris Games of 1924 were the first to have housing for the athletes, however these were in the form of temporary wooden barracks, so did not add to the post-games housing inventory. The Amsterdam Games of 1928 are not known for any innovations in the area of urban planning.

Like the Antwerp Games, the 1932 Los Angeles Games were the brainchild of a group of businessmen who wanted to promote Los Angeles and who stood to gain personally from the city acquiring the event. In the early 1920s these boosters arranged for a complicated financing arrangement to finance the initial construction of the Los Angeles Memorial Coliseum, the main stadium for the 1932 Olympics (Reiss 1981). Like the Games in Los Angeles 52 years later, the 1932 Games relied on existing locations for venues and private funds. The athletes' Olympic Village for the Los Angeles Games was the first to be made available for sale after the conclusion of the Games (Chalkley and Essex 1999: 377).

Whereas the 1920 and 1932 Games were used to promote local investment and tourism, the 1936 Games were used to advance a political philosophy, beginning a trend where the Games explicitly were used as a political tool. The Berlin grounds were originally prepared for the 1916 Games that were cancelled due to World War I. The centrepiece of the planned Games was a 32,000-seat stadium constructed with private funds. Twenty years later Adolf Hitler planned to use the Olympic Games for propaganda to further his concept of German cultural and ethnic superiority. The 32,000-seat stadium was replaced with a 100,000-seat stadium and an Olympic site that included many new facilities and a cultural centre. Driven to show the potential of the new Germany, the Berlin Games left a larger impact on the city's urban infrastructure than any of its predecessors. The Olympic Village was built outside of town to impress visitors. The legacy of the 1936 Games included many sports and cultural facilities, including the Olympic Stadium, which, after refurbishing, was used as the site of the 2006 FIFA World Cup soccer final.

The 1948 Games were hosted once again in London. London was scheduled to host the 1944 Olympics which were cancelled because of World War II. Given that resources were still scarce in post-World War II Europe, there was no development investment made for these Games. Existing sports facilities were used for all events, and the athletes' housing was a converted Royal Air Force barracks. The sombre nature of the 1948 Games earned them the nickname, the 'Austerity Games'.

Besides the sporting venues, housing became the major urban development contributions of the 1952 Helsinki and 1956 Melbourne Games. The Helsinki Olympic Village was designed to be a self-supporting, residential community after the Games were completed. The Olympic Village in Melbourne was used by the government to house immigrants (Chalkley and Essex 1999: 379). The 1960 Olympics altered the Roman infrastructure so much that it caused some to suggest that the future Games be cancelled because of the cost and the magnitude of the urban changes. The Roman municipal water supply system was replaced, new airport facilities were built, public transportation was improved. There were two centres for Olympic activity on opposite sides of the city. These two centres were connected by a new road. The city was made more attractive to tourists with new street lighting and illumination of the cities many monuments.

The IOC awarded the 1940 Games to Tokyo, but World War II cancelled the Games for that Olympiad. Ignoring a request by the IOC to moderate the degree of urban investment, the 1964 Tokyo Games generated even more urban development than the Roman Games. Japan used the Olympics as a way of announcing its reentry into the world of nations. Tokyo, wanting to show the world the modern Japan, is estimated to have spent US$2.7 billion for the infrastructure improvements made for the Olympic Games. The Tokyo freeway system was built in preparation for the Olympics. Like Rome, Tokyo replaced its water supply system. To make the city more attractive to tourists Tokyo leaned heavily on improving its environment. Tokyo added three sewage treatment plants and cleaned its rivers and streams. Tokyo also improved its city services by initiating regular trash pick-up and street cleaning. City health and food hygiene standards were improved. While these improvements were designed to enhance its image, they also served to make the Tokyo Games the first green games.

Many observers felt that the large scale investments made by Rome and Tokyo intimidated potential host cities since the number of bids to host the 1968 Games was fewer than normal. Mexico City was awarded the Games, but the country was in an economic contraction so few resources were devoted to the Games. The largest investment made during these Games was the Olympic

Village. Existing sports venues were used. These were located in various parts of the city and with no investment in public transit or roads; the Mexico City Games are remembered for their traffic jams.

The 1972 Games in Munich is an example of an urban development plan that was accelerated due to the pending Olympics. Unlike Mexico City, all of the sporting venues and the Olympic Village were to be located on one site, north of Munich. The location was an abandoned World War II airstrip. A 1963 city plan identified the area to be developed as a sports complex over a 15 to 20 year period. When Munich won the bid for the 1972 Games in 1966, the time horizon was compressed to six years. The Munich Olympic Village is used as a housing project for low and mid-income families. The Munich Games also saw the return of large-scale urban development in preparation for the Olympics. Even though the Olympic site was north of the city, the downtown area benefited from significant investments. Three expressways with 90 miles of total length were constructed. Public transp0rtation was improved and the historic section of town was restored including pedestrian streets.

The IOC's strategy of awarding the 1976 Games to Montreal backfired, and almost ended the Olympic Games. The IOC selected Montreal over larger competitors, such as Los Angeles and Moscow, to counter criticisms that the Games were becoming so extravagantly expensive that only the world's elite cities could hold successful Games. Mayor Jean Drapeau had championed the 1967 World's Fair and saw the Olympics as another opportunity to redevelop the city as well as showcase the city to the world.

Like Munich, the primary Olympic site had been earmarked much earlier as a site for recreational use. The Olympics hastened the process. Additional sports venues were located in other sections of Montreal and existing facilities were upgraded. Transportation was upgraded as the subway was extended to the Olympic site from downtown, and a new airport was built. After the Games, the Montreal Olympic Village became a residential area that is so popular that a waiting list is used to fill vacancies.

To the horror of the IOC the labour disputes and poor financial controls of the Montreal Games left the endeavour hopelessly in debt. Under the terms of the contract, the financial deficit fell to the City of Montreal. Observers place most of the blame on Drapeau, who embraced a 'politics of grandeur' rather than financial prudence. Drapeau is quoted as saying, 'Name me one Roman emperor who history remembers because he reduced taxes' (Levine 2003: 105). The end result was a stadium that was not complete a decade after the Games concluded, a city with a massive 30-year debt, and a municipal pension fund that still faces an 'actuarial deficit' of $1.7 billion because the city had stopped making payments into the pension system as a way of paying some of the Olympic and World's Fair bills (Levine 2003: 11).

The 1980 Moscow Games, known more for the boycott by Western countries, contributed far less to urban development than did the Montreal Games. Most of the sporting venues were already constructed as part of a five-year plan when the bid was awarded to Moscow. Twelve venues were completed more quickly than planned so they could be used for the Olympics. Infrastructure investments included a new airline terminal, and new telecommunication facilities. The Olympic Village now houses 14,500 Muscovites (Chalkley and Essex 1999: 384).

The 1984 Games were the first to be awarded after the Montreal Games. Rather than refuting the critics who argued that the Olympics were too extravagant for a city, particularly a smaller city, to afford, the Montreal experience reinforced these criticisms. As if to confirm these critics, only one legitimate bidder emerged for the 1984 Games. Almost by default, the 1984 Games were awarded to Los Angeles. Not unlike the 1932 Games, the bid was organised by a private group of boosters, although these boosters had less direct financial gains from promoting Los Angeles than did their 1932 predecessors.

The Los Angeles Games were as opposite of the Montreal Games as one could imagine. Los Angeles' Olympic Organising Committee (LAOOC) planned on making minimal investment expenditures and aggressively seeking revenues from broadcast rights, endorsements and merchandising. The LAOOC sold more sponsorships to the Games than ever before, and charged top rates for the sponsorships. To control costs the LAOOC used existing venues, upgrading them where necessary. There was no new investment in housing. Dormitories at the University of Southern California and the University of California, Los Angeles were used to house athletes. No additional investment was made in transportation, with the exception of a second deck being added to the international airport. Telecommunication investment was not needed since Los Angeles was already a communications hub. The 1984 Los Angeles Games improved the self- and global image of Los Angeles not only as a center for commerce and tourism, but as a well-run city, but the 1984 Games left little in the way of an urban development bequest.

What the Los Angeles Games did leave is a more than $200 million profit. That profit endowed a foundation promoting amateur athletics in Los Angeles. It also resurrected the Olympic movement showing that the Games could not only be successful athletically, but they could be financially viable. This prompted vigorous competition for the next Games to be awarded, the 1992 Games.

The 1988 Games were held in Seoul. These Games, more than any prior to 1988, emphasised the cultural aspects of the host nation, Korea. Palaces and shrines were restored, and at least four museums were opened. The environment also was a focal point of the Seoul Games. A massive effort to reclaim the Han River was undertaken, not only to improve the environment, but to make the river available for transportation. Investments were undertaken that moved sewage and industrial waste to treatment plants. Once the river became safer, beaches were created along the river's edge. The transportation investment was focused on public transit. Three new subway lines were built and 47 bus routes were extended. The cost of the environmental and transportation investments is estimated to be $17 billion.

The 1992 Barcelona Games reinforced an extensive urban development plan that had the purpose of elevating the image and awareness of the city. Many of the projects undertaken had been planned long before Barcelona was awarded the 1992 Games but once again, the on-coming Olympics gave new urgency in starting, and completing, these projects. While the main stadium was a restored facility in Montjuîc Park many new venues were built. The location of the Olympic Village necessitated a new placement of two rail lines that separated downtown Barcelona from the coastline. Originally this property had been part of an industrial area. The industrial section was replaced with beaches, which after the redirection of the train tracks, were easily accessible to downtown. The sewage system was also modernised and cultural interest in Barcelona was rekindled. Four museums and a botanical garden were renovated in preparation for the Games. The attempt at image improvement was successful. By 2004, Barcelona was the number one tourist destination in Europe.

Attempting to follow the Los Angeles model, the 1996 Games in Atlanta had little impact on non-sports development. Ten new venues were constructed, including the Olympic Stadium that was converted into the home stadium of a US Major League Baseball team. Many of the new venues were located at, and later donated to, local colleges and universities. Similarly, the Olympic Village was located on the campus of Georgia Tech, and is used currently for student housing. The Atlanta Games were projected to be self-supporting, but needed close to $1 billion dollars of public funds to be completed on time. The major non-sports legacy of the Atlanta Games is Centennial Park, a downtown park designed to improve the lives of local residents after the Games. Like Mexico City, the decision not to make transportation investments led to an overburdened transportation system during the Games. These problems, and a bombing in Centennial Park, left many Olympic officials with a bias against future bids from cities that rely on private sector funds as heavily as the Atlanta Games proposal did.

The 2000 Summer Games in Sydney was touted as the Green Games, although Greenpeace only gave the Games a narrow pass grade for their efforts. Part of the environmental awareness was necessary because the main Olympic site, Homebush Bay, was a toxic dump. Homebush Bay was zoned to be reclaimed for recreational purposes in a 1984 planning document. Once again, the Olympics prompted long planned investments to be accelerated. In keeping with the Green Games theme, the Olympic Village incorporates solar power. Some observers question whether a new stadium and arena were necessary since they seemed to duplicate existing facilities downtown. Indeed, the Homebush stadium and arena have entered into bankruptcy, as has a rail link from downtown to Homebush that was created to take Olympic visitors to the Olympic site and commuters now living in Homebush to downtown.

The 2004 Athens Games involved so much investment that it introduced a new form of continental aid to pay the bills. Hoping for a 'Barcelona Effect' the spending on stadiums and all aspects of infrastructure was so lavish that one-third of the cost was borne by the European Economic Community's development fund. Even with this aid, the debt burden on Athens and Greece is said to near $7.1 billion.[2] Many cynics claim that it is more likely that Athens will realise a 'Montreal Effect'.

Conclusion

Table 4.1 summarises the previous discussion. Those boxes marked in black indicate a significant commitment in that sector. A grey block indicates a minor commitment. A white cell indicates no or little development in that sector. No column is created for telecommunications since it is assumed that every city will upgrade its telecommunications network for their Games.

A casual look reveals that for the most part there is a steady increase from left to right in the number of filled boxes. This indicates the growing expectations that the Olympics play in urban development. From the early Games where only sport sites were built to latter-day venues which included sporting site investments, as well as infrastructure and environmental investment.

An interesting question is how much of the pattern in urban development reflected in Table 1 arises from the host city's internal development programme and how much comes from pressure and requirements the IOC imposes on the city as a condition of hosting the Games. The evidence seems to be mixed. Some urban investment, such as Barcelona's urban redefinition and Munich's sports park, had been part of the city's plans for decades before the Games were held. The awarding of the Olympics in these cases created a motivation for undertaking projects that had languished in the planning stage.

In other cases, the original plan of one host city motivates the IOC to make that area a part of the subsequent bidding process. Sydney's environmental plan prompted the IOC to ask bidding cities to follow similar protocols for future Games (SOCOG 2001: 19). In this case the host city's ideas influenced the demands made on subsequent hosts.

In still other cases, the germ of the idea starts with the IOC or even an individual member of the IOC. It is reported that the addition of a cultural component arose from Pierre de Coubertin's insistence that the Stockholm Games include cultural exhibits as a condition of receiving the Games (ACOG 1997: 146, 145). Every Games since 1912 has had some cultural component although its role and importance has varied. The motivation for the programmes of urban development is an interesting question requiring further study. This will require researchers to have access to the candidate bids

---

2 http://www.chinadaily.com.cn/english/doc/2004-08/24/content_368435.htm.

Table 4.1   History of urban investment by sector: Olympic Games 1896–2004

Year	Host	Sports facilities	Housing	Transport	Urban culture	Environment
1896	Athens	▓				
1900	Paris					
1904	St Louis					
1908	London	▓			▓	
1912	Stockholm	■			▓	
1920	Antwerp	■		■	▓	
1924	Paris	■	1		▓	
1928	Amsterdam	■			▓	
1932	Los Angeles	■	■		▓	
1936	Berlin	■	■		▓	
1948	London				▓	
1952	Helsinki	■			▓	
1956	Melbourne	■			▓	
1960	Rome	■		■		■
1964	Tokyo	■		■		■
1968	Mexico City					
1972	Munich	■			■	
1976	Montreal	■		2	■	
1980	Moscow	■		3		
1984	Los Angeles	▓ 4		5		
1988	Seoul	■			■	■
1992	Barcelona	■		■	■	■
1996	Atlanta	■		■		■
2000	Sydney	■		■		■
2004	Athens	■		■	■	■

Notes

1. Temporary housing was built for athletes. The housing structures were destroyed after the Games.
2. Little done for Olympics since most infrastructure investment was completed for the 1967 World's Fair.
3. A new terminal was built in Moscow airport.
4. The 1984 Games renovated existing facilities but built no new facilities.
5. Airport had a second deck added to accommodate departing passengers.

as well as the questionnaire posed to the candidate cities by the IOC and other bodies. No systematic attempt has been made to determine if investment in the Olympic Games and infrastructure was prudent (although in some cases conclusions may be unavoidable). The assessment is, perhaps, best made by those who live in the community.

In some ways the city's attitude to public involvement towards Olympic driven urban investment is already reflected in the commitment of resources. It is probably not a coincidence that the two Olympics in the last fifty years that relied least on public funding were Los Angeles and Atlanta, both reflecting the entrepreneurial spirit of the US. The history of other Olympic Games over the same period seems to reflect other national and regional values. The Mediterranean countries spent more and undertook more involved investments than their counterparts in other countries. In the same way, the Asian hosts of the Tokyo and Korean Games invested heavily in sewage treatment and cleaning rivers to promote a sanitary and environmentally friendly image to the world.

The urban development investments decisions are not made in an economic vacuum. Olympics held when there is a national economic contraction (Mexico City 1968) or a shortage of economic resources (London, 1948), are years where little or no urban development was generated by the Olympics. Another issue not addressed in this paper is the question of equity. In some cases urban development came at the expense of the low-income and politically weak. This leads to a normative question that cannot be answered by science.

Although no attempt has been made here to determine if the investments were prudent, it is possible to surmise which investments seemed to earn a positive return. Clearly, Barcelona falls into that category. Los Angeles, in both 1932 and 1984, also achieved a good return on the investment; if for no other reason, than the investment was relatively small. Tokyo increased its global image and the transportation investment made for those Games seem to have paid off as a contribution to making Japan one of the world's leading economies. On the other hand, Montreal and Sydney (given the high number of financial distress cases coming from the 2000 Games) seem to fall short of a positive return. It appears likely that the most recent incarnation of the Athens Games fall into this category as well.

The IOC's attitude towards infrastructure investment displays a subtle and consistent sensitivity to the host cities' (and nations) economic condition. The host cities for the Games conducted in the 1960s (Rome, Tokyo and Mexico City) all are in countries that could be classified at that time as developing. During this period, the IOC expressed concern that the infrastructure costs associated with these Games may have been rising to unacceptable levels. In contrast when London was granted the 2012 Games, the IOC welcomed the bid as being based upon regeneration. Such an apparent change in philosophy can be attributed to the fact that the IOC was not concerned about the expense London would incur in preparation for the 2012 Games because, unlike the cities from the 1960s, London in the twenty first century was a major developed economy and the investment could be better borne by the organisers, the city, and the nation.[3]

Finally, while it may be possible to see the impact of normative values and economics on the size of the Olympic driven urban investment, there does not appear to be a pattern one can rely on in predicting which strategies will most likely succeed. Cities in two developed countries, Los Angeles and Barcelona, both appear to have won the Olympic development game but used different strategies. On the other hand, Sydney, also in a developed country, put in fewer resources than Barcelona and seems not to have won, or at least not to have succeeded as well as Barcelona did. At the same time, Atlanta tried to play the Games using the Los Angeles strategy, but its success, if it was successful, was more modest than that realised by the city it sought to emulate.

References

Atlanta Committee for the Olympic Games (ACOG) (1996) *Official Report of the Centennial Olympic Games, Atlanta 1996*, Vol. 1, Atlanta: ACOG.

Baim, D. (2004) 'The Post-Games Utilization of Olympic Venues and the Economic Impact of the Olympics After the Games', *Proceedings of the First Olympic Economics and City Development Forum*, Beijing: Humanistic Olympic Studies Center, Renmin University of China.

Chalkley, B. and Essex, S. (1999) 'Urban Development through Hosting International Events: A History of the Olympic Games', *Planning Perspective* 14(4): 369–94.

Levine, M.V. (2003) 'Tourism-Based Redevelopment and Fiscal Crisis of the City', *Canadian Journal of Urban Research* 12(1): 102–23.

Preuss, H. (2004) *The Economics of Staging the Olympic Games*, Cheltenham: Edward Elgar.

Renson, R. and den Hollander, M. (1997) 'Sport and Business in the City: The Antwerp Olympic Games of 1920 and the Urban Elite', *Olympika* 6: 73–84.

Riess, S.A. (1981) 'Power without Authority: Los Angeles' Elite and the Construction of the Coliseum', *Journal of Sports History* 18(1), Spring: 50–65.

Sydney Organising Committee for the Olympic Games (2001) *Official Report of the XXVII Olympiad, Sydney 2000*, Vol. 1, Sydney: SOCOG.

---

3 In addition, the IOC may also believe, as was not clear in the 1960s, that the infrastructure investments may lead to positive returns that justify the costs. Also, the 1960s was a period before significant media rights income was available to cover the costs of the investments.

PART 2
Olympic Cities

Chapter 5

The Legacy of the 1988 Seoul Olympic Games

Hyunsun Yoon

Background

Seoul was awarded the 1988 Olympic Games on 29 September 1981 in Baden-Baden. The Olympic Movement was going through 'a very worrying time', recalls Juan Antonio Samaranch, the then President of the International Olympic Committee (IOC):

> The terrorist attack that traumatized the 1972 Games in Munich had demoralized several cities that were nurturing hopes of hosting the Olympic Games. Montreal's financial problems in 1976 exacerbated this recession. As a result in 1978 only one city, Los Angeles, bid for the 1984 Games. The 1980 boycott of the Moscow Games was a further setback. (Samaranch 1994: 406)

Only two oriental cities, Nagoya (Japan) and Seoul, were bidding for the Games and Seoul was chosen. Held in a politically divided nation, the 1988 Games was significant because athletes from all over the world met together for the first time since the 1976 Montreal Olympics. A total of 160 countries participated in the 1988 Games and the Games, despite the absence of athletes from seven countries, clearly had an impact on the Olympic Movement in that it ended the era of boycotts.

The Olympic Movement, in return, has also affected the domestic political context of South Korea. The 1988 Seoul Games has been closely associated with a dramatic and decisive process of democratisation, by the end of which the military regime in South Korea had been peacefully displaced by a new era of multi-partyism and electoral democracy (Black and Bezanson 2004: 1246). The IOC's decision to award the 1988 Games to Seoul had been understood as lending international legitimacy to the repressive military regime of General Chun Doo-Hwan (Kim 1997: 392). The IOC's decision can be seen as an occasion when it turned a collective blind eye to the abusive human rights practices of regimes, which clearly violated the principles promoted in the Olympic Charter such as 'the establishment of a peaceful society concerned with the preservation of human dignity', 'respect for universal fundamental ethical principles' and incompatibility with 'any form of discrimination with regard to a country or a person on grounds of race, religion, sex or otherwise' (Black and Bezanson 2004: 1,246). Ironically, the military-led government of President Chun for whom the bidding for the Seoul Olympics was very much a political project, was South Korea's last military regime.

The Games thus played a catalytic role in political change and there is no doubt that it also had economic and cultural impacts on major events in the Korean peninsula. These include the joint entry of North and South Korea into the United Nations in September 1991 and the first international exposition held in a developing country at Tae-Jon in 1993. The Koreans are hopeful that the 2014 Olympic Winter Games will be held in Pyeong-Chang. The focus of the campaign is the sustainable increase in winter sports participation in Asia (Jin 2007: 24) and building on the plans submitted to host the 2010 Games (Pyeong-Chang competed with Sochi (Russia) and Salzburg (Austria), Sochi won the bid).

This chapter explores the political, economic and cultural impacts of the Games on the host city and country. It examines the legacy of the 1988 Games, both hard legacy gains, such as improved infrastructure, and soft legacy gains, such as enhanced confidence and international status. The chapter concludes that the 1988 Games brought significantly positive legacies for Seoul and South Korea.

Political Impact

The Cold War era boycotts led by the US in 1980 and the Soviet Union in 1984 had boosted the term 'Political Olympics' as descriptive of the recent history of the Games (Kim 1997: 390). The boycotts clearly indicate that the Olympics have reflected the international political climate of their time. In addition to international relations, national politics also has strong links with the Olympics and, in broader terms, with sport. Sport has served the purpose of nation-building and national integration in many countries. The military-led government of General Chun (September 1980 to February 1988) found it very advantageous to make use of sports both in improving Korea's overseas image and in enhancing harmony among people at home.

South Korea became a member of the IOC in 1947 and it first participated in the 1948 London Olympics. It was in the late 1970s under President Park Chung-Hee's regime that the idea of hosting the Olympic Games was first born (Black and Bezanson 2004: 1,250). After President Park's assassination in 1979, his successor General Chun Doo-Hwan proceeded with an Olympic bid. The Koreans' response to the bid to host the Games was twofold. The Seoul Games unquestionably evoked a great surge of national pride and patriotism among the Koreans. There were, however, also objections to hosting the Games. Anti-government politicians and university students perceived the

Games as a 'pure' political project of the military government. They called the Chun government the 'Sports Republic'. Indeed, two international sports events, the 10th Asian Games in 1986 and the 1988 Games were held in South Korea in the 1980s, and during this period professional sports were introduced in the country for the first time.

According to Black and Bezanson (2004: 1,248–9), the decision to bid for the Olympics and the response of the Koreans to that decision can only be fully understood in the context of the harsh reality of the country's ongoing adjustment to a newly installed military dictatorship during the 1980s. Many Koreans hoped for a new democratic era after President Park's assassination but these hopes were dashed by General Chun's military coup. Opposition to this seizure of power was widespread and throughout the 1980s pressure for democratisation continued. The question of elections and constitutional reform became more urgent. It was when Roh Tae-Woo, then chair of the ruling Democratic Justice Party (DJP), accepted direct presidential elections and all other opposition demands, including amnesty for political prisoners and broad civil liberties, in a nationally broadcast declaration on 29 June 1987, that the crisis came to a resolution. Presidential elections took place in December 1987; Roh Tae-Woo won the election but during separate parliamentary elections in April 1988, his party, the DJP, failed to win a majority in the National Assembly, which was unprecedented for the ruling party (Kang 2003: 257).

Although the Seoul Olympics cannot claim to have *caused* the process of democratisation and political change in South Korea given the 'ripeness' of other conditions for transition, they can be deemed to have had a signal effect on the *pace* and *peacefulness* of the transition (Black and Bezanson 2004: 1,254). The 1988 Games created a deadline for decisive action and the threat of a profound national humiliation if far-reaching change was not set in train. Similarly, Weede argues that the anticipation of the Games eased and accelerated South Korea's transition to democracy (Weede 1988: 317).

The Seoul Games was very much a political project with various political consequences. Larson and Park (1993: xvii) argued that at the national level the political consequences of the Games included the use of the Olympics as a project to mobilise the nation. It was also suggested that the Games were used as publicity in South Korea's international propaganda battle with North Korea. At the grassroots level, there has been a sense of resentment about the government's policies on North Korea. It was viewed that the government should have cooperated with North Korea in hosting the Games to a greater extent (Kim 1997).

The 1988 Games was indeed a massive exercise in image politics for Seoul and South Korea; not since the Korean War occurred in 1950–1953 had such extensive worldwide attention centred on the Korean Peninsula. According to a national survey conducted immediately after the Games, most Koreans think that the Games played a very important role in enhancing a sense of solidarity among Korean people as well as increasing the nation's visibility in international terms (Kim et al. 1989). Although this indicates that the Korean government had been successful in convincing its people of the beneficial effects of the Games to the country, some argued that not all of the regions benefited from the event, especially in economic terms.

Economic Impact

The Korean economy, as a newly industrialising country, had achieved phenomenal success from the 1960s and there was an urgent need to replace the nation's war-torn image, derived from the Korean War of 1950–1953, with a new, prosperous one. From a poor developing country to one of the foremost trading nations in the world, South Korea transformed itself in only three decades. South Korea's rapid economic growth has been driven by the export market and overseas income from export sales was invested in industrial infrastructure, notably heavy and chemical industries, which resulted in the development of shipbuilding, automobile and electronic industries by the mid-1980s (DTI 1995). In 1997–1998, South Korea went through an economic crisis, which resulted in the imposition of IMF conditions, but it is considered to have made a successful recovery. In fact, South Korea's capacity utilisation ratio reached 81 per cent by July 1999, back at its pre-crisis level, and industrial production grew by over 30 per cent in 1999; in addition, consumption continued to recover, as shown by the 9 per cent increase in household consumption in 1999 (British Trade International 1999). From one of the poorest countries in the world, South Korea's per capita GNP increased to US$15,840 in 2007, which made the Korean economy the world's 12th largest (H.-S. Lee 2007). Today South Korea is poised to become competitive in the higher-technology industries such as semi-conductor chips and consumer electronics.

To focus on the figures during the years leading up to the Games, the production resulting from Olympic projects amounted to 1,846.2 billion Korean won, accounting for 0.4 per cent of the GNP (Pyun 1999). The Seoul Games showed that a city could significantly improve its infrastructure by hosting an Olympics that was, as an event, also financially viable (PricewaterhouseCoopers 2004: 20). A recent report on the economic impact of the Olympic Games revealed that Seoul upgraded its transport and telecommunications facilities, as well as constructing new urban centres with housing, retail and other community facilities that have been fully integrated into their metropolitan areas. Indeed, the Seoul Olympic Games brought about tangible and intangible economic effects. Seoul benefited from the longer-term impact, often referred to as the 'Olympic legacy', through, for example, hard legacy gains (improved infrastructure) and soft legacy gains (improved international status).

When Seoul was chosen as the venue for the Games, there were concerns that the cost of the Games would be a heavy burden on the national economy.

Indeed, 'it was a national challenge and it took an enormous public investment – some three billion dollars – to bring it off' (Hubbard 1994: 435). In fact, in the early 1980s, the balance of payments deficit was a serious problem for the Korean economy along with its growing foreign debt (Pyun 1999). Another typical concern was about a possible post-Olympic recession, considering Japan's experience of a temporary recession after the 1964 Tokyo Games. Japan's GNP growth rate fell from 13.2 per cent to 5.1 per cent in 1965 (Pyun 1999). The Korean economy, however, enjoyed sustained growth, recording a 12 per cent growth rate in 1989 and, overall, the Games proved a financial success and generated a budgetary surplus (see Table 5.1).

Table 5.1   **Financial balance of Olympic organising committees (US$m at 1995 prices)**

	Operational costs	Revenues	Balance excluding investments	Overall balance
Munich 1972	546	1,090	544	–687
Montreal 1976	399	936	537	–1,228
Los Angeles 1984	467	1,123	656	335
Seoul 1988	512	1,319	807	556
Barcelona 1992	1,611	1,850	239	3
Atlanta 1996	1,202	1,686	484	0
Sydney 2000	1,700	1,900	239	0

Source: PricewaterhouseCoopers European Economic Outlook (2004: 20).

There were several reasons for its success from an economic standpoint. First, existing facilities were used for most competitions for the Games. Out of a total 112 competition sites, only 13 were newly built (Pyun 1999). Most existing facilities reverted to their previous use after the Games. As a key part of the urban regeneration objectives of the Games, the main newly constructed accommodation for athletes and journalists – the Olympic Village – was sold as residential units after the Games, which helped to ease the housing shortage in Seoul. Second, although Seoul saw significant infrastructure investment for the Games, the city was already equipped with a relatively sufficient infrastructure. As a metropolis of over 10 million people, Seoul had a developed social infrastructure, such as good transportation facilities and accommodation to hold a mega sports event such as the 1986 Asian Games. Third, the Games-related investments were necessary for industrial development and improved public welfare. Typical examples are the expansion of Kimpo International Airport, the Olympic Freeway and communications networks. A domestically developed Wide Information Network System Service (WINS) linked over

100 sites, including countrywide competition sites, the Olympic villages, the press centre, and relevant government offices. Fourth, the Seoul Olympic Organising Committee (SLOOC) collected substantial fees for TV rights, and foreign currency revenues increased due to the influx of tourists. A sum of 841 billion Korean won was raised by the SLOOC, which covered game-operation expenses. The figure accounts for 75.9 per cent of the funds for projects directly related to the Games, which totalled 1,108.4 billion Korean won (Pyun 1999).

In brief, the Seoul Games accelerated the country's economic development. Pyun (1999) calculates that from 1982 to 1988, Olympic projects-related production amounted to 1,846.2 billion Korean won (0.4 per cent of the GNP) and 336,000 temporary, pre-event, new jobs were created. For example, in 1987 alone, Olympics projects employed 0.5 per cent of the nation's total workforce. As a result, South Korea enjoyed a trade surplus of US$14.2 billion in 1988. However, the growing trade surpluses have had various negative effects, including increased trade friction with industrial powers, pressure from market liberalisation and inflationary pressures resulting from the increase in money supply. The Games has also been criticised on the grounds of its negative role in exacerbating uneven regional development between Seoul and the rest of Korea. There were scores of conflicts over space in the construction period for the Games (Kim 1993: 398). Seoul's least well-off residents lost housing to the 1988 Games and the 1986 Asian Games developments and had to be relocated, which led to numerous, large demonstrations (Kang 2003: 71).

Seoul also benefited from soft legacy gains such as increased awareness and reputation, which contributed to the expansion of exports and diversified overseas markets. In 1988, trade volume with Eastern European countries, for example, Hungary, Yugoslavia, Bulgaria and Poland, increased 80 per cent over the previous year, amounting to US$3.65 billion (Kang 2003: 251). The increased economic cooperation with these countries led to the establishment of official diplomatic relations.

Cultural Impact

The face of modern Seoul has been described as the result of bombings (the Korean War), a booming economy (the capital city of a newly industrialising country), and the Olympic Games (Zincone 1989). The massive building projects and urban development for the Games played a significant role in the transformation of the entire urban form of Seoul. It is believed that the introduction of the aesthetic to the cityscape was one of major imports of the Seoul Olympics (Kim 1997: 394).

Over 100 organisations and commercial sponsorships under the control of the Central Council for Pan-national Olympic Promotion had been operating to encourage public initiatives for the Olympics (SLOOC 1989). The projects included the Han River Development and the constructions of the Olympic Park, Seoul Sports Complex and other competition venues. First, the Han River Development included the construction of the Olympic Highway along the riverside, the Olympic Grand Bridge over the river, and the Han River Park housing numerous recreational, green spaces. The beautified Han River became the most frequently televised backdrop as Seoul presented itself to the world.

Second, the Olympic Park was built to accommodate the Olympic Centre, the Olympic Village, the International Broadcast Centre, the Main Press Centre and other sports venues. There were also outdoor stages constructed for folk arts performance and the creation of a Sculpture Park. During and since the Olympics, the Olympic Park has served as one of the city's tourist highlights. Third, sports facilities in the Seoul Sports Complex have been refurbished and the complex housed the Olympic stadium, the main focus of the Games. The Seoul National Institute's nationwide survey revealed that Seoulers perceive the Olympic-related places – the Han River Park, the Olympic Park and the Olympic Stadium – as the most beautiful landscapes in Seoul (Kim 1997: 396).

Finally, along with these projects, scores of buildings for cultural events and entertainment have been either newly constructed or refurbished, for example, the Seoul Arts Centre, the National Classical Music Institute, the National Museum of Contemporary Arts and the Chongju Museum. These facilities served various cultural programmes during the Games such as the Seoul Olympic Arts Festival and have continued to promote traditional culture and international culture exchange.

The development of traditional Korean culture and the promotion of international cultural exchange were greatly encouraged during the Olympic period. The Korean people's increasing concern about their own culture and traditions had resulted in the construction of cultural centres and the preservation and restoration of historical heritages in Seoul (Kim 1997: 394). It was especially in the opening and closing ceremonies that the ideas of 'how to define Koreanness and how to translate it in terms of internationally communicable means' were best demonstrated (Kang 1992: 80). This re-discovery and reinvention of cultural traditions have been the part of the Korean elites' attempts to establish the unity and integrity of the new democratic government.

Seoul saw evidence of community participation in the Games events through volunteering: Seoul Olympic Sports Promotion Foundation (www. sosfo.or.kr) records that 27,221 volunteers participated. Seoul was also successful in engaging people in pre- and post-Games events. In pursuit of making 'a clean, green and cultural city' the Seoul Metropolitan Government set up the 'Environmental Beautification Programme' to mobilise its citizens to participate in beautifying the city (SLOOC 1989). It is not clear, however, whether or not, or to what extent, good environmental practice was given any significance in this programme. Environmental sustainability was not an important part of the bidding or planning process. The 17th post-Games annual anniversary events in the Olympic Park in Chamsil, Seoul and international conferences were well attended.

The Games established South Korea as a safe and pleasant tourist destination, replacing the earlier war-torn images with new prospering ones. Seoul has succeeded in attracting rising numbers of tourists during and immediately after the mega-sporting events such as the 1986 Asian Games, the 1988 Games and the 2002 World Cup in Seoul, which was advertised as a lineal descendant of the 1988 Games. For example, the number of foreign tourists increased by 16.4 per cent in 1986, compared with the average of 7.4 per cent annual increase rate for the previous decade (Kang 2003: 84). However, the evidence is unconvincing as to whether these events alone had the long-term impact on the substantial growth in tourism. Although the tourism legacy is uncertain, the entertainment, sports and leisure industries have been significantly improved and expanded. Major Korean conglomerates invested in the construction of leisure and sports facilities and in professional sports. Kang explained that this was based on the strategy of the 'commercialisation of leisure', which was made possible by the Games and the increase in GNP (Kang 2003: 296).

Conclusion

The Seoul Olympic Games are generally believed to have brought significantly favourable outcomes for Korea and Seoul in terms of legacy benefits such as improved infrastructure, urban redevelopment and improved international status. In the context of the Olympic Movement, the Games were the catalytic agent for ending the Cold War boycotts era. Research suggests that the connection between the 1988 Games and the process and timing of democratisation in South Korea is strong (Manheim 1994; Weede 1988; Black and Bezanson 2004). Black and Bezanson (2004: 1,245) argue that the experience of the Seoul Olympics in 1988 has led major games boosters to assert boldly their liberalising potential, especially in the context of the 2008 Beijing Games. South Korea also saw legacy benefits such as the commencement of trade and diplomatic relations with Eastern European countries, then the Communist bloc. As part of the Korean elites' attempts to establish the unity and integrity of the new democratic government, the re-discovery and reinvention of cultural tradition and the promotion of international cultural exchange were encouraged during the Games. It was essentially hoped that the 1988 Seoul Olympic Games would provide legitimacy at home, protection from a hostile North Korea, and serve notice to the world of Korea's arrival as an economic power (Manheim 1994: 236) and it seems the Seoul Games lived up to these aspirations.

References

Black, D.R. and Bezanson, S. (2004) 'The Olympic Games, Human Rights and Democratisation: Lessons from Seoul and Implications for Beijing', *Third World Quarterly* 25(7): 1,245–61.

British Trade International (1999) *Partnership Korea: Information Guide*, London: British Trade International.

Department of Trade and Industry (1995) *South Korea: General Information Pack*, London: DTI Korea Trade Promotion Unit.

Hubbard, J. (1994) 'The Olympiads as a Reflection of Contemporary World Tensions', in Park, S.-J. (ed.), *Stories Behind the 1988 Seoul Olympics*, Seoul: Koryo Publishing.

Jin, J.-E. (2007) 'IOC Evaluation Commission in Pyeong-Chang', *The Chosun Ilbo*, 15 February, 24.

Kang, J.-M. (2003) *History of Modern Korea: 1980s*, Seoul: Inmul and Sasang.

Kang, S.-P. (1992) 'Comparative Study of Seoul Olympics and Barcelona Olympics', Studies of Humanities and Social Sciences, Kimhae, Korea: Inje University, Institute for Humanities and Social Sciences 75–94.

Kim J.G., Rhee, S.W. and Yu, J.C. (1989) *Impact of the Seoul Olympic Games on National Development*, Seoul: Korea Development Institute.

Kim, Y.-H. (1997) 'Interpreting the Olympic Landscape in Seoul: The Politics of Sport, Spectacle and Landscape', *Journal of the Korean Geographical Society* 32(3): 387–402.

Larson, J.F. and Park, H.-S. (1993) *Global Television and the Politics of the Seoul Olympics*, Boulder, CO: Westview Press.

Lee, H.-S. (2007) 'Korea's GDP Falls to 12th in the World', *Korea Times*, 16 May.

Manheim, J.B. (1994) 'Rites of Passage: The 1988 Seoul Olympics as Public Diplomacy', *Western Political Quarterly* 43(2): 279–95.

PricewaterhouseCoopers (2004) *PricewaterhouseCoopers European Economic Outlook*, London: Pricewaterhouse Coopers Limited.

Pyun, D.-Y. (1999) 'The Economic Impact of the Seoul Olympic Games', unpublished paper presented at 7th International Postgraduate Seminar on Olympic Studies, International Olympic Academy.

Samaranch, J.-A. (1994) 'The Seoul Olympics and Me', in Park, S.-J. (ed.) *Stories Behind the 1988 Seoul Olympics*, Seoul: Koryo Publishing.

Seoul Olympic Organising Committee (SLOOC) (1989) *Games of the 24th Olympiad Seoul 1988: The Abridged Official Report*, Seoul: Seoul Metropolitan Government.

Weede, E. (1988) 'The Seoul Olympics, Korea, and World Politics', *Korea and World Affairs: A Quarterly Review* 12(2).

Zincone, G. (1989) 'Welcome to Seoul', *Abitare*, April: 218–26.

Chapter 6

The Economy of the Barcelona Olympic Games

Ferran Brunet

Introduction

Barcelona's dream of hosting an Olympic Games that would achieve the highest levels of human and sporting quality was fulfilled. In the process, the city underwent an impressive transformation. Overall, we can say, the Barcelona Games were a total success in organisational and sporting terms. The urban transformation generated by the Games had far-reaching economic and social impacts. Barcelona has been highly successfully in harnessing the impetus and legacy of the Games; for example, by 2006, the city was ranked as Europe's fifth most attractive. Consequently, the Barcelona Games, their organisation and impact, have become a model from the sporting, organisational, economic, social and urban planning perspectives. This chapter examines the following:

1. the organisation of the 2002 Games in terms of the model adopted, methods and resources used over the 1986–1992 period;
2. the impact of the investments made on economic activity, employment, income, construction, tourism and transport, with special emphasis on the 1992–2002 period;
3. the city's harnessing of the Olympic impetus to improve its strategic position with a view to the future (2002–2010).

1986–1992: Preparing for the Games

In organising the Olympic Games, Barcelona aimed to ensure sporting excellence, in keeping with the Olympic spirit, and to bring about a major urban transformation leading to the improved quality of life and an enhanced attractiveness of the city as a whole.

The Barcelona Model

The key to the success of the Barcelona Games lies in the strength of the objectives (organisational excellence and urban impact), the inter-institutional consensus, the use of special management bodies, mixed private-public funding models, and also the successful harnessing of the Olympic impetus and the attraction of investment (Samaranch 1992).

These features and the excellent results achieved (Ajuntament de Barcelona 2007) constitute a 'Barcelona model' that links urban transformation to major events. Figure 6.1 sets out the main features of this model.

Economic Resources of Barcelona'92: The Cost of the Games and Source of Funding

A distinction must be drawn between organisational costs (items not usable after the Games) and investment in building work and facilities which would continue to serve the city in the future. The organisational costs are in effect the genuine 'net cost', since their functions end with the termination of the Games. The aim was to minimise these organisational costs. In contrast, facilities and infrastructure constitute part of the Olympic Legacy, the benefits of which continue after the Games, and were, therefore, to be maximised.

The resources allocated to organisational costs and investment in facilities and infrastructure, and their impact, are set out in Table 6.1. There is a major difference between total organisational costs (S1,364 million, mainly funded by the Organising Committee) and the investments in infrastructure and facilities ($8,012 million). The latter accounted for 85.5 per cent of total Olympic spending (Figures 6.2 and 6.3).

COOB'92 closed their accounts in July 1993: spending had totalled 195,594 million pesetas, that is, $ 1,638 million (equivalent to $1,678 million at 2000 rates), with a surplus of $3 million (COOB'92 1993).[1]

Income accruing directly to COOB'92 itself accounted for 75.2 per cent of the total. The main sources of this income were sponsorship and television rights. In organisational costs, the main outgoings were for television and press facilities (International Communications Centre and technology), the competitions themselves and Olympic family services (See Table 6.1 and Figure 6.2 for the exact distribution). The main COOB'92 costs lay in services (49.9 per cent of the total), followed by investments in infrastructure (33.8 per cent).

Olympic Organising Committee Income, 1964–2008

By comparison with other Olympic Games, the Barcelona Games were outstanding for the increased Organising Committee income, investment

---

1   As the project advanced, public and private investment far exceeded initial projections: $1,984 million, April 1985; $6,435 million, March 1991, and $9,376 million, finally in July 1993. The real cost, the organisational expenses, remained fixed in current peseta rates, but the volume of investment generated by the Games rose extraordinarily.

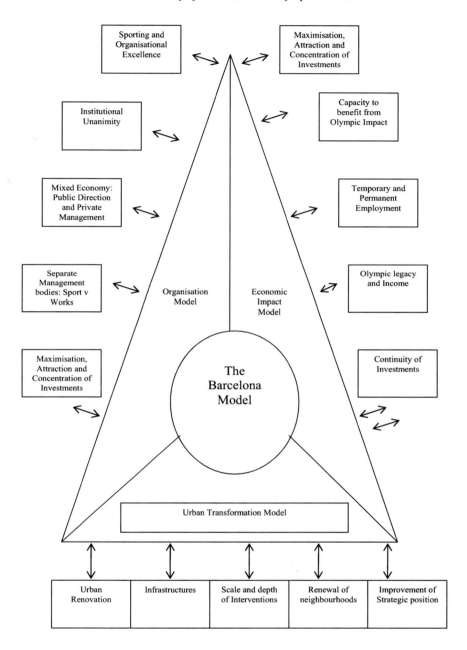

Figure 6.1   The Barcelona model

Table 6.1 **Economic resources of the Barcelona Olympic Games 1992: sources, applications and impacts**

Accumulated values 1986–1993	Pesetas (000,000)	US$ (000,000) Current	Euros (000,000) At 2000 rates	Distribution (%)	
A Source of funding	**1,119,510**	**9,376**	**11,532**	**12,474**	**100.0**	
1 Commercial income	*668,387*	*5,598*	*6,886*	*7,448*	*59.7*	*100.0*
1.1 Domestic private company investments	204,697	1,714	2,108	2,280	18.3	30.6
1.2 International private company investments	108,320	907	1,116	1,207	9.7	16.2
1.3 Spanish state company investments	130,416	1,092	1,343	1,453	11.6	19.5
1.4 HOLSA income	42,306	354	435	471	3.8	6.3
1.5 COOB'92	182,648	1,530	1,882	2,036	16.3	27.3
Television rights	54,164	454	558	604	4.8	8.1
Sponsors: monetary payment	58,152	487	599	648	5.2	8.7
Sponsors: payment in kind	42,448	356	438	474	3.8	6.4
Lotteries	20,143	169	208	225	1.8	3.0
Others	7,741	65	80	87	0.7	1.2
2. Government funding	*451,123*	*3,778*	*4,647*	*5,026*	*40.3*	*100.0*
2.1 State funding for COOB'92	12,947	108	133	144	1.2	2.9
2.2 HOLSA: MEH and AB credit	112,590	943	1,160	1,255	10.1	25.0
2.3 State budget investments	325,586	2,727	3,354	3,628	29.1	72.2
Barcelona City Hall (municipality)	22,789	191	235	254	2.0	5.1
Generalitat de Catalunya (regional government)	142,726	1,195	1,470	1,590	12.7	25.7
Spanish state (central government)	116,124	973	1,197	1,295	10.4	31.6
European Union	8,100	68	84	91	0.7	1.8
Other public administration bodies	35,848	300	369	399	3.2	7.9
B Application and use of resources	**1,119,510**	**9,376**	**11,532**	**12,474**	**100.0**	
1 Organisation (COOB'92 programmes)	*162,880*	*1,364*	*1,678*	*1,815*	*14.5*	*100.0*
1.1 Competitions	14,045	118	145	157	1.3	8.6

Table 6.1 cont'd

Accumulated values 1986–1993	Pesetas (000,000)	US$ (000,000)		Euros (000,000)	Distribution (%)	
		Current		At 2000 rates		
1.2 Ceremonies and cultural events	9,053	76	93	101	0.8	5.6
1.3 Press, radio and television	18,254	153	188	203	1.6	11.2
1.4 Preparation of facilities (building works excluded)	13,510	113	139	150	1.2	8.3
1.5 Technology	24,791	208	256	277	2.2	15.2
1.6 Olympic family services	37,023	310	381	412	3.3	22.7
1.7 Security	4,671	39	48	52	0.4	2.9
1.8 Management and corporate image	18,618	155	191	207	1.7	11.5
1.9 Support structures	22,915	192	236	255	2.0	14.1
2 Resources applied to building work (public and private investments linked to the Games) = Olympic Legacy	*956,630*	*8,012*	*9,855*	*10,660*	*85.5*	*100.0*
2.1 Roads and transport	404,514	3,388	4,167	4,507	36.1	42.3
2.2 Telecommunications and services	123,313	1,033	1,271	1,375	11.1	2.9
2.3 Coasts, water management, and parks	60,438	506	622	673	5.4	6.3
2.4 Housing, offices, and premises	139,741	1,170	1,439	1,556	12.5	14.6
2.5 Hotels	119,884	1,004	1,235	1,336	10.7	12.5
2.6 Sports equipment and facilities	87,511	733	902	976	7.8	9.1
2.7 Cultural and health facilities, and others	21,229	178	219	237	1.9	2.2
C Total economic impact	**3,107,788**	**26,028**	**32,014**	**34628**	**100.0**	
1 Direct impact	*1,165,600*	*9,762*	*12,007*	*12987*	*37.5*	
1.1 Resources applied to organisation and building work (A = B)	1,119,510	9,376	11,532	12474	36.0	
1.2 Spending by non-resident visitors	46,090	386	475	514	1.5	
2 Indirect impact	*1,942,188*	*16,266*	*20007*	*21641*	*62.5*	

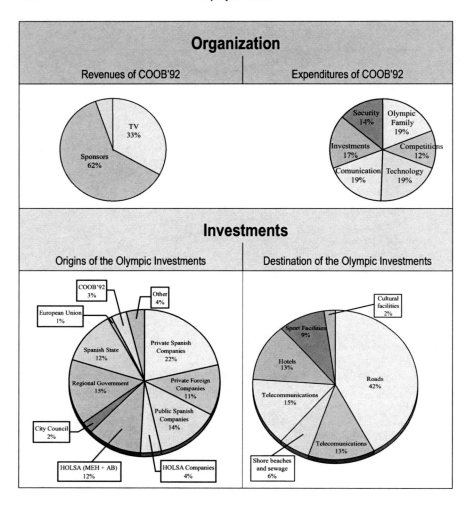

Figure 6.2   Composition of the revenues and of the expenditures in the
Barcelona Olympic Organisation and in the Olympic investments

Source:Brunet (2002).

in facilities and infrastructure, and impact (IOC 2001, 2002 and 2007). The
Games continue to have an international and city-wide impact, some 25 years
after the event. Internationally, as an organisational model – the memory of
the excellent organisational and sporting results lives on as a model of urban
transformation (Rogge 2002) and locally, since the scale of investment and
the Olympic Legacy has had a far-reaching impact through improving the
city's economic and strategic positioning. Hence, our interest in studying the

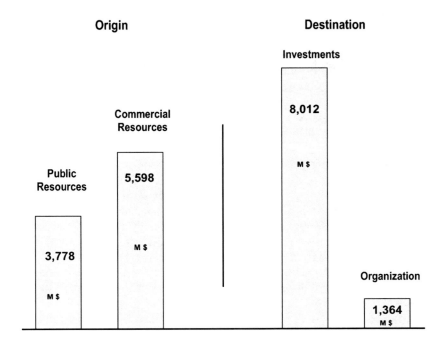

Figure 6.3   The Barcelona 1992 resources: commercial and budgetary sources and investment and organisation destinations

Source: Brunet (2002).

investment in infrastructure and facilities generated by the Barcelona Games, the city's harnessing of the Olympic legacy, and the ongoing investment and urban renewal process (Brunet 1995a and 1996).

Construction Work for the Barcelona Games

The central Spanish government and Barcelona City Hall set up a joint venture, Barcelona Holding Olímpic, SA (HOLSA), to facilitate the investment process. In an excellent example of mixed public-private funding, HOLSA built the main Olympic facilities, the bulk of the 78 km of new road infrastructure and the Olympic Village. Given the Barcelona'92 objectives, a vast amount of construction work was required, and much more was also indirectly generated, though it was not directly necessary for the holding of the Games. This is one of the aims of candidate host cities: to generate construction of as much infrastructure and facilities as possible which will serve the city in the aftermath of the event itself. Total indirect or infrastructure spending linked to the Games over the 1986–1993 period amounted to $8,012 million (for details see Table 6.1 and Figure 6.2).

The main construction work was as follows:

1. road and transport infrastructure;
2. housing, offices and business premises;
3. telecommunications and services;
4. hotels;
5. sports facilities;
6. environmental infrastructure.

A total of 61.5 per cent of Olympic funding was allocated for building work. This illustrates a key feature of Barcelona'92: its structuring effect on the city.[2] The deepest impacts of the Olympic investments in the city were long-term. The Barcelona ring-roads, the re-opening of the city to its seafront via construction of the Olympic Village, the creation of a range of new urban sub-centres and the Olympic facilities at Montjuïc, the Diagonal and Vall d'Hebron, were the main Barcelona building projects (HOLSA, 1990).

The scale of urban transformation arising from the Games was immense: new roads represented an increase of 15 per cent over those existing in 1986; new sewage systems, 17 per cent, and new green areas and beaches, 78 per cent. Another outstanding feature of the Games was regional decentralisation: Olympic investment also went to numerous sub-host cities. Of the total investment, only 38.5 per cent was located in Barcelona city. The impact was, therefore, felt throughout the region. Another important aspect was that construction of sports facilities accounted for only 9.1 per cent of the total investment. This small percentage reflects the great volume of additional indirect investment attracted by the impetus of the Games. A total of 36.8 per cent of the Olympic building work was promoted by the private sector, and one-third of this was funded with foreign capital. Private investment focused on housing, hotels and business centres. The high level of private investment was sparked by expectations of improvement in the city's attractiveness (Roldán et al. 1992).

The Financial Balance Barcelona 1992

The city's aim was to minimise public funding for organisational costs, and to direct it towards the construction of infrastructure and facilities. Public funding may rise to levels above those originally foreseen or promised. However, in Barcelona's case the greater the public investment, the greater the private investment that followed, and the greater the legacy – the additional activity and employment generated. As a result, public sector income, post-event, also rose in line with the increased investment and economic activity.

---

2   According to an urban planning perspective represented by Bohigas (1986), Busquets (1992) and Esteban (1999), among many others.

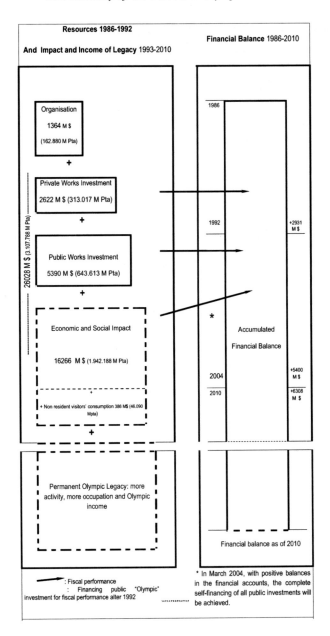

Figure 6.4   The links between the economic resources and the fiscal balance of the Barcelona 1992 Olympic Games

Source: Brunet (2002).

The financial balance sets out all the Olympic-related public administration costs and the income generated by the Games, both directly and indirectly. The Figure 6.5 sets out the financial balance of the Barcelona Games. Two periods are considered: the preparatory period (1986–1992), and the aftermath of the Games. Up to 1992, we see that public infrastructure costs were high, but so was public administration income due to taxable Olympic activities. After 1992, public Olympic-related spending was limited to maintenance of the Legacy, yet income deriving from greater private capital and economic activity generated by the Games rose sharply. Therefore, in both periods, the financial balance is clearly positive.

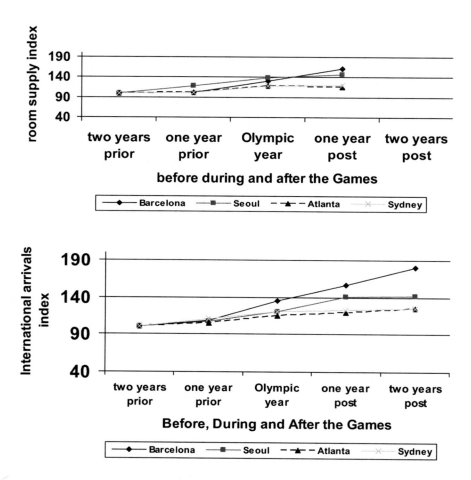

Figure 6.5   The different Olympic cities' answers to the Olympic opportunity hotel offer and visitors before, during and after the Games

Even by 2004 then, public investment in the Games had received ample returns, as shown in Figure 6.5. The financial balance presented here has been estimated with an error margin or +/– 15 per cent. However, it does not include income deriving from company social security contributions. Including this figure, the surplus would be as follows: + $6,835 million for 1986–1992; + $2,608 million for 1993–2001; + $3,873 million for 2002–2010.

1992–2004: Impact

The impact of the city's nomination as Olympic host city was immediate: unemployment underwent a dramatic fall, the housing market came back to life and, of course, the construction industry experienced a boom (Brunet 1995b). However, one decade later, it is surprising to find that this expansive trend continues: 1993 was worse than 1992 – as it was in the entire region, and indeed in all of Western Europe; however, every year since has seen new growth records on all indicators: employment, investment, income, attractiveness, etc. Not only did Barcelona react well to the Games, it succeeded in maintaining the growth generated, on a scale never seen before.

The Economic Impact of the Games

The labour market of Barcelona, and its hinterland, benefited substantially in the pre-Games period. Unemployment fell from an all-time high of 127,774, in November 1986, to as low as 60,885, by July 1992, during the Games themselves. Between October 1986 and August 1992, Barcelona's general unemployment rate fell from 18.4 per cent to 9.6 per cent, while the Spanish figures were 20.9 per cent and 15.5 per cent, respectively. In the preparatory phase, Olympic-based activity generated annual occupation rates of an additional 35,309 persons, on average (Brunet 2005).

In addition, Olympic-linked investment in infrastructure and facilities led to additional permanent employment for an estimated 20,019 people. Therefore, the average annual effect over the 1987-1993 period of Barcelona'92 was to create employment for some 59,328 persons. From this we can conclude that at least 88.7 per cent of the reduction in unemployment registered in Barcelona between November 1986 and July 1992 (66,889 fewer unemployed) was due to the Games.

After the Games, unemployment in Barcelona rose by 21,000 persons, a figure approximately equivalent to the annual employment created by COOB'92. Over the following years, unemployment fell significantly. The investment generated by the Games provided a soft mattress, breaking the fall in a context of general depression. Barcelona's economy proved resistant to the widespread recession and, after 1994, once again began to create employment. Until 1993, 41,450 new jobs had been created, representing a halving of the

Table 6.2   Employment generated by organising the Barcelona Olympic Games

Temporary employment

Generated by the BCN'02 OG
(Full-time posts, annualised average data, November 1986–July 1992)

Organisation tasks	6044
Investment works	35496
Induced impact	17788
Total	59328

Permanent employment

Generated by the BCN'92 OG impact and legacy
(Full-time posts, annualised average data, 1992–2010)

Private sector	18630
Public sector	1600
Total	20230

Source: Brunet (1994, 2002, and 2006).

unemployment figures. In 1993 and 1994, unemployment increased by 18,000 persons; however, after 1995 unemployment fell, thanks, in part, to some 20,230 permanent jobs deriving from Olympic investment (a legacy of 956,000 million pesetas in company capital). The remaining economic indicators confirm Barcelona's progress over the years after the Games. Let us take the construction sector, for example. The consumption of cement was increased by a ratio of 2.5 between 1986 and 1992. House building also expanded, despite the fact that as a city Barcelona's building potential had already been relatively well exploited.

The Response Capacity of Olympic Host Cities: Barcelona as an Exception

Between 1986 and 2000, Barcelona's hotel capacity increased threefold. Parallel to this, the number of visitors from abroad visiting the city doubled, reaching a total of 3.5 million visitors per year. In comparison with the other host cities over the last 12 years, Seoul, Atlanta and Sydney, Barcelona's results are outstanding. In some areas, they are truly exceptional, as for example, in the figures on hotel capacity and the number of foreign visitors. Barcelona's response to the Olympic stimulus has been more intense and sustained than that of the other host cities. This has made Barcelona'92 a model in so far as impact is concerned. This is where Barcelona's performance was exceptional: in its extraordinary and sustained capacity to ride the Olympic wave.

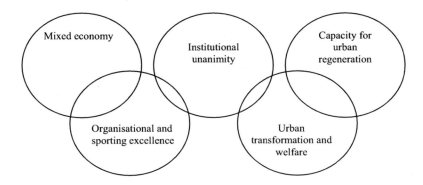

Figure 6.6   The components of Barcelona's success

The Barcelona Olympic Impact Model

The immediate impact of the Olympic Games was highly notable. However, what was truly surprising was the impact and scale of the permanent Olympic Legacy, and the continuation of this impact over the 1992–2002 period. The Barcelona Olympic Impact Model and its main results are summarised in Figures 6.1 and 6.7 as well as in Tables 6.1, 6.5 and 6.6. The key element of this model is investment in infrastructure, both in terms of quantity and quality. However, this impact model presupposes a certain organisational model for the Games and also involves urban transformation of the city.

The model is based on the maximisation of investment, attraction of further investment and temporal concentration. Given the scope of urban transformation sought, continued investment is essential. This has occurred in the case of Barcelona (see Table 6.3). Barcelona has been highly successful in harnessing the Olympic impetus and benefiting from the investment made, and this had facilitated change. The resources allocated to urban infrastructure led to temporary employment in the necessary construction work, followed by permanent employment in operation of this infrastructure. Both led to increased economic activity, although not all of it was concentrated in the city itself. The capital invested and the increased economic activity led to increased wealth, wellbeing, and social cohesion and made the city more attractive.

Comparison of Olympic Impacts, 1964–2008: Barcelona as an Exception

A database has been prepared to compare the Olympic impact of various host cities in terms of organisation, investment and resulting economic impact.[3] Barcelona's performance again stands out. The Olympic investments and their economic impact are without parallel in other host cities. Only Tokyo reached half the volume of the investment generated in Barcelona. Investment was also significant in Seoul; however, Olympic investments in Atlanta and Sydney were very limited. The projections for Athens and Beijing include major investment and impact, more along the lines of Barcelona.

2004–2010: Strategy and Perspectives

By 2004 we can see that the investment made between 1986 and 1992 was the key to the city's urban transformation and its improved strategic positioning.

Investment in Infrastructure and Urban Transformation, 1986–2010

The investments are the key element within the economic resources mobilised by Barcelona'92, and were crucial in the economic impact of the Games, the city's transformation and the subsequent increase in economic activity, income and wellbeing. The investments explain a great part of Barcelona'92's exemplary success and were notable both in terms of the quality of the infrastructure and scale of funding (€10,660 million). They constitute the Olympic Legacy which underpinned much of Barcelona's economic and social boom in the 1990s.

Not only were the investments central to the original Olympic impetus, they were also important in completing the impact and enabling continuation of the urban transformation and strategic strengthening process. For this reason, the investments made post-1992 are also set out in Table 6.3. Two central axes served to focus urban transformation in the post-Olympic period:

1. The Barcelona Universal Forum of Cultures 2004;
2. The Poblenou 22@BCN Plan.

The first involves renewal of Barcelona's eastern section, thus completing the Olympic Village seafront (Brunet 2000). Just as occurred with the Games,

---

3   On the impact of the Games, in addition to the International Olympic Committee (2001, 2002 and 2007), see, for Seoul, Kim et al. (1989) and Pyun (1999); for Atlanta, Humphreys and Plummer (2002), and for Sydney, Centre for Regional Economic Analysis – Arthur Andersen (1999) and Preuss (2004). Cf. also Organising Committee for the Olympic Games Athens 2004 S.A. (2005) and Organising Committee for the Olympic Games Beijing 2008 (2007).

the Forum will serve as a framework for large-scale urban planning projects, several of which would be difficult to undertake and complete under normal conditions. Funding is largely public. The second comprises far-reaching renovation of the Poblenou district (Brunet 1995a; Trullén 2001), adjacent to the Forum 2004 site. In this case, the investment is largely private.

These two pillars served to mobilise the investments set out in Table 6.3 in three phases:

- 1986–1992, included for comparative purposes;
- 1992–2004, in which other large-scale projects such as the AVE (high-speed train), work on the Besòs and Llobregat rivers, and the extensions to the port and airport were added to the direct investment in the Forum 2004;
- 2004–2010, in which investment still pending from earlier projects, and a major public transport initiative covering Barcelona and its hinterland, will be added to direct investment in the Poblenou area.

To complete our view of Barcelona's urban transformation process up to and beyond 2004, we must include the inner-city renovation projects (PERI) taking place in various parts of the city such as Ciutat Vella, Eixample, Gràcia, Nou Barris.

The Olympic Legacy and Barcelona's Strategic Perspectives

The new public and private capital and the permanent employment generated by the Olympic investments constitute the city's Olympic Legacy; a legacy which included the city's urban transformation, changed economic structure, increased capitalisation, increased service sector activity, heightened international role, attractiveness, centrality, productivity and competitiveness. Barcelona has been outstandingly successful in strengthening and maintaining the Olympic impetus, thus increasing its own level of economic activity and income, improving its quality of life and social cohesion, and advancing strategically.

Business confidence in Barcelona, as reflected by the willingness of foreign companies to establish there (a combination of attractiveness, availability of services, workers, market, and competitiveness) improved notably in the aftermath of the Games (Healey and Baker 2001 and 2007). In 1990, Barcelona occupied 11th position in the league table of European cities; by 1993, it had risen to 10th, by 2001 it was in 6th position; and arrived at 5th in 2006 (Table 6.4).

The city's capacity to prolong the Olympic impact has enabled it to offset impediments such as disputes between different public administration bodies, and the delay in providing certain infrastructure, such as the high-speed train (AVE). It has also enabled it to avoid drowning in a sea of uncertainty with

Table 6.3　Investment in urban renewal in Barcelona, 1986–2010

	Accumulated values in millions of euros at 2000 rate					
1986–1992		**1992–2004**		**2004–2010**		
Public and private investment related to the Olympic Games = Olympic Legacy		Investments in metropolitan economic infrastructure		Investments related to Barcelona 2004 and Poblenou 22@BCN		
Coasts, recovery work and parks	673	Environmental infrastructure	930	Environmental infrastructure	1,800
Telecommunications and services	1,375	Telecommunications (telephones and cables)	2,036	Seafront	750
Housing, offices and premises	1,556	AVE and non-regional trains	1658	AVE	2,100
Hotels	1,336	Extension of airport	925	Extension of port	800
Sports equipment and facilities	976	Extension of port	841	Port, diversion of Llobregat river and Logistics Zone	1,500
Cultural, health facilities and others	237	Electric network	589	Diagonal Mar, Forum 2004 and Sant Andreu	720
Roads and transport	4,507	Road network	1,502	Metropolitan public transport	7,295
		Metro, urban trains, trams and buses	1,394	Poblenou 22@BCN	2,675
Total	**10,660**	**Total** + Urban renewal	**9,875**	**Total**	**17,640**
Ciutat Vella	1,603	Ciutat Vella, Eixample	1,921	Ciutat Vella, Eixample, Gràcia, Nou Barris	2,400
General total	**12,263**	**General total Total**	**11,796**	**General total**	**20,040**

Source: Brunet (1994 and 2005) and Clusa (1996).

Table 6.4   Evaluation of European cities

1990	2001	City	2006
1	1	London	1
2	2	Paris	2
3	3	Frankfurt	3
4	4	Brussels	4
11	**6**	**Barcelona**	**5**
5	5	Amsterdam	6
15	9	Berlin	7
17	8	Madrid	8
12	10	Munich	9
7	7	Zurich	10
9	11	Milan	11
-	13	Dublin	12
23	21	Prague	13
16	16	Lisbon	14
13	14	Manchester	15
6	17	Düsseldorf	16
19	15	Stockholm	17
8	12	Geneva	18
14	18	Hamburg	19
25	27	Warsaw	20
21	22	Budapest	21
10	19	Glasgow	22
20	23	Vienna	23
18	20	Lyon	24
-	24	Copenhagen	25
-	25	Rome	26
-	26	Helsinki	27
24	30	Moscow	28
-	28	Oslo	29
22	29	Athens	30

Source: Healey and Baker (2001 and 2007).

regard to the seafront and urban renewal programme associated with the Forum 2004. And, although it does have certain disadvantages (it is neither a state capital nor headquarters for many multinationals, and suffers from shortcomings in public transport, language training, worker mobility and available development land, etc.), Barcelona continues to attract investment and enterprise.

Barcelona, Model and Reality

We can talk of a 'Barcelona model' in three respects:

1. a model for organisation of the Olympic Games (Figure 6.1);
2. a model for economic impact of the Olympic Games, especially in terms of investments not directly linked to the Games (Figure 6.4);
3. a model for urban transformation, improved attractiveness and strategic positioning (Figure 6.7).

The use of the term 'model' has become widespread and seems to have been accepted. In analytical terms, a model is an organised set of forms and procedures, shorn of accessories. However, in everyday usage, 'model' includes the extra content, in this case the objectives and results.

The objectives of Barcelona'92 were very clear (sporting and organisational excellence and the urban transformation of the city) and so were the procedures (institutional unity, mixed public-private funding, etc.). And since the results of this 'Barcelona model' were positive, then the term 'model' is often used in the sense of being exemplary for other cities organising similar events. It seems that it did serve as a model in this sense for Sydney, Athens and, possibly Beijing as well. Barcelona has then become a model for other Olympic Games and cities.

Conclusions

Thanks to the Olympic Games, Barcelona is now a different city. The organisation was optimum, fostering massive investment in infrastructure. Thanks to the correct use of the Olympic Legacy – increased capital investment and improved attractiveness – the urban development process has continued long after 1992.

The organisation (Figures 6.1, 6.4, 6.5 and 6.7), the investment (Tables 6.1 and 6.3), the economic and social impact (Table 6.1 and Figure 6.4), the urban transformation, the efficient use of the Olympic opportunity and legacy (Figure 6.6) were all highly positive. This is why we refer to the Barcelona Model for the organisation of mega-events in relation to their capacity to generate economic impacts and urban transformation.

Table 6.5   A synthesis of the impact of the Barcelona OG 1992: model, investments, employment, attractiveness, legacy and income

☑ **Large-scale events and urban dynamics**
OG: event requiring mass-communication
(audiences, resources managed, urban impact).
Olympic ideals, economic resources, organising capacity and attractiveness of investments

☑ **Model for OG. BCN'92**: institutional unanimity, sporting and organisational excellence, urban transformation, mixed economy. Separate management bodies (organisation and works)

☑ **Organisation of OG** (sporting excellence) Growth of investments through TV and sponsors. Financed 92% by commercial investments	☑ **Investments in 'Olympic' projects** (urban transformation: 48% urbanisation, 15% housing, 3% hotels). Financed 59,7 % by commercial investments
☑ **Minimise cost of** organisation of the Games	☑ **Maximise investments** generated by OG

Macroeconomic impact (demand, employment)
and **Microeconomic impact** (construction, entrepreneurial activity) of the OG

☑ **Fiscal balance** of the OG: considerable fiscal excess in all periods
(1986–1992, 1993–2004, 2005–2010)

Improvement of strategic position Barcelona:
Increase of *attractiveness* (businesses-capital, visitors): in 2006, Barcelona ranked 5th European city

☑ **Barcelona model** of urban development: complexity, quality, gradualness and depth of achievements

Exceptionality of Barcelona: special capacity of Barcelona
to benefit from economic impulse of OG
(comparison with Seoul, Atlanta and Sydney)

☑ **Organisation** OG + **Olympic investments** + **impact** → Olympic legacy = capacity + premium capital + premium employment → olympic income: larger and better activity and permanent income

☑ **Olympic Legacy:** Best **social and public capital** ($5390m): urbanisation, employment, transport, beltway, cultural institutions, sanitation, sporting installations, maritime facade, beaches, parks Best **private and business capital** ($2623m): hotels, locales, offices, employment, marina, companies Best **employment** (20,230 positions created) and highly-qualified workforce Best **capacities**: Organisational know-how, culture of *excellence* and of *consensus*	☑ **Olympic income:** Better and better economic *activity*: best VAT (△ $ 702m annually). Best *productivity* and competitiveness, best income, quality of life, wellbeing and social **cohesion** of residents Improved **strategic position** (2007: 5th place in ranking of European cities) More and more **Attractiveness**: more capital, residents y tourism. Fiscal benefit ($ 150m annually)

☑ **Investments 1992–2004–2010 and strategic perspectives of Barcelona**
The Olympic income and legacy has been powerfully manifested by the continuity of urban investments
In the forecast 2004 and 2010, the strategic position Barcelona seems firmly consolidated

Sources: Brunet (1994, 2002, and 2005).

Table 6.6   The Olympic strategy decalogue

The Olympic Decalogue:
A strategic way to success in the organisation and impact of mega-events

1.   The institutional agreement

2.   Mixing economy: public direction and private management

3.   Separate organs: one to organise the Games (Sports)

4.   and one to manage the investments (stone)

5.   The concentric circles principle: The Olympic resources are not cost but investment

6.   Maximise investments and minimise costs

7.   The excellence principle: In two weeks of excellence you match the past organising efforts and especially all your new future

8.   The first beneficiary of the Games is the state: At medium term always a fiscal surplus appears

9.   From a strategic perspective, the most important period begins after the Games!

10.   The Olympic investments are the legacy

11.   Continuity in investments is needed to maintain and to profit from the new strategic position of the city and of the country

---

Source: Brunet (2006).

The objective was quality, the implementation excellent, both in the preparatory and follow-up phase. Of equal importance however, was the city's capacity to harness the Olympic impetus. Comparison with other Games and cities over the 1964–2008 period, shows that Barcelona was most successful in harnessing the Olympic impetus and its impact.

The continued investment in infrastructure and development driven by such events as the Forum, and development of the Poblenou district into a high-added value information and technology area, is the key to the city's maintaining its 6th position among European cities.

The city's achievements from 1986 to 1992 and again after 1992, have been enormous. Yet the challenges facing it now and in the future are similarly daunting. The investment in urban transformation must go on. European integration and globalisation are factors which favour Barcelona, as long as the city maintains the Olympic spirit.

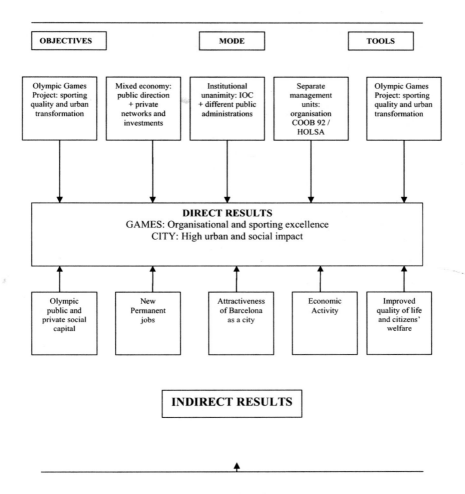

Figure 6.7   Direct and indirect legacy benefits

References

Ajuntament de Barcelona (2007) *Barcelona economia. Indicadors econòmics de Barcelona i de la regió metropolitana*, Barcelona: Ajuntament de Barcelona, http://www.publicacions.bcn.es/bcneco.

Bohigas, O. (1986) *Reconstrucción de Barcelona*, Madrid: MOPU.

Brunet, F. (1994) *Economy of the 1992 Barcelona Olympic Games*, Lausanne: International Olympic Committee.

Brunet, F. (1995a) *Dimensió econòmica i posició estratègica del Poblenou*, Barcelona: Institut Municipal d'Urbanisme.

Brunet, F. (1995b) 'An Economic Analysis of the Barcelona'92 Olympic Games: Resources, Financing and Impact', http://blues.uab.es/olympic. studies.

Brunet, F. (1996) *Anàlisi econòmica de les actuacions urbanístiques a Ciutat Vella*, Barcelona: Promoció de Ciutat Vella.

Brunet, F. (2000) 'Memoria económica de los beneficios fiscales aplicables a las actividades y obras del Fórum Universal de las Culturas Barcelona 2004 en virtud de la Propuesta Normativa para su inclusión en el anteproyecto de Ley de Presupuestos Generales del Estado / Anteproyecto de Ley de Medidas Fiscales, Administrativas y del orden Social para el año 2001', Barcelona: Fòrum Universal de les Cultures Barcelona 2004, mimeo.

Brunet, F. (2002) 'Anàlisi de l'impacte econòmic dels Jocs Olímpics de Barcelona', in Botella, M. and de Moragas, M. (eds) *Barceloma: l'herència dels Jocs, 1992–2002*, Barcelona: Planeta.

Brunet, F. (2005) 'Analyzing Impacts in a Strategic Perspective: The Olympic Games Economy', paper presented to the 'International Forum on Olympic Games', 9–10 July, Renmin University of China, Beijing, PR China.

Brunet, F. (2006) 'The Barcelona Model and the Economy of the Olympic Games', paper presented to 'The Copenhagen Conference on the Economic and Social Impact of Hosting Mega Sports Events', 1 September, Copenhagen Business School, Denmark.

Busquets, J. (1992) *Barcelona. Evolución urbanística de una ciudad compacta*, Madrid: Mapfre-América.

Centre for Regional Economic Analysis – Arthur Andersen (1999) 'Economic Impact Study of the Sydney 2000 Olympic Games', University of Tasmania, http://www.comlaw.utas.edu.au.

Clusa, J. (1996) *Les infraestructures metropolitanes de l'àrea de Barcelona. Una aproximació als projectes en curs*, Barcelona: Cambra Oficial de Comerç, Indústria i Navegació de Barcelona.

Comitè Organitzador Olímpic Barcelona 1992 [COOB'92] (1993) *Memòria Oficial dels Jocs de la XXVa Olimpíada Barcelona 1992. Volum II. Els mitjans. Escenaris, objectius i recursos [i] Volum III. L'organització. La preparació dels Jocs*, Barcelona: COOB'92.

Esteban, J. (1999) *El projecte urbanístic. Valorar la perifèria i recuperar el centre*, Barcelona: Fundació Bosch i Gimpera – Aula Barcelona.

Healey and Baker (2001 and 2007) *European Cities Monitor*, http://www. healey-baker.es/servlets.

Humphreys, J.M. and Plummer, M.K. (2002) *The Economic Impact of Hosting The 1996 Summer Olympics*, Georgia: Selig Center for Economic Growth, Terry College of Business, The University of Georgia – IRE Advisors, http://www.selig.uga.edu.

International Olympic Committee (2001) 'Marketing olympique 1980–2001', *Marketing Matters* 19, July: 1–7.

International Olympic Committee (2002) *Marketing Fact File*, Lausanne: International Olympic Committee, http://multimedia.olympic.org.

International Olympic Committee (2007) *100 Years of Olympic Marketing Evolution of Olympic Marketing During the 20th Century*, http://www.olympic.org.

Kim, J.-G. et al. (1989) *Impact of the Seoul Olympic Games on National Development*. Seoul: Korea Development Institute.

Organising Committee for the Olympic Games Athens 2004 (2005) *Annual Report 2003–2004*, http:// www.business2005.g>.

Organising Committee for the Olympic Games Beijing 2008 (2007) *Finance*, http://www.beijing-2008.orgh.

Preuss, H. (2004) *The Economics of Staging the Olympics. A Comparison of the Games, 1972–2008*, Cheltenham: Edward Elgar.

Pyun, D.-Y. (1999) *Economic Impact of the Seoul Olympic Games*, http://www.geocities.com/olympic_seminar7/papers/pyun. html.

Rogge, J. (2002) *Speech of the IOC President at the Opening Ceremony of the 113th IOC Session*, Salt Lake City, UT: SLOC.

Roldán, S. et al. (1992) *Barcelona Olímpica. La ciutat renovada*, Barcelona: HOLSA.

Samaranch, J.A. (1992) 'Discours d'ouverture par president du CIO et Pasqual Maragall, Maire de Barcelone, president de COOB'92', *Revue Olympique* 300, October: 473–5.

Trullén, J. (2001) *La metròpoli de Barcelona cap a l'economia del coneixement: diagnosi econòmica i territorial de Barcelona*, Barcelona: Ajuntament de Barcelona, Gabinet Tècnic de Programació.

US Bureau of the Census (2007) *Statistical Abstract*, http://www.census.gov.

Chapter 7

Atlanta (1996): The Centennial Games

Gavin Poynter and Emma Roberts

Introduction

Atlanta started life as a rail terminus and was incorporated as a town in 1847. Its title was derived from its aspiration to become the 'gateway to the Atlantic' for the Old Southern Confederate states. Since its inauguration, Atlanta has sought to play a significant role in the southern US economy. It was the birthplace of the Coca Cola company (1886) and is famous as the home of Margaret Mitchell, the author of *Gone with the Wind*, a novel that captures many of the attributes of resilience and enterprise that have become essential features of the official representation of the history of the city. The city was also the birthplace of Martin Luther King Jr and a centre of the civil rights struggles of the 1960s and 1970s. In some ways evaluations of the city's hosting of the Olympic Games in 1996 and its legacy, have reflected the concerns of two of its most famous citizens. The city's determination to host the Games reflected its competitiveness and entrepreneurialism, whilst the event's legacy has been critically assessed for reinforcing divisions within the city between the centre and suburbs, rich and poor and black and white (COHRE 2007; Keating 2007).

Atlanta's heritage, as a major centre of the civil rights movement, was a key selling point of the city's narrative in its bid for the 1996 Games. Being the home of the major Olympic Games sponsors, Coca Cola, was also probably important to the outcome of the bidding process (Roche 2000: 155). Atlanta competed against five other cities – Athens, Belgrade, Manchester, Melbourne and Toronto. Athens was considered to be the leading contender because the 1996 Games represented the centenary year of the modern Olympics – the event would be returning to its classical birthplace for the centenary. The Athens bid, however, was poorly constructed and the city did not have the transport or telecommunications infrastructures required to deliver the Games. Los Angeles and Seoul had set high standards of infrastructure provision, particularly as the Games, in its commercial phase, relied increasingly upon broadcast revenues as the key source of income. This was a central concern of the IOC. Atlanta presented a strong bid in relation to transportation, stadium development and telecommunications infrastructure and was selected in September 1990 by the IOC to host the Games, though its selection was subject to significant rumours that excessive gifts and bribes had been used to secure the decision (Preuss 2004: 8).

The city was divided in its aspirations for hosting the 1996 Games. The divisions were, arguably, exacerbated by the proliferation of subcommittees and associations that were set up to implement these different visions. Whilst the Atlanta Committee for Organising the Olympic Games (ACOG) was the lead agency, the Corporation for Olympic Development in Atlanta (CODA) pledged to improve 15 impoverished districts and use the Games to tackle wider problems of poverty and inner city decay. Business leaders sought a more limited commercial legacy, mainly focused upon attracting inward investment through encouraging companies to locate regional and national offices in the city, taking advantage of the broader shift in capital and employment from north to south USA that occurred in the1980s. It was the latter, business-oriented approach that eventually prevailed with public officials playing a limited role in preparing the bid and securing the Games for Atlanta. The Atlanta case illustrates the commercial model of the mega event and the consequences of this approach for the process of social and economic regeneration. In particular, it demonstrates how the construction of a commercial approach to hosting the Games is reflected not simply in the creation of the bid but also in the mode of governance and the eventual legacy that is achieved.

Inevitably, the evaluations of the Games' legacy for Atlanta vary considerably. The world's media largely considered the Games to be 'over commercialised and poorly organised' (Ward 2006) and the IOC tended to agree, taking the view that the private sector funding model with its 'down to the wire finances. have convinced the IOC of one thing, we are never going through this again' (Preuss 2004: 13). In contrast, representatives of Atlanta's business community, 10 years after the event, could point to:

> a spotless balance sheet. While Montreal is still paying off its debts thirty
> years after the event, Atlanta had enough surplus to pay for a free concert
> ... to celebrate the 10th anniversary. (Ward 2006)

Business leaders also argued that the Games provided a catalyst for the movement of capital and enterprises into the city that facilitated a significant expansion of the urban and regional economy in the latter part of the 1990s. By contrast, civic groups, community leaders and academic writers have focused upon the process of gentrification and the displacement of poorer, mainly black sections of the community, arguing that the Olympic legacy reproduced long term patterns of discrimination and impoverishment that demonstrated that the city that describes itself as 'too busy to hate is blatantly the city that is too greedy to care' (COHRE 2007: 46). This chapter evaluates these highly contested evaluations of legacy through a brief examination of the bid, the process of governance that it gave rise to and the available evidence on the outcomes achieved.

The Atlanta Bid

US cities that have bid to host the Games have established private, not for profit, organisations, to prepare and run the event. Public/private partnerships have been formed to deliver the Games, with local variations arising in the form that these partnerships have taken, typically with the private sector taking the lead. This pattern was first established by Los Angeles. City leaders in Los Angeles were concerned not to reproduce the public debt burden experienced by Montreal and were also wary of falling foul of the Proposition 13 tax limitation movement that was firmly established in California. As a result, the city's negotiations with the IOC produced an outcome that caused the latter to waive the obligation of the city to accept the financial liability or risk that accompanies the hosting of the Games. The Los Angeles Olympics Organising Committee (LAOOG) and the United States Olympic Committee (USOC) assumed the financial liability for the Games whilst it was agreed with the IOC that the event costs would be met by corporate sponsorships; in effect causing the Los Angeles Games to be the first 'private' Olympics (Andranovich et al. 2001: 162).

Atlanta broadly followed the Los Angeles 'model' though there were three key bodies that formed a Tri-Party Agreement to oversee the Games – the private sector led Atlanta Committee for the Olympic Games (ACOG), the state run Olympic Authority (MAOGA) and the city. In practice, ACOG was the lead partner (Andranovich et al. 2001:163). Unlike Los Angeles, however, where the Games were not associated with any major plans for urban development and renewal, the Atlanta organisers, including ACOG, were committed in the bid stage to promote redevelopment within the city, including a significant programme of regeneration of the inner-city area that had experienced 'white flight' into the suburbs from the 1960s and the increased concentration of mainly African American communities in poor inner city neighbourhoods. The bid also emphasised the quality of the city's communications infrastructure and the capacity to develop high quality athlete accommodation on a single site, with a delivery mechanism for housing development – the Atlanta Housing Authority's 'Olympic Legacy Program' – being established in 1991.[1]

The improvements designed for downtown Atlanta were also aimed at developing the business district of the city, with ACOG seeking to attract inward investment and the establishment of the city as the regional and/or

---

1 Original plans proposed three sites but IOC insistence reduced the three university campus sites to one.

national headquarters for US enterprises, following the Coca Cola example. In emulating Los Angeles, a further important objective of ACOG was to establish Atlanta as a 'global' city with a brand that would be recognised beyond the borders of the USA. In brief, ACOG's objectives, reflected in the bid book, combined commercial and social goals into an ambitious development and regeneration programme that would be mainly sponsored by the private sector with some publicly funded support.

For such an ambitious programme, the Games-related budget was relatively small, about $1.7 billion, drawn largely from private sources. Infrastructure development, however, did attract federal funds for housing and a local bond scheme was matched by federal and state funds to create a $375 million investment in utilities, including sewer and water systems. The Games catalysed other infrastructural improvements with, for example, the airport receiving a new concourse and extensive hotel construction took place with about 7,500 new rooms being built between 1990 and the opening of the Games, enabling Atlanta to increase the number of hotel rooms within the city to over 60,000 by 1996. The public-private partnerships that were formed to fund improvements varied but perhaps, their spirit was typified by the improvements made to the downtown sidewalks and streets. Federal funding supported the replacing of sidewalks, the introduction of signage, tree planting, new lighting and the installation of public art. In turn, a representative of city government 'leased space to temporary vendors in tents, stalls and carts creating a carnival atmosphere that became the subject of much controversy' – and no doubt a source of income for the city (New Georgia Encyclopedia 2006).

The Event

Over ten thousand competitors represented 197 nations at the Games, the largest number of participant nations achieved in the post-1945 era. The city received about two million visitors in the period leading up to the Games and over the duration of the event. The opening ceremony celebrated southern US culture and commemorated the one-hundredth anniversary of the founding of the modern Olympics movement. The first day of events, however, demonstrated flaws in the city's transport system and the Games' communications infrastructure. The international press corps and many spectators missed events due to traffic congestion and bus breakdowns. Journalists were late filing copy because computer systems failed to deliver results data from the competition sites that were located in and around the city. The Games organisers reflected upon these problems in their final assessment report of the Games, highlighting the issues surrounding the organisational relationship between 'local' venue management and Games-wide or centralised functional areas, recommending that these two management structures required clearly defined responsibilities that are effectively communicated across the whole organisation from the outset (ACOG 1997: 34).

The Games were mainly concentrated in the Centennial Olympic Park, an area of 21 acres of derelict wasteland that had been transformed to create the Olympic Stadium and green parkland. Unfortunately, the problems afflicting the event were not only organisational and technical. It was in the Olympic Park that a right-wing extremist, Eric Rudolph, planted a nail bomb during the Games that killed two people and injured more than one hundred. This tragedy overshadowed several days of the event. The mixed reviews of the Games subsequently presented by the IOC and the world's media were not, however, mainly focused upon security, the event itself had demonstrated that some features central to the success of the bid, had been poorly delivered, especially the telecommunications systems, traffic management and the financial package specifically designed to deliver the event.

The Legacy

The commercially oriented perspective prevailed with the Games providing a legacy that favoured the redevelopment of commercial downtown districts rather than neighbourhood renewal on a scale that would significantly improve the lives of the least well-off citizens of the inner city. Atlanta achieved its goal of securing the relocation of 18 major companies to the city following the completion of the Games and hosting the event was one of the key reasons for achieving the designation by the federal government as one of six 'federal empowerment zones'. With the Olympic Games, Atlanta attempted to reposition itself as a leading business and global sports centre and indeed the sporting venues have been well utilised since the Games, the main venue hosting a Baseball team and other venues taken on by colleges and universities. This repositioning ran under the title 'Operation Legacy'. Centennial Olympic Park Area (COPA) was set up by Central Atlanta Progress (CAP) and according to Paul Kelman, president of CAP, 'the park was a catalyst, but we had to come on afterwards and help it' (Dann 2004: 13). The Atlanta Chamber of Commerce developed a marketing strategy to assist this, 'Forward Atlanta' and the Department of Industry, Trade and Tourism established a simultaneous marketing campaign 'Georgia Global'. Although there was success in attracting major corporate offices to Atlanta, it has been difficult to separate out the effect of the Olympic Games on this process. Atlanta experienced high levels of economic growth during the pre and post Olympic years, which makes the isolation of the effect of the Games difficult to measure. On the other hand, the Olympics left a legacy of ill-will amongst particular neighbourhoods that lost housing and experienced severe dislocation arising from the urban developments that accompanied the event.

The housing issue has dominated post-Games assessments of the Olympic legacy. The Centennial Olympic Park and its surrounding area have attracted considerable investment in the decade since the Games. The Park was designated as an entertainment area, attracting new facilities, and private sector developers, who took over much of the Park's development on completion of the Games; creating new commercial and residential projects adjacent to it (ACOG 1997: 88). Over the past decade, the Centennial Park has provided new entertainment venues, housing and green space, all located close to the inner city. The rebirth of the city's centre also appears to be supported by population statistics which indicate a reversal of the decline experienced in the period between 1970 and 1990. Over 20,000 people moved into the city, increasing its population from a little under 400,000 to around 416,000 between 1990 and 2000 (Keating 2007). The re-birth of the city, however, has taken place via a process of what critics have called 'gentrification'[2].

The net increase in population was not matched by a significant increase in housing units. In the period 1991 to 1996 seven 'Olympic Ring Neighbourhoods' witnessed the demolition of 1203 housing units, with a total overall of 7,000 public and private sector housing units being demolished in preparation for hosting the Olympics. These were replaced by about 11,000 units, a net total increase of 4,000. The Olympic Ring Neighbourhoods housed largely poor African-Americans in the early 1990s, by 2000 five of these were 'well on the way to be gentrified and the other two had begun to gentrify' (Keating 2007: 10). The Games, according to its critics, provided a catalyst for a process of renewal that favoured the well-off and displaced the poor:

> The 1996 Olympic Games and the development plans surrounding the mega-event had provided the drama, the energy and the interest in long-held dreams of politicians and investors alike to propel Atlanta into the ranks of international cities. Today, ten years after the mega event that attracted developers and planners to try again to gain control of the city, downtown is exploding with expensive, high rise, inner-city loft and condominium construction. (COHRE 2007: 47)

Post-Games regeneration has continued in Atlanta through the establishment of the BeltLine project in 2005, a project designed to address the city's population growth, its disconnected pockets of development and renewal and the continuing problems of under investment in the inner city.

---

2   The concept of gentrification was first coined by the sociologist, Ruth Glass, describing developments in London in the 1950s. It refers to the physical renovation of older houses, the construction of new high value stock and the creation of neighbourhoods that fit the lifestyles of new owner-occupier middle-class residents; neighbourhoods that previously served the poor eventually squeeze them out, or displace them, often to other parts of the city (see Hamnett 2003: 160–61).

The BeltLine project is focused upon 22 miles of rail lines that circle the urban centre of the city; transforming these into parks, housing and cultural attractions (Franklin 2005). The project is to be funded by the creation of a BeltLine Tax Allocation District (TAD):

> The BeltLine TAD funds will be generated by new growth in the tax base within the defined TAD Redevelopment Area. Based on this growth, as private development begins, bonds will be sold and the proceeds used to fund a proportion of the total cost for acquiring land and building parks, trails, transits and other government projects. (The bonds are secured by the anticipated growth of the tax base within the TAD; the tax payers within the City of Atlanta will not be obliged to repay the bonds.) The remaining portion of the project costs is expected to be funded through various philanthropic and federal sources. (Franklin 2005: 2)

The BeltLine project appears to be continuing a process of renewal that commenced in the Olympic phase; the Games provided the opportunity for a business-led coalition to reshape the city's future development in a manner consistent with commercial interests that, in turn, has generated neighbourhood renewal that displaces lower income families and reduces the provision of low cost housing. This pattern of urban renewal, reinforcing social divisions rather than reducing them, is also reflected in the workplace.

There is little evidence of the Games creating a lasting impact upon skills and employment patterns. The Atlanta region has one of the largest city-suburban income gaps in the USA. 78 percent of those living below the poverty line in the Atlanta region, live in the inner city. The disparity between suburban wealth and inner-city deprivation has not changed significantly in the decade since the Games. The suburbs continue to have a high proportion of the wealthier, middle class community, including a significant black middle class. One consequence of this polarised society is that commuter travel distances are high and inner-city deprivation is reflected in continued low achievement in schools and colleges. This is despite the Olympic legacy seeking to attain a strong record of affirmative action in employment.

Before the Games, a study commissioned by ACOG from the Selig Center for Economic Growth at the University of Georgia estimated the total economic impact of the Games to be $5.1 billion and that there would be a creation of 80,000 jobs between 1990 and 1996. Hosting the event would generate 'Georgia's Second Gold Rush' (Rutheiser, 1996: 231). The employment impact of the Games on Atlanta is recorded by the State Of Georgia as a direct impact of 36,000 new jobs and an induced impact of 41,000. This data has to be placed in context. The Atlanta regional economy produced significant job growth in the 1980s and 1990s. 500,000 net new jobs were created, for example, in the period 1980–1990. It is likely that the Olympic employment effect mainly generated temporary employment opportunities with the overall employment impact of the Games being 'overwhelmed' by general trends such as corporate relocations to the city and corporate expansion in the region. In the decade following 1996, Atlanta achieved a 30 per cent increase in international companies being located in the city (a total of 1,600 companies by 2006). Whilst, distinguishing the Olympic employment effect is extremely difficult, a study by Baade and Matheson (Baade and Matheson 2002) suggests that an optimistic scenario of job creation in the Atlanta economy indicates around 40,000 new jobs were generated, however:

> Employment figures for 1991–93 suggest that Atlanta's recovery from the nation's recession that ended in the spring of 1991 did not seem to gather momentum until 1993. The Olympics is therefore credited with job creation that should be attributed to other developments and events [...] Those who championed public subsidies for the Atlanta Olympics contend that the impact of the Games endures. Our evidence, however, indicates that the Olympic legacy is likely to be smal l... the evidence suggests that the economic impact of the Olympics is transitory, one-time changes rather than 'steady state' change. This outcome is likely to be true unless great care is taken to ensure the Olympic infrastructure is compatible with the resident economy ... Job growth estimates for 1997 derived through adjusting the model to reflect the higher job growth induced by the Olympics indicate that between 17,706 and 32,768 jobs were 'given back'. In other words, at least 40% (and perhaps more) of the jobs were transitory. The city of Atlanta and the State of Georgia spent approximately $1.58 billion to create 24,742 permanent full- or part-time jobs in the best scenario model, which averages out to $63,860 per job created. (Baade and Matheson 2002: 144)

Perhaps the most significant legacy of the Atlanta Games for the Olympic movement was the IOC decision that the Olympic Games would never again be given to a city that,

> has no significant public sector commitment, either in the form of a financial contribution or, at the very least, a guarantee to meet the necessary costs of organising the Games. (Richard Pound, the IOC's chief liaison with ACOG, quoted in Rutheiser 1996: 259)

The IOC consequently decided that for future Games it would be necessary to ensure that public funding was behind a city's bid to insure against the risk that private funds failed to materialise.

Atlanta's Governance Structure

Governance refers to ways of bringing institutions representing the state and market into forms of public-private partnership to deliver regeneration projects. The concepts of governance and partnership are fluid, contested terms in the academic literature (Jones and Evans 2006). Partnerships between the state and private sector may vary according to the levels of cooperation and interdependence of the public and private institutions engaged in specific projects (Davies 2001). The network of institutional relations – national, local, public, private – may assume the character of 'self-organisation' in implementing mutually agreed goals or remain largely state or business centred with control firmly in the hands of business leaders or city-wide and national government officials.

ACOG was responsible for preparing and carrying out the Games. As a public-private partnership, it was run by the 'crazy Atlanta nine', a self-appointed group of individuals chaired by Andrew Young, a former aide to Martin Luther King Jr. The 'crazy nine' were thought to have little managerial experience (Rutheiser 1996: 228) and MAOGA was their 'watchdog' although, in practice, it is thought that MAOGA exercised little authority (Rutheiser 1996: 236–7). In 1992 an 'Image Summit' was held to draw together stakeholders in the Games to find an appropriate slogan for the event. Although slogans and mascots had already been created, they had not 'stuck'; perhaps reflecting the lack of a clear and cohesive vision for the Games. Two weeks after this unsuccessful 'Image Summit', the Cooperation for Olympic Development in Atlanta (CODA) was set up as a not for profit organisation that would be responsible for the revitalisation of neighbourhoods. It included members from the City Council, ACOG, MAOGA, neighbourhood groups and the business community. From the outset, however, CODA lacked a cohesive strategy. CODA was marginal to or excluded from decisions about planning and designing the Olympic Park, with ACOG keeping plans for the Park's legacy usage a secret prior to the Games. In this way, the Park became a metaphor for the 'break down' of relationships and symbolic of a planning process designed to meet private rather than public interests (Rutheiser 1996: 262), a process for which the Atlanta '96 Games has come to be remembered.

Despite the Tri-Party arrangements of governance for the Atlanta Games, business leaders dominated the policy making process, with civic leaders performing a supporting role (Andranovich et al. 2001: 158). The ACOG priorities provided the dominant conceptual framework for the Atlanta Games – privileging tourism and the visitor economy and the re-presentation of the city as a focus for the re-location of capital and the creation of urban spaces that reflect the lifestyle needs of the professional, middle classes. ACOG asserted that the Olympics were 'not a welfare program, [they are] a business venture. If they [the city government] wanted to be more involved, they should've voted to pay their own expenses' (Rutheiser 1996: 238).

ACOG's dominance in the governance framework provided the policy and practical instruments to secure corporate sponsorship for a Games that balanced its budget *and* ensured that the business perspective came to dominate the urban regeneration agenda, leaving civic and community groups at the margins of decision making. The consequence for Atlanta was that one of its main goals in bidding for the Olympics, the improvement of the lives of those living in the most deprived inner city neighbourhoods, failed to occur.

Conclusion

The commercial model emerged with the Los Angeles Games of 1984. The combination of public/private partnerships that this gives rise to may vary. Los Angeles and Atlanta had different approaches to governance, though in both cities business rather than civic leaders dominated their respective Olympic organising committees, despite the presence of elected officials. For Los Angeles, undertaking a commercially viable, even profitable, event whose costs were largely met by private sponsorship and corporate donations, was a major priority. The added value of the Games themselves were reflected in corporate terms as intangibles – place-marketing and branding – with the Games providing an important insight into the capacity for sport to become a significant vehicle for the selling of a city on a global scale.

By contrast, Atlanta embraced elements of the regeneration agenda that informed the Barcelona Games but the commercially oriented governance structure came not only to dominate the preparation for the event but also the process of urban redevelopment that took place alongside it. The mega-event provided the opportunity to utilise the Games to commence a process of urban renewal that marginalised community groups and local forms of political accountability while 'privileging investors interests' (Andranovich et al. 2001: 162). This process has given rise to claims that the Games initiated a programme of gentrification that is set to be continued in the form of the latest stage of urban renewal, the BeltLine project. The overall impact of the Games upon the economy of Atlanta and its region is difficult to measure, especially given the wider context of economic growth achieved in parts of Georgia following the end of the early 1990s recession and the shift of enterprises into the region in the latter part of the decade. Arguably, the attraction for capital of relocating to Atlanta was enhanced by hosting the Games, and was aided by the federal support for infrastructural and economic development that went with being a host city. Equally, the event produced forms of inner-city renewal that merely re-shaped rather than reduced the patterns of social and racial division that have long existed in the cities of the old south.

References

Andranovich, G., Burbank, M. and Heying, C. (2001) 'Olympic Cities: Lessons Learned from Mega-Event Politics', *Journal of Urban Affairs* 23(2): 113–31.

Atlanta Committee for the Olympic Games (ACOG) (1997) *Olympic Games Official Report*, Vol. 1, *Planning and Organisation*, Atlanta: Peachtree Publishers.

Baade, R. and Matheson, V. (2002) 'Bidding for the Olympics: Fool's Gold?', in Barros C., Ibrahim, M. and Szymanski, S. (eds) *Transatlantic Sport*, London: Edward Elgar, 127–51.

Centre on Housing Rights and Evictions (COHRE) (2007) 'Atlanta's Olympic Legacy', background paper, Geneva: Geneva International Academic Network.

Dann, B. (2004) 'Legacies of the Games: Long-term Impacts of the Olympic Games on the Host Cities of Atlanta and Sydney', Duke University, https://portfolio.oit.duke.edu/retrieve/2642/Summer+Report+updated+1-19-2005.

Davies, J. (2001) *Partnerships and Regimes, The Politics of urban regeneration in the UK*, Aldershot: Ashgate.

Franklin, S. (2005) 'Atlanta's Economic Development Plan: Year One Results and 2007 Action Plan', Atlanta: Brand Atlanta Inc., November, http://www.atlantada.com/media/EDPbrochure-webpages.pdf.

Hamnett, C. (2003) *Unequal City*, London: Routledge.

Jones, P. and Evans, J. (2006) 'Urban Regeneration, Governance and the State: Exploring Notions of Distance and Proximity', *Urban Studies* 43(9): 1491–509.

Keating, L. (2007) Resurgent Gentrification and Development Policy in Atlanta, Georgia: Georgia Institute of Technology (draft requires approval for quotation from author).

New Georgia Encyclopedia (2006) 'Olympic Games in 1996', http://www.georgiaencyclopedia.org/nge/Article.jsp.

Preuss, H. (2004) *The Economics of Staging the Olympics – A Comparison of the Games 1972–2008*, Cheltenham: Edward Elgar.

Roche, M.C. (2000) *Mega-Events and Modernity: Olympics and Expos in the Growth of Global Culture*, London: Routledge.

Rutheiser, C. (1996) *Imagineering Atlanta*, London: Verso.

Ward, A. (2006) 'Ten Years on Atlanta Takes Stock of its Olympic Legacy', *Financial Times*, Asia edition, 21 July 2006.

Chapter 8

Regenerating Sydney's West:
Framing and Adapting an Olympic Vision[1]

Richard Cashman

It is important from the outset to place Sydney's Olympic vision and its legacy – what has been promised and what has been realised – in the context of the time. Sydney's Olympic vision was framed in the early 1990s, when legacy was of much lesser importance in Olympic discourse than it is now. Legacy was then a far more informal and even haphazard practice. Although legacy was enshrined in Sydney's bid – making it more attractive to the international Olympic community and saleable to the host community – it was taken as a given which would occur as a matter of course after the Games. Few plans were put in place to implement and evaluate Olympic legacy after the Games and there was no designated post-Games authority to operate in this period.

Such legacy practice was typical of what occurred in Olympic cities in the previous century. Once the Games were over, the organising committee shut up shop and wound up the Games affairs as expeditiously and economically as possible. There was no idea that there was significant unfinished Olympic business.

The world of legacy has changed remarkably since 2001. The International Olympic Committee (IOC) had earlier recognised the importance of impacts when it created the Olympic Games Global Impact (OGGI) programme in 2001. OGGI operates over an 11-year cycle – from two years before the selection of an Olympic city to two years after the staging of the Olympic Games – and during this period there is a sustained effort to collect and capture social, environmental and economic impacts of the Games. There are a number of benefits that flow from this programme. OGGI assists with the transfer of Olympic knowledge from one Olympic city to another and it enables the IOC to better understand and manage future Olympic Games.

The organisation of an international conference at Lausanne in 2002, 'The Legacy of the Olympic Games,1984–2000', and the publication of the conference proceedings, made a cogent case for greater attention to and

---

1   The material in this chapter is drawn from my book (Cashman 2006). However, this chapter includes much new material on the adaptation of legacy since January 2006, when the book was published. Legacy continues to unfold in the decade (and even decades) after the staging of an Olympic Games.

research on Olympic outcomes (Moragas et al. 2003). It was argued at the conference that impacts are immensely important because they relate to issues of sustainability, accountability and evaluation. At the 2002 legacy conference, IOC President Dr Jacques Rogge warned about the danger of luxury developments made in the name of the Olympic Games that became white elephants – costly extravaganzas with no long-term benefit. Greater attention also needs to be paid to the development of post-Games policies and the creation of appropriate authorities so that a city can minimise negative impacts and maximise positive ones. There had been all too little evaluation of an Olympic Games and its impacts in the past. Maurice Roche, who has written extensively on mega events and Olympic Games, noted in 1992 that 'pre-event projections are seldom tested against post-event accounting' (Roche 1998: 562).

Legacy planning is now enshrined in the Olympic cycle of host cities. Five years before the London 2012 Olympic Games a 'Legacy Lives' conference was held in London on 30 and 31 January 2007. Delegates had to pay a two-day registration fee of over £1,000 suggesting that legacy had become both topical and expensive – and even big business. A one-day conference on legacy was held at Vancouver on 1 November 2006 – four years before its Winter Olympic Games. There were no such conferences in Sydney before or after the Games, though one is likely to be held in 2010 – on the tenth anniversary of the Games.

It is intriguing to speculate about how and why legacy has become so important in Olympic circles in such a short space of time. It is a reflection in part of the spiralling cost of staging an Olympic Games and the need to introduce more public accountability and to demonstrate evidence of community benefit. It is also a welcome action on the part of the IOC to better manage its events and avoid associated problems such as gigantism and white elephants. Behind this is the attempt to protect the name and reputation of the Olympic movement. Bad publicity from a past Olympic Games affects the Olympic brand and the willingness of future cities to bid for the right to stage the Games.

Argument

This chapter will consider four overlapping stages in the development of Sydney's Olympic legacy. The Olympic vision, which was articulated before the Games, was a powerful and compelling one. During the second stage, the immediate years after the Games, the city struggled to realise its legacy because of insufficient plans to implement the vision. In the third stage belated plans were developed and implemented to deal with ongoing problems. The city's Olympic vision was adapted and modified in the final stage to suit the changing post-Games environment.

Sydney's experience provides a number of lessons for future Olympic cities. While legacy plans might be good on paper, there needs to be an active plan of follow-up, evaluation and implementation. It has also become apparent that legacy does not occur on a one-off basis at the end of the Games but that impacts, positive and negative, planned and unplanned, continue to resonate in an Olympic city for years and even decades. The challenge for Olympic cities is to adapt and modify legacy plans in accord with a changing post-Games environment to secure the best outcomes for the city.

Sydney's Olympic Vision and its Implementation

Sydney Olympic Park was the city's major and most identifiable Olympic infrastructure project. While the Park was the cornerstone of Sydney's Olympic objectives, the city hoped to gain economic and business benefits, such as increased tourism and greater global positioning of the city. The majority of Olympic venues, including the largest and most prestigious, were built at Sydney Olympic Park. Almost without exception, the sports venues were new and state of the art. Sydney Olympic Park was framed by the parklands of Millennium Park and by Bicentennial Park, which included significant wetlands and facilities for passive leisure. The Park also included the Olympic village at Newington, the flats and apartments that became the post-Olympic suburb of Newington. The showgrounds, which are the site of an annual agricultural show, were located in another section of the Park, near the railway station.

The Olympic vision for the Park consisted of a number of dimensions. First, the creation of a super sports precinct that was located in western Sydney where sports facilities were most needed. Second, the development of the parklands, that enabled the provision of new facilities for active recreation (cycling and walking paths) and passive leisure (such as picnics). Third, the Park was also created to be an environmental showcase. Finally, the Park was designated a place for cultural activities. This vision addressed all three dimensions of Olympism – sport, culture and the environment. It also accorded with the IOC policy that a costly Olympic development should be of value to the community after the Games.

Homebush Bay

Sydney Olympic Park was the principal theatre for the Sydney 2000 Olympic Games and its creation involved a massive investment of public resources. Sydney's Olympic vision related to this large urban project, the remediation of Homebush Bay and the creation of a sporting precinct there, with state-of-the-art facilities. Homebush Bay consists of 760 hectares of land in the demographic heartland of Sydney – west of the city, the focus of population growth in recent decades – where world-class sporting facilities were considered most needed. Homebush Bay includes some remnant woodlands and extensive wetlands. The area is the home for a variety of mammals, reptiles, amphibians and birds. It had been the location variously of an armaments depot, abattoir and brickworks – the remnant quarry remains a feature of Millennium Park. From the 1960s, Homebush Bay became the site of unrecorded and unregulated dumping of household and industrial waste including toxic material so that it had become degraded. After the potential of the site had been identified for urban renewal in the 1970s, the State Sports Centre, Bicentennial Park and a privately developed business complex, the Australia Centre, were opened in the 1980s. The winning of the Olympic bid accelerated this development, which had been planned to occur gradually over a period of 30 years.

The remediation of Homebush Bay and the related concept of the 'Green Games' were attractive features of the bid because the environmental measures proposed were more ambitious than any previous Olympic Games. The idea anticipated the IOC's adoption of environment as the third dimension of Olympism in 1995. There had been some environmental initiatives at the 1994 Lillehammer Winter Olympic Games but Sydney's 'green' promises related to a wider range of areas – energy and water conservation, waste avoidance and minimisation, recycling of water, transportation, the improvement of air, water and soil quality, and the protection of significant cultural and physical environments. Greenpeace Australia was involved in the Sydney bid from its planning stages (Cashman and Hughes 1998). Environmental issues also shaped the contours of Sydney Olympic Park: treated and capped waste formed the basis of the man-made hills of Olympic Park since it was considered best to deal with the past problems on the site rather than exporting them elsewhere.

Homebush Bay has undergone a 'profound physical and symbolic restructuring' (Dunn and McGuirk 1999: 18–32) which has led to a 'refashioning of [its] identity' (Winchester et al. 2003: 134). This precinct, in the words of Olympic historian Harry Gordon, has been transformed in the 1990s from 'an ugly wasteland ... into ... one of the world's great sporting and industrial parklands' (Gordon 2003: 85). Geographers Kevin Dunn and Pauline McGuirk added that 'the imagery of Homebush was altered' (Dunn and McGuirk 1999: 18): the landscape was no longer considered 'a dirty, polluted industrial zone' but a 'post-industrial, clean and green space of leisure and sport' (ibid.: 32).

Post-Games Malaise

While the vision was admired before 2000 – by politicians, community leaders and the people of Sydney more generally – it soon became apparent after the Games that there were insufficient plans in place to realise this vision. The Park was frequently empty and serviced by inadequate public transport except when a major event was staged there. One commentator described the Park as a ghost town and another referred to it as a 'wasteland of white elephants' (Cashman 2006: 31). There was sustained media criticism of the Park in 2001 and 2002 because of the absence of public events there and the cost of maintaining struggling Olympic venues. (There were some notable exceptions to the rule, such as the Sydney International Aquatic Centre, which increased its patronage after the Games). Because the Park was under-used in 2001 and 2002, there was much public concern that it would become a future burden to the state government and ultimately to the taxpayers. Others suggested that it was essential to develop public confidence in the Park. Ric Birch, the acclaimed director of the Sydney Olympic opening ceremony, stated that buildings by themselves do not create 'an atmosphere' and a public attachment to the Park (Cashman 2006: 154). It was necessary then to develop a public commitment to use the Park.

The staging of the major matches of the 2003 Rugby World Cup at Sydney Olympic Park revived the Park's fortunes. The Olympic stadium was once again full to overflowing for its seven matches and the Park throbbed with life in October and November 2003. The Rugby World Cup was a great financial success because it capitalised on the already-established Olympic infrastructure. The Cup demonstrated the value of staging future mega-events in Olympic venues. The Rugby World Cup also enabled the Sydney public to reconnect with the Park.

Post-Games Planning

Planning for the future of the Park began belatedly – nine months after the Games – with the creation of the Sydney Olympic Park Authority (SOPA) on 1 July 2001. The objectives and mission statement of SOPA acknowledged implicitly some of the problems facing the Park - that it was not sufficiently 'active and vibrant' and there was too much dependency on 'ongoing funding'. It might also be noted that a struggling Sydney Olympic Park was a potential political issue at the March 2003 state election because it was the state (and the taxpayers) that had underwritten Sydney Olympic Park. A failing Olympic Park could have damaged the Government's election prospects.

SOPA's objectives were to:

- create an active and vibrant centre within metropolitan Sydney;
- develop a premium destination for culture, entertainment, recreation, tourism and sport;
- establish best practice in environmental and town planning standards;
- advance education, training and health.

SOPA's mission statement included:

- 'Sydney Olympic Park Authority will develop and manage Sydney Olympic Park, as a special place for sporting (both elite and non-elite), recreational, educational and business activities for the benefit of the community.
- Future development and management will be based on the principles of recognising the responsibility to preserve the Olympic legacy, of supporting stakeholders, of protecting and enhancing the environment, of maintaining high environmental and design values while also generating an adequate financial return to reduce the dependency for ongoing funding.[2]

The first draft master plan, adopted by 31 May 2002, provided a lifeline for the Park in that it advocated residential and commercial development. This was a frank recognition that the precinct could not survive on sport and recreation alone. The master plan recommended the creation of a town centre near the railway station to accommodate a residential population of 15,000 housed in large apartment towers. It was also planned to attract small and medium-sized offices to the Park so that there would be a daily workforce of 15,000.

Modification of the Olympic Vision

The commercial use and development of Sydney Olympic Park in recent years represents a pragmatic and significant adaptation of the plans for the Park in the interests of making the Park more self-sufficient and viable. The two hotels, the Novotel and Ibis, have had occupancy rates of over 80 per cent per annum, and another two new hotels will be built by 2008: the five-star Sofitel and the budget Formula 1 hotel. The announcement in 2006 that a major Australian bank (the Commonwealth) planned to shift almost half of its office staff to Sydney Olympic Park provided proof of its rising status and attractiveness to the business community. The bank's chief executive Ralph Norris stated that about '5000 jobs would be moved to the park by 2009' and housed in three seven-storey towers near the Olympic railway station, built at a cost of US$300 million. The move to this suburban location would reduce the rent paid by the bank. The additional 5,000 bank staff would increase the daily work force to 11,000 by 2009, augmenting the 6,000 workers who were based there by 2006 (*Sydney Morning Herald*, 13 July 2006).

Mark Rosenberg, Marketing Director of SOPA, believes that business activity has expanded impressively for two main reasons. The numerous world-class indoor and outdoor facilities had the capacity to provide for a growing number of meetings, exhibitions and conferences. The Park has

---

2   See the Sydney Olympic Park website: http://www.sydneyolympicpark.nsw.gov. au.

become Sydney's second major business events destination after Darling Harbour, which was created in 1988, in the central business district. The Park has also benefited from its location at the edge of western Sydney, which has experienced spectacular growth over the past three years, The Park is being embraced by businesses as they recognise the advantages of its location and its appeal to employees who are seeking a healthy work environment (interview, August 2006).

Negative media stories that appeared in 2001 and 2002 were replaced by positive ones by 2006. An article in the *Sunday Telegraph* of 27 August 2006, entitled 'Olympic site's building boom', catalogued the developments, which included the three Commonwealth bank buildings, two new hotels and three 20-storey residential towers to provide 679 units on Australia Avenue (near the town centre). There was also a significant rise in the number of serviced apartments built at the Park and plans were in place to create an 'Eat Street' on Olympic Boulevard, with a range of restaurants, bars and shops. There are also several private developments, particularly near the waterfront, indicating that many are attracted by the prospect of living at Sydney Olympic Park. Rosenberg believed that the second building boom at Sydney Olympic Park from 2006 to 2008 will be almost as spectacular as the initial boom from 1996 to 1999, when there was greater construction activity than anywhere else in the state.

It is significant that the first building boom related primarily to sport, culture and the environment. The second boom, by contrast, was driven more by commercial and residential imperatives. So does this represent a pragmatic retreat from the original Olympic vision? Does the development of a multi-purpose park dilute Olympic legacy?

The possible clash between an Olympic legacy vision and that of a multi-purpose Park is an intriguing issue. Because there was never a precise definition of Sydney's legacy, it is unclear whether the new developments at the Park diminish or enhance the Olympic legacy. It could be asserted that sport, culture and the environment are still prominent features at the Park, they have been merely augmented by business and housing. It is also debatable whether the establishment of banks and businesses and a permanent residential population detract from sports, cultural and environmental objectives. A permanent park population of around 30,000 may enable more Sydneysiders to access the Park's sporting, recreational and leisure options and will lead to better public transport to the Park. Undoubtedly, the move towards a multi-purpose park has led to greater community use and added value to this Olympic precinct. At the very least Sydney Olympic Park is avoiding the criticism that it is either a luxury development or a white elephant.

Promoting an Olympic Legacy

SOPA, to its credit, has taken some steps to promote an Olympic legacy and add to the symbolic significance of the Park. Two examples illustrate this point. After the Games the cauldron was removed from its lofty pedestal high in the Olympic stadium and was transformed to become an accessible and public sculpture in the nearby Overflow Park. The cauldron was reconfigured so that water cascaded from its perimeters. It thus replicated the fire and water that were central to the cauldron-lighting ceremony of the Olympic Games. The names of all Olympic and Paralympic medallists are featured at the base of the sculpture. The cauldron is lit at the time of each anniversary of the Games and on other important ceremonial occasions. A forest of 530 poles in front of the Olympic stadium, which lists the name of every Olympic and Paralympic volunteer, is another example of legacy best practice. This development, which is known as 'Games Memories', was unveiled in 2002 at the time of the second anniversary of the Games.

Since its establishment in 2001, SOPA has developed significant measures to enhance cultural programmes at the Park. It released an 'Arts and Cultural Strategy', outlining initiatives that would be undertaken from 2005 to 2015. Heritage-listed buildings at Newington (the site of a former armoury) will be used for exhibition and performances spaces and artist residences. The Park has become the site for the annual Sydney Festival. There have also been an increasing number of sports and environmental education programmes at the Park. The New South Wales Institute of Sport provides programmes for 800 athletes and the Australian College for Physical Education is located opposite the Aquatic Centre. Sport Knowledge Australia, which was established in 2004, offers courses in sports science and sports management and coaching to senior Australian and international sports managers. There have been continuing efforts to enhance the parklands. The Brickpit Ring Walk, which is a 55-metre walk on an elevated platform 18.5 metres above the sandstone floor, enables visitors to observe the unique environment below. This walk won a 2006 National Trust Award. Nearby Wentworth Common, also completed in 2006, is now one of a number of expansive public areas suitable for recreation, picnics and functions.

Flexible and Constructive Post-Games Policies

Although Sydney's legacy plans were developed belatedly, individuals and government and have responded to new post-Games opportunities. The Sydney-Beijing Olympic Secretariat (SBOS), which was established in February 2002, is a prime example of a shrewd and timely response to Beijing's success in winning the bid for the 2008 Olympic Games in July 2001. SBOS was established within the Department of State and Regional Development

(DSRD) in the New South Wales (NSW) government. Its aim was to assist local Australian business to gain access to the Chinese Olympic market. SBOS has worked well because it enlisted the active support of individuals, such as Sandy Hollway and David Churches, who had been prominent in the Sydney 2000 Olympic Games. The continuing commitment of individuals, such as Hollway and Churches, to an Australian Olympic presence in future Olympic and other Games has reaped rich dividends.

Australia has developed a highly profitable Olympic and Games export industry and continues to play a significant role in the organisation of Olympic Games at Beijing and London as well as Asian, Commonwealth and other Games. Although it is difficult to measure the precise extent and worth of this export industry, there are grounds for believing that Australia has been more successful than many other countries in securing Olympic contracts, consultancies and advisory roles. Australians have won Chinese contracts to assist in the design and construction of the National Swimming Centre, the Watercube and the Olympic village in Beijing and the sailing facility at Qingdao for instance. This author plans to document the rise of this industry in a volume entitled *The Australian Olympic Caravan: Creating and Maintaining a Unique Export Industry*. This project will be undertaken with the support of the Department of State and Regional Development and published in 2008.

Conclusions

Since 2001, legacy has become an important issue in international Olympic circles and it is likely to increase in significance in the future. The IOC has encouraged bidding cities to develop both a legacy vision and specific legacy plans. Legacy is now established as an important issue that all bid cities must seriously address. The IOC is right to stress that large-scale and costly developments made in the name of an Olympic Games should have a useful and valuable post-Games life. This will ensure that the Olympic stamp on a city continues to be a positive one in the years after the event has been held. When Sydney won the right to host the Games in 1993 and staged the Games in 2000, legacy demands were of lesser significance. While the Sydney organisers developed a legacy vision, they failed to articulate specific legacy plans before 2000. There was also no designated post-Games authority to manage Sydney's legacy. As a result, the initial few years after the Games were difficult ones.

One feature that has stood Sydney in good stead since 2000 has been the flexibility and adaptability of its post-Games planners. Solutions have been found for the problems faced by Sydney Olympic Park in 2001 and 2002. Rather than placing the Olympic precinct in mothballs or allowing it to become degraded through under-use, it is preferable that a precinct which bears the Olympic name should be of continuing benefit to the population that supported the Games. Sydney organisers have also creatively tapped into some new opportunities that were not apparent at the time of the Games. The success of the Australian Olympic export industry and Australia's event management expertise provide a model for other Olympic cities.

It has become increasingly apparent that legacy is a rich area for future study. Between 2006 and 2010 this author plans to complete four separate projects on different aspects of Sydney's legacy. The first project was published in early 2006: *The Bitter-Sweet Awakening: The Legacy of the Sydney 2000 Olympic Games*.[3] Work is under way (with Simon Darcy) on a companion volume of the legacy of the Paralympic Games, *The Benchmark Games: The Legacy of the Sydney 2000 Paralympic Games*.[4] There has been all too little substantial research and evaluation of this important part of the Olympic festival. A third project, *The Australian Olympic Caravan*, has been mentioned already. A final project, with the support of SOPA, will examine the history of Sydney Olympic Park focusing in particular on the period 2000 to 2010. This project will explore the post-Games history and transformation of this unique precinct. I hope that others will recognise the value of such research and undertake legacy studies in other Olympic cities.

In my work on the legacy of the Sydney 2000 Olympic Games it has become clear that impacts – direct and indirect, planned and unplanned – continue to resonate in an Olympic city, years after the Games. There are even some surprising twists in the post-Games realisation of legacy. Sydney's post-2001 Beijing opportunities represent a case in point. Sydney Olympic Park, for instance, is about to experience a second massive building boom in 2007 and 2008, comparable to the building boom from 1996 to 1999, when Olympic venues were erected. The establishment of a permanent residential population and an enhanced commercial presence is a response to the under-use of the Park in 2001 and 2002. The creation of a multi-purpose Park is an attempt to ensure that Sydney's legacy is sustainable and positive. I have been, and will continue to be, a keen observer of the transformation of Sydney Olympic Park over this coming decade (Cashman 2006).

References

Cashman, R. (2006) *The Bitter-Sweet Awakening: The Legacy of the Sydney 2000 Olympic Games*, Sydney: Walla Walla Press.

Cashman, R. and Hughes, A. (eds) (1998) *The Green Games: A Golden Opportunity*, Sydney: University of New South Wales, Centre for Olympic Studies.

de Moragas, M., Kennett, C. and Puig, N. (2003) *The Legacy of the Olympic Games 1984–2000*, Lausanne: International Olympic Committee).

---

3   See the Walla Walla Press website: http://www.wallawallapress.com.
4   Published in late 2007.

Dunn, K.M. and McGuirk, P.M. (1999) 'Hallmark Events', in Cashman, R. and Hughes, A. (eds) *Staging the Olympics: The Event and its Impact*, Sydney: University of New South Wales Press, 18–32.

Gordon, H. (2003) *The Time of Our Lives: Inside the Sydney Olympics*, Brisbane: University of Queensland Press.

Roche, M. (1998) 'Mega-events and Micromodernisation', quoted in Hiller, H. 'Assessing the Impact of Mega Events: A Linkage Model', *Current Issues in Tourism*, 48.

Winchester, H.P.M., Kong, L. and Dunn, K. (2003) *Landscapes: Ways of Imagining the World*, Harlow: Pearson Prentice Hall.

Chapter 9

The 28th Olympic Games in Athens 2004

Roy Panagiotopoulou

Introduction: The City

Athens has a long-lasting and close relationship with the Olympic Games. Greece is the only country that has participated in all the ancient and modern Games without exception, and Athens was the city where the first modern Games took place in 1896. Therefore, the selection of Athens to host the 28th Olympic Games in 2004 was inevitably linked with the history of the event; Olympic Movement values were re-baptised in an ethical discourse with strong references to the narrative of antiquity (Panagiotopoulou 2003).

Athens, the capital of Greece, is a very fast growing metropolis, which in the last 40 years has nearly doubled in size.[1] Nowadays, it constitutes a city of approximately four million inhabitants (including Piraeus and the suburbs) with many spatial and social problems. Until the end of the 1980s, population increase was the result of internal migration but since then the increase arises from people immigrating to Greece from other countries and immigrants now form 10 per cent of the Greek population. Many areas in the Athenian capital region have developed fast, without the necessary infrastructure and city planning. This has led to the creation of poor city-areas with very little infrastructure. Athens now has all the disadvantages of a modern densely populated metropolis (air population, traffic congestion and so on) without the benefits of pleasing architectural features and styles, and lacks parks and other recreation and green areas (Beriatos and Gospodini 2004: 192). This development has affected negatively the image of the city, a situation that is evident in the continuous decline in the number of tourists in the last decade. Nowadays, millions of tourists use Athens only as a stopover before they travel elsewhere in Greece.

---

1 According to the 1961 national census, the population of Greater Athens was 2,057,974 inhabitants, which was 24.5 per cent of the total population of Greece. In the latest census of 2001, the population of Athens was recorded as being 3,761,810 inhabitants, 34.3 per cent of the total population of the country. See Theodori-Markogiannaki et al. (1986) and National Statistical Service of Greece (2006).

Advantages and Disadvantages of Bidding for the Olympic Games

Compared with other cities, Athens had two major advantages in being selected to host the Games: its special historic ties to the Olympics and the almost universal support of the Greek people for hosting the event. Over 90 per cent of the total population considered the Games as a constituent part of their cultural heritage and national identity.[2]

For the international community and the International Olympic Committee (IOC), the choice of Athens to host the Games had an unquestionable symbolic dimension and a forceful cultural message. For Greeks, it offered a major opportunity for their country to modernise its infrastructure, reorganise many of its services, enlarge its tourist and commercial transactions, attract foreign investment, improve its international image and strengthen its role as a political force within the Balkans and the enlarged European Union (EU). Further, it offered an opportunity to support the successful sporting performance of Greek athletes, renovate or create new sporting facilities and widen the usual programme of summer cultural activities of the Athens Festival through the Cultural Olympiad offering a new stage of performance for national and international artists. An additional but also significant advantage was the convenient broadcast time of an Athens Games for European and American TV viewers.

Nevertheless, the choice of Athens in the age of globalisation constituted a considerable risk, which was initially a problem: the largest global sporting and mass media event in the world was to be organised by a small country that was not prosperous, and had no pre-existing infrastructure (for example in communication technologies, transportation, sporting facilities, and so on), nor previous experience in organising such major and complicated projects. Moreover, Greece did not have a particularly positive international image in a period of terrorist hysteria, economic recession and wars in surrounding regions (Kosovo, and later Iraq).

On the part of the large international sponsors and corporations, the choice of Athens to host the event was not particularly welcome, and they demonstrated this throughout the period leading up to the Games. In fact some companies decreased the level of their sponsorship because, as they themselves said, the market was small and the risk for them was great.[3]

---

2   In July 1996 two different public opinion polls were held regarding the candidacy of Athens as the next host of the Games. The company VPRC conducted one poll in which 93 per cent of the population accepted the organisation of the Games by Athens (4 per cent did not); the other was carried out by the company MRB, who found that 96.2 per cent accepted that the Games should be held in Athens (2.5 per cent did not) (Vernardakis 2004: 79–80).

3   According to an article published in the newspaper *Eleftherotypia*, based on provisional data, the 'TOP V' sponsors spent 'the sum of 510 million Euros. The

This reluctance was accompanied by a questioning, at every stage of the preparations, as to whether the country would be ready to organise the Games in accordance with very detailed IOC specifications. In brief, global interest focused primarily on the protection of the institution of the Games, 'the hen that laid the golden egg', which globally brings nothing but profits. At first the criticisms of Greece by the international sponsors and corporations were guarded, but they became vehement during the last year and a half before the Games. Equally, the country found itself in a continual battle with time and money to make up for delays, satisfy all the international demands and be ready for the opening of the Games.

The Bid

When, in September 1990, Atlanta won the bid to be the host city for the 1996 Olympic Games, Athens came second. This was very disappointing for Greek people because they had been keen to organise the centennial Olympic Games. However, seven years later, Athens was nominated as the host city for the Olympics 2004. Despite the fact that the Greeks had bid to host the Games in the past, it had never been made clear to the majority of the population what it meant for a small country to organise this international and hugely challenging sports event.

Athens won the right to hold the Games at the meeting of the IOC on 5 September 1997 in Lausanne (Lunzenfichter 2002; Synadinos 2004: 175–205). In March 1998 the Organisational Committee of the Athens 2004 Olympic Games (ATHOC) was founded and the first steps were taken towards organising the Games. From then until early 2000, the Games organisers were preoccupied with the search for appropriate sites for the construction of competition venues, in addition to dealing with legal and administrative actions required for the tendering of contracts for the building projects. A significant obstacle that had to be resolved before the building projects could begin was the search for appropriate sites for the sports venues in a densely populated area with very high land prices. The intention of the government was to spread the Olympic buildings over a variety of poor districts in Athens so these venues would in future provide centres of local development and entertainment, which were lacking in the city at the time (Beriatos and Gospodini 2004; Synadinos 2004: 157–64). A further significant obstacle – not particularly well known outside

---

original predictions of the ATHOC were much larger, reaching 750 million Euros' (Aggelis 2004). The number of sponsoring corporations fell to 31 for Athens 2004 (it had been 104 for Sydney), 'owing to the promise to not further commercialise the Olympic Games, but also owing to the fact that Greece is a relatively small market and therefore the interest of sponsors is lower' (Preuss 2004: 129). Further, the sponsors from the USA contributed only 64 per cent of the total sponsoring revenue (it had been 82 per cent for Sydney and 90 per cent for Atlanta) (Preuss 2004: 130).

Greece – was the fact that in Athens every square metre of soil potentially contains something of historical interest (Waterfield 2004: 322). The Central Archeological Council has the right to interrupt any building activity until the excavated area is monitored by the archeologists.[4] However, the longest delays during the first three-year period of planning for Athens 2004 were mostly caused by the slipshod manner in which the file for Athens' candidacy had been prepared and the inadequate planning for the funding of the public works (Telloglou 2004: 43).

The reasons why the IOC entrusted the Games to Athens is described in a variety of articles about the Games of 2004 (Lunzenfichter 2002; Llewellyn Smith 2004; Pound 2004; Telloglou 2004: 13–37). In a period in which both the image and the practices of the IOC had been damaged by internal scandals (Burbank et al. 2001: 2–4; Pound 2004) and the significance of the global event was in danger of being diminished, the choice of Athens appeared to be a *deus ex machina* to clear the image of the Games from the charges of gigantism and commercialisation, to reinvigorate the Olympic ideal and to rekindle the hope of many smaller cities and/or states to bid for the right to organise the event.

The Preparation Period and the Financing of the Games

The intensive preparation period for the Games started a few months before the Sydney Olympics. The new Head of the ATHOC, Mrs Gianna Aggelopoulou-Daskalaki, took control and began to speed up the planning and construction of the various competition and non-competition venues. There were 62 work sites related to the Games; 22 were directly related to the competition venues and the remaining 40 were related to non-competition venues. The 22 Olympic competition venues were located in the greater area of Athens, aiming to improve infrastructure in poor city districts, and offer new opportunities for city development and the creation of new metropolitan spaces after the Games.[5] The majority of these venues were expensive constructions and their

---

4   The Athens Metro constituted one of the largest contemporary excavations in Athens, and its construction was delayed for more than five years. With regard to the Olympic works, antiquities were found at the Marathon Rowing Centre, the Equestrian Centre and the Olympic Village (Waterfield 2004: 323).

5   The major competition venues in Athens were divided into separate zones where various athletic events took place. These zones were the Athens Olympic Sports Complex (OAKA) in Maroussi area including the Olympic Station, Tennis Center, Indoor Hall, Velodrome and Aquatic Center; and the costal zone including two areas: the Hellinikon Olympic Complex with the installations of Softball Stadium, Baseball Center, Hockey Center, Fencing Hall, Canoe/Kayak Slalom Center, Basketball Hall; and the Faliron Olympic Complex with Beach Volleyball Center, Sports Pavilion, Peace and Friendship Stadium. Other venues were dispersed in the greater Athens area: Marathon Start, Schinias Rowing and Canoeing Center, Agios Kosmas Sailing Center, Markopoulo Shooting and Equestrian Centers, Nikaia Weightlifting Hall,

reconstruction for other non-athletic, post Games, usage (conference centres, cultural spaces, water parks and so on) was costly. Many of these works were planned previously, and had begun to be built before the country took on the Games, in order to improve the quality of life in Athens, but they were also necessary to support Athens' candidacy for the Games. Indeed, the Games provided an incentive and, undoubtedly, encouraged the major changes that took place to the infrastructure of the capital city.

Many of the non-competition venues were peripheral but essential to the organisation of the Games, such as the Olympic Village, the seven press villages, and the two main communication centres (the Main Press Center and the International Broadcasting Center). Other public works were related to the upgrade of various services and facilities, such as transportation, the port of Piraeus, the public traffic network, wastewater management and aesthetic improvement projects in public areas. Works included 120 km of new road construction, six major new highway interchanges, an expanded metro system and upgrading of the old metro line stations, a new traffic management centre, a 23-km two-line tram network, a suburban railway connecting the airport with the metro and the town, an expanded bus and trolley fleet, the development of the Attica peripheral highway, the renovation of various buildings in central Athens and the unification of the ancient sites of the city. All of these works contributed to the improvement of the city's infrastructure and the achievement of a new, more attractive look to the city (ATHOC 2004b). They also considerably improved public transport and the traffic conditions in Greater Athens. In the bid-proposal for the greater Athens area, there was a plan to create green areas and reforest many areas around Athens, but only a few of these ideas materialised. By and large, the environment surrounding most of Athens did not improve. This was mainly because much of the construction work was completed only a few months before the beginning of the Games, and there was not enough time for planting and similar measures.

After the Games, the government formed a new public company, the Olympic Real Estate SA, which aimed to manage and exploit the Olympic venues. The government has repeatedly said that it does not seek to sell the venues. However, most of them are expected to be leased by companies from the private sector for a long period, because the government wants to avoid the operating and maintenance costs of the venues as well as to find sources of funding to pay off the huge public debt.[6] The maintenance and

---

Ano Liosia Wrestling Hall, Paeristeri Boxing Hall, Goudi Modern Penthathlon Hall, Galatsi Gymnastic Hall, Parnitha Maoutain Bike Venue and the old Panathinaikon Stadium at the centre of the city where the modern Olympic Games took first place (ATHOC 2004a: 79–318). A further venue was the ancient stadium of Olympia in Ancient Olympia, where the shot put took place.

6   It was estimated that for 14 installations managed by the Olympic Real Estate SA the annual maintenance cost surpassed €1 million (Ziotis 2004).

operation of such costly facilities cannot be undertaken by the various Greek sporting federations. Clearly, such problems arising in the post-Games period demonstrates that the original bid was constructed in a haphazard way, without plans for the post-Olympic use of the installations after the Games.

In the three years that have passed since the Games, many of the facilities do not operate as sporting centres and their future use has not been defined. Moreover, the public bids for their leasing to the private sector have not even been completed.[7] The only construction that was given directly after the Games (October 2004) for citizens' use was the Olympic Village, which is a residential area. It was given, after a lottery competition, to 2,229 families living on lower incomes.[8]

The Economics of Staging the Games

The public works that took place were accelerated in their completion by the timescale imposed by the Games and constitute a classic example of the catalytic role of the event, even though their final cost was considered extremely high and almost prohibitive for the country. Initially, it was estimated that many of the works would be undertaken in the form of co-funding with the private sector. Eventually, almost all of the works were funded through public sources.[9] International corporations did not show any particular interest in Greece, except in the field of security, which after the events of 11 September 2001, expanded enormously as security issues were strongly associated with the organisation, infrastructure and communications aspects of the Games. During the preparation phase private investment was consistently low across all other projects and sectors, with the exception of some architectural competitions concerning building projects, and the production of souvenirs. The Greek government and Games organisers were not sufficiently proactive

---

7   By the end of 2006 public bids for IBC, the Goudi Hall and Equestrian Center had been completed.

8   Each of the awarded families had to pay €850 per m². The management of the Olympic Village was given to a new public company, 'Olympic Village SA', which will undertake the construction of the other buildings (shops, sporting centres and so on), the maintenance of the public spaces and the security of the complex (Megas 2005).

9   This was because the conditions of funding by the private sector were not at that time attractive to domestic capital as interest rates were exceptionally high, so borrowing from banks was unprofitable. Foreign capital did not find the market attractive enough for investments. Thus, more than 90 per cent of the total cost of the Olympic works was covered by public investment. In the end, only two of the works that were specifically created for the Games were co-funded by private investors: the Olympic Village and the Press Village in Maroussi, close to the venue of the Olympic Stadium.

when forming policy and adapting bureaucracy to make inward investment attractive to international enterprises.

The discussion concerning the final cost of the Athens Games has provided material for many publications in the local and international press. Many estimates for the cost of the Games included infrastructure works that were not directly connected to the event. This approach gave the impression that the total costs of the Games were much higher than the real ones.[10] Although the economic reports of the ATHOC and the Greek government presented some slight differences, we can draw a relatively exact picture of the money spent on the preparation and realisation of the Games. As mentioned before, most of the money (80 per cent) was provided by the Greek state (Table 9.1).

Table 9.1   Sources of expenditure on Athens 2004 Olympic Games (€m)

	€m	%
Budget of the Greek state	7,202	80.4
Budget of the ATHOC	1,752	19.6
Total	8,954	100.0

Source: The Business of Sport, 12 November 2004, http://business.sport.gr/onenew. asp?id=1792.

The security system, one of the most modern worldwide, was not taken into account in the original organisational costs, and proved a serious financial burden (costing more than €1 billion). A major part of this investment proved useless after the Games. The cost of providing security may be a major problem in future preparations for the Games because it requires considerable investment, but there are few tangible legacy benefits since the physical security precautions erected for the Games are unlikely to be useful once the event is over. The security system, and its expense, however, raised considerable concerns among Greek citizens about the possible restrictions to their democratic rights during the event and in the months following its completion.

According to the official economic report of the ATHOC, the cost of the Games reached €1,967.8 million and the revenue was €2,098.4 million.

---

10   The large differences in the calculation of the final costs are partly due to the way in which the total cost is calculated and partly the result of violent disagreements between the major political parties (Kartalis 2004; Apostolopoulou and Papadimitriou 2004: 182). Apart from its financial and administrative problems, and the struggle to complete the works on time, Greece had a change of government four months before the opening ceremony of the Games. As soon as the new conservative government came into power, it started to blame its predecessor for the delays in construction and for hugely exceeding the original budget.

Table 9.2   Breakdown of state expenditure on Athens 2004 Olympic Games (€m)

	€m	%
Olympic works*	2,861	39.7
Sporting facilities and equipment	2,153	29.9
Security	1,080	15.0
Other expenses**	1,108	15.4
Total	7,202	100.0

*   Includes only works directly related to the Olympic Games.
** Includes Cultural Olympiad, environmental improvements, athlete hospitality, marketing and promotion costs.

Source: The Business of Sport, 12 November 2004, http://business.sport.gr/onenew. asp?id=1792.

Consequently, there was a surplus of €130.6 million. The revenue breakdown is presented in Table 9.3.

Table 9.3   Revenue sources for Athens 2004 Olympic Games (€m)

	€m	%
Television rights	578.7	27.6
International and national sponsorship	536.7	25,6
Contribution of Greek state	282.5	13.5
Financial transactions*	226.0	10.8
Tickets	194.1	9.2
Merchandise and commercial rights	119.7	5.7
Hospitality services	113.7	5.4
Other revenues	47.0	2.2
Total	2,098.4	100.0

*   Revenues from financial transactions result from successful changes in currency from US$ to Euro.

Source: The Business of Sport, 12 May 2005, http://business.sport.gr/onenew. asp?id=2586.

The expenses covered a variety of fields and are summarised in Table 9.4
    According to other sources, expenditure on the Olympic Games exceeded the original budget of €4,602 billion by approximately 25 per cent (PricewaterhouseCoopers 2004: 22). To this sum we must add over €1 billion for security costs, which were not foreseen in the calculations for the costs of

Table 9.4   Expenses of the ATHOC on Athens 2004 Olympic Games (€m)

	€m	%
Technological infrastructure and equipment	338.8	17.2
Games functioning	309.6	15.7
Games support	298.0	15.1
Olympic and Paralympic adjustments	190.2	9.7
Production of broadcasting signal	171.7	8.7
Torch relay, opening and closing ceremonies	133.4	6.8
Administration services	101.4	5.2
Paralympic Games (organisation cost)	99.4	5.1
Financial services and supply	93.5	4.8
Marketing and promotion of tickets, sponsors etc.	92.4	4.7
Image and identity promotion	69.8	3.5
IOC and National Olympic Committee rights	69.8	3.5
Total	1,967.8	100.0

Source: The Business of Sport, 12 May 2005, http://business.sport.gr/onenew.
        asp?id=2586.

the overall project. According to current EU estimates, expenditure on the Olympic Games raised the state budget deficit of Greece by approximately 6.1 per cent of the GDP (Moschonas 2005). This was one of the main reasons why Greece has been under EU monitoring since 2004. In her speech presenting the economic results of the organisation of the Games the Minister of Culture, Mrs Fani Palli Petralia, estimated that the Athens Games cost approximately €200 for each Greek citizen. She added, 'We held a very good Games, very safe and very expensive'.[11]

The Event

The Athens 2004 Olympic Games took place from 13 to 29 August and the Paralympic Games from 17 to 26 September. As with previous Games, two mega cultural events were included in the programme – the opening and closing ceremonies. These media events are used to attract the interest of global television viewers and promote the image of the host city and country. Athens could not make an exception to 'stage the nation' (Hogan 2003: 100–101). The opening ceremony on 13 August 2004 followed the guidelines of the Olympic Charter by being suitable to be televised as a spectacle. The concept of the opening and closing ceremonies followed the 'auteur' model and was

---

11   See http://business.sport.gr/onenew.asp?id=1786, from 12 November 2004.

commissioned by the artist Dimitri Papaioannou.[12] For the ceremonial part that referred to the host city, the opening ceremony had as its main theme the evolution of the Games since antiquity – emphasising the role of Greece. As the opening ceremony is an event with a global reach, the messages of promoting the city of Athens related both to Olympic ideals (human scale, participation, celebration, heritage) and to the 'Greekness' of the Games' history, the promotion of modern Greece and the 'metamorphosis' of Athens into a contemporary metropolis.[13]

The opening ceremony had a great impact and was able to reverse the negative image Greece had relating to the preparation of the event. Despite its references to the classic masterpieces of art and the classical era, which gave the ideals of the Olympic Movement strong symbolism that was not easily decoded by the general public, the opening ceremony received very positive comments from the Greek and international press[14] and contributed to the generally positive reception of the Games. The closing ceremony had the character of a big party and was also successful.

Eleven thousand and ninety-nine athletes from 202 countries participated in the Athens Games.[15] Most delegations resided in the Olympic Village, with a few located in cruisers at the Piraeus harbour. All 16 competition venues were well equipped and offered an optimal competition environment to the athletes and spectators. Further, the transport for athletes and visitors, one

---

12   MacAloon (1996: 37–8) distinguishes three organisational models for the OG ceremonies: a) the impresario model, where the general authority goes to an impresario from the world of film, television and advertising production, (master of the spectacle); b) the committee of cultural experts model, where there is a team of officials and intellectuals of the host country; and c) the 'auteur' model, where there is a single artist with a national and international reputation who represents the new generation. The agency Jack Morton Worldwide was responsible for the production of the two ceremonies.

13   It was a successful attempt to represent artistically a certain discourse of the Greek national identity in an elaborated and easy to understand narrative (Hall 1992: 293). The central motto during the preparation period was 'The Olympic Games are returning to Greece, their ancient birthplace and to Athens, the city of their revival'. Other mottoes used in the preparation campaign were: 'Join us in welcoming them home'; 'Welcome home Olympics'; 'Ready since ... long ago ... Greece welcomes you'; and, during the Games, 'Welcome home' (Panagiotopoulou 2004).

14   For example headlines on 14 August 2004 included: 'Theatrical mixture of ancient and modern Greece' (Reuters); 'The Games opened in a glorious way in Athens' (BBC); and 'Mythology and history met in the Athens stadium' (Republic).

15   The postmodern narrative adopted by the organisers for presenting Olympic results tends to report that various figures always surpass previous ones. According to the official statistics the Games consisted of 28 different sport disciplines, 37 sports and 301 single competitions in which 75 countries won a medal. Further, they were 3,500 doping controls and 23 athletes tested positive. See report in *Kathimerini*, the daily newspaper of Athens ('Athens 2004 in Figures' 2004).

of the most frequently mentioned disadvantages of holding the Games in Athens, worked very satisfactorily due to the special traffic measures that were taken (special Olympic lanes, new public transport schedules combining all kind of transportation, express bus lines, special transport for journalists and the media, and so on), and all previously mentioned infrastructure works.

According to a poll conducted during the 15 days of the Games at all sports venues, around 90 per cent of Greeks as well as foreign visitors were 'very' or 'rather' satisfied with the organisation of the Games (Table 9.5). This was the best reward for all Greeks.

Table 9.5   Visitors' satisfaction level with the Athens 2004 Olympic Games

Sector	'Very' or 'rather' satisfied (%)	Greeks (%)	Foreigner visitors (%)
Sport events	94.8	95.2	94.4
Opening ceremony	95.2	95.4	95.0
Closing ceremony	96.2	95.9	96.3
Venues	95.4	96.5	94.6
Volunteer services	96.0	97.1	95.4
Transportation	86.9	85.8	87.6
Security	98.4	95.4	86.8

Source: VPRC and MRB (2004), Visitors Satisfaction Measurement, 13–29 August 2004, http://www.vprc.gr.

Apart from the Games, the Cultural Olympiad, supervised by the Ministry of Culture, organised a complex programme that included events from all art forms under the motto 'For a civilization of civilizations'. The events aimed to promote artistic activities relating to the theme of the Games and to provide international artistic performances that would attract Greek and foreign visitors. The Cultural Olympiad lasted during the whole preparation period and reached its peak in summer 2004 with 249 events for the Olympic Games and 95 for the Paralympic Games.[16]

---

16   The Cultural Olympiad in combination with the 'Athens 2004 Cultural Program' organised by the ATHOC aimed to support the festive period of the Games. All festivities and art events were designed to interact with the city functions, to promote the new image of Athens and to enrich the Olympic experiences of the visitors by giving free access to the public.

Coverage by the Media

There was a heavy media presence long before the Games began, which became even more intensive for the duration of the event. It was the first time Greece had handled such a variety of media demands upon infrastructure and services. There were some 21,500 accredited journalists reporting the Games, of whom 12,000 were accredited broadcaster journalists, 7,000 journalists for the printed media and 2,500 accredited internet journalists (AOB 2004; ATHOC 2004a: 13).

The broadcasting data of the Athens Games are remarkable. According to Jacques Rogge (2004b), the president of the IOC and the Athens Olympic Broadcasting (AOB), television coverage of the Athens Games was transmitted by more than 300 television stations in 220 countries throughout the world. There was a total 44,000 hours of dedicated coverage to the Games worldwide.[17] This established the Athens 2004 Games as the most covered Games in history, as 3.9 billion people had access to the events (compared with 3.6 billion viewers for Sydney). Live coverage increased and the AOB produced 3,800 hours of live sports competitions, transmitted by more than half of the global broadcasters. Prime time coverage was up by 55 per cent compared with Sydney. More specifically, prime time transmission reached 21 per cent of the total dedicated time for the Athens Games (13 per cent in Sydney) (Exarchos 2006). There was a significant increase in the diversity of choice available to viewers as more satellite and cable channels devoted all their 24-hour programming to Olympic coverage. According to the IOC President:

> Athens has set a new benchmark with the highest audience, images of spectacular quality, expanded coverage of sports, new technologies and, I am delighted to say, a high level of satisfaction amongst our rights holding partners. (Rogge 2004a: 1)

Globally, the average viewer watched over 12 hours of Olympic Games. In Europe, the average viewing time per person reached 14 hours (50 per cent above that during the Sydney Games). In France, the average viewing time was 17 hours, in Germany 11 hours, in Greece 17.5 hours, in Spain 15 hours and in Great Britain over 13 hours. All countries had an increased average viewing relative to Sydney (Rogge 2004a: 2); clearly, from the perspective of the viewing audience, the Athens Olympic Games of 2004 were a considerable success.

The ERTSA (Hellenic Radio and Television Broadcasting Corporation SA), the public radio and television network, became a Grand National Sponsor of

---

17   This compares with 29,600 hours of dedicated coverage in Sydney in 2000, 25,000 hours in Atlanta in 1996 and 20,000 hours in Barcelona in 1992 – an increase of some 49 per cent over the previous Games in Sydney (AOB 2004; Exarchos 2006).

the Games in communications.[18] In order to fulfill its role, ERT entered into an extended programme of investment, which reached €35.5 million for the construction of new buildings, studios, transmitters, relays and broadcasting links.[19] It is clear that public television gained numerous and significant advantages from its participation in the television coverage of the Athens Games. It significantly increased its share of the Greek television viewing audience during and after the Games as well as enhancing its public credibility.

Before the Games, Athens had a negative image. This largely remained the case throughout the entire preparation period until approximately one month before the beginning of the event. Air pollution, chaotic traffic, garbage in the streets, and a number of social issues, such as inadequate state policies in individual sectors like health and transport, were the main negative aspects that were reported. Quite often, such criticism failed to recognise the gradual improvements taking place in the city (the new Metro, improved traffic management) and was mostly related to tourist activity and the problems that tourists encountered in Greece (Waterfield 2004: 322–3).

The intense scepticism that built up in the mass media for months focused on two main issues: security and the measures planned by Greece to deal with possible terrorist actions, and, secondly, delays in the completion of many building projects related to the organisation of the Games (McCall 2004). From the beginning of 2004, negative press publications and critical comments by the written and electronic media increased instead of dropping off.[20] Many articles on security issues were exaggerated and often unfair, when one takes into account that the country funded the most up-to-date security systems, and cooperated with NATO and experts from the US, Great Britain and Israel to ensure there was effective protection. Criticism also centred upon the projects that would remain unfinished or be scrapped. Press reports focused monotonously on the question of whether Athens would be ready in time to host the Games. Such ongoing negative reports tend to damage the image of Olympic cities, especially when the host city belongs to a small country that does not have a powerful international lobby with the capacity to counter such stories.

Neither the ATHOC nor the Greek government managed to come up with an effective communication strategy to reduce these overall negative press reports,[21] but in May 2004 some more positive articles about Greece and the

---

18   The total amount of the sponsorship was US$17 million (NN 2001).

19   In addition to this, ERT used 1,100 m^2 at the IBC to produce a broadcasting programme for Greece, on which 1,100 individuals worked and which transmitted 1,110 hours of television programming.

20   See *The Times* on 13 April 2004 and 16 May 2004; *Financial Times* on 6 May 2004; and the *Guardian* on 16 January 2004, 30 March 2004, 6 May 2004 and 14 May 2004.

21   Finally in June 2004 the ATHOC started undertaking advertising activities abroad (http://www.athens2004.com).

Olympic Games began to appear in the international press.[22] Finally, against the odds, comments changed and journalists started reporting that one of the most long awaited but also most doubted Olympic spectacles in history might just turn out to be one of the best (McCall 2004).

The praise and the 'apology to Greece' came too late to increase the small numbers of foreign visitors to the Games.[23] However, it should be stressed that the Athens Games had indeed held the public in suspense until the final moment as to whether the venues would be ready in time, given that the roof of the Olympic Stadium was finally put into place only in late May 2004 and that the marathon route was completed only days before the opening ceremony. This situation, combined with a number of international events (terrorist acts in Madrid 2003 and Istanbul 2004, rising oil prices, the SARS epidemic in east Asia, the increase in the value of the Euro relative to the US$, the increase in Athens hotel rates and so on) discouraged people who might have been interested in visiting Greece for the Olympics. In July 2004 the occupancy rate of hotels in the Athens region was 12 per cent lower than the rate for Sydney hotels for that same period four years ago (Delezos 2004: N14).[24]

The Athens Games were the only Games in recent times where there was a decrease in the number of tourists to the country holding them, see Table 9.6. Although there was a slight increase in the number of tourists to Athens, the rest of the country's tourism destinations faced a very poor season in 2004. The situation improved the following year.

---

22   The practice of publishing articles devoted to the city or country organising the Olympic Games is common in the large international newspapers (Moragas et al. 2003: 285). In the case of Athens, these articles were slow to appear, e.g. *Daily Telegraph* (14 January 2004), *Die Presse* (5 February 2004), *Frankfurter Allgemeine* (5 February 2004), *Seven Network* (18 July 2004), *USA Today* (5 August 2004) and *Le Monde* (7 August 2004).

23   For example, one of the many publications was an open letter from the president of the television network NBC, D. Ebersol, to the Greeks, the organising committee and the government (NN 2004).

24   The price per available room in the Athens hotels during the Games increased 261 per cent with hoteliers taking advantage of high August demand in the city centre. Occupancy reached 84.4 per cent. According to analysts of Deloitte, 'in terms of visitor numbers, the travel industry had estimated the Olympics would attract an extra 2 million tourists to the country as a whole during the summer months. However, preliminary figures suggest that fewer than half of these actually arrived. The year-to-July04 visitor numbers show a decline of 12 per cent. But, this decline was not surprising given that many "traditional" visitors chose to avoid crowds and increased prices. In the case of Athens, heightened concerns about security and the widespread publicity given to the unfinished building projects prior to the Games were also likely to have deterred some visitors.' See 'Athens hoteliers hiked Aug 04 rates by 261%' 2004.

Table 9.6   Foreign tourist arrivals in Greek airports between 2000 and 2005 (000s)

	Athens	Rest of Greece	Total
2000	3,777.4	7,744.2	11,521.6
2003	4,022.2	7,643.3	11,665.5
2004	4,250.4	7,325.1	11,575.5
2005	4,534.0	7,569.4	12,103.4

Source: National Statistical Service of Greece, http://www.statistics.gr.

The excellent range and quality of the coverage of the Olympic Games in the media may itself have influenced negatively the number of visitors who attended the Games in person.

The Legacy

The organisation of the Games in Athens was a considerable success. The challenge in the post-Olympic period lies in exploiting effectively the tangible and intangible benefits deriving from this organisation (Panagiotopoulou 2006). The legacy of the Games has three distinct components: the infrastructure and relevant facilities, the macro-economic benefits in the long term, and the intangible benefits. The most intensive debate about the post-Olympic period in Athens has focused upon the best way of taking advantage of the tangible infrastructure and facilities that remain. It was widely acknowledged that the sporting venues of Athens were among the best constructions of their sort. The macro-economic effects, apart from the directly measurable positive impact on tourism, include gaining expertise in technical and managerial issues. Finally, the intangible benefits such as new organisational patterns, new forms of governance and co-operation, organisational experience in various sectors, a new city–country image and the legacy of volunteerism have added value to the development of the city and country.

The image of the Games is made up of different interventions and tensions, which are not always under the control of those who manage officially the country image (Moragas et al. 2003).The most weakly organised element of the Athens Games was the coordination of the various agencies, which in many cases was insufficient or even impossible, with various negative consequences. For example, the communications campaign could not be coordinated effectively. Additionally, the big delays in completing the Olympic works, including the endless construction and unfinished look of the city just two months before the Games started, was another important negative factor that re-enforced the strength and validity of the negative comments in the international media.

However, Greek public opinion and those who experienced the organisation of the Games were unanimously positive. At the last minute, Athens managed to provide a festive atmosphere and present a very engaging face to its visitors. The Athenians, who had suffered many hardships for so long, deemed this abrupt change in public opinion a 'wonder' that only few believed could happen. The Games may influence public opinion and the collective memory strongly, and can become an important part of the city's history. Perhaps the success of the Athens Games may be gradually equaled by the success of its legacy. The influence of the legacy will become visible after some years, if there is a consistent and realistic plan to exploit the positive impact that the event had upon the city. Three years after the end of the Games, Greece seems, however, to be exhausted by the great effort required during the long preparation period and the staging of the event.

The general welcoming of the Games by the overwhelming majority of the Greek population was always one of the strong points working in favour of Athens. This positive public opinion may be one of the determining factors that will help the country to overcome the first post-Olympic years of inertia and nostalgia; to look at how the Olympic legacy can be best used, to work out how to meet the additional economic burdens and to create a new collective vitality in the wake of this mega event.

References

Aggelis, G. (2004) 'We Paid – the IOC Receives Payment', *Eleftherotypia* 5 September.

Apostolopoulou, A. and Papadimitriou, D. (2004) '"Welcome Home": Motivations and Objectives of the 2004 Grand National Olympic Sponsors', *Sport Marketing Quarterly* 13(4): 180–92.

Athens Olympic Broadcasting (2004) *Host Broadcast Final Report Athens 2004*, Athens: Athens Olympic Broadcasting. October.

'Athens 2004 in Figures' (2004) *Kathimerini*, 21 September.

'Athens Hoteliers Hiked Aug 04 rates by 261%' (2004) 24 September, http://www.e-tid.com/pma/22384.

ATHOC (2004a) *Athens 2004 Media Guide*, Athens: Organizational Committee of the Athens 2004 Olympic Games, Press Operations, July.

ATHOC (2004b) 'Fact Sheet prepared by the Athens 2004 Newsdesk', Athens: Organizational Committee of the Athens 2004 Olympic Games, August.

Beriatos, E. and Gospodini, A. (2004) '"Glocalising" Urban Landscapes: Athens and the 2004 Olympics', *Cities* 21(3): 187–202.

Burbank, M.J., Andranovich, G.D. and Heying, C.H. (2001) *Olympic Dreams. The Impact of Mega-Events on Local Politics*, London: Lynne Rienner.

Delezos, K. (2004) 'High Prices Keep Tourists Away', *Ta Nea* 17 May, 14 [in Greek].

de Moragas, M., Belen Moreno, A. and Kennett, C. (2003) 'The Legacy of the Symbols: Communication and the Olympic Games', in de Moragas, M., Belen Moreno, A. and Puig, N. (eds) *The Legacy of the Olympic Games*, Lausanne: International Olympic Committee, 279–88.

Exarchos, G. (2006) 'Olympic Games and Television: The Global Image and the Greek Heritage', in Panagiotopoulou, R. (ed.) *Athens 2004: Post-Olympic Considerations*, Athens: General Secretariat of Communication, 106–16 [in Greek].

Hall, S. (1992) 'The Question of Cultural Identity', in Hall, S., Held, D. and McGrew, T. (eds) *Modernity and its Futures*, Cambridge, MA: Polity, 273–326.

Hogan, J. (2003) 'Staging the Nation: Gendered and Ethnicized Discourses of National Identity in Olympic Opening Ceremonies', *Journal of Sport and Social Issues* 27(2): 100–23.

Kartalis, K. (2004) 'Miracle … in Athens About the Costs of the Games', *Imerisia*, 27 November [in Greek].

Llewellyn Smith, M. (2004) *Olympics in Athens 1896: The Invention of the Modern Olympic Games*, London: Profile Books.

Lunzenfichter, A. (2002) *Athènes, Pékin 1896–2008: Choix Epique des Villes Olympique*, Paris: Atlantica.

MacAloon, J.J. (1996) 'Olympic Ceremonies as a Setting for Intercultural Exchange', in de Moragas, M., MacAloon, J., Llines, M. (eds) *Olympic Ceremonies and Cultural Exchange*, Lausanne: International Olympic Committee, 29–43.

McCall, J. (2004) 'Analysis: Marketing Opportunities for 2004 Olympics Proved Solid', *PR Week*, 30 August, http://www.jackmorton.com/pdf/JMcCall_PRWeek_8_30_2044.pdf.

Megas, C. (2005) 'They Want +20% On the Shops', *Eleftherotypia*, 12 January.

Moschonas, K. (2005) 'Almunia: Your case Falls Under Article 104§9', *Eleftherotypia*, 7 February [in Greek].

National Statistical Service of Greece (2006) *Hellas in Numbers*, www.statistics.gr/gr_tables/hellas_in_numbers.pdf.

NN (2001) 'Greek National Radio – TV Also Becomes Grand National Sponsor', *Athens 2004 Olympic News*, Issue 5, June.

NN (2004) 'NBC: Sorry and Congratulations', *Naftemporiki*, 9 October [in Greek].

Panagiotopoulou, R. (2003) '"Join Us in Welcoming them Home": The Impact of the Ancient Olympic Games' Legacy in the Promotion Campaign of the Athens 2004 Olympic Games', in de Moragas, M., Belen Moreno, A. and Puig, N. (eds) *The Legacy of the Olympic Games*, Lausanne: International Olympic Committee, 346–52.

Panagiotopoulou, R. (2004) 'The Communication Strategy of the Olympic Games Athens 2004', *Zitimata Epikoinonias* (Communication Issues) 1(1): 38–56 [in Greek].

Panagiotopoulou, R. (2006) 'Introduction', in Panagiotopoulou, R. (ed.) *Athens 2004: Post-Olympic Considerations*, Athens: General Secretariat of Communication, 17–27 [in Greek].

Pound, D. (2004) *Inside the Olympics. A Behind-the-Scenes Look at the Politics, the Scandals and the Glory of the Games*, Chichester: Wiley.

Preuss, H. (2004) *The Economics of Staging the Olympics. A Comparison of the Games 1972–2008*, Cheltenham: Edward Elgar.

PricewaterhouseCoopers European Economic Outlook (2004) 'The Economic Impact of the Olympic Games', June, http://www.pwcglobal.com/gx/eng/ins-sol/spec-int/neweurope/epa/EEOJun04_SectionIII.pdf.

Rogge, J. (2004a) 'Global TV Viewing of Athens 2004 Olympic Games Breaks Records', *15th International Sports Television Convention*, Monaco, 12 October, http://www.olympic.org/uk/news/olympic_news/full_story_uk.asp?id=1117.

Rogge, J. (2004b) 'I Am a Very Happy IOC President', interview 29 August 2004, http://www.athens2004.com/el/LatestNews/newslist?item=4ac042b9 38aef00VgnVC, accessed 30 August 2004.

Synadinos, P. (2004) *The Game of a City*, Athens: Kastaniotis [in Greek].

Telloglou, T. (2004) *The City of the Games*, Athens: Estia [in Greek].

Theodori-Markogiannaki, E. et al. (1986) *Basic Statistics at Prefecture and Regional Level*, Athens: Center for Economic Planning and Research [in Greek].

Vernardakis, C. (2004) 'Greek Public Opinion and the Organization of the Olympic Games: National Consent and Critical Voices', *Zitimata Epikoinonias* 1(1): 79–92 [in Greek].

VPRC and MRB (2004) 'The Image of the Olympic Games', Panhellenic poll conducted between 17 and 27 September 2004, Athens, September (mimeo) [in Greek].

Waterfield, R. (2004) *Athens. From Ancient Ideal to Modern City. A History*, New York: Basic Books.

Ziotis, Ch. (2004) 'Long Term Leasing Instead of Selling the Olympic Property, *Eleftherotypia*, 27 August.

Chapter 10

The Economy of the Beijing Olympic Games: An Analysis of Prospects and First Impacts

Ferran Brunet and Zuo Xinwen

Introduction

Since its nomination to host the 2008 Summer Olympic and Paralympic Games, Beijing has developed rapidly. The city has benefitted from considerable investment and experienced extensive social change as a result of its preparations to host the Games. This chapter explains the major infrastructural and socio-economic developments that have taken place in Beijing and its surrounding region over the past five years. The chapter charts Beijing's progress toward a 'post industrial' service-based economy and reveals how becoming an Olympic host city has assisted China's capital to affirm its twenty first century status as a 'global city'.

Transforming the Patterns of Economic Growth

Some 15.8 million people live in the Beijing urban area of 1,041 km^2. In 2006, the GROSS DOMESTIC PRODUCT (GDP) of the Beijing region reached 772 billion yuan. Primary industry contributed added value of 9.8 billion yuan, secondary industry achieved an added value of 221.7 billion yuan, and the tertiary sector experienced continued development by contributing an added value of 540.5 billion yuan. The city's financial revenue reached 111.7 billion yuan, an increase of 21.5 per cent over the previous year, while the city's expenditure was 129.2 billion yuan, a 22.1 per cent increase. Over recent years a series of significant changes have occurred to the trajectory of the city's economic and social development.

The preparation for the Games has accelerated change in the pattern of Beijing's urban development. The period between 2002 and 2007 has witnessed one of the most sustained phases of economic growth since the city's entry into the reform period (post-1979) and its opening-up to domestic and external influences. The annual urban economic growth rate has increased by 12.1 per cent in the past five years; 1.3 per cent more than that achieved between 1997 and 2001. In 2006, the value of the city's economic activity amounted to 772 billion yuan (2.1 times that of 2001) enabling the city economy to achieve the rank of 10th in China. The per capita Gross Domestic Product (GDP), calculated according to permanent residents, rose to US$6,210, 1.9 times that of 2001. The goal of reaching US$6,000 per capita GDP by 2008 was realised two years before the target date. While the aggregate of economic activity has significantly increased and development enhanced, the pattern of economic growth has witnessed important changes (China National Statistical Administration 2007).

Economic growth has occurred alongside a reduction in the levels of energy consumption and environmental pollution; the quality and benefits of economic growth have been significantly improved. Over the past five years, Beijing has sustained 12 per cent economic growth based on a rise in energy consumption of 6 per cent; 1.14 tons of standard coal consumed for every 10,000 yuan GDP in 2001 fell to 0.8 tons by 2005: 104.9 cubic meters of water was consumed for 10,000 yuan GDP in 2001 and this level fell to 44.4 cubic meters in 2005. Chemical Oxygen Demand (COD) and sulphur dioxide emissions decreased by 35.4 and 12.6 per cent respectively in comparison with the levels achieved in 2001. This data indicates an important change that Beijing has made in the trajectory of its economic development. Equally, the growth in consumer prices has been kept at a comparatively low level. In 2005 and 2006, annual consumer prices went up by 0.4 per cent in each year. Local revenue exceeded 100 billion yuan. By 2006, general budget revenue stood at 111.72 billion yuan, 2.5 times that of 2001. Between 2002 and 2006, the local budget revenue aggregate was up to 390.74 billion yuan, 2.6 times the level achieved between 1997 and 2001 (Development Research Center of the State Council, 2005).

In the period of preparation for hosting the Games, Beijing's industrial structure has shifted toward the creation of higher value added products and services with the service-oriented economy continuing to dominate and expand. By 2006, the tertiary sector accounted for 70 per cent of the Beijing economy, 3 per cent higher than that in 2001. Services, hi-tech industry and manufacturing have served as the main instruments for achieving sustained economic growth. The service sector, represented by financial and information services, cultural creativity and technology research and development, accounted for 47 per cent of Beijing's value added, while the value added produced by hi-tech industry represented 7.8 per cent. Six 'high end' industrial areas, including the Zhongguancun Science Park, the Beijing economic and technological development zone and new business and financial services centres, have taken shape and started to play an increasingly dominant role in the capital's economy (Beijing Municipal People's Congress 2006b: 12).

Consumer demand has strengthened considerably over recent years. Investment was 337.15 billion yuan and consumption 327.52 billion yuan in

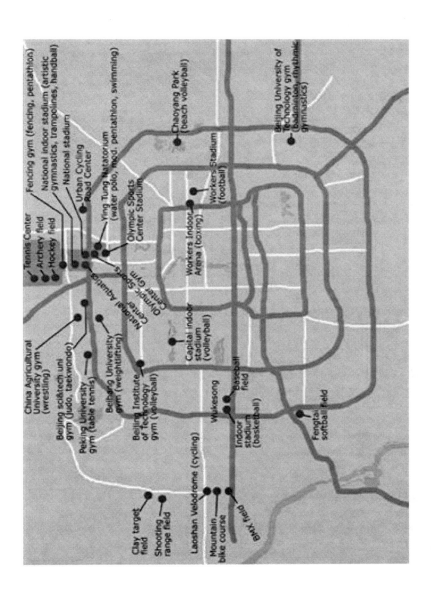

Figure 10.1 The Beijing Olympic venues

2006, 2.2 times and 1.8 times the levels achieved in 2001. The annual growth rate of total retail sales of consumer goods rose to 12.3 per cent between 2002 and 2006, 0.8 per cent up when compared to the growth rates obtained between 1997 and 2001 and the patterns of consumption are shifting to higher value added commodities. Automobiles, housing and telecommunications have maintained a strong growth momentum. Tourism, sports recreation and entertainment have also been developing at a fast pace. Investment, with clear priorities, conforms to the guidance and requirements of the state's 'macro' controls and regulations. Over the past five years, Beijing's fixed asset investment increased by 17.4 per cent annually, up 6.1 per cent by comparison to the growth achieved between 1997 and 2001 (China National Statistical Administration 2007).

Technology development has accelerated, making a greater contribution to economic growth. In 2006, Beijing invested 85 billion yuan in science and technology development of which Research and Development spending was 45 billion yuan (5.8 per cent of GDP) and 1.2 per cent more than that of 2001. Beijing approved 11,238 patents, 80 per cent more than in 2001. Among them, there were 3,864 invention patents, 3.1 per cent more than that of 2001 (Cheng et al. 2003.) A large number of innovative results have occurred and many new enterprises have emerged.

The Resources of the Beijing Olympic Games Organising Committee

The Beijing Organising Committee for the Games of the XXIX Olympiad (BOCOG) established a budget of US$ 1625 million for the Games. TV rights (International Olympic Committee 2001) are the main revenue (43.6 per cent), with a further 20.3 per cent of income derived from sponsors and licenses, 11.1 per cent from lotteries and 8.6 per cent from the sale of tickets (Table 10.1) The current operations of the BOCOG assume a total spend of 88.3 per cent of the budgeted expenditure. Expenditure financed by BOCOG represents 11.7 per cent of the total budget.

Investment in the Beijing Olympic Games

Investments related to the Beijing Games are estimated as US$ 14,256.6 million. Three items constitute the main expenditure – environment protection (60.5 per cent), transport (25.8 per cent), and sports facilities (10.0 per cent).

The level of investment for Beijing 2008 has been much higher compared to other Olympic host city's (Brunet 1994 and 2003; Poynter 2006). Much of this investment has been in large scale infrastructure projects. Current figures are not definitive; the total investment catalysed by the Games is likely to be much larger – between $20 and $30 billion dollars – especially when the private

Table 10.1   Budget of the Beijing Organising Committee of the Olympic Games 2008: revenues and expenditures

Revenues	US$m	%	Expenditure	US$m	%
1 Television rights	709.00	43.63	B1 Capital investments	190.00	11.69
			13 Sports facilities	102.00	6.28
2 TOP sponsorship	130.00	8.00	Olympic Village	40.00	2.46
3 Local sponsorship	130.00	8.00	MPC and IBC	45.00	2.77
4 Licensing	50.00	3.08	MV	3.00	0.18
5 Official suppliers	20.00	1.23			
			B2 Operations	1,419.00	88.31
6 Olympic Coins Programme	8.00	0.49	14 Sports events	275.00	16.92
Philately	12.00	0.74	Olympic Village	65.00	4.00
7 Lotteries	180.00	11.08	MPC and IBC	360.00	22.15
			MV	10.00	0.62
8 Ticket sales	140.00	8.62	15 Ceremonies and Programmes	100.00	6.15
9 Donations	20.00	1.23	16 Medical Services	30.00	1.85
10 Disposal of assets	80.00	4.92	17 Catering	51.00	3.14
11 Subsidies	100.00	6.15	18 Transport	70.00	4.31
National Government	50.00	3.08	19 Security	50.00	3.08
Municipal Government	50.00	3.08	20 Paralympic Games	82.00	5.05
12 Others	46.00	2.83	21 Advertising and promotion	60.00	3.69
			22 Administration	125.00	7.69
			23 Pre-Olympic events and coordination	40.00	2.46
			24 Other	101.00	6.22
25 Shortfall			25 Surplus	16.00	0.98
Total	1,625.00	100.00	Total	1,625.00	100.00

Notes

1   US dollar/RMByuan exchange rate used in preparing the budget: 1:8.27.
2   Date of finalisation of the budget: 14 December 2000.

Source: BOCOG (2007).

Olympic Cities

Table 10.2   Investment in the City of Beijing 2008

Capital investments	Construction cost (US$m)								
	2001	2002	2003	2004	2005	2006	2007	2008	Total
Planned non-Olympic specific expenditure									
Environmental protection	1,000.00	1,000.00	1,500.00	1,500.00	1,500.00	1,300.00	827.00	0	8,627.00
Roads & railways	547.00	592.00	636.00	636.00	636.00	313.00	313.00	0	3,673.00
Airport	12.00	30.00	31.00	12.00	0.00	0	0	0	85.00
Olympic-related expenditure									
Sports venues	212.57	425.13	495.99	283.42	12.01	0	1,429.12		
Olympic Village	110.62	158.87	134.74	38.25	442.48				
Total	1,559.00	1,622.00	2,379.57	2,573.13	2,742.61	2,055.29	1,286.75	38.25	14,256.60

Source: BOCOG (2007).

sector contribution is added (Zhang and Zhao 2007). The scale of investment in infrastructure is reflected in, for example, transport and communications.

Table 10.3   Investments related to the Olympic Games

Olympic city	Infrastructure investment – actual sums (US$ billions)	Sources of investment: public sector (% of total investment)	Sources of investment: private sector ((% of total investment)
Barcelona 1992	8,012	61.5	38.5
Sydney 2000	3,03	64.4	36.6
Beijing 2008	14,257	85.0	15.0
London 2012	13,7	64.2	35.8

Source: Poynter (2006: 15).

Transport and Communications

The Games has given rise to new opportunities for the construction and development of the communications infrastructure in Beijing. Several key communications projects have been programmed and built in preparation for 2008:

Railway Transportation

116.6 km of new municipal rail construction has occurred in the city and 3 new municipal railways have been built (82.1 km) in the suburbs, costing an estimated total investment of 63 billon yuan; achieving 200 km of new municipal railway development across Beijing (China National Statistical Administration 2007). The projects are as follows:

- Subway Line No. 4 (28.2 km);
- Subway Line No. 5 (27.6 km);
- Subway Line No. 9 first phase (5.8 km);
- Subway Line No. 10 first phase (24.6 km);
- OG branch (5.9 km);
- Airport Line (24.5 km).
- Yizhuang Line (18.8 km);
- Fangshan Line (29 km);
- Changping Line (34.3 km)

Highways

Beijing has accelerated the process of highway construction with the development of a new express way as its focal point; speeding up the process of integration of the city and its suburbs. The goal of the express way is to directly link the centres of counties and districts in the outer suburbs with the city centre; creating a new mileage of 15,400 km (including the express way 890 km) with total investment amounting to 30 billon yuan). The projects are as follows:

- western section of the 6th ring road (88.4 km);
- Jingcheng express way the second and third phases (108.6 km);
- the northern line to airport (10.8 km);
- the second express way to airport (23 km);
- Jingbao express way (25.9 km);
- the northern channel of Jingjin express way (35 km);
- the southern channel of Jingjin express way (35 km);
- Jingping express way (69 km);
- Jingkai express way (7 km).

Urban Roads

Beijing has constructed ten new roads each of approximately 6 km in length, including Lianhuachi Xilu Street, and has constructed a new network of roads of over 200 km – Benchenxi Road, Beichengdong Road and Aotizhong Road – to support the Games by increasing road density and improving the circulation of traffic.

Building the Transportation Hub

Passenger communication hubs such as Dongzhimen, Xizhimen, Beijing Zoo, Liuliqiao, Yimuyuan, Sihui, West Railway Station, Beiyuan, Songjiazhuang and Wangjingxi, have been set up to shorten the distance of transfer and provide additional convenience to passengers.

City Public Transportation

Thirteen municipal railways of about 300 km in length, 60 km large capacity bus and tram routes (BRT), and a 350 km quick bus and tram transport network have been constructed. Following completion of these projects it is estimated that travel by public transport will rise from 27 per cent to 60 per cent, with municipal railways and large capacity bus and tram systems taking up to 40 per cent of the total public transport.

Intelligent Traffic System

A modernisation project for communications and administration and the creation of a comprehensive information platform is being introduced to further improve the communications administration system.

Communications

Beijing is seeking to facilitate extensive coverage of the Games by broadcasters and the press. Beijing will provide the world media with high quality working, living and transportation conditions to ensure the fast, efficient and successful coverage of the event. There will be no restrictions on journalists reporting the Games.

The opportunity to host over 17,000 accredited members of the world media is, from Beijing's perspective, one of the most exciting prospects as well as a major challenge of the Games. The close proximity of the Media Production Centre, International Broadcast Centre, the Media Village and the fourteen competition sites in the Olympic Green shows the priority given to, and the convenience provided for, the media coverage of the Games, including the Opening and Closing Ceremonies. (Beijing Municipal People's Congress 2006a) An overall plan for media operations and services includes the following:

- *comprehensiveness* – comprehensive and accurate information and data will be provided by the Olympic news service to facilitate the media's coverage of the OG;
- *efficiency* – the latest network technology and a well trained staff of media professionals and selected volunteers will be engaged to provide media with easy access to data and information;
- *convenience* – a 24-hour shuttle bus service will be provided for the media from Media Village and media hotels to the MPC and IBC;
- *comfort* – the accredited media will be provided with comfortable and well equipped living and working environment. Free food and drinks will be provided in the MPC and IBC as well as in all competition venues, subpress centres. Restaurants in the Media Village and media hotels will be open round-the-clock (Brajer and Mead 2003.)

Industrial Restructuring

Beijing's Municipal Congress recognised the opportunities to use the Games as a catalyst to promote industrial restructuring and urban development. In 2006, for example, it published a statement that reflected its aims to rapidly develop a knowledge-based service economy in Beijing, achieving the attributes often associated with the post-industrial global city:

> To achieve rapid and sound development of the capital city's economy, we should speed up the adjustment to the economic structure substantially and transform the growth mode. We should strive to realize the coordination of the speed, structure, quality and efficiency of economic growth by increasing industrial and technologic competence, magnifying scale and concentration effects, and promoting resource saving and efficient utilization. (Beijing Municipal People's Congress 2006b: 17)

Its policies are designed to:

*   develop high-end industries;
*   prioritise, in particular, modern service industries;
*   vigorously push forward new and high-tech industries;
*   moderately develop modern manufacturing industry and to substantially upgrade modern agriculture.

The Authority, in developing modern service industries in the capital, is seeking to steadily upgrade the 'core' industries where it has comparative advantage in finance, culture and real estate and to nurture industries showing real potential, for example tourism, the convention and exhibition industries and modern logistics (Blake and Li 2007; China National Tourism Administration, 2007.) According to the policies of the Municipal Authority, industry level developments are designed to reflect and enhance the dynamic nature of China's economy and the aspirations of Beijing to be internationally and domestically recognised as a city that may be compared with other global, service-oriented cities such as London, Tokyo and New York. The city plan provides a detailed exposition of the steps being taken to transform the Beijing service economy and refers to a wide range of industrial sectors and specific projects being undertaken in each. The sectors include finance, the cultural and creative industries, the real estate industry and logistics; with proposals developed for each of these to establish new market conditions and forms of regulation that are favourable to inward investment and extensive modernisation (Beijing Municipal People's Congress 2006b: 18–19).

The Municipal Government Plan refers to several other important developments in service-related industries. The Plan emphasises the significance of speeding up the modernisation of key sectors while also addressing the necessity to phase out lower value added and environmentally hazardous industries. Sectors identified for rapid development include the high technology sector, especially software and mobile communications, and the development of research in bio-technology. In these industries, the city government is seeking to;

build Beijing into the national centre for information services, a major hub for international information service providers and one of the most important telecom pivots in the Asia-Pacific region. (Beijing Municipal People's Congress 2006b: 20)

The plan refers to the clustering of high technology industries into a pattern of regional development that facilitates the creation of networks of large and medium sized companies that are capable of achieving high levels of research and development activities and establishing internationally recognised brands. It also refers to the restructuring of manufacturing and process industries, such as automobiles and petrochemicals, the development of traditional Chinese and modern 'chemical' medicine and the relocation, or phasing out, of polluting industries such as coke and steel plants.

The environmental or green agenda has made an important impact upon Beijing over recent years. Two significant factors have played important roles in ensuring the prioritisation of environmental improvements in the city. First, the underlying shift of the economy toward the dominance of services has created opportunities for the scaling down of polluting production industries and, secondly, the designation as host city for the Olympic and Paralympic Games has lent added legitimacy, as well as a clear timescale, for the development and implementation of green policies. The city has developed policies designed to nurture recycling industries, encourage green consumption and establish the exemplary role of pilot projects (Wei and Yan 2005).

The city authority has set up a comprehensive evaluation of industrial projects, using an indicator system of resource evaluation and environmental protection as a guide to project selection. The evaluation system includes land investment intensity, input/output efficiency, water consumption, energy consumption, environmental requirements and other indicators as major considerations in project reviews and land provision. Equally, the city authorities are seeking to strictly control projects with high consumption, high emissions and low socio-economic benefits. Plans for regulating production and encouraging the development of recycling industries have been accompanied by the development of new approaches to the regulation of consumption through government procurement of green products, the encouragement of green power projects, the designation of energy labels for products, the introduction of energy and water saving certificates, environmental labels, and green, organic labels and measures to reduce excessive packaging and throwaway products.

Improvements in the green management of production and consumption have been matched by commitments to improving the city's general environment – air, water systems, waste disposal and noise levels – with 2008 providing a deadline for the completion of several projects:

Clean energy conversion of 3,000 existing units of coal-burning boilers under 20 tons in eight urban districts of Beijing must be completed before 2008, while desulphurization, de-nitrogen, and highly effective de-dust treatment projects of coal-burning power plants and large coal-burning boilers should be implemented in a bid to slash soot pollution. The fourth motor vehicle emission standard of the state will be executed comprehensively in 2008 to further improve automotive fuel standard, accelerate the phasing out of high emission automobiles and control the pollution conducted by motor vehicles. (Beijing Municipal People's Congress 2006b: 34–5)

Finally, city plans have been developed to combat the desertification of areas affecting Beijing and Tianjin; these plans include the reforestation of Yan Mountain and Taihang Mountain, the development of a forest protection programme surrounding key water sources and the creation of eco-towns and eco-villages in the areas adjacent to China's capital city.

Government and the Market

As the environmental and industrial policies reveal, Beijing's Municipal Authority and China's national government continue to produce detailed state plans for the management of the economy. At the same time, government officials recognise that economic growth and development is driven by 'market players'. In recognition of this complex relationship between state intervention and the market, the Chinese authorities are seeking to shift the focus of government economic management to:

serving and creating a sound environment for market players through system and policy innovation as well as service efficiency improvement. A satisfactory, more creative and easy environment for enterprises will promote the development and transformation of the capital's advantageous resources and help to release its potential. (Beijing Municipal People's Congress 2006b: 26)

Attempts to achieve this are reflected in the commitment to further open markets, provide seed capital to promote innovation and research and development and to develop 'incubator' units to support the growth of private enterprise:

We are resolute to break monopolies, straighten out and eliminate restrictive regulations and practices that impede development, especially in education, medical care and cultural services, to relax control over market access. In addition, we should improve the project management system, combine verification and approval systems, perfect 'one-stop' services, execute notification and commitment systems and build a more standardized and transparent management and service system. Apart from attracting capital investment, we should give more emphasis to introducing technology, management, talent and the improvement of the production and operation environment. Moreover, we should strengthen the rule of law and credit cultivation to make investors more reassured and satisfied. (Beijing Municipal People's Congress 2006b: 26)

The capacity to stimulate this programme of marketisation, relies heavily upon the success of policies aimed at sustaining social harmony within a society that is experiencing significant change; here policies focus, in particular upon employment, health, education, social security provision and the promotion of stable urban/rural relations.

Social Change and Social Stability

An urban/rural employment and social security system has been established in part to manage the significant growth in Beijing's labour force that has occurred in recent years. In 2005, there were 8.78 million employees in Beijing, 2.49 million more than those in 2001. Olympic Games related employment peaked in 2005, with a little over 50,000 jobs being created directly by the preparation for the Games. The registered unemployment rate remained at a relatively low level of 2.57 per cent in 2006.

The coverage of the urban social security system has expanded through the implementation of improvements to the basic pension, medical care, unemployment insurance, work injury insurance and maternity insurance systems. Up to 2006, there were over 6 million people with basic pensions, 6.8 million covered by basic medical care, 4.8 million with unemployment insurance and 4.653 million people insured against work injury; these were respectively 1.8 million, 4.6 million, 1.95 million and 2.6 million more than those covered by such schemes at the end of 2001.The minimum allowance provided by the social security system has been increasing year on year (Brunet 1997 and 2007). Rural minimum living standards and a new cooperative medical system have been promoted. The rural minimum living standards security system was initiated in 2002, and within five years its coverage had extended to 150,000 residents and 80,000 farmers. A new rural cooperative medical system has achieved extensive coverage; by the end of 2006, the system included 86.9 per cent of residents living in rural areas and a pilot plan in respect of rural pensions has started, with 448,000 participants. The Beijing authorities have also sought to increase enrolments into higher education and improve public health provision:

> The Beijing education service continues to develop with 99 percent of
> school age children receiving education in 2006. The enrolment rate at high
> school was over 98 percent and the gross enrolment rate of higher education
> reached 56 percent, 11 percent higher compared with 2001. Beijing was the
> first city to significantly expand higher education; a policy that is exemplified
> in the provision of textbook and other grants and living subsidies for poorer
> families and the disabled. (Beijing Municipal People's Congress 2006b: 28)

In relation to the Public Health Service, at the end of 2006, there were 4.44
licensed doctors and 3.84 registered nurses for every 1,000 persons, a level
that compares favourably with international comparators. Community health
developed rapidly, with an 81 per cent coverage rate achieved by the end of
2006. The system of unified purchasing and distribution with zero differences
in prices of the commonly used medicines has been widely implemented.

In summary, the Beijing Municipal Authority has undertaken significant
changes to the relationships between the city and its hinterland; with
improvements occurring in welfare systems and the infrastructure that connects
the countryside to the city. The Beijing-Pinggu Express Highway, for example,
is over 1000 km long and is set to open prior to the commencement of the
Games in 2008. This intensive period of investment and urban development
has impacted upon living standards and the quality of life in the city.

Living Standards and the Quality of Life

Over the past five years, Beijing has witnessed rapid urban development.
Total investment in infrastructure between 2002 and 2006 was 283.89 billion
yuan, or 1.8 times greater than that achieved between 1997 and 2001. Between
2001 and 2007, investment in communications and transportation exceeded
110 billion yuan, more than four times greater than was achieved between
1997 and 2001. By the end of 2006, the mileage of urban public transport in
operation was 19,000 km, an increase of 5,399 km over that in public use in
2001 (Owen 2005).

Demand for electricity in Beijing is 61.16 billion kilowatt hours, 52.9 per
cent up compared with that at the end of 2001. Natural gas supply has risen
from 1.6 billion square meters in 2001 to 3.8 billion m^2 in 2006. The number
of sewage treatment plants has increased from 12 in 2001 to 49 in 2006. And
the ratio of sewage treatment in the eight districts (Dongcheng, Xicheng,
Chongwen, Xuanwu, Chaoyang, Haidian, Fengtai and Shijingshan) has
reached 90 per cent, 48 per cent up when compared to the end of 2001. The
harmless treatment ratio of domestic garbage in these districts has been raised
from 89.1 per cent in 2002 to 96.5 per cent in 2006. The Jing-Jin Sandstorm
Source Control Project has completed its development of green belts around
the city. The per capita area of parks and greenbelts reached 12 square meters

in 2007. The green coverage rate within the city achieved 51 per cent in 2007, 7 per cent up compared to 2001. In 2006 there were 241 days when the quality of air was rated as 2-grade or better – 66 per cent of the calendar year. This represents a 15 per cent improvement compared to 2001 (China National Statistical Administration 2007).

The overall urban planning and positioning of Beijing's districts and counties have been reformed. Functional districts have taken shape, such as the finance quarter, the central business district, Zhongguancun high-tech Park, the Olympic zone, the airport economic zone and Wangfujing Mall and Xidan Cultural Plaza. An emergency management system has been introduced and the management of urban transport has improved with priority given to the development of public transport. The percentage of people regularly using public transport has risen to 30 per cent in 2007, increasing from 26 per cent in 2001.

A series of campaigns have been staged to practice the values of the 'humanistic' Olympics, including a manners and etiquette education campaign – 'Welcome the Olympics, Improve Manners and Foster New Attitudes'. A survey conducted by the Beijing Civilisation Office shows that spitting has dropped to 4.9 per cent from 8.4 per cent in 2005 and littering to 5.3 per cent from 9.1 per cent – these figures are based on an accumulative 1700-hour observation of about 230,000 pedestrians at 320 public sites (BOCOG 2008).

Patterns of private consumption have changed with spending on communications, telecommunications, education and entertainment by the city's residents increasing respectively by 32 per cent, 27 per cent, 7 per cent and 5 per cent compared to 2001. People spent more on high-grade, fashionable brands with cars and housing becoming their main high cost expenditures. By the end of 2006, there were 1,810,000 private cars registered in the city, 2.9 times more than the end of 2001. The living space area for each urban citizen and the housing space for each rural citizen are respectively 20.1 m^2 and 39.1 m^2, increasing by 2.5 m^2 and 8.1 m^2 as compared to 2001 (Cousins 2004). Cultural life within the city has been enhanced with the building of the capital library and the capital museum and grass-root cultural facilities have been popularised. Beijing's citizens now take holidays at home and abroad and many surf on the Internet. In 2006, there were 4.7 million 'netizens', a 42 per cent increase compared to 2001.

Conclusion

Over the past 5 years, Beijing has carried out some important development goals, taking advantage of the opportunities of hosting the 2008 Olympic and Paralympic Games. Preparation for the Games has played an important role in the city's development in several ways. From 2002 to 2006, the average annual economic growth of Beijing rose to 12.1 per cent, 1.7 per cent higher than the

Table 10.4   Beijing real estate dynamics

	Total investment	Marketable buildings under construction	New construction of this year	Floor space of marketable buildings completed	Floor space of marketable buildings sales
2001	783.8	5,966.7	2,789.8	1,707.4	1,205.0
2002	989.4	7,510.7	3,206.0	2,384.4	1,708.3
2003	1,202.5	9,070.7	3,433.8	2,593.7	1,895.8
2004	1,473.3	9,931.3	3,054.3	3,067.0	2,472.0
2005	1,525.0	10,748.5	2,965.9	3,770.9	2,803.2
2006	1,719.9	10,483.5	3,179.4	3,193.9	2,607.6

Source: China National Statistical Administration (2007).

10.4 per cent growth per annum achieved in the previous 20 years. The reason lies not only in the developing characteristics of the capital's economy but also because of the catalytic effect of the Games. The Olympic economy has provided a new impetus to the upgrading of the capital's industrial structure and directly stimulated the development of several industries, including construction, communications, transportation, tourism and exhibitions. It has also accelerated the development of the finance, insurance, information and business services and the leisure and cultural and creative sectors.

A group of Chinese enterprises and brands have been formed and become leading sponsors of the 2008 Games. Legend Group is the one enterprise participating in the international TOP VI program and seven enterprises whose headquarters are in Beijing have become partners of BOCOG, including the Bank of China, PICC, CNPC, SINOPEC, CNC, China Mobile, Air China. SOHU and Yanjing Beer. These corporations have improved their brand awareness and raised their domestic and international profiles through this engagement with the Games.

Olympic-related economic development has made Beijing one of the most dynamic cities for domestic and foreign investment. In the past five years, investment and consumption in Beijing have achieved rapid growth, especially in relation to cultural consumption, tourism, sports, transportation and communications. Between 2001 and 2006, the number of foreign visitors increased from 2.858 to 3.903 million. Through its preparation for the Games, the city's operational management, general support capability and range of services have improved to meet the challenges presented by hosting the event and a series of plans for the Games in respect of transportation, security, food security and medical care have been worked out, laying the foundations for the city's development post-2008. The preparation for the Games has made Beijing more open to the outside world. The total value of Beijing's imports and exports in 2006 has reached US$158.18 billion, 3.1 times greater than that achieved in 2001. From 2002 to 2006, direct foreign investment reached US$15.1 billion, 49.4 per cent higher than was achieved between 1997 and 2001.

The development of the Olympic economy has provided opportunities for increasing employment and improving wage levels. In the past five years years, the city's annual growth in new employees was about 0.62 million, mainly in the fields of construction, high-technology, modern manufacturing, financial services and social services, with the latter playing an important role in the absorption of new workers into the city. In relation to the environment, the focus has been placed upon strengthening the prevention and management of pollution, and the protection and construction of the ecological environment.

The city's preparation for the Games has addressed the economic and social context in which it is taking place. Beijing has utilised the event to facilitate a significant expansion of its higher value added service industries and achieve major developments in infrastructure whilst also seeking to develop its social welfare and housing policies to manage the inevitable consequences of rapid social change. It is likely that the 2008 Games will affirm Beijing's status to the rest of the world as a post-industrial, 'global city'.

References

Beijing Municipal People's Congress (2006a) *International Forum on Olympic Business Opportunity and Venues Operation after Olympic Games*, Beijing: Beijing Municipal Commission of Development and Reform.

Beijing Municipal People's Congress (2006b) *The Outline of the Eleven Five-year Program for the National Economic and Social Development in Beijing*, Beijing: China Population Publishing House.

Beijing Organising Committee for the Games of the XXIX Olympiad (BOCOG) (2007) http://www. beijing2008.com.

Beijing Organising Committee for the Games of the XX1X Olympiad (BOCOG) (2008) 'Manners to Make a Better Olympic Games', hhtp://www.beijing2008.com.

Blake, A. and Li, S. (2007) 'The Economic Impact of International Tourism on the Chinese Economy: A Computable General Equilibrium Analysis of Beijing 2008 Olympic Games', paper presented at the 1st Conference of the International Association for Tourism Economics, Palma de Mallorca, 25–27 October.

Brajer, V. and Mead, R. (2003) 'Blue Skies in Beijing Looking at the Olympic Effect', *Journal of Environment and Development* 12(2), June: 239–63.

Brunet, F. (1994) *Economy of the 1992 Barcelona Olympic Games*, Lausanne: International Olympic Committee.

180 *Olympic Cities*

Brunet, F. (1997) 'The Economic Impacts of the Olympic Games', in Brunet, F., Carrard, F. and Corrand, J.-A. (eds) (1997) *The Centennial President*, Lausanne: International Olympic Committee, 1–10.

Brunet, F. (2003) 'The economic impact of the Barcelona Olympic Games, 1986–2004', http://olympicstudies.uab.es.

Brunet, F. (2007) 'The Barcelona Model and the Socio-economic Strategy of the Olympic Games and Mega-events', paper presented at the 4th International Olympic Forum organised by the Humanistic Olympic Studies Center of the Renmin University of China, Beijing, 24–25 June.

Cheng, H., Zhang, Z. and Huang, W. (2003) 'A Study of CGE Model of Policy Analysis in High-tech Industry Based on Social Accounting Matrix', *Journal of Wuhan University of Technology (Transportation Science and Engineering)* 27(3): 333–6.

China National Statistical Administration (2007) http://www.stats.gov.cn.

China National Tourism Administration (2007) http://www.cnta.org.cn.

Cousins, S. (2004) 'Beijing Cuts Olympic Costs', *Business Beijing*, Beijing: Information Office of the Beijing Municipal Government, http://www.btmbeijing.com.

Development Research Center of the State Council (DRC) (2005) *The Effect of Infrastructure Development on Poverty Reduction in China*, Manila: The Asian Development Bank.

International Olympic Committee (2001) *Host City Contract for the Games of the XXIX Olympiad in the Year 2008*, Lausanne: International Olympic Committee.

Owen, J.G. (2005) 'Estimating the Cost and Benefit of Hosting Olympic Games: What Can Beijing Expect from Its 2008 Games?', *The Industrial Geographer* 3(1) Fall: 1–18.

Poynter, G. (2006) 'From Beijing to Bow Bells: Measuring the Olympic Effect', Working Paper in Urban Studies, University of East London, London East Research Institutes, March.

Wei, X.Z. and Yan, P. (2005) 'The Olympic Games Will Add 0.8% in annual GRP Growth for Beijing', *Beijing Youth Daily*, 9 September, A1 [in Chinese].

Zhang, Y. and Zhao, K. (2007) 'Impact of Beijing Olympic-related Investments on Regional Economic Growth of China: Interregional Input–Output Approach', *Asian Economic Journal* 21(3): 261–82.

PART 3
London 2012

Chapter 11

London: Preparing for 2012

Gavin Poynter

Introduction

I feel it would be madness to bid for the Olympics, quite apart from whether we can actually get them. There are all kinds of reasons why. First of all is the cost. Nobody knows what the cost would be. (Kaufman (Chair, DCMS Select Committee) 2003)

London is recognized as having an outstanding technical bid which has helped generate genuine excitement. A London Games would be a winner for the whole of London, kick-starting the regeneration of the Lower Lea Valley and focusing the world's attention on every aspect of our great city.

It would also be a winner for the whole UK. Our bid has cross-party political support, and real and growing backing from the British public. With our extensive infrastructure, global reputation, and combination of the richest history and incredible dynamism, London would make an exceptional host city. (Livingstone (Mayor of London) 2005)

The inevitability is Paris will win. Longer term we should host an Olympics sometime not at the moment because I don't think we are ready. We don't deserve it and Paris does. (Hoey[1] 2004)

London's bid to host the 2012 Games has attracted considerable public debate in the UK over recent years with critics focusing on the issue of costs and supporters emphasising the importance of the regenerative legacy to East London and the boost to the global reputation of London that arises from hosting the Games. This chapter reviews the 'story so far'. It examines the

---

1 Kate Hoey is a Labour MP (Vauxhall, London) and was Labour Sports Minister 1999–2001. She was appointed in May 2008 as an unpaid adviser on London 2012 to the new Mayor of London, a Conservative, Boris Johnson. Johnson defeated Livingstone in the mayoral race which took place on 1 May 2008 by achieving 53 per cent to Livingstone's 47 per cent of the vote. Ken Livingstone was a critical figure in preparing London's 2012 bid and winning support from government for it. Livingstone was seeking a third (four year) term as Mayor of London and was defeated by a candidate reported widely in the international press, such as CNN, as a 'maverick'.

origins of the bid and its association with the renewal and regeneration of East London. It outlines some of the main promises and policies that central, city and local government agencies aspire to achieve and also explains the complex governance structures established to deliver these aspirations. Finally, the chapter discusses one of the key social issues raised by the emphasis on the catalytic role the Games may play in the process of urban regeneration in East London.

The Genesis of the London Bid

The process commenced in 1997 when the British Olympics Association (BOA) commissioned a feasibility study into a London bid to host the 2012 Games. The failures of the Birmingham and Manchester bids for the 1992, 1996 and 2000 Olympic and Paralympic Games, convinced the BOA that only a London based bid was likely to taken seriously by the IOC. The feasibility study was prepared by David Luckes, a member of the British hockey team that played in the Atlanta Olympics in 1996. The study ran to over three hundred pages and presented options for locating the Games in West or East London (Lee 2006: 6). In 2001, the feasibility study was submitted to the government and Mayor of London (then Ken Livingstone) and it was the latter who insisted that the Games bid was focused upon East London, with the sporting benefits complemented by a firm commitment to enhancing an existing urban regeneration agenda. This regeneration focus, the positive public support revealed in a 2001 ICM poll – with 81 per cent of UK respondents supporting a bid; the success of the Manchester Commonwealth Games in 2002; Beijing's success in beating Paris in July 2001 to win the right to host the 2008 Games – thus opening the possibility of a European city hosting the 2012 Games; the positive global images of the Sydney Games (2000) and the desire to address the failure of projects such as the Millennium Dome and Picketts Lock (an aborted attempt to construct a new national athletics stadium in North London) were all factors that pushed the government into serious consideration of a bid to host the 2012 Games.

In 2002, a consultancy company, ARUP was commissioned by the government to provide a report on the capacity for London to host the 2012 Olympic and Paralympic Games. A summary report was published in May 2002 and contained a financial analysis of the cost of hosting the event. The analysis focused upon the costs and income for bidding, preparing and staging the Games, provision for risk and 'an estimation of the residual values of the assets created' (ARUP 2002: 4). The report estimated total expenditure to be £1.79 billion with income estimated at £1.3 billion, leaving a shortfall of about half a billion pounds that could be reduced significantly according to ARUP, since the report's authors had been conservative in their estimates of income. The government established a cabinet subcommittee to examine the

ARUP report and requested a senior civil servant to review carefully ARUP's estimation of costs.

The civil servant, Robert Raine, found the ARUP report to underestimate costs by about £800 million. A revised figure of $3.8 billion (£2.4 billion) was eventually agreed (it was this figure that was submitted in the Candidate File to the International Olympic Committee (IOC) by the London bid team). The £800 million 'gap' was addressed through discussions between the then Secretary of State for Culture, Tessa Jowell, and the Mayor of London, Ken Livingstone, with a financial package created that covered the Games £2.4 billion costs, a package that included lottery funding via an Olympic scratch card game, London Development Agency investment and an increase in the council tax in London that would realise a rise of £20 per tax payer per annum for a maximum of ten years (Lee 2006: 13). The financial package prompted the government to finally support a bid following a cabinet meeting on 15 May 2003 (BOA 2007).

London's Success

The London bid was considered to be second or third favourite behind Paris and Madrid, when in July 2005 the final presentations were made to the IOC in Singapore. London's success was attributed to its focus on urban regeneration and the importance attached to the sporting legacy to be provided for generations of young people as Jack Straw (then Secretary of State, Foreign and Commonwealth Office) commented in parliament on the day following the announcement in Singapore:

> London's bid was built on a special Olympic vision. That vision of an Olympic games that would not only be a celebration of sport but a force for regeneration. The games will transform one of the poorest and most deprived areas of London. They will create thousands of jobs and homes. They will offer new opportunities for business in the immediate area and throughout London … One of the things that made the bid successful is the way in which it reaches out to all young people in two important respects: it will encourage many more to get fit and to be involved in sport and, whatever their physical prowess, to offer their services as volunteers for the Olympic cause. (Hansard 2005)

Straw's statement provides a compelling interpretation of why London's bid was successful with its emphasis on non-sports related outcomes and its focus on using the Games as a vehicle for the pursuit of non-elite participation in sport and exercise. These values struck a cord with the IOC in its post-commercial phase, and were consistent with the prevailing values of the UK government's own health policies and its appropriation of sport as a vehicle for the articulation of 'new' Labour's social values and policies, including its commitment to social inclusion.[2] The government's attachment to the Olympic event as a vehicle for the promotion of its own political and social policies presents a significant challenge to those implementing the regeneration agenda in East London. From the outset, the achievement of 'a successful Games' was closely associated with the effective construction, preparation and holding of the event and the attainment of a transformative legacy that impacts upon East London and the wider Thames Gateway.

On receiving the news of London's successful bid for the 2012 Games, the media descended upon East London, particularly Stratford, to discover local people's views. Broadly supportive comments carried caveats about who might win and lose as a result of the implementation of the urban renewal programme that was associated with hosting the 2012 Games[3]. In the months following the announcement of London's victory, East London's community and civic centres were filled with leaflets proclaiming the positive benefits to be derived from hosting the Olympics and political and civic leaders lent enthusiastic support in local newspapers and on countless TV and radio programmes. Olympic-related events commenced almost immediately with, for example, Newham local authority, launching free entrance to sports facilities for young people and school students were encouraged to spend their holiday time doing structured sports activities. Youth crime in the borough fell by 25 per cent in the summer months of 2005 (Muir 2005).

The positive Olympics-related 'effects', it seems, commenced within weeks of the announcement of the London bid success. The supportive local response to the success of the bid to host the Games was reflected more broadly within the UK. A study published in January 2006 indicated that UK taxpayers were willing to pay a total sum of around £2 billion for London to host the 2012 Games (Atkinson et al. 2006). The show of popular support for 2012 provided its organisers with a positive starting point for managing the interface between the London Organising Committee of the Olympic Games (LOCOG), the agencies responsible for delivering the event and its legacy and the various interests groups, or stakeholders, who seek to benefit from the significant investment required to host the Games.

In the period since 2005, public enthusiasm for hosting the Games has been severely tested by the international protests over the Beijing flame relay that

---

2   Labour's commitment to sport was reflected in its renaming of the Department of Heritage as the Ministry of Media, Culture and Sport in 1998. This commitment has been critically evaluated as successive Labour governments have, some argue, used sport as a vehicle for the expression of their own therapeutic and paternalist social policies including projecting social cohesion around the superficial representation of a 'new' national identity. See, for example, Blake (1999).

3   Perceptions gathered from local people within a week of the announcement of the success of London's Bid for the 2012 Olympic Games (Cohen and MacRury 2005).

attracted protestors concerned about human rights in China and, in particular, Tibet; a national debate about costs and local concerns over compulsory land purchases, the displacement of local businesses and other community-based issues. Often negative national media coverage has been countered by the publication of policy documents and promises or commitments from government, the Mayor of London and LOCOG about the social and economic benefits to be derived from the Games. This 'legacy' debate has been conducted in a context in which a complex framework of governance for the mega event has emerged.

The Governance of London 2012

The Games are overseen by government, the Mayor of London and the British Olympics Association. The agency acting on their behalf is LOCOG (the London Organising Committee of the Olympic Games – whose composition reflects this coalition) and their delivery, via the Olympic Development Authority (ODA), is trusted to a private sector consortium. The key government ministry responsible for the Games is the Department for Culture, Media and Sport (the DCMS has a Government Olympic Executive responsible for the oversight of London 2012) , while the Minister with direct responsibility for 2012, Tessa Jowell, is located in the Cabinet Office. The land designated for use as the Olympic Park was compulsory purchased by the London Development Agency (LDA).

The LDA is funded by central government though responsibility for its strategic management rests with the Mayor of London (from 4 May 2008, Boris Johnson who defeated Ken Livingstone in the London mayoral elections of May 1st). The Olympic Delivery Authority Board consists of representatives from the public and private sectors and works with the London Development Agency (LDA), Transport for London (TfL), Thames Gateway and five designated Olympic local authorities – Greenwich, Hackney, Newham, Tower Hamlets and Waltham Forest. The Nations and Regions Group (NRG) has the responsibility for ensuring the whole of the UK benefits from the 2012 Games. It is made up of twelve senior representatives from UK business and sport: nine from the English regions and one each from Scotland, Wales and Northern Ireland – the 'home nations'[4] (see Figure 11.1).

In its June 2007 report on the preparation for the Olympic Games, the House of Commons Committee of Public Accounts indicated its concerns relating to the governance structure:

> Two new bodies have been set up. The Olympic Delivery Authority will provide the facilities, and the London Organising Committee of the Olympic

---

4   http://www.London 2012 Group.com/about.

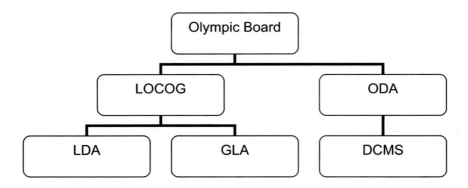

Figure 11.1   London 2012: governance structure

Games and Paralympic Games (LOCOG) will stage the Games. They are overseen by the Olympic Board, and a new team within the Department for Culture, Media and Sport (the Government Olympic Executive) will co-ordinate the contributions of other parts of government to the Games.

The Olympic Board will play a leading role in progress monitoring and risk management, supported by a Steering Group of senior officials and the Olympic Programme Support Unit which provides independent advice to the Board. No one individual has overall responsibility for delivering the Games, however, and the large number of bodies involved presents significant risks, for example to timely decision-taking. (House of Commons Committee of Public Accounts 2007: 1)

The House of Commons Public Accounts Committee identified the problem of governance from the perspective of effective risk management, especially in relation to costs and the finite timescale for delivery of the project. Such a perspective tends to perceive governance as arising from a 'top down' or hierarchical approach driven essentially by the management of risk. Such an approach may focus upon the managerial requirements for effective project or event management but does not address the necessity for a wider social engagement with the legacy related process of urban renewal and regeneration. The experience of previous host cities suggests that the legislative framework required for the planning and construction of Games venues and associated infrastructure projects and the powers given to the Games organisers tends to diminish local forms of accountability and dilute local democracy, with the result that regeneration happens to local communities rather than being influenced by them (LERI 2007).

The potential for governance to become a serious issue in the lead up to 2012 may depend upon the engagement with, and outcome of, public consultations taking place in 2008 over the shaping of the Olympic 'legacy', an example being the plans for the Olympic village. 'Lend Lease' the chosen developers, produced plans for new homes schools, healthcare and community facilities and these were made available for public consultation in the autumn of 2007. In their defence of the system of governance and its associated consultation procedures, government, LOCOG, the Mayor of London and local authority representatives have argued that London has given more consideration to legacy issues, and at an earlier stage, than any previous host cities in the history of the modern Games, as Sir Robin Wales indicated in his comments to the House of Commons DCMS Select Committee on 15 January 2008:

> One of the things, I think, that is frustrating in this debate is that we are trying (Athens did their legacy after the Olympics) to work this through early, and if we do not have answers it is because we are actually trying to raise the question so we can find answers. At the moment, it seems to me that some of those answers are coming forward in a timely manner. Rightly, we will be raising questions about the costs during the Games, but we have raised questions about the costs building up to the Games, and some of that has been answered. (DCMS 2008).

Undoubtedly, 'legacy' was integral to the London bid and its scope has been subsequently refined through the publication of a series of policy statements and promises. The implementation of these and the degree of civic engagement with consultative processes will provide some indication of the success or otherwise of the London 2012 governance structure in delivering its ambitious regeneration plans.

Unlike Atlanta (1996), the agencies engaged with London 2012 are not dominated by a coalition of primarily commercial interests, the state – in the form of national government and the Mayor of London – has been the key agent in strategic decision-making relating to 2012, especially in creating the funding packages to build the Park and its associated infrastructure. LOCOG, a short-life private sector company, whilst being responsible for preparing and staging the Games, has no independent source of funds beyond those allocated by the state and that secured from the IOC and official Olympic partners – members of the IOCs Olympic 'family' who include Coca-Cola, Atos Origin, GE, McDonalds, Omega, Samsung and Visa. In this sense, LOCOG's capacity is largely confined to operational issues and the development of aspirational plans which require a 'socially responsible' commercial partner to provide the funding to implement. By contrast, the LDA, an organisation apparently lower in the 2012 hierarchy compared to LOCOG, is formally the owner of the land that constitutes the Olympic Park and is, therefore, likely to play a key role in shaping the Games legacy for East London.

The London 2012 Legacy: 'Plans and Promises'

The DCMS has outlined *Our Promise(s) for 2012*. These include;

- Making the UK a world-leading sporting nation;
- Transform the heart of East London;
- Inspire a generation of young people to take part in local volunteering, cultural and physical activity
- Make the Olympic Park a blueprint for sustainable living
- Demonstrate the UK is a creative, inclusive and welcoming place to live in, visit, and for business (DCMS 2007).

In January 2008, the then Mayor of London, Ken Livingstone (2008) also produced a set of five legacy commitments – increasing opportunities for Londoners to be involved in sport; ensuring Londoners benefit from new jobs, business and volunteering opportunities; transforming the heart of London; delivering a sustainable games and sustainable communities and, lastly, showcasing London as a diverse, creative and welcoming city. LOCOG published a sustainability plan in 2007, *Towards a One Planet 2012* that emphasises a thematic legacy around climate change, waste, biodiversity, social inclusion and healthy living.

These public policies and promises have been complemented by publications exploring the opportunities for the regions in the UK to benefit from 2012 and by in-depth studies of specific issues such as employment, training, housing and the environment produced by institutions such as the Commission for Architecture and the Built Environment (CABE), business groups, such as the London Chamber of Commerce, and 'think tanks', such as Demos.[5] London boroughs have produced their own Olympic strategy policies and documents and several have established strategy groups. In particular, the five designated London Olympic boroughs have allied existing regeneration plans to the opportunities presented by 2012 with Newham, for example, focusing upon the synergies to be achieved through its major regeneration scheme referred to as Stratford City. This will be one of the largest mixed use developments in the UK, developed by a private sector partnership involving Chelsfield plc, Stanhope plc and London and Continental Railways. The plans include 465,000 m² of offices, 4,850 new homes for around 11,000 people, 150,500 m² of retail space and up to 2,000 hotel bedrooms, a drop-in health centre and primary care centre and community facilities. The Stratford City development, adjacent to the Olympic Park, is taking place in a region that is also designated as a major regeneration area, the Thames Gateway.

---

5   See, for example, CABE (2007), London Chamber of Commerce (2005), Mean et al. (2004) and Demos andTims (2007).

The Thames Gateway scheme was initiated in 1990 by the South East Regional Policy Guidance plan formulated at the time of the Conservative government and was championed by the then Secretary of State for the Environment, Michael Heseltine. At that time, regeneration was focused upon a region that had suffered major decline in areas of traditional employment – docks, dockyards, manufacturing – and a shortage of affordable housing for its resident population. The decision in 1991 to route the Channel Tunnel Rail Link through North Kent and into central London via Stratford, provided an important catalyst for improvements in road and rail infrastructure and by 1995 the Thames Gateway Task Force drew up plans for 30,000 new homes and 50,000 new jobs being established in the Thames Corridor by 2021 (Buck et al. 2002: 84–5).

Since 1997 successive Labour governments have continued to provide vigorous support for the Thames Gateway scheme through the Office of the Deputy Prime Minister (ODPM) and a variety of partnership agencies, including the Mayor's Office, the Greater London Authority (GLA) and LDA and all the local authorities located within the region. The ambitions for the development of the Thames Gateway have correspondingly risen with, for example, the proposal to develop a new bridge crossing for the Thames and an expansion of plans for house building and the development of new townships along the Thames corridor. These plans were incorporated into the government's 'Creating Sustainable Communities' (2003) in which the number of new houses to be built increased to 120,000, with many of these located in fourteen 'zones of change'. Since the success of the Olympic bid in 2005, the total number of new homes planned for the Thames Gateway has risen to 160,000, to be achieved by 2016, with 225,000 new jobs also being created in a similar timescale (Thames Gateway, The Delivery Plan (2007), London: Department of Communities and Local Government).[6] Clearly, the policies and promises arising from hosting the 2012 Games sit alongside ambitious targets for the Thames Gateway – itself a project to which the government has committed £9 billion in public funding (Thames Gateway, The Delivery Plan 2007:2). Regrettably, public debate in the UK concerning the legacy of the 2012 Games and its relationship to an extensive programme of state-led regeneration along the Thames Gateway has been less about what might constitute good city building and more about the question of cost.

---

6   It should be noted that the Thames Gateway development is overseen by the Department of Communities and Local Government while London 2012 is the responsibility of the Department of Culture, Media and Sport.

Delivery, Deadlines and (Avoiding) Debt

In November 2005 David Higgins became Chief Executive of the Olympic Delivery Authority. He performed a similar role for the Sydney 2000 Games. His immediate task was to realign the delivery strategy to contain costs. He began to do this by setting aside an existing 'informal' shortlist of contenders involved in the procurement contest for the contract to manage the construction and delivery of the Olympic site at Stratford and the other venues dotted around the UK. When the formal process of tendering was initiated in February 2006, the contract framework favoured the creation of consortia that came from big business, companies that had a strong track record in delivering large infrastructure projects.[7] Parallel to this process, the revision of the Olympic Village design at Stratford took place, reducing the requirement to relocate local small enterprises and re-positioning the Media and Aquatics Centres within the security zone of the village itself and in close proximity to the new Stratford City development.[8] These steps represented the initial phase of realigning plans to fit a delivery budget of approximately £1.7 billion. Despite this realignment, further revisions to the budget were required.

Additional costs attributed to the Olympic Park (£1.04 billion) caused the government to announce a further revision to the Games budget, a revision that amounted to an increase from £2.4 billion to £3.4 billion. By 2007, another revision was announced to include contingency (£2.747 billion), £836 million for tax, a rise in security costs to £600 million, an increase in the Olympic Development Authority's programme delivery budget from £16 to £570 million and a decrease (from £738 to £165 million) in the anticipated private sector contribution toward meeting the costs of the Games. The consequence of these adjustments was that the public sector funds available to meet the costs of the Games and associated infrastructure development were required to increase by about £4.7 billion net, including £2.7 billion contingency. The 'gap' of between £2 and £4 billion in the public funding estimated to be needed at the time of the bid and that required by spring 2007 was primarily attributable to the underestimation of tax (Value Added Tax (VAT) – a cost to the Games paid out by government but returned to the Exchequer) and the poor initial assessment of security costs, Park remediation costs and the expenditure associated with the logistics costs of the ODA (the initial budget for ODA costs had been estimated as if it were a small

---

7   The emphasis in the tender documentation shifted from applying financial penalties for failures to deliver projects on time to rewarding the delivery partner for the effective risk management of the whole construction project. See Boles (2006).

8   See ODPM (2006a), ODPM (2006b) UK-London and Construction project management services 2006/S 33-036394 Contract Notice http://ted.publications.eu.int/ official.

Urban Development Corporation, the complexity of delivering the project management for the Games was ignored). Government and wider public concern over costs prompted the National Audit Office (NAO) to commence a series of reports on the preparations for London 2012. Its first report, in February 2007, focused upon risk assessment and management and reported upon the necessity for a finally agreed budget estimate to be settled, something achieved almost one year later. The report also commented upon the risks arising from a 'cumbersome' decision-making process, an observation that had not been addressed by early 2008 (NAO 2007).

The 'technically' polished London bid was deeply flawed in relation to estimating clearly identifiable event-related costs, including contingency and the attribution of tax; the expenditure required to clean-up the highly contaminated Park land was also, more understandably, under-estimated. Such errors, however, are not unusual in the planning and construction of major projects and mega events, especially when such events are related to a wider process of urban regeneration or development as the Beijing and Athens Games have revealed. Event-related and infrastructure costs in Beijing, for example, have, according to several estimates, exceeded the bid book by over $20 billion and, as a recent study of mega projects and risk has revealed, across the world nine out of every ten transport infrastructure project costs exceed initial estimated costs by between 50 and 100 per cent (Cousins 2004; Fylvberg et al. 2003: 15) .

A benign observer could suggest that the overall event and non-event related infrastructure costs of hosting the Olympics and developing a part of East London – a figure of around £18 billion, including a cost overrun of approximately £5 billion – places the '2012' mega-project at the lower end of the spectrum of the 'calamitous history of cost overruns' (Flyvberg et al. 2003: 11). This was not, however, the interpretation or response typically to be found in the UK media. The initial acclaim arising from the UK's successful bid was quickly replaced by articles critical of the uncertainties surrounding the budget, the continuous revisions of budget costs by government and the elaboration of more specific criticisms of the costs associated with the creation of the widely derided Olympic logo, the design and cost of the Olympic Park sporting arenas, the salary costs of LOCOG senior staff and, by early 2008, the revised estimates of land values emerging from the economic problems posed by the downward turn in the international economy, the so-called 'credit crunch'. One journalist from the popular press summed up much of the media's perspective on the Games and 'money' in concluding that Olympic funding had gone from 'joke to scandal' (Routledge 2008).

The Sustainability Games?

Other important challenges facing London 2012 have sparked less controversy but are, arguably, more fundamental in determining the capacity of the Games to catalyse social renewal in East London. Employment, training, housing and environmental programmes are all part of the 2012 project and the degrees of success in their implementation will determine the social impact of the Games beyond the event itself. In this sense, 'sustainabililty' refers to the capacity for regeneration to build a momentum beyond the event stage, avoiding 'white elephants' and the downturn in socio-economic activity that has accompanied the aftermath of the Games in other host cities such as Athens and Sydney. Several of these issues are discussed in subsequent chapters; here the question of employment and training is used to illustrate the sustainability issue.

Employment arising directly from the Olympics is typically temporary and short term in industries such as construction, tourism, hospitality, catering and security. The contribution to the local economy may arise from, for example, the opportunity to experience work for those who are amongst the long-term unemployed (Donovan 2006: 6). Sustainable longer term or more permanent job opportunities for the local population of working age may emerge as a spin-off from training and education programmes initiated during the Olympics phase and from any inward investment attracted by the positive publicity that East London achieves arising from hosting the Games and developing its transport, technological and environmental infrastructures. In its January 2008 Annual Report on Skills and Employment, the LDA identified a target of creating 10,000 new jobs via inward investment between 2006 and 2016 (LDA 2008) through its internationally-oriented 'Think London' campaign.

In the construction industry, contracts are awarded through competitive tender, with project completion being highly time-sensitive. The proportion of employment opportunities going to local workers is affected by the capacity to match local skills profiles with the specialist requirements of the industry over the period 2008-2012, with 2010 being a peak point in the demand for labour. There is relatively little lead-in time for overcoming any mismatch between the skill requirements of construction companies and the existing skills profile of the resident East London workforce. In January 2006, the London Development Agency commissioned a major skills study for the London 2012 Games (LDA 2006). The study was designed to identify the range of skills needs, drawing upon best practice experience from previous Olympic host cities. LDA financial support for training was fixed at £12 million and this has been supplemented by other training grants, such as the European Social Fund (ESF) grant of £6.2 million awarded to the East of England Development Agency to support the introduction of training programmes for local people. In addressing the skills requirements of the construction industry such reports and training programmes face several structural labour market issues such as the mobility of labour between major construction sites – the completion of Terminal Five at Heathrow may induce a migration of skilled labour to East London and the migration of skilled labour from other EU states where the construction industry may be less buoyant. The 'ready' availability of this mobile labour has to be balanced alongside the provision of employment opportunities for the local workforce.

In part to address these structural questions, in October 2006, a London Employment and Skills Task Force (LEST) Action Plan was initiated by government to provide 'a comprehensive and coherent programme of activity' (LDA 2008:3) on labour market issues to address the opportunities presented by 2012. According to an LDA report published in January 2008, considerable success was achieved within two years of this plan being introduced:

- the proportion of the construction workforce from the five local host boroughs is currently 19 per cent as at December 2007. This equates to 359 local workers from a total workforce of 1896. Monthly figures since July have been averaging at just over 20 per cent;
- 52 per cent of the workforce come from London;
- 11 per cent of the current workforce on site were previously unemployed;
- 17 per cent of the construction workforce come from BAME communities, just above the industry average;
- over 300 construction and ancillary workers placed into roles on the Olympic site via local five borough and Jobcentre Plus employment support;
- in excess of 1,000 construction short courses offered to residents in the 5 East London Host boroughs;
- 375 people completed the pilot phase Personal Best volunteering Programme;
- the opening of London's only plant training school on the Olympic Park site at Eton Manor;
- over 500 contractors have won contracts to deliver the Games to date worth over £1 billion in total;
- over two-thirds (68 per cent) of successful businesses are small or medium sized;
- half (50 per cent) of all contracts have gone to London companies;
- one in ten (11 per cent) is based in the one of the five east London host boroughs;
- the substantial completion of the land acquisition and assembly of the Olympic Park in July 2007, safeguarding 98 per cent of the 4,750 jobs previously based on the site;
- further employment creation re-located businesses;
- a wholehearted and significant commitment from all partners to the employment and skills agenda associated with the Games, equating to almost £85m to 2012;

- a further £30 million committed to broader socio-economic benefits from the Games, including enterprise, sports and physical activity programmes and engagement (LDA 2008).

Aside from the construction sector, the Olympics provides a further, wide range of temporary employment opportunities in sport and exercise, transport, media, health, education, cultural industries and in leisure, tourism, hotels, food and catering. These sectors have diverse structures ranging from the relatively integrated and large scale – health and education sectors – to those dominated by small businesses and sole traders – restaurants, food outlets etc. Establishing an effective framework for the development of training and education opportunities for local residents is a significant task. Equally, what constitutes an East London labour market is a complex affair with the inner London boroughs containing variations in economic activity/inactivity and skills profile. Those boroughs in closest proximity to the Olympic development site – Hackney, Newham and Tower Hamlets – have higher proportions of the workforce with no qualifications than the London-wide and national averages and the characteristics of current employment and occupational patterns have strong ethnic and gender dimensions. The potential for the polarisation of temporary employment opportunities arising from the Olympic Games to be divided with local people undertaking low skill jobs and specialist and higher skilled labour being recruited from outside the region remains, though the evidence derived from the LDA Report, January 2008, suggests that some progress in addressing these underlying labour market issues is being made.

Conclusion

A glance at the British media coverage of preparations for the 2012 Games in the three years since the successful London bid would suggest that Gerald Kaufman's comments in 2003 were prescient. The rising costs of the Games have dominated public debates about the London Olympics and much parliamentary select committee time has been taken up with the monitoring and evaluation of each revision to the budget. The National Audit Office has joined the monitoring process and the government department with overall responsibility for the Games, the DCMS, has sought to manage concerns about lottery funds being diverted from arts and cultural organisations to pay for the extensively revised budgets for 2012. Parallel to the budget debate, government, LOCOG, The Mayor of London and other agencies have published numerous policy documents and promises relating to the regeneration legacy to be achieved via the investment in 2012. These promises and policies have attracted less public scrutiny than the balance sheet for the Games. A likely consequence of this focus on the finances is that the Games is perceived and evaluated by its organisers and critics alike as a 'project' that is subject to 'audit' rather than as a social process whose outcomes and achievements may be contested.

From a broader social perspective, London 2012 has some distinctive features. Whereas the Beijing Games celebrated a dynamic economy and a society announcing its entry onto the world stage, the London Games reflects the aspirations of a less dynamic economy and society for whom 'regeneration' consists of addressing a lengthy period of under-investment in the infrastructure and social development of its capital city, particularly in a part of the city that has long been neglected. The hosting of the 2012 Games lends legitimation to a programme of state-led urban renewal on a significant scale and in a timeframe that is much more rapid than the normal 'organic' process of urban regeneration (Preuss 2004:79). Set in this context, the costs associated with the Games are less 'madness' or 'scandal' and more a public investment in a process of social re-engineering of London's east end. It is this social process that deserves greater public debate and attention.

References

ARUP (2002) 'London Olympics 2012: Costs and Benefits', London: ARUP (mimeo).

Atkinson G., Mourato, S. andSzymanski, S. (2006) 'Are We Willing to Pay Enough to Back the Bid?', London: London School of Economics and Political Science (mimeo).

Blake, A. (1999) 'These Sporting Times', *Soundings* 13 Autumn, http://www.amielandmelburn.org.uk/collections/soundings/13_10checkedblakeintro.pdf.

Boles, T. (2006) 'Amec and Balfour Beatty team up for Olympic Gold', *Sunday Times*, 19 February.

British Olympics Association (2007) 'London 2012 Bid – An Eight Year Journey', http//:www.olympics.org.uk.

Buck, N., Gordon, I., Hall, P., Harloe, M. andKleinman, M. (2002) *Working Capital – Life and Labour in Contemporary*, London. London: Routledge.

CABE (2007) 'Olympic, Paralympic and Legacy Transformation Masterplans', *Design Review*, 23 March.

Cohen, P. and MacRury, I. (2005) 'Hopeful or Worried but not yet Jumping for Joy: Some Emerging Themes from a Pilot Study of the London 2012 Bid', *Rising East Online* 2, http://www.uel.ac.uk/risingeast/archive02/features/happyworried.htm.

Cousins S. (2004) 'Beijing Cuts Olympic Costs', *Business Beijing*, Beijing: Information Office of the Beijing Municipal Government, http://www.btmbeijing.com.

Demos and Tims, C. (2007) 'The Post-Exotic Games', http://www.demos.co.uk/fil/postexoticgames.

Department of Communities and Local Government (2007) 'The Thames Gateway Delivery Plan', http://communities.gov.uk/publications/thames gateway/deliveryplan.

Department of Culture Media and Sport (2007) *Our Promises for 2012*, London: DCMS.

Department of Culture Media and Sport (2008) House of Commons Select Committee (uncorrected) minutes, 15 January.

Donovan, P. (2006) 'East London's Economy and the Olympics, London: Global Economic Perspectives', London: Global Economic Perspectives (mimeo).

Flyvberg, B., Bruzelius, N. and Rothengatter, W. (2003) *Megaprojects and Risk*, Cambridge: Cambridge University Press.

Hansard (2005), House of Commons Debates 'London 2012 Olympic Bid', 6 July.

Hoey, K. (2004) 'London 2012 Bid Has No Chance', BBC Sport, 10 December.

House of Commons Committee of Public Accounts (2007) 'Preparations for the London 2012 Olympic and Paralympic Games – Risk Assessment and Management Thirty-ninth Report of Session 2006–07'.

Kaufman, G. (2003), 'Olympics Debate Set to Reignite', BBC News, 23 January, http://news.bbc.co.uk.

Lee, M. (2006) *The Race for the 2012 Olympics*, London: Virgin Books.

Livingstone, K. (2005) 'Livingstone – London 2012 Olympics Would Be Exceptional', *Politics.co.uk* 15 February.

Livingstone, K. (2008) *Five Legacy Commitments*, London: Mayor of London.

London Chamber of Commerce (2005) 'A Sporting Chance – Ensuring London Firms Benefit from the 2012 Olympic Games', sponsored by KPMG, London: LCC.

London Development Agency (2006) 'London Employment and Skills Taskforce for 2012 – An Action Plan to Maximise the Employment and Skills Benefits of the London 2012 Olympic Games and Paralympic Games', January, London: LDA.

London Development Agency (2008) Annual Report 'Employment and Skills Activity Associated with the 2012 Games', London: LDA, January.

London East Research Institute (2007) *A Lasting Legacy?*, London: LERI.

Office of Deputy Prime Minister (2006a) Olympic Delivery Authority (Planning Functions) Order 2006, London.

ODPM (2006b) Consultation Paper and European Communities – Services – Competitive Dialogues, London.

Mean, M., Tims, C. and Vigor, A. (2004) 'After the Gold Rush, London: IPPR.

Muir, H. (2005) 'Sporting Drive Sees Drop in Crime for Olympic Borough', *Guardian*, 8 August.

National Audit Office (2007) 'Preparations for the London 2012 Olympic and Paralympic Games – Risk Assessment and Management', Report of the Comptroller and Auditor General HC252 Session 2006–7, 2 February, http://www.nao.org.uk.

Preuss, H. (2004) *The Economics of Staging the Olympics – A Comparison of the Games 1972–2008*, Cheltenham: Edward Elgar.

Routledge, P. (2008) 'Ken's Gold Muddle', *Daily Mirror*, 18 January.

Chapter 12

London 2012 and the Regeneration Game

Penny Bernstock

For more than three decades East London has been at the centre of policy debates and initiatives on urban regeneration. These have raised a number of questions concerning what characterises successful regeneration: Who should pay for it? How we should we evaluate it? Who should benefit? Whilst almost every UK urban initiative has been tested in East London, three schemes stand out in particular for their claims to bring benefits to the immediate area and beyond; London Docklands, the Thames Gateway project and London 2012. While most analysis of the potential impact of the London 2012 Games takes as its starting point experiences in other Olympic cities, it will be argued here that it is equally important to explore other urban regeneration projects that have taken place or are underway in East London. This chapter, drawing on evidence from these other projects, considers alternative scenarios concerning the housing legacy of London 2012.

One of the most well known urban development projects in Europe is London Docklands. Here the focus of analysis is specifically on housing development, concentrating mainly on the Isle of Dogs. According to many indicators Docklands has been a success but from the perspective of existing communities gains have been limited and the area has become synonymous with an increase in social polarisation between rich and poor communities. Described as the largest development project in Europe, the 'Thames Gateway', like London 2012, has committed to the provision of significant proportions of affordable housing. Following a review of these two major projects, the chapter concludes with an analysis of the potential housing legacies' of London 2012 through an exploration of the plans for the Olympic Park and an adjacent development, Stratford City.

London Docklands

Here we briefly review the impact of the London Docklands Development Corporation(LDDC) on housing and housing need. The LDDC was not a housing authority, but in 1981 was given development control powers for parts of three Docklands boroughs – Newham, Southwark and Tower Hamlets. It was argued that the regeneration of these areas, given their strategic significance to the regeneration of London and the country as a whole, should be developed in the 'national' rather than the 'local interest', embracing a Thatcherite approach to planning in which the market, unfettered by government controls, would be the central agent of regeneration. The LDDC was answerable only to the Secretary of State, overriding the power of democratically elected representatives, and agendas and minutes of LDDC board meetings were not available to the public (Brownill 1989).

Plans had been drawn up by the respective local authorities to use vacant lands to meet local needs. However, the LDDC's brief was simply to bring 'land and buildings into effective use'. The role of the agency reflected central government's concern to promote owner occupation and reduce the role of government and indeed they were successful in this regard with owner occupation increasing from five per cent in 1981 to 44 per cent by 1989 (Brownill 1989: 67) The LDDC argued that it was necessary to create a balanced community by attracting the more affluent to Docklands.

Between 1981 and 1998 (when the LDDC was disbanded) some 24,402 properties were built across the Docklands area, 17,789 of which were for direct sale (77 per cent of the total), and a further 722 for sale through shared ownership schemes. On the Isle of Dogs, 4965 properties were built. The majority of these (84 per cent) were for owner occupation, with a small proportion of these for sale through shared ownership; in addition 783 properties(16 per cent) were developed by housing associations for social rent (LDDC 1998). In Wapping and Limehouse 4601 properties were built over the same period and more than 90 per cent of these were owner occupied (LDDC 1998).

In addition, the London Borough of Tower Hamlets lost more than 400 homes as a result of the construction of the Limehouse link (Foster 1999) and thousands more through the right to buy scheme, so that the proportion of social housing available in the borough declined from 82 per cent in 1987 to 46 per cent in 2004 (London Borough of Tower Hamlets 2005). The pattern was similar in Surrey Docks, now known as Surrey Quays where a total of 8088 properties were built, of which 79 per cent were for private sale, with a small proportion of these available for sale through shared ownership. The pattern of housing completions in the Royal Docks, however, was different. Between 1981 and 1998, 6,422 units were built of which 3,562 were for private sale and a further 229 were developed for shared ownership, accounting for some 59 per cent of the total. In the Royal Docks, 2,055 properties were developed by housing associations for social rent and a further 576 by the local authority for social rent, generating a very different tenure mix (LDDC 1998).

One explanation for the lower proportions of rented housing in Wapping and the Isle of Dogs relates to the comparatively high land values of properties given their proximity to Tower Bridge. Land in the Royal Docks was much cheaper and more affordable to housing associations wishing to develop, whereas the cost of developing a new site in Wapping or on the Isle of Dogs was prohibitive as the market led model meant that housing associations had to compete with private developers to purchase sites. Moreover, developments in the Royal Docks began a little later than those close to the City and by 1988, the LDDC, following extensive public criticism of the polarised nature of development, placed a greater emphasis on meeting local need with the introduction of 'community gain' agreements, which explicitly linked development with community benefits. . The London Borough of Newham's community gain agreement resulted in the provision of 1500 social housing units in the Royal Docks (Brownill 1989).

It was always a policy objective of the LDDC to present its strategy as beneficial to local people. The proportion of local people purchasing the new housing became an important point of debate, with the LDDC claiming that significant numbers of local people had purchased these properties, whilst other studies questioned this data (LDDC 1988; GLC 1984; Docklands Forum 1987). Moreover, despite the government's commitment to promote a free market approach to regeneration, attractive financial incentives were given to private developers to enable them to develop sites, so that in some instances sites were sold to private developers at half their market value (Brownill 1989; Foster 1990). In return, developers were expected to enhance local take up of schemes. Developers were required to cap a proportion of the units at £40,000 which was the figure deemed to be affordable to local residents, and exclusion clauses essentially gave local people first preference on new properties.

The LDDC claimed that by 1985, 40 per cent of new properties had been purchased by local residents (Brownill 1989). However, a GLC study found that the proportion of local people buying houses was decreasing over time, as house prices increased (GLC 1984). The proportion of housing available at under £40,000 declined significantly as property prices almost doubled between 1985 and 1987 and as land values reached £4-6 million per acre in some parts of London Docklands (LDDC 1988; Brownill 1989). Indeed developers suspended local exclusion clauses because so few applicants were applying (GLC 1984). The cheaper housing tended to be located in Beckton with the implication that those living in Tower Hamlets would have to relocate to Beckton should they wish to purchase a home (Foster 1999). There was also evidence of fraud with local residents selling their rent books to would be purchasers and using fake addresses, thus questioning the reliability of the data (Brownill 1989). However, local income surveys demonstrated that for the majority of residents, owner occupation was not an option, with this problem compounded as property prices rose (Docklands Forum 1987).As new properties were built across the three Docklands boroughs, the mismatch between housing need and housing supply became apparent. Reviews of housing need indicators suggested that housing waiting lists, homelessness and overcrowding continued to be major problems (London Borough of Tower Hamlets 2005; London Borough of Newham 2003a; London Borough of Southwark 2006). Rather than creating 'mixed/balanced' communities in areas such as Wapping and the Isle of Dogs there is considerable evidence

of polarisation both in incomes and lifestyles (London Borough of Tower
Hamlets 2006). In 2005, 43 per cent of households in Tower Hamlets had
an income of less than £10,000 and 67 per cent of council homes in Tower
Hamlets fell below the Decent Homes Standard (London Borough of Tower
Hamlets 2005). Equally, those who bought properties in the area, either as
speculators, investors or purchasers, have made considerable capital gains.
Data for the period April to June 2007 indicated that property prices increased
by 18.9 per cent in Tower Hamlets with the average price for a flat costing over
£300,000 (BBC News 2007a).

The regeneration of London Docklands has been a physical success, the
urban landscape has been transformed but the project has come to symbolise
both a post-industrial Britain and a post Thatcher divide between the 'haves'
and 'have nots'. It was through the enduring commitment of local communities
to highlight these contradictions that the legacy of 'Canary Wharf' will always
be identified by these inequities:

> This is an area which suffers from its image. It may have been redeveloped
> but it hasn't been regenerated. Side by side with housing that is available
> only to the richest few there are overlooked pockets of severe poverty and
> urban stress. (Time and Talents 1997: 3)

What relevance does this have then to the potential housing legacy of London
2012? As will be demonstrated below, there are circumstances that create the
possibility that Stratford City will be characterised by the same patterns of
social polarisation that has come to define the London Docklands, and, in
particular, the Isle of Dogs.

Thames Gateway and Affordable Housing

The second project briefly reviewed is the Thames Gateway, it straddles both
sides of the River Thames,stretching from London Docklands to Southend
in Essex and Sittingbourne in Kent, and includes the site of the London 2012
Games. The Thames Gateway has been shaped by a post-Thatcherite planning
regime which attempts to reconcile private profit with Community Gain, through
the implementation of section 106 agreements. Section 106 agreements were
introduced as part of the Town and Country Planning Act 1990. These place
conditions on developers linked to the granting of planning permission. The
intention of Section 106 is to mitigate the impact of any new developments by
ensuring that developers contribute toward necessary infrastructure including,
for example, constructing new schools and roads. Agreements may also include
wider benefits such as a contribution to youth provision/community centres in
an area; the creation of open public spaces or ensuring local people get access
to job opportunities generated from the construction of the development.

These agreements include specific recommendations related to housing, and may specify the proportion of affordable housing required to be achieved by a scheme, including the balance between social rented housing and other types of affordable housing such as 'shared ownership' and the housing mix in terms of number of bedrooms (Bernstock 2008). Indeed, the provision of affordable housing delivered through S106 agreements is increasing to the extent that in 2006 more than half of all new affordable housing was provided in this way (Monk et al. 2006). Targets for affordable housing have increased with the Greater London Authority arguing that 50 per cent of all new housing should be affordable and reflected in S106 agreements (GLA 2005). It will be through this mechanism that affordable housing and a range of other legacy benefits will be achieved on the London 2012 site.

The development of Thames Gateway and the delivery of affordable housing have become synonymous, with targets of 50 per cent for London Thames Gateway and 35 per cent for the region as a whole (GLA 2004; DCLG 2006). Between September 2005 and March 2006 a research project was undertaken that aimed to provide a detailed picture of current practice regarding S106 planning agreements on all schemes of 100 plus units across the Thames Gateway that had either been planned or developed between January 2000 and September 2005. 82 agreements were analysed. The project identified huge variations in the way in which these agreements were applied (Bernstock 2008).

There was wide variation in the proportion of affordable housing specified in the agreements ranging from 7–100 per cent and an average of 28 per cent across all schemes. Moreover, despite the GLA requirement that schemes should include 50 per cent affordable housing, the study found that levels of affordable housing only exceeded 35 per cent on schemes led by Registered Social Landlords, with profitability often presented by developers as an argument for lower proportions of affordable housing. There was though a clear trend overtime towards increasing proportions of affordable housing being required. Whilst data on the proportion of affordable housing was available on all schemes, definitions of what constituted affordable housing and a more detailed breakdown of the type of affordable housing being provided were not systematically recorded by many schemes. In the main, affordable housing, where it was defined, comprised of housing for social rent and housing on a part buy/part rent (shared ownership) basis. There were widespread variations in the proportion of housing allocated for social rent, ranging from zero to one hundred per cent, with lower levels of social rented housing often rationalised as a way of achieving more 'balanced communities', irrespective of need. Similarly there were very few attempts to determine affordability levels on the part buy/part rent schemes. This lack of focus on what constitutes affordable housing is problematic given the failures in London Docklands discussed above.

If the needs of lower income groups were at the margins of the development of London Docklands, the regeneration of Thames Gateway has been similarly problematic.

Data on housing type was not systematically recorded on all schemes but it was available in eight of the 11 authorities reviewed. This indicated that 70 per cent of all new properties were flats and in terms of bedroom type, 34 per cent of these properties were one bedroom; 47 per cent two bedroom and 19 per cent three bedrooms or more. This data was then analysed against information on housing need and revealed a mismatch in most Thames Gateway authorities between the type of housing needed and the type of housing being built. Indeed the GLA's guidelines on property types recommends that 32 per cent of all properties should be one bedroom; 38 per cent two and three bedroom and 30 per cent of properties should have four bedrooms or more. The provision of larger properties was rare on the schemes examined (GLA 2005). A reliance on the private sector to deliver affordable housing may create a mismatch between the type of housing built and the type of housing needed.

The study identified a trend toward building at densities that exceeded many of the respective authorities own guidelines as stipulated in their Unitary Development Plans. Indeed, building at increasingly high densities has become a policy goal in itself encouraged by central government directives in response to the shortage of land; the need to ensure a critical mass that will generate high quality services; and, for developers, building at high densities offers a way of maximising profit and meeting affordable housing targets . However, in some parts of Thames Gateway higher densities have not led to the development of high quality services, as individual schemes although built at high densities, remain spatially isolated.

The trend toward constructing high density flatted accommodation raises crucial issues about families and their quality of life. Will those families with more resources move further down river to purchase more affordable family housing, and what of those families dependent on rented accommodation, what will be their housing options? Policy makers appear to assume that people purchasing this housing will be childless, but clearly this situation may change and families may become trapped in unsuitable housing.

The government itself has raised crucial questions about the housing built in Thames Gateway, questioning its quality and the lack of family housing (DCLG 2006). In many senses the development of the Thames Gateway is a continuum of the trend towards mainly owner occupied units targeted at young childless couples working in the city. There continues to be a mismatch between the type of housing being built and the type of housing needed, exacerbating the housing crisis for low income families.

London 2012 – Social Inclusion or Social Polarisation?

A number of potential housing legacies may arise from London 2012. These are mapped out below by examining the extent to which the emerging Stratford City will be characterised by the type of social polarisation that is associated with the Isle of Dogs or whether a more inclusive model will be achieved that serves as an exemplar of good practice.

Displacement and Housing Loss

There is some evidence that mega-events such as the Olympic Games have a detrimental effect on poor populations living in close proximity to the Games' main sites. A recent report explored the displacement impact of the Games over the last 20 years estimating that some two million people have been displaced and that this displacement disproportionately affected minority groups, the poor and the homeless (Centre on Housing Rights and Evictions 2007). There are two main groups of residents that have been displaced from the London 2012 site, the residents at Clays Lane and 130 travellers who lived on two traveller sites within the designated Olympic Park zone.

On the Clays Lane site some 450 social housing units have been demolished and 425 residents re-housed. The Centre on Housing Rights and Evictions advocates a code of good practice and those involved with re-housing the tenants at Clays Lane would indeed argue that they have worked with tenants to ensure positive outcomes and have pursued good practice offering a range of choice to those affected (Jowell 2008). Nevertheless, many did not want to leave their homes, and local residents expressed disappointment that more was not done to facilitate a community move (Games Monitor 2008). On the other hand, for those other local residents in housing need in the area, their prospects of being re-housed have been adversely affected as the residents at Clays Lane received priority in housing allocations. Similarly, whilst relevant agencies can claim they worked with travellers to ensure positive outcomes this does not negate the fact that the travellers did not want to move and attempted to have the compulsory purchase order over-turned in the High Court (BBC News 2007b; Piper 2007).

There is another legacy commonly associated with the hosting of mega-events such as the Olympic Games, this is rising land and property values. As we enter a period of financial uncertainty and economic recession in the period leading up to 2012, this effect becomes more difficult to estimate in the context of East London Two possible scenarios are considered below, the first based upon a rise in land values, and the second on falling land prices.

Rising Land and Property Values and the Housing Legacy of London 2012

It has been estimated that land values increased by 25per cent in the first 18 months after the announcement of London's successful bid to host the Olympic Games and the government is predicting that there will be a considerable profit from the sale of land after the Olympics, with a possible quadrupling in prices after 2012 (Temko and Campbell 2006). Rising land values are good news for a government that may seek to sell the land to recoup some of the cost of the Games, but this may have similar repercussions to London Docklands where only the highest bidders can afford to buy land, resulting in the development of more exclusive forms of housing. Such an effect could be mitigated in part by current government and Mayor of London commitments to the provision of affordable housing as an important component of the 2012 legacy.

Rising house prices have also been an enduring legacy of mega-events such as the Olympics (GLA 2007). A study undertaken by Halifax estate agents explored changes in house prices from the second quarter of 2005 to the third quarter of 2006 and found that whilst house prices had increased by 15 per cent overall in London, in those areas surrounding London 2012 increases had exceeded this. For example, house prices increased by 23 per cent in Leytonstone, 21 per cent in Hackney and 13 per cent in Leyton. However, in Stratford itself, price increases had been below the London average at eight per cent for the same period. The same study also explored the impact on house prices in Barcelona, Atlanta, Sydney and Athens and found that all cities experienced an increase in house prices compared to house price increases for their countries as a whole over the same period (*About Property* 2007). The study also explored price rises in Manchester in the lead up to the Commonwealth Games and found that house prices increased by 102 per cent for Manchester in the five years leading up to the Games, compared to 52 per cent for the North West Region and 83 per cent for London as a whole (*About Property* 2007) Halifax predicted that house prices in Hackney would continue to rise even as prices elsewhere had begun to fall because of the Olympics effect (*Financial Times* 2008). There has been much less work done on rising rental values but a recent report by the East Thames Housing Association identified this as a particular problem. People living in privately rented accommodation in the area reported rapidly increasing rents (East Thames Housing Association 2007).

Whilst rising house prices may be good news for those owning properties in the area, it may have a detrimental effect upon those hoping to buy or indeed rent. Moreover, whilst 'affordable housing' features as a key part of the legacy debate, the reality is that East London has traditionally been a source of more affordable housing, simply by virtue of its lower house prices. Indeed, the Halifax study noted that despite these increases, house prices in eight of the 14 districts close to the Olympic site were 25 per cent below the London Average. Therefore, an unintended consequence may be to create increased demand for more formal affordable housing options, as cheaper sources of market housing in the vicinity of the Olympic site diminish.

Falling Land Values and their Impact on Legacy

London 2012 is dependent on increasing land values in order to realise the costs of funding the Olympics. If land values continue to fall, demand for the land may fall and this in turn may be detrimental. It may mean that expenditure on the lasting legacy dimension is cut and this could, in turn, lead to poorer quality social housing and less expenditure to enhance the public realm. Indeed, developers have expressed concern about the impact of a large number of properties becoming available and potentially flooding the market, with London and Continental Railways suggesting they may require a government subsidy to cover any losses (Pocock and Gadher 2006). There is some speculation that a large private renting scheme could be developed on the Olympic Park site (Marshall 2008).

A fall in land values may be positive for those dependent on social housing. In London Docklands when house prices began to fall and developers found it hard to sell new homes, registered Social Landlords were able to purchase this housing at a lower cost, increasing the overall supply of social housing, and leading to more socially inclusive outcomes.

How Many New Homes?

One of the unique features of the London 2012 bid was its commitment to deliver a lasting legacy in terms of regeneration benefits and in particular speed up the process of regeneration leading to the construction of a water city in the Lower Lea Valley comprising some 30,000–40,000 new homes (GLA 2006). According to Sebastian Coe (2007):

> The regeneration will create between 30,000 and 40,000 new homes in the area. It will be a catalyst for investment that will create new, quality housing – much of which will be 'affordable housing' available to key workers such as nurses or teachers.

However, the claim that regeneration will lead to the construction of 30,000–40,000 new homes is tenuous and based on a view that London 2012 will speed up the broader regeneration process in East London. We can assume that this number of homes is unlikely to be completed in the near future, and will not be reflected in any performance indicators developed to measure the legacy.

More specifically it is anticipated that more 9,000 homes will be located on the site of the Olympic Park. Initially, it was claimed that 50 per cent of these will be affordable, however, official websites now refer to 'many of these being affordable', and according to a recent document published by the GLA:

> The games will provide a legacy of 9,000 high quality homes on site, many
> of which will be available to Londoners on low incomes. (GLA 2008)

The GLA document suggests that about 30 per cent of these homes will be
affordable, representing a downward shift in the affordable housing legacy
(GLA 2008).

The Athletes' Village and its Housing Legacy

Original plans made clear that the Athletes' Village at London 2012 would be
temporary and converted to housing after the Games. After London won the
right to host the Games a new set of plans emerged, integrating the Athletes'
Village development with Stratford City in order to reduce remediation costs
(*Financial Times* 2006). This integration of the two projects raises the question
as to whether the anticipated housing legacy of the Athletes' Village will be
incorporated into the 5,000 homes that were already planned as part of the
Stratford City development prior to the IOC's decision that London should
host the 2012 Games.

In February 2007 planning applications were submitted to convert 529 of
a total of 1,252 homes at the Athletes' Village after the Games had ended.
The proposed scheme comprised five blocks ranging in height from three to
eleven storeys. In common with other schemes across the Thames Gateway
there is a predominance of one and two bedroom flats. It is proposed that
50 per cent of these would be affordable, divided between 50 per cent social
rented and 50 per cent intermediate housing options, and indeed whilst the
London Plan suggests a split of 70:30 in favour of social housing, Newham
made clear in a discussion of the planning application that it would prefer
a lower proportion of social rented housing, i.e. under 21 per cent, as the
authority was concerned that a higher percentage may lead to a concentration
of benefit dependent residents. Newham also expressed concern about the low
proportion of family housing and the failure to provide community facilities
as part of the scheme (London Borough of Newham 2007a). Discussions are
continuing with regards to the allocation of this housing, and it is likely that
allocations will be drawn from throughout London.

Stratford City

Initial plans for Stratford City were agreed as part of an outline planning
application in February 2005 and included a commitment to providing 30
per cent affordable housing increasing to 35 per cent if it could be proved
to be financially viable. The rationale for this relatively low proportion of
affordable housing was agreed partly because Stratford had a large proportion

of residents living in social housing and this proportion would help to create a more 'balanced community' (London Borough of Newham 2003b).

In May 2007, a planning application was submitted to the ODA outlining some alterations to Zone One. Zone One is significant as it will be at the centre of the new Stratford City. It was originally designated as a mainly retail hub, with 500 residential units, and this has been revised to include commercial and office space and an increased number of residential units. The new plans include an increase of 640 residential units achieved through a rise in density. The proportion of affordable housing remains the same at 30 per cent, but does not include any social rented housing.

Details were also submitted related to the site wide strategy for the scheme, confirming a total 5,453 units to be built on the site, of which 3,830, or 70 per cent, will be private. The remaining 1,623 will be affordable housing units and of these 60 per cent (978) will be for social rent with 140 of these comprising supported housing and social rented housing. The intermediate housing options include shared equity; shared ownership and discount market rental. In this most recent document it is proposed that there be a reduction in the proportion of larger units for sale, whilst still affirming the previous commitment that 40 per cent of housing for social rent comprise larger units. This proposal challenges models of regeneration based on mixed communities, and may potentially result in a concentration of disadvantaged families living in the family housing (London Borough of Newham 2007b).

Table 12.1   The London 2012 housing legacy

Housing legacy: balance sheet*	No. of units	Proportion of affordable housing
Stratford City (already planned)	5,453 (additional 640 units added since July 2005)	(30%) 1,623 units
Athletes' Village	1,252	631 (50%)
Total	6,705	2,254 (34%)
Shortfall	2,795	1,865 (67%) to reach 50% target 727 units to reach target of 30%

*   As at Spring 2008.

Table 12.1 shows that plans are now in place for the delivery of 6,705 units on the Olympic Park. However, nearly 5,000 of these were already agreed prior to London winning the bid. The net gain in relation to affordable housing is the 631 units planned at the Athletes' Village, and indeed when we take into account the 425 units lost at Clays Lane, the net gain in terms of affordable housing as a result of the London 2012 bid is negligible.

There is a danger, however, that we may become sidetracked into focusing on the number of houses built as a measure of whether the government and relevant agencies have been successful. It may be more important to focus on the qualitative dimensions related to the liveability and inclusivity of the scheme. If, for example, 5,000 homes were built of high quality that housed a cross section of London's population and became a demonstration project for successful urban living then perhaps we should consider the scheme as a success. In addition to the actual legacy anticipated for the Olympic Park, there is also the long term legacy related to speeding up regeneration across Stratford and the Lower Lea Valley. We will now consider in more detail the emerging Stratford High Street as a window into the area post 2012.

Stratford High Street 'Post 2012'

For anyone travelling on the Docklands Light Railway from Stratford it would be hard not to be surprised at the extent of development taking place along Stratford High Street. Cranes, half finished towers and newly completed apartments dominate the landscape. For sale and for part sale boards are attached to these new and emerging developments. Interspersed between these developments we can see Old Stratford, the 1960s tower blocks and high density council housing. It is for these communities that the question of legacy is particularly pertinent. Will they be forced to move to other areas as land values increase or will the housing legacy provide a future for them in the area as it becomes more prosperous?

A study on housing needs undertaken for Newham and published in 2003 identified higher levels of people who were unemployed at 6.72 per cent compared to 5.58 per cent for inner London and higher levels of the population without qualifications, at 35.58 per cent compared to 23.73 per cent for London as a whole. Moreover, average incomes in 2002/3 were below the national average and significantly below regional averages (London Borough of Newham 2003a). There were also significant variations in income between those living in different housing tenures. Owner occupiers with mortgages had average incomes that were more than three times greater than those living in council or Housing Association housing. The income gap between those living in private rented housing and those living in social housing was also considerable with private renters having on average double the income of those in social rented housing, but significantly less than those with mortgages. The study also explored income across the eight subregions of Newham and found that those living in Stratford had the second lowest income at £12,534 per annum compared to £16,952 for all regions and the highest proportion of households living in unsuitable housing at 22.9 per cent compared to 15.7 per cent across the borough as a whole, however, they also had the highest proportion of social housing and it is generally within this sector that housing need is more prevalent (London Borough of Newham 2003a).

Overcrowding was the most significant factor linked to unsuitable housing, followed by children living in high rise accommodation at 1,839 households, and yet as we will see below the type of housing being built in Stratford is mainly flatted accommodation in high rise blocks. The study explored the potential for the market to resolve the housing problems confronting those in housing need and concluded that 96.4 per cent of families needing to move within the borough could not afford to buy market housing. **The study** suggested that around 25 per cent of those in need could afford intermediate housing purchase options, if they were priced at a level just above social rented housing (London Borough of Newham 2003a).

Having explored housing need in the area, we will now review some of the schemes that have either been agreed or submitted as planning applications. Both the London Plan and the Newham Unitary Development Plan focus decision making upon planning applications. The London Plan aims to ensure that new developments meet housing need and recommends that 50 per cent of housing should be affordable, with 70 per cent of this being available for social rent, with a mix of units including at least 30 per cent that are four bedroom or more (GLA 2005). The London Borough of Newham, on the other hand, wants to encourage a change in tenure in the area, to counter-balance the high proportion of socially rented housing. Newham is committed to permitting schemes with lower proportions of affordable housing and lower proportions of housing for social rent than recommended in the London Plan (London Borough of Newham 2003b)

In May 2006, a planning application was submitted to construct a 30-storey tower. The developer was required to pay £50 million per hectare to buy the land and the scheme attempted to maximise profit through the construction of a 30-storey tower which would include 334 residential units and a hotel (GLA 2007). The scheme was rejected by the Greater London Authority, but provides an insight into the types of development that are emerging.

On the other side of Stratford High Street, a small tower can be seen behind the bingo hall. This is one of a number of developments led by Registered Social landlords in the area. This is a 20-storey block, and comprises 164 mainly one and two bedroom properties, including live work units, just 2 per cent of the units have three bedrooms, substantially below that indicated in the London Plan. Whilst the housing is categorised as affordable, only 11 per cent is available for social renting, and the remainder is available on a part buy basis. This is again considerably below the 70 per cent recommended in the London Plan (London Borough of Newham 2004a).

On the opposite site of the road on the junction of Stratford High Street and Lett Road planning consent has been given for a ten storey mixed use development scheme, including 90 residential units. Again the development comprises mainly one and two bedroom flats, with just 6 per cent of the units having three bedrooms. The proportion of affordable housing agreed is 35 per cent which again falls short of the 50 per cent stipulated in the London Plan.

The social rented units will be provided off site and linked to the regeneration of the nearby Carpenters Estate, potentially contributing to social polarisation (London Borough of Newham 2007c).

Within the Carpenters Estate another development is nearing completion, the Stratford Icona, comprising a number of blocks including an eighteen storey tower. The scheme includes 35 per cent affordable housing, and in this instance was justified due to the lack of social housing grant. The affordable housing comprises 44 per cent social renting and 56 per cent intermediate housing options, again lower than that recommended in the London Plan. The 2012 factor has clearly had an effect on sales with all of the private housing sold off plan prior to completion (London Borough of Newham 2004b).

The site under construction at 160–188 High Street Stratford is being developed by a consortium of Registered Social Landlords and again comprises a number of blocks, the tallest of which is a 19 storey tower. This is a mixed use development, including 275 mainly one and two bedroom units, justified because the high rise nature of the development was considered unsuitable for children. One hundred and twenty-four (45 per cent) of the units will be for sale on the open market, a further 53 (19 per cent) are for sale through shared ownership with 25 (9 per cent) aimed specifically at key workers for shared ownership. The remaining 73 (27 per cent) units will be social rented. The proportion of housing for social rent again falls short of that recommended in the London Plan, but was considered acceptable due to the already high proportion of social rented housing in the area (London Borough of Newham 2004c).

At 80–92 High Street Stratford, on the site of a disused tyre sales centre, another high-tech landmark is under construction, Stratford Edge. This includes a 27-storey tower and 202 residential units, again the development comprises mainly one and two bedroom flats. The scheme includes 35 per cent affordable housing, 60 per cent of which is for social rent and 40 per cent for intermediate housing, though the bulk of social rented housing will again be provided off site (London Borough of Newham 2005).

As we move closer to the Bow interchange and the end of Stratford High Street, we see that another 25-storey tower is under construction, Stratford One. A hoarding informs that all private units are sold. The scheme includes 327 units, 50 per cent are affordable and of these 69 per cent will be social rented. Initially, the scheme included a lower proportion of affordable housing but attained a social housing grant from the Housing Corporation. The proportion of social rented housing meets London Plan guidelines at 69 per cent with the remainder being shared ownership housing. The scheme again comprises mainly one and two bedroom flats but includes a larger proportion of three bedroom properties than neighbouring schemes at 8 per cent, though this is still far less than London Plan Guidelines Density is high at 1,122 habitable rooms per hectare, which was seen as a compromise in achieving 50 per cent affordable housing (London Borough of Newham 2005).

There is considerable development taking place along Stratford High Street, however, the area continues to be characterised by neglect, evidenced in the rubbish littered on empty waste lands, the polluted waterways, and vacant factories. New spaces are emerging that are quite different from those that have been there before. It is the extent to which these new spaces open up possibilities for the existing disadvantaged communities living in the area, as compared to simply bringing in new populations, that will be the measure of their success.

Conclusion

Three major urban regeneration programmes in East London have been reviewed. These projects have a common commitment to bring benefits to an area far greater than the immediate spatial boundaries in which they are located. Whilst London Docklands has clearly been a success in relation to physical regeneration, the anticipated positive 'trickle down' effect leading to social and housing improvements for local communities did not occur. There is the potential for a similar outcome in Stratford arising from the impact of London 2012. Despite the high levels of housing need , there has been a commitment to facilitate a type of regeneration that is based on attracting more affluent populations to the area.

It might be argued, that what sets the London 2012 approach apart from London Docklands is its commitment to the delivery of 'affordable' housing. Though this was a strategy latterly pursued by the LDDC, with limited results because the affordable housing became unaffordable as land values rose. The current emphasis on Section 106 agreements, will constitute a substantial proportion of the affordable housing delivered on the Olympic Park and therefore much more attention must be given to the details of funding mechanisms to ensure that it is available to a wider range of low income groups. Just as the developments in London Docklands were shaped by proximity to the city, the developments in Stratford may take a similar form, with areas away from Stratford City offering the potential for more inclusive uses.

The planned housing legacy of London 2012, will be shaped in part by the impact of external factors, particularly the global credit crunch. In relation to the net housing gain, this may be relatively minimal and it will therefore, be important to ensure that what is built is of high quality and does embrace the theme of inclusivity, a theme that was deployed to win the Olympic bid. If land values continue to rise as has been the case in other Olympic Cities it may mean that the traditional source of cheap market housing becomes inaccessible and accelerates dependency on other 'affordable' type housing schemes in the area. Moreover, as the government attempts to recoup the costs of staging the Olympics through the sale of land, the incentive could be to sell to the highest bidder and this may mitigate against a more socially inclusive form of urban regeneration.

In order to ensure that a positive legacy is secured from London 2012 greater emphasis is needed on imagining possible socially inclusive futures and putting in place the mechanisms to achieve these. Current housing plans and developments appear to be reliant upon mechanisms that have already been tested and found wanting on other regeneration projects. What distinguishes London 2012 from these other projects is not so much its plan, but the lack of local community voices advocating more inclusive outcomes and calling the London 2012 agencies to account. During the 1980s a range of posters were produced by campaigners who sought a greater community benefit from the Docklands development, one slogan seems particularly pertinent in the lead-up to 2012, 'Big Money is moving in. Don't let it push out local people'.

References

About Property (2007) 'House Prices Soar in Olympics Area', 2 February.

Bernstock, P. (2008) 'Homing in on Housing', in Cohen, P. and Rustin, M,J. (eds) (2008) *London's Turning: The Making of Thames Gateway*, Aldershot, Ashgate.

Brownill, S. (1989) *Developing London Docklands? Another Great Planning Disaster*, London: Paul Chapman.

BBC News (2007a) http://bbc.co.uk/1/shared/spl/hi/in_depth/uk_house_prices/ html/bg.stm, updated 17 September.

BBC News (2007b) *Gypsies Lose Land to Olympics*, 1 March.

Centre for Housing Rights and Evictions (2007) *Fair Play for Housing Rights: Mega-events, Olympic Games and Housing Rights*, Geneva: COHRE.

Coe, S. (2007) 'It's Ludicrous to Claim the Olympics will Lead to Evictions and Poverty, *Guardian*, 15 June.

Department of Communities and Local Government (2006) *Thames Gateway: Interim Plan*, London: Crown Copyright.

Docklands Forum (1987) *Housing in London Docklands*, London: Docklands Forum.

East Thames Housing Association (2007) *Home Games: A Study of the Housing and Regeneration Legacies of other Olympic and Paralympic Games and the Implications for Residents of East London*, London: East Thames Group.

Financial Times (2008) 'South East and Scotland Forecast to Buck Slowing Price Trend', 4 January.

Foster, J. (1999) *Cultures in Conflict: Worlds in Collision*, London: UCL Press.

Games Monitor (2008) Response from evicted resident to Jowell, T., Parliamentary question, http://www.gamesmonitor.org.uk/node/558.

Greater London Authority (2004) *The London Plan: Spatial Development Strategy for Greater London*, London: Greater London Authority.

Greater London Authority. (2005) *London Plan Supplementary Planning Guidance – Housing*, London: GLA.

Greater London Authority (2006) *Lower Lea Valley Development Framework*, London: GLA.

Greater London Authority (2007) *Planning Report PDU/1263/01*, 27 February.

Greater London Authority (2008) *Five Legacy Commitments*, London: GLA.

Greater London Council (1984) *Housing and Employment in London Docklands*, London: GLC.

Jowell, T. (2008) House of Commons Written Answer, 31.01.2008 re: displacement of local authority tenants.

London Borough of Newham (2003a) *Newham Housing Needs Survey*, London: LBN.

London Borough of Newham (2003b) *P03/0607 Stratford City Planning Application*, Development Control Committee Papers, February.

London Borough of Newham (2004a) *Planning Application P/04/1142*, Development Control Committee, 25 January.

London Borough of Newham (2004b) *P04/0608 Planning Application*, Development Control Committee, 1 September.

London Borough of Newham (2004c) *P03/0667 Planning Application*, Development Control Committee, 24 May.

London Borough of Newham (2005) *P05/0700 Planning Application*, Development Control Committee, 21 September.

London Borough of Newham (2007a) *LBN Consultation Response: Olympic Village Part and Legacy Residential Planning Application*, Development Control Committee, December.

London Borough of Newham (2007b) *ODA, LBN Response – 07/900006 AODODA – Stratford City, London E15*, Development Control Committee, June.

London Borough of Newham (2007c) *06/01246 Planning Application*, Development control Committee, May.

London Borough of Southwark (2006) *Housing Needs in Southwark*, London: LBS.

London Borough of Tower Hamlets (2005) *Housing Strategy Statement 2005/6-2007/8*, London: LBTH.

London Borough of Tower Hamlets (2006) *Local Development Framework*, London: LBTH.

London Docklands Development Corporation (1988) *London Docklands Housing Review*, London: LDDC.

London Docklands Development Corporation (1998) *Housing in the Renewed London Docklands*, London: LDDC.

Marshall, T. (2008) 'Going for Gold', *Roof*, January/February.

Monk, S., Lister, D., Lovatt, R., Ni Luanaigh, A., Rowley, S. and Whitehead, C, (2006) *Delivering Affordable Housing through Section 106: Outputs and Outcomes*, York: Joseph Rowntree Foundation.

Piper, J. (2007) 'Councils Consulted Travellers Moved on by Olympics', *Guardian*, 14 June.

Pocock, I. and Gadher, S. (2006) 'Olympic Village to Cost £400m', *Sunday Times*, 19 November.

Temko, N. and Campbell, D. (2006) 'Olympic Site to Deliver 4 million Windfall After the Games', *Observer*, 3 December.

Time and Talents (1997) Time and Talents Newsletter, London.

Chapter 13

'Race', Sport and East London

Kevin Hylton and Nigel D. Morpeth

The overarching vision for the London 2012 Olympic Games and Paralympic
Games is to host inspirational, safe and inclusive Games and leave a sustainable
legacy for London and the UK.

(Olympic Delivery Authority 2007: 2)

There is so much inspired joy on the playing field that it's easy to forget how
people in power use sports to advance their own narrow agendas.

(Zirin 2007: 171)

Introduction

The ODA (2007) and Zirin (2007) exemplify some of the contradictions and
competing tensions in any Olympic project. London 2012 is not immune to
the dominant narrative and counter-narrative discourses and as such this
chapter chooses to emphasise some of the complexities and contradictions
bound up in the consideration of 'race', sport, the East End and the London
2012 Games. Some of the complexities of the Olympic Games are apparent
in competing discourses in addition to each host nation's local-national
backdrop which contributes further social concerns for serious consideration.
In East London foregrounding urban renewal and legacy promises driven by
one event are massive challenges in London's most multicultural and resource
deprived areas. This chapter also considers UK sports development's historical
failure to include black and minority ethnic communities as participants and
influential voices and how this is likely to be perpetuated in East London.

Mega-events such as the Olympic Games provide a convenient conduit for
expressions of chauvinism, nationalism, patriotism, imagined and idealised
aspirations of nationhood and so called national identity camouflaged by
a heady mix of sporting celebration. The focus on the *global* and *national*
arguably has implications for the national/local nexus and how we recognise
and understand the *local* and the concept of community in contemporary
Britain. Further, it has been suggested that sport, unlike other key arenas in
society, is a vehicle for black people in the UK to become integrated or even
assimilated into 'British culture' (Whannel 1992; Polley 1998). Polley's (1998)
argument that sport has delivered a level of recognition and respect to black

people that they would not have achieved so readily is instructive especially where sport consistently delivers good news about black people more often than most other areas of social life. The success of black people in high profile sport has led to a 'quickening' in the establishment of albeit diverse, black cultural identities (Whannel 1992). Sport is symbolic in highlighting a regular mutual experiencing of togetherness in black communities that it is perhaps much harder to see elsewhere, even in politics. Where we can agree on the transitory nature of identities, whether real or imagined, we can also accept that sport has the capacity to liberate and constrain, unify and divide in a most profound way. Whannel (1992: 130) has spoken of the 'black cultural resonances' of the 'blackwash!' banners held up in celebration of a West Indies cricket Test victory against England. Also sport can bring disparate people together in ways unimagined and it is anticipated by Olympic authorities that the communities in east London will not only cohere where they are not already strong but if the rhetoric is correct should also become more active in sport; and as citizens more employable; more healthy; and better educated (LERI 2007). The potential for sport to mobilise in the UK through racialised politics does have some evidence too as Member of Parliament, Diane Abbot, who was brought up in a white suburb in Harrow and was schooled in a girls grammar school where she was the only black girl, was inspired by Tommie Smith and John Carlos on the podium in the Mexico Olympic Games in 1968 and motivated into joining a black liberation movement that 'made me proud of my race [sic]' (Abbot 2006: 94). Jenkins (2008: 36) writing in *The Guardian* newspaper, argues that:

> The Olympics are not essentially about sport, the sports being almost 'minor' ones. The longstanding ploy of the International Olympic Committee in inflating the nationalist significance of the Games and thus sustaining the extravagance of the spectacle has made them ... a grotesque display of chauvinism that only the richest state can play.

These states he argued are 'drenched in national prestige' and that due to the inevitable politicising of the Olympics that they should be regarded as 'a festival of politics as well as of sport and civil engineering'. What is clear is that the tensions between 'race', sport and politics will be evident in east London before, during and after the 2012 Olympic Games however the outcomes of these tensions are likely to be less transparent.

The Olympic Delivery Authority highlights the importance of diversity in the planning, implementation and considerations of the legacy outcomes of the London 2012 Games. How could we not fail to be moved by the signifiers of diversity in the London bid when a multi-racial group of children accompanied Lord Coe to hear the decision of the International Olympic Committee. Bramham (2008) suggests that a reading of this moment might lead observers to believe that the beneficiaries of the new Olympic facilities were going to be them. However, as a signifier of the London Games they also denote the rich diversity in the five London boroughs in the east of London surrounding the Lea Valley where the bulk of the major facilities find their homes; Newham (East), Tower Hamlets (West), Greenwich (South), Hackney (N. West) and Waltham Forest (North). London is relatively more diverse than the UK as a whole – with the five boroughs more diverse than London as a whole. In the UK 8 per cent of the population is black ('non-white' sic) compared to London (29 per cent) and the host boroughs at 42 per cent (ODA 2007: 10). Further, ethnic diversity in the five boroughs summarily reflect the UK's multicultural society but is much more a vision for the future of ethnic diversity for many locations outside of east London. In addition to the cultural complexities in the five host boroughs, three of the five score 11 or less on the index of multiple deprivation where 1 is the most deprived and 354 the least deprived. Incumbent with these statistics are the ancillary concerns around employment, education and social exclusion. Power and Mumford's study (2003) of the East End of London describes an area with the highest poverty levels in the capital where many communities relying upon social housing and related services feel disempowered. The traditional identity of an 'East Ender' is also disrupted as the contradictions of diversity 'insiderness' and 'outsiderness' all describe the postmodern condition of the East End. Clearly some communities are more established than others but they are not easily differentiated by traditional views of homogeneity of identity, 'race' or ethnicity, 'English or Britishness', but rather their differences and similarities lie in their experiences of living in this part of London, and living in England as racialised, classed and gendered individuals in social networks. Any legacy impacts or benefits from the London 2012 project will therefore impact neighbourhoods, individuals and communities of interest and cultural affinities in a variegated fashion. On this note the Olympic authorities' consideration of the complex ethnic communities in east London will dictate the long term benefits accrued in this part of the capital.

The Greater London Authority 'Lasting Legacy for London' (LERI 2007) report identifies that the planning of an Olympic legacy should be part of an existing regeneration plan, a plan for urban renewal within the London Borough's hosting the Olympics. With the report identifying that 'Cities assess legacy in their own terms and as an important part of the governance process' (LERI 2007: 10). Whilst articulating a binary division between 'soft' and 'hard' legacy and an understanding that 'hard' legacy is about improved infrastructure and amenity (including a reconfiguration of city spaces), the recognition of what constitutes the measurement of 'soft' legacy is more problematic; problematic in the sense that it is about the recognition of intangibles which might take longer to be measured. What also needs to be evaluated in the long-term is the veracity and validity of the 'Olympic-speak' that underpins the promises of legacy benefits for residents in the east of London.

Local People, Marginalisation and Olympic Progress

Much is made of the capacity of the Olympics to engage and enervate local communities. The impacts of previous Olympic Games have been widely advertised through bidding committees as benefiting local communities (LERI 2007). The LERI's more sober evaluation of these benefits is such that it challenges this view, and in particular the 'legacy' effect for the people of east London. In summary they argue that employment growth is inconclusive and for those in east London who are long term unemployed or 'workless' the message is that there is no evidence of things changing for them in the post-Games period. This advice is also a rider to arguments that there is likely to be an increase in social capital as a result of the fantastic influx of volunteers to the Games 'family'. *There is little evidence of volunteer skills transferring to the post-Games economy* (LERI 2007: 9).

Whilst the semiotics of bidding city images are awash with eager residents, the televisual scrutiny of the Games in situ is almost exclusively locked into the arenas of sporting drama. How the dramas of the 2012 Olympics emerge for the east London communities is yet to be documented however, the invisibility of residents was particularly apparent during the 1968 Mexico Olympics, when protesting and rioting Mexico City displaced shantytown residents who remained invisible and did not sully the harmonious televisual sporting narrative of the Games. Raco (2004: 35) reminds us that:

> The failure to build on the *existing strengths and continuities* of regeneration areas has resulted in many flagship projects and spectacle-based forms of development failing to engage with local communities' needs and aspirations. ... often implicit in such programmes is the need to change 'problem' communities entirely through processes of gentrification and displacement. (Emphasis added)

The final preparations for the smooth running of the Beijing 2008 Olympics has included a further fettering of both political dissidents and also the quelling of protest from people displaced from newly created Olympic territory. There are early signs of acts of displacement and the *decanting* of people out of their home areas in order to create Olympic facilities within London. The erection of the Lea Valley Olympic fence has demarcated Olympic territory into what was previously part of the environment of a range of local communities. Representative of these diverse communities are so called 'Travellers'. As a wider backdrop to the displacement of these communities, Trevor Phillips the Chief Executive of the Commission for Equality and Human Rights has highlighted unsatisfactory London local authority engagement with travelling communities.

The shift in residential experience and specific discussion of the issues of rising real estate prices for the multi-ethnic east London communities are beyond the scope of this chapter to cover in detail but nevertheless remain critical factors in determining the legacy elements of an Olympic Games. These issues will result in significantly reordered urban spaces currently inhabited by local communities. However, what happens in east London and how it is reported to the national and global community is not necessarily the same *story*. Rutheiser's (1996) *Imagineering Atlanta* highlighted that it is possible to offer the outside world a vision of a symbolic city, a mythologised city which 'airbrushes out' an uncomfortable racist past and continual racial fault-lines, and 'celebrates' multiculturalism to deflect attention away from these uncomfortable realities. Rutheiser's imagery of the Olympics as a stage set with elements of perfomativity and spectacle, suggests a suspension of political realities for the duration of the 'Olympic celebration'. Arguably previous Olympic Games have through the effectiveness of image making and 'imagineering' made invisible the political and ethnic fissures which characterise host populations. This has implications for how London 2012 seeks to represent the diverse multi-cultural communities in which the 'Olympic territory' occupies.

Space, 'Race' and Sport

The multicultural history of the east of London has imbued it with racialised markers. These markers have demarcated sections of the city in such a way that communities and locations are symbolised in spaces and places, these are the spaces and places likely to be disrupted by the Olympic development process. Recent work on racialisation has suggested that spaces are contested and their use is encoded by individuals and communities in complementary and divergent ways (Murji and Solomos 2005; van Ingen 2003; Durrheim and Dixon 2001). Lefebvre's (1991: 292) view that the 'illusion of a transparent, 'pure' and neutral space has permeated Western culture' is one of the main reasons offered by van Ingen (2003) for the lack of research in this area. Clearly the mapping of an area by planners and policy makers is but one crude vision of a space that offers little insight into the dynamics of those spaces and the meaning of the spaces and the activities practiced in and around them (Hylton 2008).

There has now been a significant volume of activity in this area in relation to the city (Cross and Keith 1995), urban planning (Thomas 2000) and well-being (Dines et al. 2006) that has explored the ways that people experience and attribute meaning to space in the city, and in sport sociology this work has been complemented by others focused on interpreting how space is structured in relation to the social and cultural practices of communities (Williams 1994; Carrington 1999), racial groups in South Africa (Durrheim and Dixon 2001), gender and sexuality and 'race' (van Ingen 2003) and sports (Andrews 1997). Van Ingen in particular utilises a triad of concepts from Lefebvre (1991) to offer a dynamic insight to how spaces are *perceived, conceived* and *lived*. These ideas present a view of sport that systematically challenges functionalist orthodoxies with respect to how sport can be used to integrate social groups as this dialectical model suggests that our lived spaces (spaces of representation) are instrumental in how we imagine other spaces (conceived spaces) and how we manage our spatial practices (perceived space) so that we may see as formal/ informal bounded spaces for sport and recreation (van Ingen 2003).

The racialisation of spaces is commonly considered in relation to our lived spaces 'black', 'Asian', 'Chinese', 'white' areas (cf. Andrews 1997; Lacy 2004) and we know too little about how spaces are conceived of or imagined by social groups. Further the creation, (re)creation and contestation of public spaces in terms of how our spatial practices structure how we experience sport (passively and actively) is under researched and under examined and makes us doubt that the London 2012 planners see more than simple places and people in making their claims about legacy and community. Increases in the bricks and mortar stock in the five boroughs and not in the wider infrastructure of sport and related areas of social provision makes the unsubstantiated claims of the Olympic authorities to be pure window dressing or the 'Olympic-Speak' that we have already become accustomed to. The necessity for governing bodies of sport to focus on diversity, equality and specifically in relation to this chapter on 'race' sport and the East End it can be demonstrated through research by the Government's sport development body, Sport England who showed for the first time that there are many unmet needs amongst minority ethnic groups in comparison to their white peers and from this it is hard to see how the legacy promise of increased participation is somehow going to affect these structural fractures as a result of London 2012 (Sport England 2000). For instance, a glance at the Sport England Sports Equity Index (2002b) would reveal a hierarchy of participation symptomatic of a public sports development system that reinforces patterns of inclusion and exclusion on the intersecting issues of ethnicity, class, gender and disability (Sport England 2002b). Curiously Sport England's (2000: 6) survey's 'light touch' on the racialised processes causing these outcomes made very little of the one in five respondents who experienced racism. This 'silence' on racism is typical of institutional responses to such issues and even in the midst of such groundbreaking research on sport and ethnicity and the promise of Olympic salvation the hegemonic values and assumptions underpinning public sector sport remain unproblematised and undisturbed.

The ODA rhetoric of monitoring for ethnicity, encouraging partners and reflexivity must contend with the inability of Sport England a much longer constituted public sector sport agency to police itself. In 1999 Sport England's research into its own activities found that minority ethnic communities similar to those in east London (Derby, Leicester and Nottingham) did not have equal access to them. To counter this problem they identified a need for greater coordination of sports opportunities, a need for community groups to work together, and a need for racial equality support for local governing bodies of sport/sports clubs (Wheeler 2000). These are long-term strategies that Olympic authorities must incorporate into their plans if the legacy promises are to succeed. Stark warnings from Carrol (1993) and Horne (1995) and Swinney and Horne (2005) have concluded from their research into public sector sport that there is often a policy implementation gap between the formulation and implementation of race equality strategies. This in itself has implications for the prospects of success in any organisation. Horne in particular developed three classic types of local authority provider and labelled them from the least effective 'gestural' that involved purely internal equality practices around employment; 'reactive' organisations that showed evidence of awareness of service delivery and employment practices that they were prepared to respond to; and finally the least common 'proactive' organisations that actively promoted racial equality and independently addressed discrimination. Documented experiences of sport and recreation organisations' inability to work consistently towards racial equality lead writers and practitioners to look in more detail at the reasons for this lack of success in the provision and service of sport for black people. What is clear in sport for black people in east London is that they have the same chance to win when on the pitch, court or poolside as anyone else but the political, economic and cultural resources available to them are invariably unequal (Jarvie 1991a, 1991b; Hylton/ILAM 1999; Carrington and MacDonald 2008; Spracklen et al. 2006).

Summary

MacClancy (1996) rightly argues that sport and its related activities cannot be understood outside of the power relations that constitute it. The Olympic Delivery Authority (ODA) has the responsibility for developing and building the new venues and infrastructure for the Games upto and beyond 2012. The ODA works in partnership with the London Organising Committee, The Greater London Authority, the Department for Culture Media and Sport, the London Development Agency, the five host boroughs, transport agencies, employment agencies, national unions, the private sector and the voluntary and community sector. They promise to do something in sport that has not happened with any deal of consistency in the past and that is for it to 'reach all communities and segments of the population ... and leave a lasting legacy of equality ...' (ODA 2007: 3). As one of the key agencies for London 2012 the ODA intends to ensure the east London communities are involved in the phase leading up to and post-Games through implementing an equality framework. This framework is planned to ensure the ODA is able to ask searching questions about *what* they build and leave behind; *how* they go about creating buildings and provision; *who* from diverse groups does the work; and *whom* the ODA listens to in making its decisions. In aiming to 'set a new benchmark for equality and diversity practice' (ODA 2007: 5) they must consider the failures of sport in the UK public sector in achieving or even working towards this goal (Horne 1995; Swinney and Horne 2005). Who plays, where they play, who organises, are all outcomes of relations socially constructed and played out in private and public (MacClancy 1996). Here agency and structure meld to the point that it becomes imperceptible how opportunity or constraint lead to decisions and outcomes affecting play and work.

Field (2003) agrees that networks can promote inequality due to their restrictive access to the means of accruing social capital through association. However, sport networks have been seen to operate with a noticeable inability to include others from an ethnically diverse background, thus reinforcing the marginalisation and power differentials black people face in other social arenas. Some connections are clearly more useful than others in terms of their ability to bond across communities and build bridges and open up opportunities. This has become particularly emphasised by the emerging literature on racial exclusions, racism and sport (Lyons 1991; Verma and Darby 1994; Long et al. 2000; Carrington and McDonald 2001; Hylton 2008). The potential for 2012 to break a racialised cycle of inequality and hierarchy of opportunity is highly desirable, if debatable, given that these issues have been part of the sporting landscape for many years. The results of local government sports policies have consistently excluded black people in local communities (Lyons 1991; Sports Council 1994; Verma and Darby 1994; Sport England 2002b). Women and black people in particular have experienced the fall out of local government recruitment and provision (Talbot 1988; Cross and Keith 1993).

The ODA, like the DCMS, has developed a strategy that draws on the discourse of valuing diversity, active communities, partnership and devolution (DCMS/LMU 2001). On many levels the voice of organised black voluntary groups is being courted to provide knowledgeable points of reference for public bodies. Further, the Home Office recognises that policy analysts and policy makers need to consider more fully the structural constraints and power dynamics pressing upon black groups and black participation in society. Where the new Olympic bodies are doing this we must be thankful and wish them every success because an area for concern for the Home Office (2001a) was a need to recognise that there needs to be a 'race'-centred approach to policy, as a 'colour-blind' approach only reinforces racial disadvantage in policy formulation. Otherwise, marginalising 'race' and ethnicity causes inconsistencies and fragmentation in service delivery (Gardiner and Welch 2001). This has been underlined by the emphasis placed upon the importance of working with black communities by the Home Office (2001b) and Race on the Agenda.

References

Abbot, D. (2006) *The Guardian Weekend*, 6 May: 94.

Andrews, D. et al (1997) 'Soccer's Racial Frontier: Sport and the suburbanization of contemporary America', in Armstrong, G. and Giuliannoti, R. (eds) *Entering the Field: New Perspectives on World Football*, Oxford: Berg.

Bramham, P. (2008) 'Sports Policy', in Hylton, K. and Bramham, P. (eds) *Sports Development: Policy Process and Practice*, London: Routledge.

Carrington, B. (1999) 'Cricket, Culture and Identity: An Ethnographic Analysis of the Significance of Sport within Black Communities', in Roseneil, S. and Seymour, J. (eds) *Practising Identities Power and Resistance*, London: Macmillan.

Carrington, B. and McDonald, I. (eds) (2001) '*Race', Sport and British Society*, London: Routledge.

Carrington, B. and McDonald, I. (2008) 'The Politics of "Race" and Sports Policy in the United Kingdom', in Houlihan, B. (ed.) *Sport and Society*, London: Sage.

Carrol, B. (1993) 'Sporting Bodies; Sporting Opportunities', in Brackenridge, C. (ed.) *Body Matters, Leisure Images and Lifestyles*, Eastbourne: LSA Publication 47, 106–14.

Cross, M. and Keith, M. (eds) (1993) *Racism, the City and the State*, London: Routledge.

DCMS/LMU (2002) *Count Me In – The Dimensions of Social Inclusion through Culture and Sport*, London: DCMS/Leeds Metropolitan University.

Dines, N., Cattell, V., Gesler, W. and Curtis, S. (2006) *Public Spaces, Social Relations and Well-Being in East London*, York: Joseph Rowntree Foundation.

Durrheim, K. and Dixon, J. (2001) 'The Role of Place and Metaphor in Racial Exclusion: South Africa's Beaches as Sites of Shifting Racialization', *Ethnic and Racial Studies* 24(3), May: 433–50.

Field, J. (2003) *Social Capital*, London: Routledge.

Gardiner, S. and Welch, R. (2001) 'Sport, Racism and the Limits of "Colour Blind" Law', in Carrington, B. and McDonald, I. (eds) '*Race', Sport and British Society*, London: Routledge.

Home Office (2001a) 'Strengthening the Black and Minority Ethnic Voluntary Sector Infrastructure', www.homeoffice.gov.uk/acu/strng2.html.

Home Office (2001b) 'Strengthening the Black and Minority Ethnic Voluntary Sector Infrastructure', Foreword by Paul Boateng, www.homeoffice.gov. uk/acu/strng1.htm.

Horne, J. (1995), 'Local Authority Black and Ethnic Minority Provision in Scotland, Moray House Institute/Heriot-Watt University', in Talbot, M. and Fleming, S. (eds), *Sports Policy* (Eastbourne: LSA Publication 95).

Hylton, K. (2008) '*Race' and Sport: Critical Race Theory*, London: Routledge.

Hylton, K/ILAM. (1999) 'Where are the Black Leisure Managers?', *Leisure Manager*, September.

Jarvie, G. (1991a) *Sport, Racism and Ethnicity*, London: Falmer Press.

Jarvie, G. (1991b) 'There Ain't No Problem Here?', *Sport and Leisure* November/December: 20–21.

Jenkins, S. (2008) 'The Olympics is a Festival of Politics Worth Every Penny to a Fascist State', *The Guardian* 15 February: 36.

Lacy, K. (2004) 'Black spaces, Black Places: Strategic Assimilation and Identity Construction in Middle-class Suburbia', *Ethnic and Racial Studies* 27(6): 908–30.

Lefebvre, H. (1991) *The Production of Space*, Oxford: Blackwell.

LERI (2007) *A Lasting Legacy for London? Assessing the Legacy of the Olympic Games and Paralympic Games*, London: London Assembly.

Long, J., Hylton, K., Dart, J. and Welch, M. (2000) *Part of the Game? An eExamination of Racism in Grass Roots Football*, London: Kick It Out.

Lyons, A. (1991) 'The Racial Equality Plan, Sport and Leisure', November/December:12.

MacClancy, J. (ed.) (1996) *Sport, Identity and Ethnicity*, Oxford: Berg.

Murji, K. and Solomos, J. (2005) Racialization: Studies in Theory and Practice, Oxford: Oxford University Press.

ODA (2007) *Equality and Diversity Strategy*, London: Olympic Delivery Authority.

Raco, M. (2004) 'Whose Gold Rush? The Social Legacy of a London Olympics', in Vigor, A., Mean, M. and Tims, C. (eds), *After the Gold Rush: A Sustainable Olympics for London*, London: IPPR/Demos.

Polley, M. (1998) *Moving the Goalposts: A History of Sport and Society Since 1945*, London: Routledge.

Power, A. and Mumford, K. (2003) *East Enders : Family and Community in East London*, Bristol: The Policy Press.

Ruitheser, C. (1996) *Imagineering Atlanta: The Politics of Place in the City of Dreams*, New York: Verso.

Sport England (2000) *Sports Participation and Ethnicity in England: National Survey 1999/2000*, London: Sport England.

Sport England (2002a) *Sports Equity Index for Regular Participation*, London: Sport England.

Sport England (2002b) 'Active Communities Experimental Projects', http://www.sportdevelopment.org.uk/html/activecommunitiesintro.html, London: Sport England.

Sports Council (1994) *Black and Ethnic Minorities and Sport: Policy Objectives*, London: Sports Council, London, Sports Council.

Spracklen, K., Hylton, K. and Long, J. (2006) 'Managing and Monitoring Equality and Diversity', *UK Sport, Journal of Sport and Social Issues* 30(3) August: 289–305.

Swinney, A. and Horne, J. (2005) 'Race Equality and Leisure Policy: Discourses in Scottish Local Authorities', *Leisure Studies* 24(3) July: 271–89.

Talbot, M. (1988) 'Their Own Worst Enemy?', in Wimbush, E. and Talbot, M. (eds) (1988) *Relative Freedoms: Women and Leisure*, Milton Keynes: Open University Press.

Thomas, H. (2000) *Race and Planning: The UK Experience*, London: UCL Press.

Van Ingen, C. (2003) 'Geographies of Gender, Sexuality and Race: Reframing the Focus on Space in Sport Sociology', *International Review for the Sociology of Sport* 38(2): 201–16.

Verma, G.K. and Darby, J. (1994) *Winners and Losers: Ethnic Minorities in Sport and Recreation*, London: Falmer Press.

Whannel, G. (1992) *Fields in Vision: Television Sport and Cultural Transformation*, London: Routledge.

Wheeler, J. (2000) *Leicester Racial Equality and Sport Project Preparation Report*, Leicester: Leicester City Council.

Williams, J. (1994) 'Rangers is a Black Club', in Giuliannoti, R. and Williams, J. (eds) *Game without Frontiers: Football, Identity and Modernity*, Aldersho: Arena Publications.

Zirin, D. (2007) *Welcome to the Terrordome: The Pain, Politics, and Promise of Sports*, Chicago: Haymarket Books.

Chapter 14

London 2012 – Winning the Olympic 'Green' Medal

Paul Toyne

Introduction

Today the Olympic Games are intrinsically linked to the need to be 'green'/ sustainable. This means that throughout its development, the running of the event and its legacy (how what it leaves behind operates and sustains itself), the Games will seek to have limited negative environmental and social impacts, and wherever possible positive impacts. The Olympic Games cannot afford to be anything other than a force for good, simply because of its huge impacts in terms of changes to local infrastructure and the global media frenzy that watches the construction of the Olympic site, the running of the Games and what happens after the Games has left. This media attention focuses on all aspects of a host nation's behaviour, as seen in the run up to the Beijing Olympics, particularly the controversy surrounding China's human rights record. The Olympics has been viewed as both a force for change and a potential reason for repression.[1]

This chapter explores the development of the 'Green' Olympic Games, and describes the approach and aspirations for London 2012. It briefly explores past Olympic Games for their approach to sustainability, reviews the current policy framework for the London 2012 Games and offers a personal insight into the potential outcomes for which the 2012 Games may be judged. In this chapter emphasis is placed on the activities surrounding the hosting and running of the Olympic Games in London, however many sporting competitions will occur outside of London, for example, sailing at Weymouth and Portland, rowing at Eton Dorney and BMX cycling at Weald Country Park, Essex. Much of the discussion and conclusions are general and can also be applied to these sites. Lastly, where relevant I have provided a reference to supporting evidence in the form of a http web address.

---

1   http://news.bbc.co.uk/1/hi/world/asia-pacific/7325754.stm;http://www.amnesty. org/en/news-and-updates/report/what-human-rights-legacy-beijing-olympics-2008 0401; accessed 24 May 2008.

Origins of the Olympic 'Green' Movement and How the IOC formalised Policy around the Environment

Origins of the Green Olympics

The International Olympic Committee (IOC) did not formally include the environment or sustainability as part of their selection criteria until the competition for the 1996 Games, won by Atlanta in the USA. Prior to that, nearly all Games by their sheer scale have considered how to manage their impact. For example, host cities such as Rome (1960) and Montreal (1976) implemented changes to their urban transport systems that reduced car use and provided an improvement in air quality. The Tokyo Games in 1964 provided Japan with an opportunity to tackle its capital's environmental problems. These problems included water quality, waste disposal, air pollution, industrial diseases and a poor public transport system caused by rapid post-war reconstruction and economic growth at the expense of public health. The Tokyo authorities decided to use the Games to create change for the whole city, not just the city sites that would be used. That meant improved water and waste-water management including three new sewage treatment systems, the clean up of the polluted Sumida River, and improved refuse disposal and street cleaning. The most notable improvement was the introduction of the *shinkansen* high-speed bullet-train, running between Tokyo and Osaka, which has subsequently been introduced throughout Japan, and which a generation later was echoed in the TGV and the other high-speed rail networks within Europe. The decade after the 1964 Games saw a number of similar environmental improvements in all Japan's cities, whose end results included measurable improvements in air and water quality, and in public health.

The environmental impacts of past Olympic Games has caused concern and created a backlash that has influenced IOC thinking. A key turning point was the negative environmental legacy of the 1992 Winter Olympics held at Albertville, Canada. The bid had proposed an ambitious programme linking together infrastructure at 13 small sites across a large area of relatively unsettled natural landscape. A great deal of road construction as well as the building of a new hotel and competition facilities was required. Many heavily forested areas were cut down to clear the ground for the building of the new infrastructure, and without much concern for the local biodiversity. The impacts were considered an environmental disaster by green groups and local inhabitants alike. Clearly that kind of legacy needs to be avoided, and to safeguard against these threats the IOC started to formalise an approach.

Formalising the 'Green' Olympics

During the 1990s, the IOC formally adopted an environmental position. It was largely drawn from the outcomes of the 1992 United Nations Conference on Environment and Development in Río de Janeiro, namely Agenda 21. Agenda 21 describes the concept of sustainable development at the local/ community level. The concept of 'sustainable development' became part of the global agenda of the United Nations. The IOC responded by debating how to adopt this concept for the Games. The outcome of the discussions at a meeting in Paris in late 1994 was the establishment of an IOC Commission on Sport and the Environment. This was tasked by the IOC with holding biennial conferences on the issue. As a result, in 1995, the environment joined sport and culture to make up the 'three pillars' of the Olympic Charter. The current Charter includes amongst the mission and role of the IOC item 13 of 18:

> To encourage and support a responsible concern for environmental issues, to promote sustainable development in sport and to require that the Olympic Games are held accordingly. (IOC 2004: 12)

Building on the 1995 statement the IOC, in 1999, published a fully itemised Olympic Games Agenda 21, whose principles were followed by the Sydney Games. Agenda 21 offers a global understanding of the environment. It understands the provision of air, water, food and recreational space of sufficient quality to promote health and well-being as basic human rights, and recognises that in order to achieve this fundamental provision, global issues have to be addressed. In the words of the IOC's own Agenda 21 document,

> The starting point of sustainable development is the idea that the long-term preservation of our environment, our habitat as well as its biodiversity and natural resources ... will only be possible if combined simultaneously with economic, social and political development particularly geared to the benefit of the poorest members of society ... in view of its universal nature, the Olympic movement accepts that it has a special responsibility to share in the implementation of this concept of sustainable development. (IOC 1999: 17)

The IOC's Agenda 21 provides a framework for potential hosts of the Games to consider how their bid will deliver to the aspirations of the Olympic movement.

The Sydney Games in 2000 sought the 'green' label and collaborated with environmental NGOs to help achieve it. It was the first Games to be audited by Greenpeace, who issued a positive report. The following Games in Athens was audited by Greenpeace and the World Wildlife Fund (WWF), according to the Sydney benchmark, and scored poorly. . Of interest is the low scoring of carbon related management in Athens after the promising actions taken in Sydney.

The future environmental impact of the Games in Beijing and London will be judged according to the Sydney benchmark, and therefore cooperation with NGOs (in information sharing, planning and execution as well as establishing

Table 14.1   Sustainability scorecard of the last four Olympic Games

	Barcelona 1992	Atlanta 1996	Sydney 2000	Athens 2004
Guidelines drawn up with NGOs	0	0	2	2
Clean-up and return of waste land to social and economic use	1	1	2	1
Renewable energy use	0	1	2	0
Water use and recycling	1	0	2	1
Waste management and recycling	1	1	2	1
Transport infrastructure and 'green' fuel	1	1	1	1
Biodiversity maintenance	1	0	2	0
Carbon: event footprint management	0	0	1	1
Carbon: visitor footprint management	0	0	0	0
Sourcing: sustainability	0	0	2	1
Sourcing: fair trade	0	0	0	0

*Source*s: Adapted from the Sydney report card (Greenpeace 2000) and Greenpeace's and World Wildlife Fund's joint scoring of the Athen's Games (WWF 2004).

the principles of construction, raw materials procurement, etc.) will be vital. In considering this the London 2012 Organising Committee for the Olympic Games (LOCOG) has set up stakeholder panels and engagement groups that deal with specific issues, for example, procurement. The next section looks at the London 2012 Games and reviews their potential to deliver a sustainable Olympics.

2012 London Olympics – Vision, Governance, Policy Frameworks and Legacy

Vision of London 2012

London won the 2012 Olympic and Paralympic Games with a vision 'to stage inspirational Games that capture the imagination of young people around the world and leave a lasting legacy'. Other important factors in deciding London's selection were the desire to use the Games as a catalyst to stimulate the regeneration of a 500-acre site in East London, and its ability to promote and inspire future generations of sportsmen. The East London site, the Olympic Park, is located at the heart of the lower Lea Valley, just four miles north from Tower Bridge and close to Stratford.

Governance

Tasked with delivering this 'vision' is a wide array of stakeholders, but the principal accountability lies with two bodies – LOCOG and the Olympic Delivery Authority (ODA). LOCOG will organise, publicise and stage the 2012 Games. It will also report directly to the International Olympic Committee on London 2012; whereas the ODA is the delivery body responsible for creating the infrastructure for the Olympic and Paralympic Games. In addition, it undertakes some operational work whilst the Games are underway, such as the provision of transport. The ODA also '… want London 2012 to be the first 'sustainable' Games, setting new standards for major events'.[2]

The London Sustainable Development Commission, in partnership with the national Sustainable Development Commission and equivalent regional structures, has established an independent assurance function – a watchdog for the Games – The Commission for a Sustainable London 2012. It was established in 2007 and its remit is to assess annual progress against the overall objectives of each of the main bodies LOCOG, the ODA and official stakeholders. It will also verify every two years – to take into account evolving policies, standards, best practices and technology – each organisation's actions against specific objectives, key performance indicators and targets.[3]

Whilst The Commission for a Sustainable London 2012 provides the external governance, internal decision-making is governed by an auditing structure that comprises of the Olympic Board together with the Boards of Stakeholder organisations. They will ensure the delivery against these sustainability objectives through the following measures – integrating sustainability principles into the day-to-day management of LOCOG and the ODA and by working closely with the host London Boroughs, the GLA Group, nations and regions, central Government, British Olympic Authority, British Paralympics Authority, sports authorities and the International Olympic Committee (see http://www.cslondon.org/). The 2012 Olympic and Paralympic Games have a vision and have the governance set up to check deliver against that vision, but what exactly are the Games hoping to achieve in the area of sustainability?

---

2   http://www.london2012.com/plans/sustainability/index.php; accessed 24 May 2008.
3   http://www.londonsdc.org/discover_more/lsdc/. accessed 24 May 2008.

Policy Framework

To deliver the 'sustainability' vision the London 2012 Organising Committee has developed a sustainability policy and accompanying plan, which set out the concept of One Planet Living and actions to achieve it. One Planet Living is a term developed by WWF and Bioregional in the UK whereby our living requirements are within the ecological limits of the planet – the one planet Earth that we have – rather than the present consumption behaviour in western Europe and North America which requires three planets (World Wildlife Fund 2004).

The policy sets out the following legacy goals:

- make the UK a world-leading sporting nation;
- transform the heart of east London;
- inspire a new generation of young people to take part in local volunteering, cultural and physical activity;
- make the Olympic Park a blueprint for sustainable living; and
- demonstrate the UK is a creative, inclusive and welcoming place to live in, visit and for business.[4]

It focuses on five headline themes: climate change, waste, biodiversity, inclusion and healthy living. These themes were chosen because they represent areas where the organisers believe that the 2012 Games can make the biggest impact and achieve the most beneficial outcomes.

Climate change   Climate change is a global issue and the organisers see the Games providing a platform for demonstrating long-term solutions in terms of energy and water resource management, infrastructure development, transport, local food production and carbon offsetting. The aims are to minimise the environmental footprint and carbon emissions of the Games and legacy development, notably by optimising energy efficiency and energy demand through the use of low carbon and renewable energy sources.

Waste   The organiser's aim is for the construction of the Olympic site to be a catalyst for a new waste management infrastructure in East London and other regional venues, and for the construction of all the facilities to demonstrate exemplary resource management practices. During the demolition and construction phase companies will need to minimise waste at source, divert construction waste wherever feasible and all Games-time waste away from landfill, and promote the waste hierarchy of 'reduce, reuse, recycle' to facilitate long-term individual behavioural change.

---

4   http://www.london2012.com/documents/locog-publications/london-2012-sustainability-policy.pdf, accessed 15 May 2008.

Biodiversity   As well as the economic regeneration of the area, the natural river system of the Lower Lea Valley and its surrounding habitats will be restored. This will involve the dredging of canals, widening rivers and the creation of three nectars of wetlands. The restoration will involve the planting of native species such as oak and hazel to create a wildlife haven in East London. These aims are entirely achievable, and the success of the Barnes wetland reserve provides a working example of a recent habitat restoration success in West London.

Inclusion   The London 2012 Games seek to promote access, celebrate diversity, and facilitate the physical, economic and social regeneration of the Lower Lea Valley and surrounding communities. This will be supported by the provision of new infrastructure and facilities and the creation of employment, training and education opportunities. Communities across the rest of London and the UK will be encouraged to identify and take full advantage of direct and indirect opportunities arising from the Games.

Healthy Living   The organisers will use the Games as a springboard for inspiring people across the country to take up sport and develop active, healthy and sustainable lifestyles.

2012 Construction Commitments

A key aspect of delivering sustainable Games will be ensuring that the construction of the Games' infrastructure is sustainable. With this goal in mind in 2006 the UK government signed up to a set of construction commitments designed to deliver the vision of the London 2012 Games. The commitments were developed with the construction industry with the aim that, if implemented, they would demonstrate the very best in British construction practices using the Olympics as a live example. The '2012 Construction Commitments' cover six key areas of the construction process and are designed to promote collaborative working and ensure the successful delivery of the Games infrastructure, buildings and subsequent legacy. To this end they reinforce and underpin the Olympic Delivery Authority's (ODA) procurement policies and those appointed as the delivery partner to work with the ODA and manage the programme to build the Olympic park are required to adhere to them.

   The Commitments were developed by the Strategic Forum for Construction's 2012 Task Group in conjunction with the Department of Culture, Media and Sport and the Department of Trade and Industry. Areas covered include:

- *Client leadership* – client leadership is vital to the success of any project and enables the construction industry to perform at its best. Eight aspects are covered in this section ranging from client attitudes to procurement and commitments to best practice.

- *Procurement and Integration* – a successful procurement policy requires ethical sourcing, enables best value to be achieved and encourages the early involvement of the supply chain. An integrated project team works together to achieve the best possible solution in terms of design, buildability, environmental performance and sustainable development – eight aspects are covered that included risk identification and project team responsibilities;
- *Design* – the design should be creative, imaginative, sustainable and capable of meeting delivery objectives. Quality in design and construction utilising the best of modern methods will ensure that the Olympic sites meet the civic needs of all stakeholders, both functionally and architecturally, for 2012 and beyond. Six aspects are covered including IT based collaborative tools and exploring the use of prefabrication techniques;
- *Sustainability* – sustainability lies at the heart of the delivery of the Games. A sustainable approach will bring full and lasting environmental, social and economic benefits through regeneration and legacy. Seven aspects are covered that include developing policy in accordance with the One Planet Olympics ideals and setting targets on sustainability issues;
- *Commitment to People* – valuing people leads to a more productive and engaged workforce, facilitates recruitment and retention of staff and engages local communities positively in construction projects. Eights aspects are covered including commitments to local employment, community engagement and training for staff; Health and Safety – Health and safety is integral to the success of any project, from design and construction to subsequent operation and maintenance. Six aspects are described that cover commitments to incident and injury free and occupational health.[5]

The Commitments were the result of detailed discussions with a wide range of stakeholders representing all parts of the construction supply chain and represent a partnership and collaborative working between industry, Government and Olympic organisations. So far the background, the policy intent and some of the issues around delivering a sustainable Games have been described. The theory has been explained but what of the reality? This next section provides a more personal opinion of what to expect.

---

5   http://www.strategicforum.org.uk/pdf/2012ConCom.pdf. accessed 19 May 2008.

What Can We Expect London 2012 to Deliver?

The London 2012 Games could be a force for good and create change around its five key themes of climate change, waste, biodiversity, inclusion and healthy living. Its 'green' success will depend on a number of factors – how influential it can be in shaping and informing national policy; whether it will be a catalyst for innovation that delivers use closer to a low waste and low carbon economy; and, lastly, the extent to which it demonstrates the capacity to build a more inclusive society. Below I consider some of these areas and pose questions that can only be answered with the progress of time.

Contribution to the National Policy Debate

London 2012 must be used as an opportunity to consider how its objectives should be drivers for the need for nationwide policy reform. Why? Scarcity of resources and increasing problems related to environmental and social issues mean that we are not delivering at the pace required to address the problems. Let us consider healthy living: What is in place to transform the UK population from an ageing, obese population with unsustainable consumption patterns? Can the Games transform the population into considering a healthy lifestyle with exercise and diet? Probably not, but it can be used to generate best practice and lessons that could be applied to other regions and at a national level. This is an important objective as the UK, like most of Europe and North America, is suffering from an obesity epidemic, affecting all age groups and resulting in other health problems such as diabetes – being more active and participating in sport is part of the solution. The challenge will be to consider how to use London 2012 to engage with the public, raise awareness and actually encourage them to change their behaviours to diet and exercise. For this to happen what else needs to be in place? What access to resources – literature, venues, equipment and support will people need?

Similar questions can be posed concerning the other themes of the London 2012 Games, for example, waste and carbon management. The construction of the infrastructure of the Games will provide an excellent opportunity for construction companies and their supply chains to demonstrate new ways of working and feed these lessons back into their operations, creating a business transformation in how they deal with waste and carbon. But what supporting legislation and enabling conditions are required to ensure that activities around the Olympics are not just one-off initiatives but do actually have the intended impact of creating transformations in the market place? The UK Government has set the draft target of halving construction waste to landfill by 2012, within the construction lifetime of the Games. If the Games-related construction projects are successful in achieving this goal, the lessons learnt can be implemented across the UK construction sector as a whole. That would be a powerful and much needed step-change.

Similarly, the current national policy framework requires that all homes built in 2016 and all non-domestic dwellings built in 2019 are zero carbon. Pushing to develop the Games infrastructure with as lower carbon footprint as possible could create an extremely important first step in meeting these targets. It would also show how the Olympic sustainability movement has moved on from the Sydney Games and recognised the significant public and political concern over climate change. What could this mean in practice? Aside from construction, will we see event management and the visitor carbon footprint being managed to promote a low carbon Games using minimal amounts of energy and resources? What part will hoteliers, transport and catering companies play?

One aspect that may be hugely beneficial for the push on sustainability is scale (size and time of the development), because if actions can be made economically – as well as socially and environmentally – viable, then there is the possibility of raising the bar in terms of subsequent performance in other developments. A flip side maybe that the lessons learnt may not translate into smaller developments and only be relevant to large scale projects and events.

Innovation

Transformation of business and public behaviour to meet the requirements of One Planet Living will require innovation. Without innovation it will simply not happen. So the challenge here will be how to stimulate innovation. Here the vision, policies and objectives for the London 2012 Games provide a catalyst to stimulate thinking and generate ideas. Innovation can also come from collaboration and some unlikely partnerships that may result from those set up around the Games. LOCOG and the ODA are developing active partnerships with non-Governmental organisations, community groups, businesses, professional bodies and academia to help leverage the opportunities provided by the Games and to utilise the power of the Olympic brand to mobilise enthusiasm and maximise benefits in a number of areas, for example, procuring goods, services and sponsorship sustainably with an emphasis on supplier diversity, fair employment and environmental attributes, as well as other social and ethical criteria as appropriate. Time will tell if it leads to innovation that creates a positive step change in these areas.

Employment, the Skills Agenda and Technology

Previous Games have led to the implementation of new technology for example in Tokyo as mentioned at the start of this chapter; also in the regeneration of Barcelona and its improvements in the control of river pollution, and waste water management; and in Atlanta where the production of an event allowed business to experiment in clean technologies such as solar panels and low-energy lighting. The Sydney Games set targets on energy efficiency and the use of sustainable materials for buildings and as a result industry innovated to meet those requirements.

London 2012 should be no different, and companies will be applying new methods of working, and applying technology in the pursuit of a low carbon stadium and accommodation. New technology will also be employed in the running and communicating of the Games, visitors to the Games will need to stay in accommodation and be provided with other services, like catering, that meet the one planet living requirements. The challenge will be to ensure that all these goods and services meet sustainability criteria outlined by the ODA green procurement guidelines, and that there is the technical support to ensure it works and can be maintained without any problems, not just for the Games but after them. Can the London 2012 Games demonstrate its positive social force by addressing poverty reduction through creating opportunities for producers and workers who have been economically disadvantaged or marginalized by the conventional Olympic procurement system? Could it be the first Games to achieve Fairtrade status?

The True Legacy of the Games – What Can be Expected?

It is often forgotten or little mentioned that economic sustainability is an important component of sustainability. Will there be an economic benefit from hosting the Games? If so, what will it amount to? If not, will there be other benefits that compensate and make the whole event worthwhile. Critics have suggested that most Olympics are expensive to run and result in debt to host nations; this is certainly true if you look at past Games such as Montreal (1976). The UK government's own Strategy Unit came to the conclusion that we should not bid to host the Games. This advice was dismissed. Why? Presumably because there are other factors to consider – the feel good factor to the UK public, the global media attention promoting Great Britain. But these will wane over time.

So what will be the long-term legacies? Hopefully, the regeneration of the Olympic site into a sustainable community, which offers a community access to local employment, education and a quality of life that promotes a healthy sustainable lifestyle. If this can be achieved and sustained then it should provide a blueprint for transforming other parts of Britain. In many ways it is an experiment and there are many risks that may result in the legacy not being delivered. One of the many risks will be the lack of investment to provide economic opportunities for the new community. Without that investment manifesting itself as enterprise, providing work to the community it will fail to function as intended.

So what legacy is likely? The upskilling and training opportunities within the construction sectors supply chain and the trailing of new technological innovations will happen. For this to be a sustained legacy it will need to be employed elsewhere and the policy drivers of building zero-carbon homes and non-domestic buildings should ensure that this happens. There will be an employment boom for construction workers. It is suggested that more than 9,300 people will be directly employed in the Games construction when activity peaks in 2010 with many more employed indirectly.[6] Where will these people come from and how will they be employed after the Olympics? A worthwhile legacy will be the ability for the social disadvantaged in the local communities where the Games take place to benefit from sustained employment, thus breaking the cycle of unemployment within families.

Smaller, less talked about issues surrounding the London Games may be where the legacy has the strongest opportunity to be delivered. Will both public and private procurement be changed for the future, incorporating measurable sustainability evidence from suppliers as a criterion for their selection? Will the concept of supplier diversity live on after the Games? Demonstrating you are a responsible employer and procuring your goods and services locally, will go a long way to meet the aims of One Planet Living, regardless of whether you are a large scale communication company or a niche boutique hotelier. Ultimately, whether the Games are a green success or not will come down to the judgement of the NGO community and the Games' performance benchmarked against the Sydney Games. There have been enough pointers of what London 2012 should do, ranging from Fairtrade status, to being a low carbon Games and offering the Olympic tourist an opportunity to trial One Planet Living, at least for the duration of their visit.

References

Amnesty International (2008) 'People's Republic of China The Olympics Countdown – Crackdown on Activists Threatens Olympics Legacy', London: Amnesty International ASA 17/050/2008, http://www.amnesty.org/en/library/asset/HSA17.

Greenpeace (2000) 'How Green the Games? Greenpeace's Environmental Assessment of the Sydney 2000 Olympics', Greenpeace International and Greenpeace Australia Pacific, http://www.greenpeace.org.au/archives/olympics/watchdog.html.

International Olympic Committee (1999) 'Olympic Movement's Agenda 21: Sport for Sustainable Development', Lausanne: IOC Sport and Environment Commission.

International Olympic Committee (2004) *Olympic Charter*, Lausanne: IOC.

World Wildlife Fund (2004) 'One Planet Living', http://www.oneplanetliving.org.

---

6   http://www.citb.co.uk/news/whatsinthenews/20060605-csn.asp, accessed 15 May 2008.

Chapter 15

Technology, Space and the Paralympic Athlete

Allan Edwards, Otto J. Schantz and Keith Gilbert

... all I need is a pair of wheels.

Rick Hansen (Hansen and Taylor 1987, 179)

Introduction

Our physical space defines us in the world and influences the perceptions which other people may have of us. What happens therefore, when the physical space colonised by some members of society is not similar to the physical space taken up by a majority of the 'normal' population?

It is estimated that somewhere near 300 million people worldwide occupy what could be termed a 'disabled body space'. Some of these disabled people often retreat into a world of helplessness and pity, while others go out and occupy their physical space in the community through Paralympic sport participation. On the journey to increase their self esteem, success and ultimate self satisfaction many of these Paralympic sport participants have the first hurdle of wheeling, stepping, crawling or being carried through the space that is the front door of their home. Once out into the community they take up and develop strategies to manage the community space around them. Who then are these Paralympic athletes who roll, limp, stagger and swagger through our community space? Do they perceive themselves as being anybody different and are they aware that the bodily space which they take up is different from the space taken up by the non disabled person? This chapter attempts to make sense of the Paralympic athlete, the disabled body and its 'struggles over the use of space' (Bale and Vertinsky 2004). It reviews the history of the Paralympic movement, and discusses the notion of the body and the disabled body and their relationship to space in the Paralympic context. In short, this chapter asks more questions than it answers as it is the first of its genre from which hopefully more research will be forthcoming. What follows is an historical review of the Paralympic movement.

A Brief Introduction to the Paralympic Movement

In July 1948, when the Games of the XIVth Olympiad opened in London, the neurosurgeon Ludwig Guttmann organised at Stoke Mandeville hospital in England a small sports competition for 16 World War II veterans with spinal cord injuries. His vision was that 'one day the Stoke Mandeville Games would achieve world fame as the disabled men and women's equivalent of the Olympic Games' (Guttmann 1994, 24). This contest grew to become the second largest multi-sports event in the world. Despite the fact, that the Paralympic movement is a rather recent sport phenomena compared to other sports movements, it has undergone tremendous changes in the last 20 years. These developments have run in parallel with the societal treatment of people with disabilities. Historically, there have been sports competitions for people with different disabilities since the end of the nineteenth century. However, competitions for people with physical disabilities often resembled 'freak' shows rather than serious sporting events (Schantz 2006). In point of fact the first disability groups to organise sport activities were the people with sensorial disabilities (visual impairments and deafness). For long time physical activities for people with disabilities were merely seen as a means of rehabilitation and adapted physical activities had been part of the medical field.

The sport movement for people with disabilities has grown quickly. In Rome in 1960, 400 athletes from 23 nations participated in the first Paralympic Games. Forty years later in 2000 at the eleventh edition of these Games in Sydney, there were almost ten times more (3.824) and coming from 122 countries (plus a delegation from East Timor). In Athens there were over 4,000 athletes. It is predicted that in London 2012 there will be close to 6,000 athletes.

The modern disabled sport movement owes much to Sir Ludwig Guttmann's efforts as founder of the British National Unit for Paraplegics in Stoke Mandeville. In his daily contact with veterans with injured spines, Guttmann noted the benefits of sport activities in the improvement of these veterans psyche and social life. As mentioned previously Guttmann organised his Stoke Mandeville Games to coincide with the 14th Olympic Games in London 1948. Four years later he founded the International Stoke Mandeville Games Federation (ISMGF) which later came to be known as the International Stoke Mandeville Wheelchair Sport Federation for wheelchair athletes.

In 1960 in Rome, one of Guttmann's dreams came true: the ties between Olympic Games and International Stoke Mandeville Games become stronger with the two events taking place one week apart in the same city. The Rome Games are considered to be the first Paralympic Games, even though they were exclusively reserved to wheelchair athletes. Progressively these Games opened up to the athletes with amputation, and visual disabilities (Toronto 1976), with cerebral palsies (Arnhem 1980) and to the category 'les autres', the 'other' people with disabilities (Stoke Mandeville 1984). The disabled sport movement gradually grew in prominence. The founding of international sports federations (IOSDs) in 1976 was the first attempt to create organisations gathering all athletes with disabilities under distinct umbrellas of organisation. Initially this representation was limited to the sportswomen and –men with amputations, skiers with disabilities and the category 'les autres' (the others). In 1983 the International Coordinating Committee (ICC) was formed to coordinate efforts in organising athletes with disabilities. The committee had no judicial authority or statutes and did not have the mandate to represent sport for people with disabilities at international authorities such as the IOC or UNESCO.

Tired of disputes between the different federations and anxious to be able to participate in decisions at the international level, the national disability federations requested during a Seminar in Arnhem in 1987 that a federation be created to represent and provide overall control of all the different types of disabilities. The International Paralympic Committee (IPC) was founded on 22 September 1989 as an international non-profit organisation run by 162 National Paralympic Committees (NPCs) from five regions and four disability specific international sports federations (IOSDs).

Howe indicated:

> Since 1988 the major event of contemporary Paralympic sport – the Paralympic Games – has gone from being a pastime enjoyed by the performers to a spectacle that has attracted increasing media attention…the Games receive a significant amount of media coverage, especially bearing in mind that little media attention is paid to sport for the disabled in between the quadrennial Games. (Howe 2006, 206)

At present, the Paralympics is the second largest multi sport event in the World behind the 'traditional' Olympic Games. However, studies have shown that media coverage is still substantially less than the Olympic Games (Schantz and Gilbert 2001; Schell and Rodriguez 2001). There is a kind of philosophy guiding the Paralympics which is that athletes with disabilities have an equal opportunity to pursue their goals in sport as the able bodied athlete. Paralympics represents a commitment to excellence that allows elite athletes with disabilities to achieve these goals (According to the 'official' etymological interpretation of the IPC, Paralympics means parallel to and associated with the Olympics). The notion of the disabled body and its relationship to space however has not been attempted before and in order to understand the disabled body we have taken a closer look at the 'normal body' and its interactions with sporting space.

Space and the Technological Body

The body as we understand it whether in the context of disability or normality
is changing. From the outset it must be stated that there is a geographical
and biological connection between the body, whether it be disabled or not,
and space. However, there are members of our society who choose to see
the disabled physical space which occupies community geographical space
in specific ways. We categorise these beliefs concerning the disabled as (a)
interpersonal (invisibility, courtesy); (b) institutional (systematic, systemic); (c)
societal (everyday, cultural).

Interpersonal disabled attitudes are a reflection of varying degrees of
dislike from individuals or those that perceive disability differences as a basis
for engagement or entitlement. It refers to people that openly discriminate
against another based on perceived inferiority based upon ability to perform
normal functions. This polite form of disability sentiment uses coded language
on a surface level to signify difference. Institutional disability attitudes go
way beyond the individual or interpersonal levels in their scope, style, and
impact. It pertains particularly to the intent (systematic) or effect (systemic)
of excluding or denying someone because of who they are, how they live, and
what they look like. Societal disability attitudes occur through either everyday
or cultural interaction patterns where people often unknowingly perpetuate a
'disabled social order'.

Biological and Geographical Space

Western conceptions of geographic space and the body, arising from new
projections of proportion and symmetry, are witnessed in contemporary
aspirations of the complex mapping of the body. This of course is a much
more complex task when attempting to map the disabled or Paralympic
body. In contemporary examples, the projects such as the human genome, or
neurological mapping of the brain and its functions aim to clarify the body's
tendencies, to eliminate possible imperfections and mutations. How does this
mapping support the body which already had imperfections and mutations?
In such projects, we see a particular understanding of an informational code
that provides a systematic basis for the correct understanding of the body and
its possible forms. The subsequent creation and recreation of other bodies
provokes the challenge of thinking the body anew, or as will be discussed,
rethinking thought as related to thinking through the body, of the impossibility
of thought outside the body, as a necessary departure when considering new
bodies of a post-human world and where they fit into the new dimensions of
space. The genome map serves as a project to solve the puzzle of the body,
charting its territory and providing answers for the above question. By charting
biological space, the vast research community surrounding the genome project
seeks to provide an increasingly rigid understanding of the body's structure

and development. However, at no time does it look into aspects of the less than perfect body. This connection with the Paralympic body could serve as an important epilogue to the Western conquest of geographic space and the disabled persons use of the space. However, there is much more to the relationship between the disabled body and post-humanism.

Community attitudes toward difference are hopefully changing. For example, in 2003 the World Transhumanist Association hosted a 'transvision' conference to explore the prospects of a post-human world. The conference explored a range of topics. Speakers supported the notion of cloning and genetically engineering human beings; human-animal chimera; human-machine interface; and the creation of super-intelligent machines, among others. Transhumanists want to attain immortality through advances in technology, including the prospect of embodying consciousness in machine. This form of embodiment has already occurred in the Paralympic context, where already athletes are utilising space in different ways than previously used. Athletes use the machine as a method to throw, run, wheel, swim and jump further which argues for the embodiment of 'man and machine' as a viable method of performance enhancement.

In other words, the body as cultural construct is no longer a mere biological given, but a contested site for inscribed meanings and readings of identity, class, gender, race, and state control. The post-human is, to Hayles (1999, 23) 'a point of view' that 'configures human being so that it can be seamlessly articulated with intelligent machines' This articulation has enabled disabled athletes to move into spaces which they would never have been welcome or suited to in the past. In other words, 'life spaces' have opened up to everyone including the severely disabled and sporting spaces are no exception to this rule. Advances in sports technology and its relationship to the disabled body has therefore been responsible for increased movement through common and sports space by the disabled athlete. For many these advances have been life changing and signify the freedom of athletes to move between and into sport spaces that were previously off limits to them.

The interesting work by Hardt and Negri (2000) argues that the condition they call Empire is now what Katherine Hayles (1999, 22) calls the 'post-human', signifying it is no longer possible to imagine daily operations that are not surrounded by, immersed in, and /or intersecting with technology. Just as the idea of the body has evolved from the 'natural' to the 'constructed', so too has technology evolved from 'tool' to 'systems,' which include structures of artificial intelligence. Indeed, as Dennett (2003, 270) professes:

> As we learn more and more about human weaknesses and the way technologies of persuasion can exploit them, it can seem as if our vaunted autonomy is an unsupportable myth.

In this way the Paralympic body is gradually transgressing into the realm of the so called normal body and by utilising technology it has changed the way in which the disabled person moves around in the space which was previously alien and off limits to that individual. Technological advances in sport then have supported the movement of Paralympic athletes in space in a positive and life changing manner. Further to this statement in the mid 1990s, at about the same time as the cyborg came to be widely recognised as a new ontological entity, the development of a similar conceptual formation, the post-human, saw a return to some of the ideological questions originally tackled by Haraway (1991). Although by the early twenty-first century, the post-human and the cyborg are often used interchangeably, they are in fact separate terms that evoke quite different kinds of arguments and analyses, albeit often about the same issue. The cyborg, as a part-human and part-machine hybrid, operates as both a critique and an emblem of the effects of modern science and technology on human identity. In contrast, the post-human does more, and less than, simply hybridise the human with the machine: the post-human is an attempt to formulate how the cultural and intellectual changes of the late twentieth century affect how we think about categories or features of identity (like human or machine) that have traditionally been taken for granted. This form of thinking has had profound effects on the Paralympic athletes use of space. For example, wheelchair basketball athlete's now have highly advanced lightweight maneuverable chairs in which they can excel at their sport and move in and out of space a vastly improved speed and maneuverability. If this trend or approach to sport is not adhered to then success cannot follow, as Berger (2004) comments on in his study on wheelchair athletes 'Melvin arrived at his first wheelchair basketball game in one of those heavy hospital wheelchairs. With the other players in lightweight sports chairs, he trailed behind them the entire time – he was not in the game' (Berger 2004). Stahl (2004) comments that this 'Technological progress plays no small part in this intensification', and as such it is safe to conclude that advances in the sophistication of the informal infrastructure have relevance for the use of space for the disabled athletes across all disciplines within the Paralympic movement.

Such a 'political landscape' and relationship to Paralympic sport and the body has also recently been highlighted by Gambs (2005): 'In the late twentieth century, sociology's interest in social phenomena related to human life was extended to "the body" – meaning the human body.' Scholars in the sociology of science have suggested that new technologies are drawing us to theorise bodies in ways other than simply human' or as we argue 'inhuman bodies in human spaces'. Indeed, when describing her training Gambs (2005) identifies:

> The expanded treatment of social bodies, beyond the level of the human
> organism through the movement and transformation of bodies at the

cellular muscular level ... Our bodies were positioned and moving amongst global configurations of money, information, technology, and power. Our organismic bodies are gendered, raced, bodies of sexuality, and nation. Our bodies are our becoming.

With these thoughts in mind it could be argued that we have utilised technology to support the Paralympic athlete but if it keeps progressing then we are interfering with the notion of biological space.

The Post-human Body as it Relates to Paralympians' Space

The post-human is, to Hayles 'a point of view' that 'configures human being so that it can be seamlessly articulated with intelligent machines' (1999, 23). Paralympians are surrounded by post-humanism, transhumanism and a morphing between man and machine. Wheelchair rugby athletes require Mad-Max style wheelchairs (Zupan and Swanson 2006), use bionic prosthetics, neural implants and cyber specified rehabilitation apparatus and are subjects to supersonic advancements in medical nanotechnology. Hardt and Negri's (2000) unquestioning support of the totality of technological development, something that they proclaim to be expressions of the desires of 'the multitude' (2000, 215), as Edwards and Skinner (2006, 215) comment, go so far as to call for the 'recognition ... that there are no boundaries between ... the human and the machine' and thus, 'the acceptance of ourselves as cyborgs'. Some Paralympians then become 'cyborgs in space'. For them the project of technologising life – i.e., biotechnology integrated with cybernetics – is desirable and necessary, simply because it exists (Edwards and Skinner, 2006). This is no more evident than in disability and in particular Paralympic sport. The use of spring loaded cybernetic legs, the adaptive technology of sit-skis (or pulk) and poles/picks for winter sports, sledge (sleigh apparatus) and ice pick poles for ice picking (skating activity) and sledge or ice hockey, specially designed foot or hand prostheses for rock climbing, scuba diving and swimming, specially designed crutches, canes, or walkers for running, hiking, skating, skiing and soccer, water ski bra, ski boom, hydro slide and monoski for waterskiing and adapted rowing or cycling ergometers and wheelchair treadmills to name a few are designed to move the disabled body faster, and more biomechanically sound through space. Indeed 'Changes in wheelchair design have been dramatic. Various wheel sizes are available now, as well as various handrims, adjustable camber, and adjustable seat size and inclination' (DePauw and Gavron 1995, 165).

This form of morphing into space all adds to the possibility and probability of the cyborgation of space. In dissecting the link between disability and the cyborg more thoroughly, Figueroa-Sarriera and Mentor (1995) in Edwards and Skinner (2006) break the Cyborg down into four main categories.

Cyborg technologies can be restorative, in that they restore lost functions and replace lost organs and limbs; they can be normalising, in that they restore some creature to indistinguishable normality; they can be ambiguously reconfiguring, creating post human creatures equal to but different from humans ... and they can be enhancing, the aim of most military and industrial research ... the latter category seeks to construct everything from factories controlled by a handful of 'worker-pilots' and infantrymen in mind-controlled exoskeletons. (14)

Deconstructing this statement allows us to see the extent of the intimacy of the relationship that exists between cybernetic discourse and the quad rugby athlete and the intimacy which exists between athlete and space. Firstly, during rehabilitation the athlete is essentially being restored to their maximal and optimal level of functioning and utilising space in a differing manner. After initial injury and rescue, adaptive hyper-modernistic space age equipment is used from the injection of morphine and narcotic laced drugs, to the X-ray, to the initial whirring and hammering of MRI scans and implicit surgical procedures following SCI, to the 'clear plastic tubes in my mouth, down my throat, up my nose, into my arms and even inside my penis' (Zupan and Swanson 2006, 97), to the neck brace itself.

Secondly, once life is restored, secured and maintained then rehabilitation begins to bring about normalisation. Individuals are normalised into space. The technologies used in the rehabilitation of SCI are expansive and enormative. Electro-stimulation therapy, adaptive gym equipment and devices allowing quadriplegics to defecate, transport themselves and advances in psycho-therapy are a necessity. As Zupan and Swanson (2006, 133) put it 'I was hooked up to various electrodes, flexing again and again, when I felt the tiny shock stimulating my muscles'. Thirdly, the rehabilitated and normalised subject then takes on the reconfigured form and the reconfigured self. The technology has in fact once again penetrated human space. The life form which now exists is one which is a merger between man and machine and they are viewed in that way by others. In the same way that Shogan (1999) suggests that the technologies associated with the machinery for adding up and capitalising time in sport actually penetrate individual bodies as part of a disciplinary process, the quad rugby athlete becomes their human form merged on a subliminal level with their machines in space. They can therefore move in and out of space in a more efficient manner. This is reinforced by Collinson (2003) who highlights that many athletes become their times (in sporting events), and identify others by their times in specific events. Many QRPs become their chairs and can therefore become larger than life in their own space. They become their technology which in turn enhances the ways in which they move in their space. They become a hyper-evident display of their new found cyborg status and this changes how they are perceived by others in 'life space' and 'sports space'. And finally, the quad rugby player is an example of enhancing what is previously not considered possible – the ability to play sport. It becomes predetermined that the Paralympic athlete becomes a new identity when they sit into their hyper-technologised, futuristic and threatening looking chair. They morph into the chair as if it were a piece of highly developed instrument of warfare. The Mad-Max analogy used in Murderball© by Zupan and Swanson (2006) is a self recognition that this is the case. The chair provides a feeling of indestructibility which the now quadriplegic athlete uncontrollably craves. Indeed, they morph into new spaces and develop as individuals. Once again their newly found cyborged self can harvest and project feelings of being tough, physical, athletic, fearless, powerful, competitive, aggressive, superior and ruthless which may even be enhanced from how they felt before SCI and how they act in space. Indeed, with the extreme competition, the big hits, the mechanic, the objectification of the opponent the sport-war analogy has rarely been more evident in any activity.

As Zupan and Swanson (2006, 7) suggest, this objectification may even rise above and beyond previous manifestations of war and sport as 'it's not like we are going to break our necks. Again'. The quad rugby player is a cyborg competing in an X-game. This argument certainly parallels theory suggested by Miah (2003), who argues that 'post-humanity is already present in elite sporting practices' and 'athletes are recognised as post-human in their biological constitutions and in the manner of approaching technology as an enhancing resource'. He argues that 'sport is identified by the pursuit of excellence, by defining human boundaries and moral understanding' (Miah 2003, 10). For the QRP this can open up an extensive panache of arguments and ethics where human and post-human barriers are crossed and blurred. Miah (ibid.) highlights 'This might translate into a normalising of supposedly transhuman technologies; such is evident by the acceptance of some kind of technologies, including altitude chambers'. Indeed, the use of hyper-advanced chairs in quad rugby becomes a very central part of the sport itself. However, how far can the development of the chair progress? Where do performance advancements stop in favour of personal safety? Indeed, Coakley (1994) warns that this technology poses a potential threat to the athlete. Sage (1998, 156) expresses concerns and fears that sport has become 'a project in engineering whose objective is producing levels of performance with seemingly little understanding of – or even interest in – what the consequences might be for the athlete'. This is evident for the QRP where 'violent chair-on-chair collisions ... sound like dynamite exploding in a rubbish bin. Players hit so hard that they bend rims, crack frames or pop tyres ... Injuries range from broken fingers, ribs and noses to concussions' (Zuapn and Swanson 2006, cover). This enhancement shows how it is not only humans who are being injured, but the very machines which the humans have morphed into are being battered and fragmented in new spaces. From an inverted perspective to this view, should the sport have evolved and progressed further with more technological enhancement?

As Miah (2003, 4) suggests, medical technologies have limitations as the new technologies aim to repair humans, rather than enhancing them. He identifies that medico-technologies perpetuate trans-humanist ideals, which are based upon 'restoration rather than the creation of new levels of human capability through such repair'. The ideal of what is considered acceptable has shifted and this technology is now considered acceptable and normal for humans to access. Athletes continually aspire to reach for their goals and defy human limits and according to Miah (2003, 7) are 'ambassadors of trans-humanism, placed at the cutting edge of human boundaries of human capability'. Elite sports strive to gain competitive advantage by helping athletes seek enhanced technologies. Could we see a chair developed to intentionally destroy another? Will the sport turn into a game of robot wars with the human at the centre of the machine controlled by 'worker pilots' (Figueroa-Sarriera and Mentor, 1995) who set out to seek and destroy in a confined space which they call the court? Clearly, the boundaries between reality and fiction are blurred in this instance, not only between right and wrong within sporting endeavour, but also between sport and all out war. These enhanced cyborgs have long been prominent in postmodern popular culture and cinematic representation, not just in the Matrix trilogies. Indeed looking at popular culture and cinematic representation, the human has been enhanced into ultra violent weapons. Take, for example, the film *Robocop* where 'it is Detroit in the future: a bleak urban landscape dominated by anarchy and crime. A badly injured cop is reconstructed by science: part human, part machine, he takes on the forces of evil. *Robocop* (1987) was one of the new breed of postmodern films that magnify a playful mixing of images and reality, a dislocation and erasure of personal history and identity' (Appignanesi and Garrett 1995, 146). Within the realms of Murderball© and quadriplegic rugby it becomes easy to see the difficulties between defining the boundaries of reality and hyper-reality. In essence however, it provides us with a new reality. 'The icon of postmodern cinema is Arnold Schwarzenegger. His muscle-bound physique, lack of emotion, total absence of sweat and inability to act serve as an ideal blank on which to over-write coded messages of considerable postmodern sophisitication' (Appingnanesi and Garrett 1995, 147). In films such as *Terminator*, *Total Recall* and *Last Action Hero* he undertakes a plethora of identities within a multitude of presented realities. Indeed, the case of Oscar Pistorius highlights some interesting challenges for the IPC leading into London 2012. Chief amongst the concerns are the use of technology and what the boundaries are between the human and the machine.

Paralympic Athlete Village as Geographical Space

In this section we explore for the first time the concept of the Paralympic Athlete Village as place. Disability becomes the norm and the external able bodied space of the community is suspended for the duration of the Paralympics.

Edward W. Soja argues in *Postmodern Geographies: The Reassertion of Space in Critical Social Theory*, that space is directly implicated in specific material structures as well as in urban and suburban geographies. Space implies a location or place. Augé (2002) identifies characteristics of space as place and nonplace. He suggests that place and nonplace have the potential to intersect within any given space, he nevertheless establishes clear differences between the two in terms of spatiality and inhabitability. In 'anthropological place,' he argues, space serves as a means of discovery 'by those who claim it as their own' (2002, 43). In such inhabitable places – including homes, villages, and other 'places of identity ... relations ... and history' (2002, 52) – stability maintains and sustains lasting relations to space such that 'to be born [in an anthropological place] is to be born in a place, to be "assigned to residence"' (2002, 53). As places of shared identities, relations, and histories, anthropological places promote a communal or collective relationship to inherited geography, an act of placemaking that often develops from inhabitants' physical and spiritual connectedness to place.

Bringing together these elements in a single public space such as the Paralympic Athlete Village alludes to the past but at the same time allows for the (re)organisation of intersectional and communicative relations and identifications, where, individual itineraries such as disability can intersect and mingle. If the Paralympic Athlete Village represents a historicised place, then the stadium space represents its (at least partial) negation, a dehistoricised nonplace. Augé (2002, 94) explains, 'the word "nonplace" designates two complementary but distinct realities: spaces formed in relation to certain ends (transport, transit, commerce, and in the case of the Paralympics-leisure), and the relations that individuals have with these spaces'.

The Athlete Village space, which we argue epitomises the transitory and dehistoricised place, serves to amplify the disabled athletes solitariness from society. This exists in a vacuum only for the duration of the games. The place of the Athlete Village is qualitatively different from any local community. It is not constructed as a permanent, self reproducing social system. It is marked by lack of permanence. Unlike a real village, the Athlete Village cannot be seen as a 'microcosm'. Its main users, the athletes, pass through. The athletes involved in reproducing the Athlete Village as a social system are transitory in time and replaced every four years ... the kinds of interaction within the athlete village whereby disability is focused and normalised are identical but little changes in the outside able-bodied place.

Displaced from the sense of connectivity characteristic of anthropological place, disabled athletes experience both an isolation and homogenisation of individual and group identity. In the Athlete Village, where athletes are paradoxically unified in their shared disabilities, neither singular identity nor social relations are created, only a realisation of similarity in difference. Reality of disability is suspended momentarily in time to be replaced after the games by the solitude of the disabled physical space. What then are the implications of changes in conception of biological and geographical space and place and non place for the Paralympics returning home to London in 2012?

Coming Home: The London Paralympics 2012

There is little doubt that sixty years after their very beginning, in London 1948, that the Paralympic Games are coming back to their birthplace in a different landscape. For Ludwig Guttmann it was a highly symbolic act to organise a competition for people with disabilities at the same time that the Games of the XIVth Olympiad opened in London. The organisers of the 2012 Games should be conscious of this symbolism and should together with the IOC make, after 60 years, another symbolic act towards sportswomen and men with disabilities. This could for example be the official recognition of the 800m women and 1500m men wheelchair races, included in the Olympic program since 1984 as so called demonstration events, as full medal events. This would mark another step towards the fully respect and inclusion of people with disabilities in the sports movement in accordance to the principles of the Olympic charter and to the dream of Ludwig Guttmann.

London's Paralympic Legacy

London's achievement in winning the right to stage the 2012 Olympic Games and Paralympic Games has created the greatest opportunity in generations for the UK to promote a contemporary, progressive attitude to sport, design, culture and social inclusion. The winning bid promised a combination of world-class sporting facilities, an unparalleled spectator and competitor experience, a legacy of sustainable large-scale regeneration, as well as inspiring young people to get involved in sport. An underpinning priority was commitment to inclusive design, aimed at ensuring that London 2012 is 'the most accessible Games ever'. To reinforce this, the London Organising Committee of the Olympic Games and Paralympic Games (LOCOG) for London 2012 will come together under one organising committee, with the aim of giving each a distinctive feel and sense of experience whilst making no distinction between them in the approach to planning, delivery and standard of service or the commitment to priority objectives.

The Paralympic Games in 2012 will take place from Wednesday 29 August to Sunday 9 September, using the same Village and many of the same venues as the Olympic Games. Working with key partners, LOCOG will take account of the need for accessibility for athletes, support staff, spectators and the media alike for both the Olympic and Paralympic Games. The London 2012 Paralympic Games is set to be the most compact in history, designed to minimise travel disruption and maximise accessibility. Most of the 20 Paralympic venues are set in two zones – the Olympic Park and the River Zone. These two zones are just 15 minutes apart.

London Research Reveals a positive attitude towards the Paralympic Games:

According to a survey published by the London Organising Committee of the Olympic Games and Paralympic Games (LOCOG) on 1 May 2008, 93 per cent of the UK public see Paralympic athletes as good role models for young people. Sixty-nine per cent of those polled say that there should be more media coverage of Paralympic sport. Other key findings in the research are that 85 per cent of the UK public believe that Paralympic athletes are as professional as able-bodied athletes. Of those polled, most agreed (93 per cent) that disability sport requires just as much skill as non-disability sport. Nearly all respondents (96 per cent) said that being disabled should not prevent people from taking up the opportunity to play sport – strong evidence of a positive attitude in the UK towards disabled people. Athletics, Wheelchair Basketball and Swimming topped the list of sports that the public associate spontaneously with the Paralympic Games. When prompted with a list of sports, there was also high awareness of Archery, Shooting and Table Tennis. The survey showed that 69 per cent of respondents could not name a Paralympian. Whilst 94 per cent of the UK public have heard of the Paralympic Games, they did not have a good understanding of the Games and its participants. The survey indicates a lower awareness of the Paralympic Games and of Paralympians amongst younger age groups, particularly those under 24. As a consequence of this research. London 2012 and its partners intend to focus efforts to raise awareness through new media outlets including broadband TV and sports networking sites.

A number of in-depth interviews with prominent correspondents in the sports and news media, conducted simultaneously with the poll of the general public, showed a media interest in personality led Paralympic features. Respondents suggested that the gap between the close of the Olympic Games and the opening of the Paralympic Games should be as short as possible to maintain public interest.

London Organising Committee Chairman (Lord Coe), said:

> We want to use the power of the Games to inspire change, and one of the key legacies the London 2012 Paralympic Games can leave is to change public and media attitudes towards people with a disability.

He adds:

> We will build on the high level of awareness, and, working with the
> International Paralympic Committee and the British Paralympic Association,
> make sure we take every opportunity to educate, engage, inform and inspire
> the UK public and the world over the next four years and deliver a truly
> memorable Paralympic Games in 2012.

Certainly one consideration and ongoing legacy concerns the planning of
disablity friendly facilities and spaces at the London site.

Paralympic Place and Non-place

Legislation and IPC regulations provide basic requirements for athletes with
disabilities attending and participating at the Paralympics. The requirements
for facility accessibility, including sport stadiums, are laid out. Despite the
progress that has been made since the IPC's enactment, host cities have faced
obstacles in implementing the provisions of the IPC into their programs and
facilities. These obstacles include physical barriers to accessibility, financial
constraints in providing additional resources, services, and equipment for
people with disabilities. Full participation and equal opportunity in sports
have historically been a challenge for people with disabilities. Whilst the
initial studies on participation rates for people with disabilities have primarily
focused on the role of the participant in sport or recreation activities there is an
emerging awareness of the need to also provide an accessible environment for
participants and spectators with disabilities. From the perspective of a sport
facility, this raises the need for a dual emphasis in service provision: providing
not only a physically accessible environment (i.e. ramps, elevators) but also
an 'accessible' living environment, one that is inviting and accommodating to
people with disabilities

The IPC policy to assess living conditions in the athlete village and venues
builds on the site requirements of the IOC. The following ten themes can be
seen to be part of the planning process: barriers and facilitators related to the
built and natural environment; economic issues; emotional and psychological
barriers; equipment barriers; barriers related to the use and interpretation
of guidelines, codes, regulations, and laws; information-related barriers;
professional knowledge, education, and training issues; perceptions and
attitudes of persons who are not disabled, including professionals; policies
and procedures both at the facility and community level; and availability of
resources.

London has taken the step of seeking input from the disability community
as an initial step in the construction of the new stadium, athlete village and
sport venues. It is argued that maintaining a relationship with the disability
community needs to be an ongoing process through the London Paralympic
planning cycle, rather than a one-time event when the stadium, village and

venues are built. Many of these requirements are to be implemented in London after conducting focus groups with athletes and spectators with disabilities. Architects, fitness and recreation professionals, IPC officials, as well as city planners and venue managers, categorise the barriers and facilitators to participation.

Conclusion

This chapter has attempted to make sense of the physical, biological and geographical space of the Paralympic athlete. It reviewed the history of the Paralympic movement, and discussed the notion of the body and the disabled body and their relationship to space in the Paralympic context. In short, this chapter sought to conceptualise Paralympic athletes in an innovative way so as to stimulate more challenging research on the concepts of space and place as they relate to Paralympic athletes.

If we take the Games one step back to their cradle, we notice that the London Paralympics Games will penetrate the same space as the Olympic Games, but not at the same time. It would be highly symbolic to strengthen the link between the Olympics and the Paralympics by adding to this fusion of space at least partly a fusion of time. The London Paralympics could be the starting point of a real universal Olympic area that brings together, at the same place and in the same time like the Greek tragedies, the heroes and demiurges of a bodily elite: the best athletes and cyborgs of the world, intermingling in the same space and at the same time, human nature, culture and technology, and thus deploying an ethics and aesthetics of human multitude.

References

Appignanesi, R. and Garratt, C. (1995) *Postmodernism for Beginners*, Cambridge: Icon Books.

Augé, M. (2002) *In the Metro*, trans. Tom Conley, Minneapolis: University of Minnesota Press.

Bale, J. and Vertinsky, P. (2004) *Sites of Sport: Space, Place and Experience*, London: Routledge.

Berger, R.J. (2004) 'Pushing Forward: Basketball, Disability, and Me', *Qualitative Inquiry* 10(5): 794–810.

Coakley, J.J. (1994) *Sport in Society. Issues and Controversies*, Boston: McGraw Hill.

Collinson, J. (2003) 'Running into Injury Time: Distance Running and Temporality', *Sociology of Sport Journal* 20(4): 331–50.

Dennett, D.C. (2003) 'The Mythical Threat of Genetic Determinism', *Chronicle of Higher Education* 49: B7–B9.

DePauw, K.P. and Gavron, S.J. (1995) *Disability and Sport*, 2nd edn, Champaign, IL: Human Kinetics Publishers.

Edwards, A. and Skinner, J. (2006) *Sport Empire*, Aachen: Meyer and Meyer Sports.

Figueroa-Sarriera, H.J. and Mentor, S. (eds) (1995) *The Cyborg Handbook*, London: Routledge.

Gambs, D. (2005) 'Training Movement', *Qualitative Inquiry* 11(2): 157–69.

Guttmann, A. (1994) *Games and Empires. Modern Sports and Cultural Imperialism*, New York: Columbia University Press.

Guttmann, A. http://www.spitfirechallenge.ca/Sir%20Ludwig%20Guttmann%20early%20history.htm24.

Hansen, R. and Taylor, J. (1987) *Rick Hanson. Man in Motion*, Vancouver and Toronto: Douglas and McIntyre.

Haraway, D. (1991) 'A Cyborg Manifesto: Science, Technology, and Socialist-Feminism in the Late Twentieth Century', in *Simians, Cyborgs and Women: The Reinvention of Nature*, New York; Routledge.

Hardt, M. and Negri, A. (2000) *Empire*, Cambridge, MA: Harvard University Press.

Hayles, K.N. (1999) *How We Became Posthuman*, Chicago: University of Chicago Press.

Howe, D. (2006) *The Cultural Politics of the Paralympic Movement. Through an Anthropological Lens*, London: Routledge.

Miah, A. (2003) 'Dead Bodies for the Masses: The British Public Autopsy and the Aftermath', *CTHEORY: International Journal of Theory, Technology and Culture, Event-Scene*, E119.

Schantz, O. and Gilbert, K. (2001) 'An ideal Misconstrued: Newspaper Coverage of the Atlanta Paralympic Games in France and Germany', *Sociology of Sport Journal* 18: 69–94.

Schell, B. and Rodriguez, S. (2001) 'Subverting Bodies/Ambivalent Representations: Media Analysis of Paralympian, Hope Lewellen', *Sociology of Sport Journal* 18: 127-135.

Soja, E.W. (1989) *Postmodern Geographies: The Reassertion of Space in Critical Social Theory*, London: Verso.

Zupan, M. and Swanson, T. (2006) *The Story Behind the Star of Murderball*, New York: HarperCollins.

Chapter 16

Where is London, England in Contemporary Britain – and Will the 2012 Olympics Help Us to Find It?

Andrew Blake

> Britain is a creative leader, but, with the new sense of energy and focus on our country that the Olympic Games will bring, it is a realistic ambition to make Britain the world's creative capital.
>
> (DCMS 2008a)

Anyone visiting one or more of the many symposia on the cultural and creative industries and the UK economy held during the second half of the 2000s (and they were legion) will have been struck by the recurrent references to the 2012 Olympics. Regional representatives from around the UK – as well as those from the north, west and south of London – were united in their desire to claim some regional benefit from the Games and from the money being poured in to regenerate the east end of London and the 'Thames Gateway', its Essex/Kent hinterland. Many of the claims were couched in the official discourse, reproduced above from a 2008 'strategy document for the creative industries'; but most speakers acknowledged anxiously that the real creative capital was London, and argued for a more equitable distribution of funding and opportunity.

In order for this to happen – and/or to decide whether it should – we need to think carefully about the ways in which the area of London currently being prepared to host the Games relates to the rest of London, and London in turn to the rest of the United Kingdom. In particular, it will be argued here, the Games afford the opportunity for a new assessment of the place of London within England, and of England within Britain. Politically, geographically, historically and culturally, the 'United' Kingdom has fractured, and England is the least stable element within it. While Northern Ireland, Wales, Scotland, and London itself all have a political and cultural framework within which to reinvent themselves, England does not, and this chapter will examine this problem within the discussion of the role of 'culture' in the preparation for and staging of the London 2012 Olympic and Paralympic Games and their aftermath.

What Use is Culture? Part 1: Culture and the Creative Arts in their Political and Economic Context

'Culture' took a new turn within the UK in the mid-1990s. The New Labour government which came into power in 1997 quickly revamped the old Department for Heritage, which had dealt with public monuments and the encouragement of tourism. It became the Department for Culture, Media and Sport (DCMS). As the title implies, the new ministry was given a wide brief – but the overall focus was not simply to preserve and defend the national imaginary through the preservation of aspects of the past, nor merely the encouragement of cultural production and sporting success, but to strengthen the contribution of these areas of life and work to the UK economy.

This was in its way a radical agenda, challenging the post-Second World War settlement which had funded a high-culture sector which was claimed to be above commerce. In this view 'the arts', narrowly conceived as painting and sculpture, the literary novel and poetry, serious drama, classical music, opera and ballet, were seen as 'good' in and of themselves. They were produced and performed by well-trained and gifted people for the rest of us to enjoy and learn from, and they should be paid for as such through public subsidy. This settlement was consensual for 30 years, but, firstly, the Conservative administration of the 1980s tried to submit some of these activities to the disciplines of the market, and then a wider view of culture and its uses began to spread within political circles. In the word of the New Labour government's 1997 election manifesto, 'Art, sport and leisure industries are vital to our quality of life and the renewal of our economy. They are significant earners for Britain. They employ hundreds of thousands of people'.[1]

Thus the new government virtually called into existence 'the creative industries', seeing them simultaneously as a sign of modernity; an export earner; and a provider of work in which people from disadvantaged areas and ethnic groups might actually be interested. They would thus provide social inclusion, widening participation and economic regeneration at a stroke. The new DCMS quickly produced an audit of these activities, a 'creative industries mapping document', which first appeared in 1998 and was updated in 2001 (DCMS 2001).[2] Through a raft of policies such as the 'new deal' for musicians (a mentoring scheme designed to ease young performers and composers into profitable self-employment), and the requirement for all local authorities to produce cultural policies of their own, the government attempted to reinforce the message that culture-as-industry was a viable way of modernising society and economy alike.

---

1   http://www.labour.org.ukm, accessed 5 May 1997.

2   The Creative Industries Mapping Documents 1998 and 2001 are available on http://culture.gov.uk accessed 12.9.2003.

Subsequent debates within government and its think-tank hinterland have indicated that there is still some room for an old-fashioned view of 'culture' as the best that has been thought and said, something which is provided for most people by the extravagantly gifted, even as the arts should try to become – and to represent themselves as – vehicles for participation, social inclusion, the celebration of multicultural and diverse Britain, and economic prosperity.[3] In response, the principal distributor of high-culture subsidy, Arts Council England, reinvented itself as an agency aiming for social inclusion and the celebration of diversity alongside its more usual elitist activities – and for a decade it was rewarded with significantly increased funding.[4]

The new government's key 1997 election pledge had been to improve education provision in order to widen social and economic participation. The two concerns were brought together in the creation of the National Endowment for Science, Technology and the Arts (NESTA), which is overseen by the DCMS. Using funds from the National Lottery (which is also overseen, as a whole, by DCMS), this quango has supported projects in education as well as other kinds of applied research, in order, again, 'to provide a real boost to the UK's economic, cultural and creative capital'.[5]

Given the above range of political concerns for the role of education and culture in the regeneration of local economies and communities, it is unsurprising that those arts providers which have survived and prospered, or which intend to do so in the future, have embarked on ambitious but synergistic relationships, working across all these areas. The result is an emerging model of arts council, local council and University collaboration in using the 'arts centre' as a nexus of provision for education, small business and artist support and creative-industries career development, as well as professional and amateur performance. The Arc, Stockton-on-Tees, for example, is home to professional theatre, music, comedy, dance and films; amateur/community events and education provision in association with the Universities of Teesside

---

3 For aspects of the debate over 'aesthetic value' versus 'economic value' see e.g. Tessa Jowell, then Secretary of State at DCMS (2004a), among whose very many rejoinders were Cowling (2004); Holden (2005a and 2005b) and Kathy Koester (2006). A few years later the same arguments were revisited, the Jowell position reworked in the McMaster review, *Supporting Excellence in the Arts. From Measurement to Judgement* (DCMS 2008b), which was almost immediately contradicted by the Department for Innovation, Universities and Skills' White Paper *Innovation Nation* (DIUS 2008).

4 See e.g. DCMS (2004b) and its evidential precursor, Evans and Shaw (2004); DCMS (2004c); British Academy (2004). The arguments for democratisation of access were presented in e.g. Johnson (2004), but also in policy; e.g. in the mid-2000s the Council ran its *Decibel* programme, which encouraged (and supported financially) non-white participation at all professional levels of creativity, performance and administration.

5 http://nesta.org.uk , accessed 12 September 2003.

and Durham.[6] Similarly the Sage Gateshead, housed in a purpose-built Norman Foster building on the south bank of the River Tyne, offers a degree programme in collaboration with Newcastle University, while in the more prosperous South East of England, Folkestone was given £620,000 by Arts Council South East for the renovation of town centre properties which will be let to artist and creative businesses in a creative quarter which includes higher education provision via Kent Institute of Art and Design and Canterbury Christ Church University (Arts Council South East 2004, 3). Developments such as these –whether or not they succeed in the long term – fuel the dream of Britain as creative capital.

Responding to this wide-ranging agenda from the heart of the capital itself, the Mayor of London (2003, 16–17) mapped out the city's cultural goals in April 2004. Four aspects of the emergent policy are worthy of particular note in the context of the cultural possibilities associated with the 2012 Olympiad.

- 'The creative and cultural industries need to be recognised as a significant contributor to London's economy and success', and the document further emphasises that 'in an area dominated by self-employment and small companies, support structures for small businesses and to nurture new talent need to be established' (ibid.).
- 'Education and lifelong learning must play a central role in nurturing creativity and providing routes to employment'. In particular, 'Black and minority ethnic groups, and people with disabilities, may need more support to be able to gain the education, training or experience they need to fill the many jobs in the cultural sector', and the document promises to 'explore ways of using major new cultural developments to maximise opportunities for black, Asian and minority ethnic groups' (ibid., 17–18).
- 'There should be a spread of high-quality cultural provision across London and at all levels – local, sub-regional and regional', to realise which the Mayor should 'facilitate strategic partnerships to maximise growth of cultural provision – coordinating development to the east as a new area of growth' (ibid., 19, 22).
- 'Cultural quarters must be developed as key contributors to London's creative capital and the development of the broader economy', in order that 'achieving a better balance between the cultural facilities of inner and outer London can go some way towards reducing the social and economic inequalities between different parts of the city'; to realise this the Mayor must 'support the development of cultural quarters and promote their role in regeneration, encouraging creative industry developments in the Thames Gateway region' (ibid., 22–3).

---

6 http://arconline.co.uk accessed 12.08.04

The Thames Gateway London Partnership (a coalition of local and strategic authorities, higher education institutions, health authorities, and the London Skills Council) responded to the Mayoral document by stressing the potential excellence of the Stratford Cultural Quarter, and claiming that 'opportunities for innovation and knowledge transfer by University of East London and London Metropolitan and Queen Mary Higher Education institutions as well as the work of Lewisham, Newham, Tower Hamlets and Greenwich further education colleges provide a rich input to the development of cultural and heritage quarters in East London' (Thames Gateway London Partnership 2003, 6).

East London is, then, no stranger to this type of development. The collaborative relationship between the three-auditorium Stratford Circus Arts Centre, Newham 6th Form College, and the University of East London is one example. It has made the Circus building the foundation point for a 'Stratford Cultural Quarter' providing incubator units and support for new small businesses alongside a range of vocational short courses, foundation and honours degrees in the performing arts and arts management, as well as professional music and dance performances. The Circus building adjoins the Theatre Royal, Stratford, and a cinema. Such clusters are not unique in East London. Rich Mix, in Bethnal Green, offers a similar combination of three-screen cinema, performance and exhibition spaces, recording studios for training, and workspaces for small-business creative industry start-ups. The redeveloped Broadway Theatre, Barking, contains a flexible auditorium space for music, dance or drama, while the basement level houses an education suite of dance, stagecraft, music recording, drama and technology rooms. The project forms part of the borough's ambitions for a 'cultural hub' mixing artists' studios, a lifelong learning centre, and library and exhibition facilities in the central area of Barking – to which end the nearby Malthouse building has also been refurbished to provide workspace for cultural industries and arts groups, and the adjoining site has been purchased by the London Development Agency for more of the same. The London Development Agency has also acquired one of the UK's major television and film studios, Three Mills Studios in East London, which Tony Winterbottom, director of regeneration and development at the LDA, described as 'a key part of east London's creative hub';[7] the Three Mills site also houses the London New Music Academy, a training facility for rock and pop musicians whose programmes include foundation degrees validated by London universities.

As these examples should indicate, there was already fierce regional and local competition for the cultural-regeneration pound well before the success of the London 2012 bid. Indeed, it might already be the case that even before the raft of developments which the Olympiad is projected to generate or influence there were simply too many cultural centres in East London fighting

---

7   http://lda.gov.uk press release, accessed 12 August 2004.

both for the same slices of public funding, and for the same market in potential resident artists, students, administrators, and audiences. Nonetheless it might also be argued that any working model which manages to combine education, community provision, local business support and professional performance will in the current climate be likely to succeed.

A key question here, then, is how far the cultural provision building up to and centred around the 2012 Olympic Games will impact on this evolving model, in which the goal of producing workers for the cultural and creative industries is carefully embedded. Many local cultural workers assume that 'culture' – whether poetry readings, art installations, street theatre or live music – will consist of big-name events which are parachuted in to East London for the events, paid well from the National Lottery money taken from the general cultural pot to support the Games, and then exit stage right as soon as possible thereafter. Culture and creativity in East London might, in this model, lose out twice over.

What, then, of the proposals for the cultural Olympiad itself? Most of the consultants and quangos already taking an interest in the question of the Olympic culture festival in the late 2000s proposed activities which were close to the bid's diversity-driven view of 'culture'. LOCOG, for example, promised 'Astonishing Opening and Closing Ceremonies that honour the Olympic traditions by celebrating the creative innovation, artistic strength and cultural diversity of the UK', and 'Cultural, ceremonial and educational programmes in a form that reflects the huge creative strength of the UK'; its ideas included [with my occasional comments in square brackets].

> *Olympic Proms* – a month's proms, which would showcase musical styles and commissions by young composers from many countries [it wasn't specified whether this event would complement, clash with, or be part of the BBC's annual Proms season of classical concerts]
>
> *Live Sites* – big outdoor screens across the UK to broadcast the Games and other elements of the Culture and Education programme, programmed with the help of young people and local communities
>
> *Artists Taking the Lead* – a network of artist communities and organisations across the UK involved in planning the largest-ever celebration of British cultural life
>
> *World Cultural Festival* – every nation competing in the Games would be invited to bring their own culture to London and the UK. Over 200 national pavilions will be 'created'
>
> *5 Rings Exhibitions* – a UK wide museum and gallery partnership between the visual arts, social history and science, offering new interpretations of our shared histories
>
> *Olympic Carnival* – a 5 day carnival bridging the close of the Olympic Games and the opening of the Paralympic Games [which, again, might complement or compete against the long-standing Notting Hill event]

Paralympic/Disability Culture Congress – Britain founded the Paralympic Games and is a pioneer of the Disabled Arts Movement. A World Congress in 2012 will acknowledge milestones achieved and the potential for future development.[8]

What might 'culture' represent here? Youth and diversity, yes; the work of UK-based artists, yes; the most important British contribution to Olympism, yes; cultural production specific to East London, London, or the UK, or dealing with specifically London/UK issues other than the celebration of diversity, probably not.

What use is Culture? Part 2: London, England and the UK – a Problematic Relationship

What then, we might ask, is 'culture' supposed to do, at this time when a global event is located in London? How might 'culture' be made to work on behalf of a particular time-space and set of issues? How might the cultural festival represent, for example, not just our 'shared histories' but the current British political entity? If it doesn't do any of the above, what's the use?

To my mind the cultural festival could, nay should, attempt to address a particular problem which is arguably going to be exacerbated by the situating of the Games in London. The legal and political status of the constituent parts of the United Kingdom of Great Britain and Northern Ireland has changed markedly since 1998, when the peoples of Wales and Scotland voted for limited political autonomy, with their own elected assemblies, and the peace process in Northern Ireland resulted in the eventual return of devolved government to the province, with the potential of closer ties to the Republic of Ireland; consequently the former Arts Council of Great Britain has been dissolved and replaced by locally funded entities. Meanwhile London – with a population greater than that of either Scotland, Wales, or Northern Ireland, and with an economy worth more than all three together – has since 2000 had its own elected Mayor and Greater London Assembly, with its own cultural programme.

These developments within nations and regions raise the curious question of what and where 'England' might be, since the country has no similar political existence. As Benedict Anderson (1983) has claimed, the 'imagined community' is crucial to modern nationhood. An England imagined only through its British past, and without a legislature of its own, can hardly be said to exist in the present. Indeed, the geographical area 'England' is virtually alone in the world in having a passionately supported 'national' football team, but no national government. Its MPs share the United Kingdom Parliament

---

8   http://www.londoncouncils.gov.uk/doc.asp?doc=16767&cat=2222.

with Scots, Northern Irish and Welsh representatives, but there is no reciprocal arrangement in the local assemblies. Proposals for elected assemblies in the English regions elicited no public support, despite being promoted enthusiastically by some Labour politicians – who have meanwhile imposed unwanted, expensive, unelected, and otherwise entirely useless, 'regional assemblies'. But despite this yawning democratic deficit no major political party has proposed an English parliament. Politically, it seems, 'England' does not and should not exist. The central state of the UK has begun to lose both its periphery and its capital city, without gaining a firm legal or political identity of its own; this makes it more difficult for an 'imagined community' to form successfully around the notion of England or Englishness, or of any associated culture or cultural shift.

There are a number of related problems. Geographically, the 'England' segment of the UK remains within stable boundaries, but there have been an important set of changes which have changed the way the English geography works within the imagination. The divisions between town and country, and between London and the rest of England, have all widened in the last thirty years. The differences matter because of the importance of the countryside in the national imaginary. The national cultural heritage is deeply associated with parts of the country – for example Suffolk is associated with the painter John Constable, mid-Hampshire with novelist Jane Austen, and the Malvern hills with composer Sir Edward Elgar. Thus a tourist-centred representation of the countryside is seen through these relations, and conversely the arts can be seen to deliver a version of the English landscape which the tourist can then experience. While there are urban equivalents – the writings of Dickens or Martin Amis connect strongly with London, and the art of L.S. Lowry represents the Manchester conurbation, for example – this patterning of culture and countryside remained dominant throughout the twentieth century and beyond. We must remember that in the most powerful current representation of Englishness, J.K. Rowling's Harry Potter novels, a boy escapes from a small town in Surrey – in essence a commuter-suburb of London – and goes to a school located in the (presumably Scottish) countryside and served by a village. London is represented in these books as a metropolis with a Dickensian dark side (though it has good shops), and as the seat of an incorrigibly corrupt government.

The English countryside has, since the early nineteenth century when the industrial revolution took the mass of the population from the country to the city, been imagined principally as a place of rural peace and gentle prosperity for its residents, and as a collectively shared public space for walkers and other urban exiles. Although the countryside contains the living relics of feudalism in the aristocratic landed estates, many of these have been sold piecemeal to farmers or pension funds, or opened to the public through institutions such as the National Trust. The political settlement produced by the 1945 Labour government had produced National Parks in areas of outstanding natural beauty such as the Lake District; and the Ramblers' Association had ensured that most of the rest of the countryside was also open to respectful leisure walkers.

Since 1945 the countryside has developed in two directions as leisure facility. Firstly, there has been the more or less respectful commodification of the past which is often identified as 'heritage culture'. This works through institutions such as the National Trust, and museums like the Weald and Downland Open Air museum in Sussex, which provides visitors with a contextual experience of historic buildings and their uses. These exhibits now usually include not just past objects and structures but also actors in historic roles, interacting with visitors and presenting a selective, and sanitised, but 'living' past which is presented as culturally, rather than politically, different. The Conservative government of 1979–1997 valorised and supported this through the Department of Heritage (which was subsequently modernised by New Labour into the DCMS).

Secondly, much of the leisure industry has been involved in the modernisation of the countryside. Aristocratic estates such as Beaulieu and Longleat have helped in their own preservation not merely by opening grand houses and parks to the public, but by changing land use to include wildlife parks, museums, and rock concerts (the Reading Rock Festival originated in jazz concerts held at Beaulieu, which also has the country's biggest motoring museum). In other words the countryside is open in different ways to most of the population. Complementing the workings of the heritage industry, adventure parks such as Alton Towers, and music festivals such as Glastonbury and Homelands (a dance music festival held in downland outside Winchester) have opened the countryside to the hedonism of urban popular culture. Dotted with second homes and cottages for holiday rent, and offering a wide range of leisure experiences, the countryside seemed to exist in amiable relationship with the town.

All, however, is less than idyllic. 'Heritage culture' hid the fact that most of the countryside had been relentlessly and ruthlessly modernised as agricultural enterprise. Most of the countryside had been devoted to capitalist agriculture since the seventeenth century. For the 30 years after the Second World War, farmers lived well on state and European subsidies for grain, meat and milk production, while paying their workers very low wages, and abusing the land using high-impact fertilisers and pesticides, to the detriment of plant and animal wildlife as well as their crops and livestock. But as supermarkets began to act as cartels, forcing prices down at the farm gate while keeping them high in the shops, the farmers were abused in their turn. During the last quarter of the twentieth century this chain of abuse began to implode. A sequence of damaging revelations about the quality of food production, culminating in the devastation of the meat industry by structural diseases such as BSE (which is transferable, and fatal, to humans) and foot and mouth disease (which is easily transmittable *by* humans, who are therefore kept out of infected areas) proclaimed that the countryside was in economic and biological crisis.

There was also a *cultural* crisis in the countryside. The New Labour government which came to power in 1997 had promised to end fox-hunting, a practice which had become popular in the countryside since the invention of the railway, but which had been regarded with horror by many people (though it has a faint echo in Olympic sports, the horse-riding Three Day Event). The attempt to ban fox-hunting early in the 1997 parliament prompted a massive backlash in which the proponents of other traditional country sports such as fishing and shooting joined the hunters, and a quarter of a million enthusiasts paraded through London in defence of their pursuits. On the back of this division the organisers of the march, the Countryside Alliance, proclaimed a cultural division between the city and the country. Using the political language and strategies of left-wing protest groups, this conservative organisation represented itself as the voice of an oppressed minority.

Meanwhile the suburbs and cities have become distinctively different from the countryside in far more than occupation and population density. Richer in ethnic variety, more confident in social, cultural and political experiment, the cities also experienced the same period, the quarter century after 1980, as a time of profound social change. In most parts of Britain there was rapid movement away from a patriarchal or class-based organisation of the relations of employment and production, and towards a consumerist society increasingly based around the individual and her or his rights. Housing was privatised, and many of the former 'working class' became part of this consumerism. Many others, however, could not. This movement necessarily created new social victims, as social and welfare services were streamlined and cut. In many city areas and in parts of the larger towns a group of people, sometimes labelled the 'underclass', seemed to exist on or beyond the edges of routine employment, education, and opportunities for upwards social mobility.

If there were cultural divisions between town and city, the biggest single division, though it is both under-recognised and under-theorised, was between the rest of England and London. The establishment in 2000 of a professional Mayor of London and elected assembly has increased this division between capital and country, and the problem of the location and identity of England is all the greater while London is both culturally unique, economically dominant, and politically separate, and England has no political representation of its own.

The capital city is indeed unique, as to be fair it has been for much of its history. London has a deeper mix of all the above social problems, but its prosperous and its poor alike share one characteristic – they were and are less likely to be British by birth or by historic connection than those living elsewhere in the UK. The trading centre on the Thames had been an important point of contact among peoples since Roman times, and the capital city of the Victorian empire had been the most multiracial city in the United Kingdom. The relaxation of exchange controls in the 1980s had encouraged the immigration of many rich people from all over the world. Governments made it easier for foreign firms to work in Britain, and most of them – most importantly the financial businesses which have taken over the City of London – have located in the capital, bringing key workers with them.

Successive waves of poorer immigration (both legal and illegal) from the 1950s onwards also focussed on London. Since the recruitment of people from the former colonies in the Caribbean and South Asia to work in Britain in the 1950s, other cities have become ethnically mixed; and since the accession of east European states to the EU, the countryside has also seen an influx of new, cheap immigrant labour. But – the point should be emphasised, since it is key to any understanding of contemporary Britain – whereas the other imperial trading cities such as Bristol, Glasgow, Cardiff, Liverpool and Birmingham are now *post-imperial* cities, with populations whose mix can be related back to those historic connections of Empire, London is a *world* city, with a population drawn from everywhere else in the world, and whose axial cultural geography is more closely connected to Los Angeles, New York, Paris and Singapore than it is to the smaller cities in England within an hour's train journey of London such as Winchester, Salisbury or Chichester. With this shifting population and sense of global connectedness which marks it out from the rest of the UK, the capital city still receives the lion's share of spending on the arts, and far more than its share of prestige architectural projects. It has become to many in the outside world a separate entity, far more attractive, desirable, and just plain visible than the England of heritage-culture tourism. Questioned at Calais early in 2001, a number of young Iranians, Romanians and Slovaks, each looking for a lift through the Channel Tunnel in order to immigrate illegally, was united in their desire to build their futures, not in England – a concept wholly alien to them – but in London.

Enter 'culture'. London is the centre of the government's much-desired creative and cultural industries, as it is of subsidised elite culture. But we need to ask, continually and repeatedly, what this means; what culture can do for us. Culture can indeed work to address significant political and social issues, to be more than the aestheticised museum of 'the arts' or merely the entertainment-based aspect of an economy. Indeed, it usually is; but only if we interrogate it as such.

Take two novels by well-known authors. It was to those potential immigrants' keenly imagined and desired London, and not to the 'England' through which they passed in order to arrive there, that Saladin Chamcha and Gibreel Farishta came, in Salman Rushdie's novel *The Satanic Verses*. The novel opens with a surreal episode in which Bollywood actor Farishta and voice-over artist Chamcha, travelling between Bombay and London, fall from their aircraft, landing miraculously alive on the beach at Dover. Chamcha is treated as a dangerous illegal immigrant, subject to the tyrannical

British police who treat immigrants as monsters, not people. Sure enough, he apparently begins to turn into a goat-like devil, while Farishta thinks of himself as an angel. Written in the late 1980s, the novel comments repeatedly and critically on Prime Minister Margaret Thatcher's London, with its mix of ostentatious private wealth and decaying public infrastructure, its racist police, and its constantly strained race relations. In a witty fantasy episode Gibreel Farishta, convinced that he has been transformed into an angel flying over London, imagines that he can transform it into a tropical city, and he describes the positive changes this would make on the cold, unimaginative and unwelcoming white population: 'Religious fervour, political ferment, renewal of interest in the intelligentsia. No more British reserve' (Rushdie 1988, 355). Since the book's publication London has become more like the city of Gibreel Farishta's imagination. Interest in the intelligentsia is probably a step too far, but thanks to the immigrant populations, it is no longer a secular city, the political ferment is obvious and troubling, and that 'British reserve' is fading fast, perhaps fatally compromised by the public response to the death of Princess Diana.

Writing in the following decade, another novelist offered an overview which takes the loosening of reserve as an index of national decline: 'An individual's loss of faith and a nation's loss of faith, aren't they much the same? Look what happened to England. Old England. It stopped believing in things. Oh, it still muddled along. It did OK. But it lost its seriousness' (Barnes 1998, 237). In his 1998 novel *England, England* Julian Barnes provides a sardonic commentary on the heritage-industry approach to that question. In the near future an entrepreneur sets up a massive theme park, taking over the whole of the Isle of Wight (the island in the Solent at the bottom of the map of England). England, England, as the island is now called, represents (and sells to tourists) an Englishness drawn almost entirely from the past. Teams of actors play historic roles which mix history and myth. Here is Robin Hood, eternally fighting the Sheriff of Nottingham; up there is the Battle of Britain, perpetually keeping the Nazi invader from polluting the white cliffs of Dover; presiding over all is the royal family. Transport is by black taxis and red double-decker buses, Manchester United always wins, and there is marmalade for breakfast. Meanwhile mainland England itself, abandoned by the financial services sector which had dominated its trade for the twentieth century, gradually reverts to an unromanticised, low-technology, country. Barnes's vision of the future of the 'real' England sees it as poor and rural, celebrating its identity in a village fête whose carnival-inspired echoes of the multicultural 1990s are all that differentiates this from the utopian vision of *News from Nowhere*, by the late-Victorian socialist and craftsman William Morris (1891) – a text in which 'London' survives as a garden, and the values of art and craft have replaced those of industry.

The mid-1990s seemed a particularly apt home for this kind of writing, as another chapter in the uneasy mix of culture and heritage was played out on the verge of New Labour's first election victory. For a while pop music tried to recreate the soundworld of the 1960s, as the various bands of the 'Britpop' moment – notoriously, Blur and Oasis – vied for public attention by recording music which sounded very like that of the Beatles and the Kinks. In its symbolic architecture, too, it felt difficult to move with the times. The national library, rebuilt at King's Cross after twenty years of delays and budget cuts, at least offered some kind of integrity and novelty of design. Other architectural showpieces were less fortunate. 2000 was the year of the Millennium Dome. The concept seemed audacious and positive: a vessel 320 metres in diameter, suspended in mid-air by a series of 12 100-metre steel masts, dominating a festival site of 130 acres of land which had been reclaimed from a wasteland poisoned by industrial use, the building seemed to signify the emergence of Britain from its manufacturing past. It also incorporated contemporary technologies, but in a way which, unlike its 1851 Great Exhibition forebear the Crystal Palace, relied almost wholly on the past for its design image. The audacity was represented in a backward-looking structure, a retrolutionary fantasy which owes a great deal to the science fiction comics of the 1950s, and to the futuristic designs which characterised a previous exhibition, the 1951 Festival of Britain.[9] Both building and contents proved unpopular with visitors; even the recruiting of Pierre-Yves Gerbeau, a young Frenchman from Disneyland Paris, as its chief executive could not make them appeal. In the mid-2000s it was sold, re-invented and commodified as the 'O2', with large and medium-sized music performance arenas; at the time of writing its success in this new commercial guise was uncertain.

As comprehensively awful was the decision to build a new national football stadium on the site of the existing one at Wembley in North London. Politicians and sports entrepreneurs quarrelled over the design parameters; contractors then quarrelled over payments for the work, making the project very late and well over budget. 'England', without a national parliament and existing in the public imaginary largely through the (pedestrian and uninspiring) efforts of its passionately supported football team, had no national football stadium for the first six years of the millennium.

Even in this issue, the problem of London haunted 'England'. Transport connections and population density might indicate that Birmingham or Manchester should have been the site for a new national football stadium, as they might have been for the nation's Millennium building, or indeed the national library. But London is so embedded in the *global* imaginary, at the expense of the rest of England, that the concept of a non-London national stadium for any major sport is unthinkable. A bid from Manchester for the 2000 Olympic Games – the event which took place in Sydney, Australia – was politely smiled at by a world which, as subsequent events showed, wanted to

---

9   For the idea of 'retrolution' see Blake (1998 and 2002).

see the games in London again, but like those potential immigrants at Calais, does not have the slightest interest in the rest of 'England'.

We need in concluding, therefore, to return to the problematic differences between the UK, England, and London. The establishment in 2000 of a professional Mayor of London has increased the division between capital and country, and moves to regionalise some aspects of government (such as policing and health provision) will do nothing to solve the problem of the location and identity of England while London is both culturally unique and economically dominant, and while England has no political representation of its own to support a counter-culture. It is the task of politicians and imagineers now and in the near future to address these problems and bring the two images together. If we are to progress with a workable vision of this particular nation state's future, England must be brought closer to London culturally, politically and ethnically; and London and the other cities must be brought into a more meaningful relationship with the countryside. Having an England-inclusive Olympic Games in 2012, and in particular making 'culture' work in a way which is sympathetic to existing provision both in East London and in England as a whole, may well be necessary steps in this process.

References

Anderson, B. (1983) *The Imagined Community*, London and New York: Verso.

Arts Council South East (2004) *News from Arts Council South East*, Brighton, April.

Barnes, J. (1999) *England, England*, London: Picador.

Blake, A. (1998) 'Retrolution: Culture and Heritage in a Young Country', in Coddington, A. and Perryman, M. (eds) *The Moderniser's Dilemma. Radical Politics in the Age of Blair*, London: Lawrence and Wishart, 143–56.

Blake, A. (2002) *The Irresistible Rise of Harry Potter*, London: Verso.

British Academy (2004) '"That Full Compliment of Riches": The Contribution of the Arts, Humanities and Social Sciences to the Nation's Wealth', January, http://www.britac.ac.uk/reports/contribution/index.cfm.

Cowling, J. (2004) *For Art's Sake: Society and the Arts in the 21st Century*, London: IPPR.

DCMS (2001) 'Creative Industries Mapping Document', http://www.culture.gov.uk/reference_library/publications/4632.aspx/.

DCMS (2004a) 'Government and the Value of Culture' (by Tessa Jowell), http://www.culture.gov.uk/reference_library/publications/4581.aspx/.

DCMS (2004b) 'Culture at the Heart of Regeneration', http://urbact.eu/fileadmin/subsites/ISN/pdf/cathr_summary_of_responses.pdf.

DCMS (2004c) 'Leading the Good Life: Guidance on Integrating Cultural and Community Strategies', http://www.culture.gov.uk/reference_library/ publications/4554.aspx/.

DCMS (Department for Culture, Media and Sport) (2008a) 'Creative Britain, New Talents for the New Economy', http://www.culture.gov.uk/reference_ library/publications/3572.aspx/.

DCMS (2008b) 'Supporting Excellence in the Arts: From Measurement to Judgement' ('The McMaster Review', by Sir Brian McMaster), http:// www.culture.gov.uk/reference_library/publications/3577.aspx/.

DIUS (Department for Innovation, Universities and Skills) (2008) *Innovation Nation*, London: DIUS.

Evans, G. and Shaw, P. (2004) 'The Contribution of Culture to Regeneration. A Review of Evidence', London Metropolitan University.

Holden, J. (2005a) 'Capturing Cultural Value. How Culture has become a Tool of Government Policy', *Cultural Trends* 14(1) March: 113–28.

Holden, J. (2005b) *Capturing Cultural Value. How Culture has Become a tool of Government Policy*, London: Demos.

Johnson, G. et al. (2004) *New Audiences for the Arts*, London: Arts Council England.

Koester, K. (ed.) (2006) *Creative Nation: Advancing Britain's Creative Industries*, London: The Adam Smith Institute.

Mayor of London (2003) 'London – Cultural Capital', consultative document, March.

Morris, W. (1891) *News from Nowhere*, London: Reeves and Turner.

Rushdie, S. (1989) *The Satanic Verses*, Dover, DE: The Consortium.

Thames Gateway London Partnership (2003) Response to Mayor's Cultural Strategy, unpublished paper, 15 September.

Chapter 17

London, Beijing and the Role of Culture in Reconstructing Society

Andrew Calcutt

Imagine there is no such thing as society, only episodes of ruthlessly individualistic self-interest followed by slack periods of listless inactivity. Of community, there is little sign; of solidarity, even less. On the other hand, imagine a society that brings itself into being by enabling all of us to express ourselves; where self-expression is the realisation of a social selfhood which incorporates shared values and common understanding alongside individuality, cultural identity and mutual recognition. This would allow for simultaneous verification of the individual and validation of the social. It would be a society of mutual respect.

In this chapter, written in 2007, I speculate that ruling elites in Beijing and London are hoping that hosting the Olympic Games in 2008 and 2012 respectively will help to reconstitute society as an *agora* of self-expression and self-recognition.[1] Despite considerable cultural differences and vastly different roles performed by China and the UK in the globalised economy, both capital cities are calling upon the Olympics to address a common problem of historic significance, namely, that the political realm is failing to constitute civil society while the market continues to undermine it, even as the market also continues to produce preconditions for the civil society which politics can no longer constitute. Hence, from opposite poles and contrasting roles in the global economy, the turn to culture is common to both, as ruling elites address themselves and their wider populations to culture in the hope that culture will call into existence the civil society which politics is now incapable of sustaining.

In a political context defined by the absence of significant political parties which define themselves against the market, i.e. when there is no alternative *in*

---

1 In elections for Mayor of London in May 2008, the Tory candidate Boris Johnson beat Labour's Ken Livingstone, who had held that office since its inception in 2000. At City Hall, the Conservative administration seems not to harbour such great expectations of culture, either as engine of economic growth or catalyst for the good society. However, as I write this footnote immediately prior to publication, the MPs' expenses scandal is in full swing and public alienation from UK politics has never been more intense. Equally, the demand for something other than politics to hold society together, is ever more urgent. As yet, there is no other candidate for this but culture.

politics, then for most people there seems little point *to* politics. In the context of the historically specific relations of capitalist production, for as long as it hinged on the possibility of transforming society, the political – comprised of ideas and organisations either for or against this transformation – was social in character, i.e. it contained (supported and limited) the tendency within capitalism for social production to be fully realised as such. In keeping with this capaciousness, modern politics could capture the imagination and win the loyalty of large numbers of people – and frequently succeeded in doing so; but it retained this capacity only for as long as it remained oriented towards the possibility of social transformation. No longer hinged on this possibility, the political is either unhinged from the lived experience of equally large numbers of people – as in the case of today's Westminster Village, which is of intense interest only to the small number of its inhabitants; or else it has become managerial rather than political, as exemplified in the latter-day Chinese Communist Party.

Having experimented with the possibility of living without society and relying almost entirely on the market, and in the process having frightened themselves with the prospect of 'bowling alone' (Putnam 2000), all around the world ruling elites have come round to the question of how to continue the social by means other than the political. Even when there is no alternative *in* politics, their hope is that culture can serve as the alternative *to* politics in its socialising role. When conflicts remain but without expectation of their resolution through the collective pursuit of contested interests; moreover, when the spectre of *anomie* haunts those in government as anarchy once terrified their antecedents (Arnold 1969), culture is the only apparent alternative to the market and its brutally episodic character.

In this context, both London and Beijing have adopted the Olympic Games as perhaps the most significant tactic in their cultural strategies. This is not just routine social engineering via sport and culture, as has been widely practiced and is generally recognised in, for example, the role of muscular Christianity in establishing some of the world's best-known football clubs; it is more like an attempt to engineer society itself at a specific time and in particular areas where it is or is perceived to be especially at risk.

This is my thesis, i.e. the short form of my attempted appropriation of social reality. In what follows I shall identify the sequence of developments which prompted Beijing and London to prioritise culture as the means to reconvene the social. I go on to show that the configuration of the Olympics as part of the attempted reconstruction of society is the aggregate of rational responses by elite men and women who have experienced both power and powerlessness in circumstances not of their own choosing. In the final part of this chapter I consider some of the attractions of their adopted cultural strategy and a few of the problems inherent in it.

I should point out that when speaking of 'culture' I am reaching for Williams' usage of the word to mean the description of a particular way of life in its entirety (Williams 1965, 57). I would also like to qualify my own work up to now by registering it as no more than a preliminary sketch and this on the part of an untutored artist with no previous experience of depicting the second of my main figures, namely, Beijing.

In doing this I am emboldened by the need not to let cultural difference be the last word. If cultural difference were as predominant in reality as it has been in some literature, there would be insufficient common ground upon which to recognise it even as difference. In this light and on this occasion, therefore, it seems not only legitimate but even urgent to emphasise that in Beijing as in London the Olympics are being deployed in response to the common question of early twenty-first century governance: how to sustain the social without the political?

The Construction of Politics

Approaching London via the M11 as the motorway cuts through the north-east section of the city's circumference, the line of one's eye is drawn to a succession of tall buildings – the oldest of which, the NatWest Tower, dates from the 1970s. But when flying over London to City Airport, the city is flattened underneath you like a map. In this horizontal rendition of East London, area is more eye-catching than height, and perhaps the most striking construction is public housing. It is scattered throughout the region but, taken together, comprises a vast acreage of houses and flats built by local councils and the erstwhile regional authority, the Greater London Council, for rent by working class Londoners. Colour these areas red and they would dominate the map of East London just as the British Empire loomed largest in early twentieth-century maps of the world.

Public housing was the concrete expression of the politics of labour in an historically specific context. Its construction resulted from the social weight of working class people and the influence exerted by their 'labour movement', especially from the 1920s onwards. By contrast, public housing programmes were suspended, and council houses sold off, as and when the labour movement was defeated by the Thatcher government of the 1980s, and the working class in Britain came to be marginalised as a political force.

Not only a reflection of those times before Thatcher, the politics of labour was a key factor in the construction of the period, making it what it was. The role of organised labour as a determining factor is thus embedded in great swathes of housing built in response to the needs of organised, working class people by institutions and organisations claiming to represent their best interests. Labour representation, as in the Labour Representation Committee which immediately preceded the modern, national Labour Party, constituted in 1921, is what this housing – and that historical period – were largely made of.

In East London as elsewhere in the UK, that sprinklings of so-called affordable housing have come to replace concerted, public housing programmes is a measure not only of the diminution of publicly funded construction, it also signifies the decline of the public itself. In Britain since the mid-nineteenth century 'the public' has been the means of conceptualising the unstable unity born of contest between classes formed in the flux of a social order that contains the possibility of further social transformation, even as it acts against such possibilities. But in the UK today, this public and the spaces previously occupied by it are noticeable by their absence.

Organised in pursuit of their material interests, classes created 'public space' as the place where needs such as decent housing were articulated with ideas, beliefs and worldviews so as to form the substance of social democratic, political debate – an historically specific substance formed insofar as the politics of social democracy was the means of addressing and, according to its left-wing critics, containing the possibility of social transformation inherent in the dynamic character of capitalist social relations.

Now, however, this stuff has been knocked out of politics, and the activities of the town hall and the Westminster Village are seen by the many as either marginal and therefore hardly worthy of attention, or, what amounts to the same thing, as unalterable to the point where paying attention is again not worth the effort. Where I have written 'social democracy', which in Britain took a Labour turn, Bauman has referred to 'liberalism'; but the upshot is the same. Politics is no longer the inclusive contest between material interests articulated with the possibility of social transformation. Instead of being the arena for the pursuit of widely shared and deeply contested, collective interests, it is of interest only to a few individuals, and matters little to the many:

> Liberalism today boils down to the simple 'no alternative' credo. If you wish to find out what the roots of the growing political apathy are, you may as well look no further. This politics lauds conformity and promotes conformity. And conformity could as well be a do-it-yourself job; does one need politics to conform? Why bother with politicians who, whatever their hue, can promise nothing but more of the same. (Bauman 1999, 4)

That the catchment area of politics is now so narrowly restricted, gives rise to a kind of degradation which is widely felt even by those who do not acknowledge it as such or recognise themselves in this process. The object of degradation – that which is being degraded – is the fabric of society itself.

Impersonal Relations

Modern, urban existence has been comprised largely of impersonal relations, i.e. relations between people who have not chosen to know each other as individual persons. For as long as we have existed in this way, there has been a tendency for all such relations to become something like economic transactions; but for this transactional tendency to be played out fully would also be to declare the war of all against all; or rather, to declare that such a war is all there is of human interaction beyond the immediate range of family and friends.

In the recent historical period, chief among the counter-acting tendencies has been politics, which operates through the acting out of relations that are largely impersonal yet not reductionist, i.e. political relations do not reduce human beings to the level of atoms competing against each other in the market; rather they have been the means of addressing the chaotic character of the market, and of human beings seeking to establish their humanity in the face of the market and its chaotic character.

Across society, therefore, politics has been the most significant point of non-economic contact between people who do not encounter each other primarily as individual personalities. Even where their point of contact was the subject of disagreement, a matter for contestation, political debate and even physical conflict, this was contact nonetheless, and out of this contact civil society was continually constructed and re-constructed. Here politics was the axis of relations which were at the same time impersonal (alternatively, impersonality was also a form of relation). However, with the relative demise of politics, such impersonal relations have been disaggregated: either relations are increasingly personalised, or they are reduced to the most transitory transactions. This disaggregation is thus the degradation of civil society.

Alongside the above-the-line realm of political struggle and debate – the level at which material interests were visibly articulated with the prospect of social transformation – politics were practised as a complex set of below-the-line connections between people who related to each other politically and thus came to be related not so much by their personal characteristics as by political affiliations and allegiances. Either at work or outside it, or both, most East Londoners were touched by at least one node of this network. If they were council tenants, for example, where the council was a Labour creation and so too was the housing which that council had built, it was their immediate habitat: they ate, slept, conceived and brought up their children in it. The labour movement and its ramifications permeated the life of London: it sent the city to war as well as, more famously, setting the terms of the domestic peace in 1945.

The radical Labour programme of 1945, formulated in large part by perhaps the foremost sociologist of East London, Michael Young (Young and Willmott 1957) was issued alongside and in competition with programmes published by Conservatives and Liberals. For every important political programme, there was a commensurate social base comprised of people whose interests it represented, whose hopes for the future were based upon it, and who were positioned in society – one to another, many to many – according to their affiliation to one or other programme. Beyond the conflicting interests of different sections of society, the very existence of modern society was based largely upon a combination of above-the-line interaction on the part of elected representatives and below-the-line connections between those represented.

Thus, in modern times, there has been much more to society than either private interests as pursued in the market or interpersonal relations occurring outside it. In between the two, largely beyond them both, civil society has been mainly a function of the political; and if we were to abstract momentarily from party political differences, politics would emerge as the programme which jointly produced modern civil society, over and above the preconditions for society which are inherent but not yet acted out in the relations of the market.

Unlike the impersonality of modern, urban politics, any place where everyone knew everyone else could only be a village of sorts. Equally at odds with modern civil society, a kingdom held together by force of arms and iconic images would be a medieval theocracy – again characteristic of the parochial and equally opposed to the urbanism of which London was the early exemplar. In the modern period, by contrast, as bodies of armed men tended to move into the background (without ever disappearing altogether), and religion ceased to be the only means of embracing all, so politics came to the fore as both the extension and the antithesis of market relations, as the aggregate of impersonal relations in which individuals came to recognise themselves and were forced to recognise others as human subjects – the subjects of civil society.

Strictly Personal

Today, however, most East Londoners see themselves in anything but politics – career, family, sport, popular culture, religion, brands, but not politics; and, increasingly, only those people who are personally, individually identified are recognisable as anything more than 'other'. Anyone not known to me personally (to emphasise what is now the eccentricity of my own usage, here I am using 'me' impersonally, as a generic) is not known to be the same as me; moreover, to be unidentifiable with me is to be unidentifiable by me, and anyone in this position is likely to be 'blanked'.

'To blank' is the verb used by some young people to describe how they regularly rule out of mind those beyond personal acquaintance who are of no immediate concern (threat or opportunity?) or transactional interest (what's in it for me?). Used in this way, 'to blank' is the nightmare of Britain's ruling elite. It describes the point where, on the one hand, personalisation, and, on the other hand, the tendency to reduce all non-personal relations to the transactional, jointly comprise the demise of those impersonal relations upon which politics and civil society have hitherto depended.

In such conditions the future of London is also cast into doubt. Not that the physical fabric of the geographical area designated 'London' is anywhere near the point of collapse (although some of the Victorian sewerage system is in just this condition), but London as the nexus of impersonal relations of which this capital city is comprised and by which its boundaries are set, looks as if it may be superseded by digital villages, part local, part global, constituted by individual villagers and the personalised lists of other, individual villagers embedded in their mobile phones.

Such is the disconnection between digital villages emerging from inside the shell of analogue London that the Mayor of London, whose office was recently established partly in an attempt to re-create the sense of London as a unified, tangible place, presided in 2006 over a publicity campaign with the message that 'We are Londoners, We are One' (Office of Mayor of London 2006). But if this were widely known to be the case, why would Londoners need to be persuaded of it by advertisements? What was presented as reality in this campaign was really an example of exhortation – a normative statement of what, according to Mayor Ken Livingstone, ought to be.

Unanswered by any amount of publicity, the question remains: how can London as a social imaginary and collective entity – be brought into existence after the breakdown of the modern, political means of constructing it? The answer, or so it seems to many, lies in culture and the growing number of those taking part in it. This answer then becomes the policy of growing the numbers of people participating in culture. Especially since, in the words of (then) UK culture secretary Chris Smith, 'like tomato bags ... culture is for growing people in' (Smith 2000).[2] More accurately, in the eyes of policy makers, culture is for bagging people up in the hope that they will grow together.

Capital Growth and its Social Limitations

Livingstone first came to prominence as leader of the Greater London Council which until it was abolished in 1986 attempted to maintain a popular sense of civil society against the rampant individualism of the Tories under Prime Minister Margaret Thatcher. The instinct of Thatcherite Conservatives was that a dynamic market would suffice to make self-interest reciprocal; and reciprocal self-interest – a nation of self-helpers – was as near to society as we needed to come. Where government intervened, as in London's Docklands, it should not be to create the social – for as to society there was, infamously, no such thing, but to clear the ground for wealth creation. Meanwhile in nearby Wapping, where unionised printers were locked out of work and thus forced to lock horns with the management of Rupert Murdoch's News International,

---

2   Smith said he was quoting from a private conversation with Sheila McKechnie, (then) Director of housing charity Shelter, and attributed the observation to her.

the full force of the state was working to clear away organised labour and its capacity to obstruct the manager's right to manage.

In attacking organised labour and the social order of which it was a constituent element, Margaret Thatcher and her ministers gave politics a brief, new lease of life; but also presaged its demise. They lured the labour movement out of a position of compromise, and were uncompromising in destroying its influence. In so doing they also helped to destroy the political terrain in which compromise had been constructed from class conflict. Above and beyond conjunctural conflicts with what turned out to be the dinosaurs of the labour movement (the extinction of organised labour was by no means a foregone conclusion, however), dependence on the market produced perhaps more problems than it solved. *Malgre lui*, it showed that there is a need for such a thing as society and that society cannot be constructed by the market alone.[3] The era of faith in the free market thus alerted Britain's ruling elite to the question of how to make society without reliance either on a rigidified labour movement or the uncontrolled movements of the market.

In East London, the visibility of Canary Wharf has served to emphasise the unreliability of the market. If only it were not so distinctive, if the Wharf had been made indistinct by widening, increasingly inclusive circles of equally monumental wealth creation, perhaps capitalism would have become truly popular among Londoners. Instead, in that its skyline has remained the exception, Canary Wharf bears witness to the uneven nature of capitalist development, to the limited areas and numbers included in its growth, and to the large numbers of people left behind. In spite of 'Big Bang' and the concomitant explosion of financial and business services, share-owning democracy and wealth for all (though this was never taken to mean that all would be equally wealthy) were found wanting as the new common weal.

The Antisocial Society

Throughout modern history, developments exemplifying the uneven character of capital are as ubiquitous as capital accumulation itself. But to grasp the antisocial aspect of capitalist production relations as an essential characteristic rather than a contingent one, examples from recent history will not suffice; logical reconstruction is required. This task is undertaken, at the highest level of abstraction, by Marx in Chapter 1, Volume 1 of *Capital*. In

---

3   David Willetts MP, erstwhile Thatcherite policy worker, now a member of David Cameron's shadow cabinet, recently admitted as much. On the BBC Radio Four programme *Start The Week*, introduced by Andrew Marr, he reported that Christianity had provided Margaret Thatcher with a social dimension to match her faith in the free market; but for those to whom Christianity is inapplicable, Willetts continued, there needs to be another means of supplying this dimension.

my short chapter, there is no space to rehearse these relations as Marx blocks them out; but suffice to say that, in his logical reconstruction each episode of commodity production ends with producers estranged from the commodities they have made and connected to each other only indirectly through those commodities. Moreover, in market exchange commodities enjoy the universal, direct relations which their producers are denied. This is what Marx meant by 'the fetishism of commodities' – not a psychological dysfunction, but 'how things really are': direct relations between things and indirect relations between people (Marx 1983).

Accordingly, the production relations of capital put commodities centre stage and propel people to the wings where they must wait for another episode of production to begin. In the sense that they bring people together only to marginalise them, capitalist social relations are ultimately antisocial. Moreover, whether episodes of commodity production do indeed succeed each other, or whether the series grinds to a painful halt, depends in no small part on what happens outside the capital accumulation and the market, on the existence of other kinds of relations which have human beings, not commodities, as their subjects. By this analysis, the market alone cannot be expected to construct anything approaching human society, since it calls into being a society of commodities, with human beings consigned to secondary status and a role subordinate to the social life of things. Politics, and the civil society in which the political has occurred, typically serve to reconnect human beings whom the market alone would leave either atomised or restricted to the necessarily narrow range of interpersonal relations.

In the UK, the essentially antisocial character of capitalist economic development has been compounded by the contingencies of its own lack of dynamism. While civil society has never resulted from the market alone, periods of economic expansion have often given added impetus to the reclamation of relations between people even as they are usurped by relations between things. Thus periods of high growth, when capital throws ever-increasing numbers of people together even as it also atomises them, are frequently accompanied by a flowering of civil society. But the British economy has not experienced high growth rates since the post-war boom petered out in the 1970s. In this context, the hope must be that civil society will find a new way of flowering that is cut loose from sluggish economic trends as it is divorced from modern politics and their exhaustion.

In the 1980s and early 1990s, the effects of a faltering economy were said to be experienced largely (though not exclusively) outside London and the South-East. In recent years, while it has been the boast of Gordon Brown, first as Chancellor of the Exchequer and latterly as Prime Minister, that the UK is enjoying an unprecedentedly long period of economic growth, the rate of growth has been unusually low – in effect, lower than it is long, and this is so even in London. In a recent report the World Trade Organisation observed that while 'the world economy expanded by 3.3 per cent in 2005', Europe's economy 'continued to record low GDP growth' (WTO 2006, 1). Indeed 'the four largest economies in Europe (Germany, France, UK and Italy) all recorded GDP growth below 2 per cent' (WTO 2006, 2).

In the UK, growth rates for 2006 seem to have been less disappointing than for 2005, but not by a large margin:

> For 2006 as a whole UK GDP grew by 2.7 per cent compared with 1.9 per cent in 2005. Last year [2006] the service sector drove the UK economy, growing at a very healthy 3.7 per cent, up from 2.9 per cent in 2005. Meanwhile output of the production industries once again dragged down on the economy falling by 0.1 per cent in 2006. (GLA Economics 2007, 3)

It is no secret that in the most developed nations more investment in research and development is required to produce significant and sustainable acceleration of economic growth. But in Britain the Treasury (the government department of the Chancellor of the Exchequer) sees little precedent for this in the recent period:

> The UK faces a major challenge in trying to increase its R&D intensity towards the level of the other major developed countries in Europe and beyond. To do this real R&D expenditure would need to rise at a faster rate than trend economic growth (expected to be around 2.5 per cent per annum). In the 10 years between 1992 and 2002, annual R&D growth rates only exceeded 2.5 per cent by a significant margin on two occasions. (HM Treasury 2006, 53)

While British manufacturing is in absolute decline and R&D investment remains relatively low, the expansion of the financial services sector has done much to keep the economy afloat. Based on the National Accounts Yearbook issued by the Office of National Statistics, a survey by a private sector research company, International Financial Services (IFS), of 'the economic contribution of UK financial services', reports that 'financial services' share of UK GDP has risen strongly in recent years to reach 8.5 per cent in 2005, up from 5.5 per cent in 2001' (IFS 2006, 1). The IFS also reports that 'financial services are heavily concentrated in London which accounted for 42 per cent of value added by the sector in 2003' (ibid.). If the sector is so consistently buoyant, one might expect many more employees to have been drafted into it, and indeed the IFS report suggests bullish expansion of financial services as an employment sector:

> A broader estimate of 'City-type' jobs in Central London compiled by the Centre for Economic and Business Resources, which covers both financial and professional services, shows how employment has picked up since 1999.

> Apart from a dip in 2002, 'City-type' jobs have risen steadily from 294 000 in
> 1999 to 332 000 in 2006. (Ibid., 2)

Yet the rise is more steady than dramatic: less than new 40, 000 jobs in seven years; fewer than 6,000 new jobs a year. Even if increased productivity among financial services employees, recently estimated by IFS to be 'about twice the UK average' (ibid.), helps to reduce employment figures, this is hardly what's expected from the most dynamic sector (financial services) in the regional powerhouse (Greater London) of a national economy (Britain) enjoying an allegedly unprecedented period of growth.

Figures from GLA Economics, the economic analysis unit at the Greater London Authority, also indicate slow growth rather than market-led dynamism. In January 2007, it reported that 'London's employment rate is still more than five percentage points below the UK's employment rate.' (GLA Economics 2007, 9) In 2005 the largest job gains occurred in business services, public services, and hotels and restaurants. In 2006 these gains were offset by job losses in construction and in hotels and restaurants, while there were further gains in financial and business services, and 'a small recovery in manufacturing' (ibid.).

All in all, it seems that Poynter (2006, 16) is correct to emphasise the lack of market dynamism in the British economy:

> Far from the market having a voracious capacity to extend its influence over
> all aspects of contemporary social and economic life in the UK, the state
> is directly engaged in propping up an un-dynamic private, corporate sector
> and ensuring employment for many of those who work in it.

The British economy seems neither dynamic enough to produce the conditions for a new society nor forceful enough to destroy the old one. On the contrary, the experience of many corporate executives is of slack years in which capital accumulation, urban regeneration and social reconstruction have trudged along relatively slowly. To this effect, the account given by Nick Balmer, development manager of building contractors Edmund Nuttall, is worth quoting at length:

> Quite large numbers of us have been involved for many years in doing
> developments like Canary Wharf, the Docklands and other things, and we
> were very disappointed when it slowed down. And we think we've lost 10–15
> years ... We've been in a form of managed decline and retreat for many
> years.
>
> I cut my teeth in the Middle East and I know that we could build
> huge townships in very short periods of time. We could make enormous
> differences. And it's really frustrated us for many years that this hasn't
> happened here. (Balmer 2006).

Throughout the protracted period of London's 'managed decline and retreat' (ibid.), the economy has failed to throw large numbers of people together in new combinations and thereby create a popular sense of participating in a twenty-first-century city. Where this may possibly have occurred in miniature, it has been in isolated pockets such as Canary Wharf which by their splendid isolation tend to confirm the experience of uneven development to the point where it mitigates against the sense of a unified city.

Furthermore, if exclusion is unsurprising, given the episodic and essentially antisocial character of the market even as it creates the preconditions for society, what is unprecedented is the low uptake of politics as the preferred means of instating the human subject into social relations from which the market alone would have us marginalised. Instead a kind of convergence has occurred between the inability of the market to create civil society, even though modern social conditions could not have been created without it, and the failure of politics to realise and sustain it. This is the double whammy to which the Olympics as cultural strategy are meant to respond.

The Spirit of Society

'We have got about three million kids in this country who think they are going to be medal winners.' Giving evidence to a Parliamentary Select Committee in November 2006, Tessa Jowell, Secretary of State for Culture, Media and Sport, was quizzed about the financial cost of delivering London 2012, but she kept coming back to the significance of the Games as 'a catalyst' in 'enthusing' and 'involving' young people (Jowell 2006). Similarly Sir Robin Wales, Mayor of Newham, one of five London boroughs in which parts of the 2012 site are located, has said that sport itself is no justification for the financial outlay, which might otherwise be laid out on matters of more immediate concern. The real benefit is the rare opportunity to engender a new 'spirit of Newham' (Wales 2006). As cost estimates spiral and promises of a hard legacy are less forcefully put (lest they are too costly to deliver), if only by default soft legacy comes to the fore; and this soft legacy turns out to be the inhalation of Olympic spirit by Londoners who may be spiritless otherwise, or even animated by destructive drives.

Supposing large numbers of young Londoners really are of the alienated disposition that led to the suicide bombings of 7 July 2005, then hosting the Games in London, as had been announced only the previous day, becomes the appropriate mechanism for rescuing psychotically alienated youth, thereby rescuing the city of London from destructive episodes arising from the lack of mutual assurance felt so keenly among its wider population. Eighteen months later, during the winter of 2006–2007, the spate of South London teenagers shooting other teenagers dead again pointed to the level and intensity of disconnection between young people and social institutions, and among young people themselves. It also pointed up the potential role for a mega-event such as London 2012 in overriding social exclusion by the intensity of its inclusion.

The Olympism chapter in London's candidate file promised 'an Olympic and cultural programme that will connect with the wider world' (London 2012 2004, 5), but its primary role is closer to home – to make connections between disaggregated Londoners, in the hope of re-aggregating the city itself. Similarly, the programme was billed as the means to 'celebrate the renaissance of East London, made possible by the Olympic Games' (ibid.); but while the ongoing significance of the hard legacy remains in some doubt, it seems that 'to celebrate' can be one and the same thing as 'the renaissance' of East London. If only enough people are brought together in volunteering or some sort of participation in Olympic preparations, this will be the region's rebirth. In which case, not only is the road to 2012 built on good intentions, good intentions between Londoners are the desired outcome.

The Olympism chapter in the candidate file took as its text the famous line by John Donne, 'No man is an island' (ibid.); recognition of our common humanity was its theme. Whereas Olympism is usually seen as uniting different nations with one another, spuriously or not, in this instance the Olympic church of unification is intended to serve first within this island, among the disconnected digital parishes emerging in post-political London and the UK. Congregations are notoriously fickle, however; and there is no guarantee that Londoners will congregate as they are bidden so to do. The precedents are not strong. 'No host country', noted the Parliamentary Select Committee for Culture, Media and Sport, 'has yet been able to demonstrate a direct benefit from the Olympic Games in the form of a lasting increase in participation.' (PSC 2007, 37) But even if there were relatively few converts from among the wider population, the Olympics might yet provide the new clerisy with a sense of mission.

When Mayor Ken Livingstone welcomed the Olympics as 'a sword of Damocles' which by hanging over the heads of those in power would spur them into action on urban regeneration, he made this rhetorical flourish at Thames Gateway Forum, the largest, annual networking event for those professionally involved in the regeneration of East London and the surrounding region. (Livingstone 2006) In other words, Livingstone was speaking at an event which institutionalises the practice of regional governance as a process of continuous dialogue among governance professionals, to the point where the process is one of its own major outcomes (Calcutt 2008).

One of the organisations represented at Thames Gateway Forum was the East of England Development Agency (EEDA). One of its board members, Stephen Castle, also represents eastern England on the Nations and Regions Group for the Olympics. As a witness called to give evidence to the DCMS Parliamentary Select Committee, Castle explained the significance of the Olympics in connecting and galvanising those already engaged in urban regeneration and social reconstruction.

> It is not necessarily about doing lots of new things; it is about achieving
> existing targets and priorities and using the Games ... as the magic dust to
> try and actually accelerate the delivery of some of those existing priorities.
> (PSC 2007, 45–6)

In the world of professional politicians and urban regenerators, to be dusted by
the Olympics will have magical, galvanising effects, and all those galvanised –
who have shared the dusting – will therefore have partaken of the same magic.
Thus the Olympics are called upon to serve as a kind of communion among
urban policy professionals in the UK; and this is a significant sacrament,
regardless of how many of the wider population take it, or are taken by it.

China: It's Not the Economy, Stupid

Whereas in London and the UK the post-political problem of how to
construct society, is posed more starkly by the absence of market dynamism,
in China the very force of the market has brought different pressures to bear.
In both countries, however, the one-sidedness of the market is only one aspect
of the key problem facing ruling elites. The problem they face acquires its dual
character not only from the inadequacies and inequalities derived from market
relations but also from the inefficacy of politics in addressing them. In China,
as in the UK, there seems to be no systemic alternative to the workings of the
market, albeit with significant, state-sponsored modification. Meanwhile the
political is unworkable; and the Olympics are being called upon to construct
what politics cannot.

There is no need here to rehearse the growth rates exhibited by the Chinese
economy, except to note that with GDP growth nudging or exceeding 10 per
cent per annum for more than a decade, China alongside India is set to provide
the biggest ever boost to the world economy (Woodall 2006, 3). Yet in China's
case especially, the biggest ever boost to the global, capitalist economy has
been occurring along lines which are not classically capitalist. Opinions differ
as to how much of the Chinese economy operates according to the law of
value rather than rulings of the state and the Chinese Communist Party. In
2005, the OECD reckoned that the private sector accounted for 57 per cent of
non-farm output; but far from being definitive this figure was an extrapolation
from 160,000 companies surveyed between 1998 and 2003 (OECD 2005). In
any case China's capitalism is clearly anomalous, as noted in the bulletin of
China Economic Quarterly:

> Relative to the past, the private sector is enormously important in China
> today. Relative to any other major country (Russia perhaps excluded), China
> remains by far the most state driven economy in the world today. (*China
> Economic Quarterly* 2005, 5)

Noting this anomaly, its instability, and the social unrest which economic growth often entails, various observers have been wondering how China can free up its economy still further, and asking whether China will develop liberal political institutions in keeping with economic liberalism and in accordance with Western models. Concerned by 'China's lagging political development' (Pei 2006, 4) and 'growing imbalances in society and polity' (ibid.), Minxin Pei warns of 'erosion of state capacity' (ibid., 13) and the possibility of 'an incapacitated state' (ibid., 214) which would both result from and contribute to economic slowdown 'should China's rise fizzle' (ibid., 213). The current state-led state of affairs, Pei says, is unsustainable. China must move further towards market relations and concomitant political relations, but the danger is of transition trapped by the very institutions which were the instruments of recent economic growth, namely, the state and the Chinese Communist Party.

In Britain, political economist and public intellectual Will Hutton has made similar observations in *The Writing On The Wall: China and the West in the Twenty-first Century* (2006). Hutton also noted that political institutions in the West are far from healthy, and called for their revitalisation as a key factor in both the development of China and developing East-West relations. However, to assume that China either is or should develop along lines previously established in the West, even while exhorting Westerners to live up to the traditions which they themselves developed, is to substitute a ready-made model of social development for analysis of historically-specific current conditions from which emerging or modified institutions suggest themselves. It would indeed be exceptional if China were to follow Hutton's directions and emerge as a highly politicised society at just the moment when depoliticisation is among the clearest trends in the West. In any case, China is not new to modern politics. It is superfluous, if not chauvinist, to call for the politicisation of China and for China to be introduced to democratic politics, since this round of introductions occurred more than a century ago.

Those such as Fincher who argue against Chinese exceptionalism[4] also reckon that Chinese democrats gave a good account of themselves at least until such time as the First World War brought about a sharp modification in the regional balance of forces:

---

4   'There is no more reason to charge the Chinese than the Netherlands, English or French revolutionaries with a cultural predisposition to defer to despots. The point could be driven further by comparing or contrasting Chinese experience with unsuccessful as well as with successful early modern European revolutions: across the Eurasian land mass from China, Pugachev's 1774 rebellion in the southern region of European Russia made its adherents servants of a "liturgic state". The autocracy of that rebellion was scarcely gentler than that of the mid-nineteenth century Taiping rebellion of south and central China' (Fincher 1981, 25).

> Judged by its progress from 1905-13, Chinese democracy was faring better at
> that moment and by the standards of its own history than were democratic
> reform movements in the largest contemporary Western polities, Russia and
> America, at that moment in *their* histories. (Fincher 1981, 23)

China's democratic reformers came close to success, Fincher claims: 'The First
Liberal Republic in China nearly produced a partnership between financial
and political power not unlike that between 'the City' and 'the Court' in the
Glorious Revolution of 1688 in England' (ibid., 263) By such accounts, Chinese
history of a hundred years ago was not that of cultural exceptionalism, but
a familiar narrative of nationalism and capitalist development in a period
dominated by two, overlapping struggles: between workers, peasants and
capital, and between imperialist rivals. This makes Mao's turn to the peasantry,
the move upon which was built the one-party state in China, an act of modern
politics at a time when neither Chinese capital nor the Chinese working class
was strong enough to withstand imperialist pressure.

In other words, the Chinese social order of the past half-century was a
continuation of modern politics by one-party means. Similarly, that the
rhetoric of the Chinese Communist Party was also the *lingua franca* of Western
political conflict from the Paris Commune at least until the incorporation of
the European working class in the post-war political settlement of 1945, is
not only a matter of semantics but speaks of the volumes of modern *political*
history in which hundreds of millions of Chinese have already lived and died.
When it comes to politics, although their long march has taken a different route
from that of Labourist Britain, the people of China have already been there
and done that. To expect today's Chinese population to enter once more into
the realm of politics, a ruined realm in East and West alike, is simultaneously
a position and a projection of cynicism or naivety, or perhaps both.

In China itself, unsurprisingly, there is little sign of such trends. Thus there
is no take-up of trade unions as the epicentre of relations between wage labour
and capital. Metcalf and Li have noted that the All China Federation of Trade
Unions boasts membership of 137 million, but that unions 'are virtually
impotent when it comes to representing workers' (Metcalf and Li 2006, 24).
They date the emergence of a labour market in China to 1994, but observe
that 'there is no evidence whatsoever of a parallel development in functioning
unions', concluding instead that unions are 'likely to remain largely nugatory
in China' (ibid.). Similarly, there is no new emphasis on 'social rights' with a
welfare state at the heart of a new political order:

> There is not a shred of evidence that, in aggregate, social spending has
> risen higher on the government's priority list ... Despite government talk
> of increased compassion, social service spending actually grew a bit slower
> than expenditure as a whole. (Kroeber 2006, 3)

This is the context, from which state welfare is noticeably absent, in which rural labourers who have migrated to work in Beijing, on finding themselves unemployed often prefer to commit suicide, sometimes by jumping off cranes on the building sites where they had been working, rather than experience the shame of returning workless to the countryside and becoming a burden on their families. In China today there is neither a welfare state nor a social movement demanding its construction.

Environmentalism is perhaps more in evidence than either unionism or welfarism. In a paper for Chatham House, Yiyi Lu (2005, 2) noted that 'environmental civil society has become highly visible in China since 2003'. She went on to report the sector's first big success:

> In 2003 the media and environmental NGOs mobilised public opinion against a planned dam near Dujiangyan, an ancient site that has been designated a World Heritage site. Eventually the plan was dropped. (Ibid.)

Lu's paper positions environmental non-government organisations (NGOs) – 'among the most dynamic civil society organisations', as potential harbingers of a newly politicised China. But the political success story cited by Lu also suggests a different interpretation of the role of such organisations, and indicates the possibility that a different turn may be occurring – a turn to something other than and different from politics – on the part of Chinese officials and intellectuals.

The plan for the Dujiangyan dam was dropped because it was a violation of Chinese tradition. The Chinese cultural tradition is said to be based on harmony between people and between people and nature – a cultural tradition which when conceived as such would have been brought into disharmony by the dam and its discordant effects. Here environmentalism is oriented towards the preservation of culture; its orientation to cultural tradition stands as a counterpoint to the increasingly central role of the market. Alternatively, it could be said that orientation towards cultural tradition is here couched as environmentalism: the turn is to culture; its form is the preservation of natural harmony in place of industrial and economic strife. Thus it is traditional culture not modern politics which is being invoked against economics and market domination.

Cultural Tradition as Social Insurance

NGOs are not the only ones making the turn to cultural tradition. Online fantasy games of the 'sword and sorcery' genre are a 'cash spigot' (Yeh 2004, 47). There is sizeable demand for cultural tradition by hi-tech means. The popular resonance for these games further suggests that the private sector may even gain legitimacy as well as profits by supplying commodities to meet this demand. On a much larger scale, there are great expectations of the cultural and creative industries in Hong Kong and the Pearl River Delta, the peculiar strength of which is said to be derived from 'the same pre-historic cultural system' of Lingnan (Hui 2006, 4).[5] In a policy study for the Centre for Cultural Policy Research at the University of Hong Kong, Hui advocated a cultural industries taskforce along lines established in Creative Britain during the late 1990s.[6] But by his own account creativity seems to have more to recommend it when associated with Chinese cultural tradition, rather than the shock of the new as espoused in British popular culture in the 1960s, and recapitulated in the construction of Creative Britain in the 1990s.

On behalf of China's state sector, with culture sandwiched between productive forces and the will of the majority, Jiang Zemin's report to the sixteenth National Congress of the Communist Party of China, indicated high-level recognition of the centrality of culture, at least in official rhetoric:

> The Party must always represent the three requirements of the development of China's advanced productive forces, the orientation of the development of China's advanced culture, and the fundamental interests of the overwhelming majority of the people in China. (Zemin 2002)

If the centrality of cultural tradition were only a rhetorical construction, it would be of little use to the Chinese Communist Party, which is already weighed down with the baggage of political rhetoric. But party and state are doing more than culture talk; they are investing heavily in cultural tradition, an investment which is embodied and embedded in the grand design of the Beijing Olympics.

The harmonious role required of culture in Beijing 2008 is encapsulated in the designation of the Games as 'humanistic'. In his presentation to the Host Cities conference produced by the University of East London in 2006, Professor Jin Yuanpu, Associate Director of the Humanistic Olympics Studies Centre at Renmin University in Beijing, described the Beijing Olympics as simultaneously Green, Hi-Tech and Humanistic, with the latter further characterised as follows:

---

5   'Geographically, both Honk Kong and the Pearl River Delta belong to the same prehistoric cultural system. The local cultural system has its roots in the Lingnan culture. In terms of local tradition, this embodiment of Lingnan cultural content and characteristics is revealed in all aspects of ideology, education, literature, arts, architecture, craftsmanship, dialects, tradition and gastronomy' (Hui 2006, 4).

6   'This integrated platform could start with an organisation consisting of representatives from the respective sectors. We might call this the Cultural and Creative Industries Commission/TaskForce (hereinafter referred to as the TaskForce)' (Hui 2006, 25).

> [confirming] the centrality of mankind in the scheme of things by developing
> human-beings in a well-rounded, harmonious manner. (Jin 2006)

The Humanistic Olympics, continued Professor Jin, will give priority to 'traditional Chinese folk art and culture', with cultural representation of all '56 groups that form the nation', each with 'their own sports, games and competitions.' (Jin 2006) The theme of harmony through creative industry and cultural tradition was also much in evidence at the Fourth International Forum on the Beijing Olympic Games in July 2006, which I attended at the invitation of Professor Jin.

The slogan of the July 2006 conference, and of the Beijing Games themselves, is 'One World, One Dream'. At such gatherings the slogan is given an international inflection. But the creation of 'one world', or even the dream of creating such a world, is just as important domestically, within China itself. More accurately, there is no such fixed thing as 'China itself'; instead China will have to be fixed and fixed again in today's turbulent conditions, and it seems that cultural tradition is an important means for achieving this. As deployed in and around the Olympics, cultural tradition is a mechanism which allows the elite to get a fix on China today – over and above the market and as a socially constructive counterpoint to its corrosive effects – and disseminate this to the masses.

Noting that 'China used to be poor but homogenous, but now a polarising trend has suddenly appeared', Hai Ren (2005, 3) of Beijing Sport University identified the adoption of 'harmonious society' as a government goal:

> China has entered a critical stage with opportunities as well as formidable
> challenges. The most difficult one is to continue the reforms, at the same
> time maintaining social stability. So construction of a harmonious society
> has been proposed as the next goal by the government.

This is the goal to which the Beijing Olympics are oriented. It has an external aspect, thus staging the Games 'will help China to meet with and integrate into the world and establish a friendly and harmonious external environment.' (ibid., 4) But domestic outcomes are just as highly prized. It is hoped that 'by facilitating social cooperation', this will 'allow everyone involved to recognise the values of others' (ibid.). Similarly, the Olympics are expected to have positive effects in 'improving social behaviour' (ibid.); that where there is evidence of the 'decline of social morals' and the 'system of social trust' has been put in jeopardy', staging the Games can 'change the situation mainly through the Olympic volunteer campaign' (ibid., 5). The Games are also called upon to help in 'disseminating the key values of modern society: openness, tolerance, friendship and care of the environment' (ibid.).

Much of this script could have been written in and for Newham, or any of London's five Olympic boroughs. Yet it would be wrong to suggest that the social agenda for Beijing 2008 is exactly the same as that of London 2012. In Beijing there is a much greater sense of international display, on a scale and with the panache to match China's spectacular re-entry into the world economy. With this ostentatious intent the Beijing Olympics are comparable to Colin Welland's infamous Oscars night declaration, 'the British are coming', but written a million times larger and delivered – in painfully sharp contrast to the British film industry, or British industry, come to that – a billion times over. However it is notable that a dramatic economic entrance which in reality dates back little more than the last two decades, is couched in terms of 4,000 years of Chinese cultural tradition and the two weeks in which to present it to the rest of the world. (Jin 2006) As in London 2012, for Beijing 2008 culture is central, both as a key credential for hosting and staging the Games, and as the most highly prized outcome, or soft legacy.

Countering Economy

Orientation towards culture is not primarily culturally specific, since it is being applied in both London and Beijing. Instead it turns out to be historically specific, i.e. a phenomenon prompted by particular historical conditions in which it is widely accepted that politics cannot work, and that the market is as insufficient as it is unavoidable. This, however, is not to say that there are no cultural differences or historical variations between Beijing and London, or that the former do not impinge upon the latter, and vice versa. Thus, if culture is similarly at the centre of things in both London and Beijing, and if both cities are to be centred on culture, then the orientation of culture itself is different in each city.

In Beijing, within living memory of the 'cultural revolution' and its disastrous consequences, the emphasis is on cultural continuity. Meanwhile in London, culture is highly regarded insofar as it connotes change, to the point where historian Tristram Hunt recently complained about the creation of 'history-free' zones (Hunt 2006). Thus the portmanteau term 'culture' is packed with either tradition or novelty depending on where you open it – in Beijing or London respectively. The irony is that the underlying economic trends in both of these cities are the direct opposite of the ideas of culture with which each seeks to be identified.

Yet this contradiction is also consistent with the ambition for culture to continue the social by means other than politics. For continuing the social means carrying on where economics leaves off; and if culture is called upon to constitute society by countering the antisocial aspects of the market, it must be recognisably other than today's market conditions, i.e. the non-identity between market and culture should be explicit. Thus in the most dynamic economy in the world it is the traditional aspect of culture which is more often invoked. Meanwhile in the slow-growth economy of the UK, 'culture' connotes innovation without necessarily delivering it. In each instance, and in both of these different inflections, culture meets one of the key criteria for social, post-political reconstruction: it is identifiably other than the current character of the national economy.

Seen in this expanded capacity both the Beijing and the London Olympics may be described as a social imaginary, but their success or failure in this role will have real not just imaginary consequences. Having indicated that the other worldliness of culture to economy is a precondition for culture's social role as constructive counterpoint to the corrosively antisocial effects of the market, I now turn to a brief consideration of whether in its Olympic guise culture is fit for the social purpose thrust upon it. Some observations in my short prospectus will be confined to the London Olympiad. When referring to Beijing I shall do so only in general terms.

Contradiction Compounded

That the Olympics is not only a cultural, non-economic event but also a capital-expending, revenue-generating extravaganza, is a contradiction which may be largely ignored by Londoners and others in Britain; or it could become a source of conflict which disqualifies the London Olympiad from playing its intended social role. So far, the popular grumble has been that Londoners are being asked to pay too large a surcharge to help cover the costs of the Olympics, while some corporations are set to make profits from it. Such grumbles are derived from a difficulty located at the heart of the modern Olympics. Although cast as a socially inclusive net which will fish for all humanity, the Olympics are also an instance *par excellence* of capitalist property relations. Aside from transcending the antisocial character of the economy, the Olympics also represent it.

Thus all may be called to take part in staging the Games, but, as noted by the parliamentary select committee for culture, media and sport, only a tiny elite has the property rights to call their activities 'the Olympics', 'the Games', 'London 2012', or anything remotely resembling these designations:

> We note that, in theory, the promotion of a school or village event termed 'Summer Games' or '2012 Competition' might be caught under the Act ...
> The London Olympic Games and Paralympic Games Act 2006 ... applies the principle of an Olympic association right to London 2012 Games ... [it] confers exclusive rights in relation to the use of any representation in a manner likely to suggest to the public that there is an association between the London Olympics and goods and services. (PSC 2007, 43)

Secretary of State Tessa Jowell gave evidence to the DCMS Parliamentary Select Committee of her department's ambition to create a brand that does not fall foul of 'the commercial relationship.' (Jowell 2006) There can hardly be a more succinct summation of the conundrum: in an image conscious, brand-aware world where the aim of the game is for large numbers of people to recognise themselves and each other in staging the Olympics, how can there be brand recognition which does not also impinge upon and infringe the property rights of the International Olympics Committee (IOC) and their 2012 proxies, the London Organising Committee of the Olympic Games and the Olympic Delivery Authority?

Here culture as general participation is in contradiction with the logic of commodified culture – culture as a commodity which only its specified owner may rightfully dispose of. Whether this logical contradiction translates into recurring, real life conflict, remains to be seen; but the potential for it to become a problem is inherent in the tactical use of the Olympics – not only a gift to the world but also the intellectual property of the IOC – in the attempted reconstruction of civil society by cultural means.

There is also the mercurial character of culture, hence (thankfully) the difficulty of fixing it as a social reagent. Culture is so much like quicksilver that it is dangerous to be schematic with it in analysis, never mind in social engineering. Suffice to say that culture is continually constituted through external and internal contradictions. As previously noted, culture must be in some sense external to the economy; but that which is external to it, namely economic conditions and their effects, must also be represented in culture if it is to retain its currency. Meanwhile, in its own terms, as regards the forms in which it functions, culture is the result of creative tension between change and continuity, innovation and tradition, experimentation and familiarity; and there is always the possibility of this tension being lost.

In Beijing's cultural policy the overwhelming emphasis on tradition is perhaps not conducive to retaining this tension, and there is a possible danger of unmanageable disjuncture – schism rather than tension – between Chinese tradition (partly invented, significantly manipulated) and a modern economy with its own modernist aesthetic. For the visitor to Beijing, there is an enjoyable *frisson* in the contrast between the angular suits and shirts worn by many Chinese men, a high modernist outfit which would not look out of place on a London Mod, and the Bird's Nest stadium, so-called because its rounded-out structure seems to aspire to the organic as the embodiment of tradition. But the contrast between ancient and modern is not necessarily enjoyed by Chinese people themselves; at some point they may feel the need to choose, which may in turn lead to a culture war waged within China itself. If perhaps these words of warning sound as lightweight as a Beijing suit, bear in mind that with heavy social investment in culture, when the cultural is called upon to carry the social weight previously sustained by politics, it is sensible to assume that the effects of this investment will indeed be weighty – whether they are measured in terms of success or failure.

In London, the risk is that 'anything goes' will be so lacking in creative tension that it does not go anywhere. As I write, among some of those involved in preparations for London 2012, there is a readiness to accept the Cultural Olympiad as one part re-badging the existing activities of leading British cultural institutions, and another part re-staging existing community arts practice as an Olympian Fringe. But the former already have as much of an audience, domestically and internationally, as they are likely to get; and the latter is often so introspective – concerned largely with relatively untutored practitioners finding themselves and each other in a process of only local relevance – that it would not withstand wider exposure, or maintain the interest of those to whom it might seek to expose itself. There is not much here to write home about: one is the arts business as usual; the other promotes access above all other criteria, i.e. it is cultural policy as usual. Neither of these complacent approaches will allow young people in London to, literally, write a new home for themselves by cultural participation. I sincerely hope that this will not be the case, but if it turned out that this is all there is to it, London's cultural policy would be found just as wanting as politics – and a lot sooner.

Yet for all these current, contingent limitations, the ambitions which now appear in their diminished form as cultural policy, can be traced back to the pre-political phase of the modern period, when Herder and others formed a view of humanity as primarily expressive, in which 'human life was seen as having a unity rather analogous to that of a work of art, where every part or aspect found its proper meaning in relation to all the others' (Taylor 1979, 1). Where Herder tended to nationalise human subjectivity, i.e. he posited the unified, expressive subject as the property of particular nations and their specific cultures, Hegel historicised it, i.e. he saw the realisation of humanity in reciprocal relations with historically specific conditions: we are the *zeitgeist*, and the *zeitgeist* is us.

I readily acknowledge such abstract formulations are really asking to be brought down to earth. Nonetheless, if it could be said of the Olympics in Beijing and London that they were both authors and instruments, subject and object, of the times in which we live, then they could surely be counted as a success – and they might even be the moments in which early indications of a new kind of society came to be widely recognised. For there is something to be said for a civil society of self-recognition; and for the time being it may be the only kind of society which we can expect. It all depends on what we recognise ourselves in, or how we encourage others to recognise themselves. Are we so cynical of humanity that we see ourselves and others in the mere process of cultural participation, where it doesn't matter what we are participating in so long as it produces a healthy glow in the cheeks and a temporary sense of conviviality? Or are we committed to the pursuit of excellence, and inspired by previous generations which have raised the bar by prostrating themselves before universal standards of human achievement? In Beijing and in the run-up to London 2012, this, surely, is the question at the heart of social and individual reconstruction. We will have failed our own times and our own people if our answer does not measure up.

References

Arnold, M. (1969 [1869]) *Culture and Anarchy: An Essay in Political and Social Criticism*, Cambridge: Cambridge University Press.

Balmer, N. (2006) 'The Olympics: Potential Opportunities and Risks Outside the Olympic Zone', Thames Gateway Forum 23 November.

Bauman, Z. (1999) *In Search of Politics*, Cambridge: Polity Press.

China Economic Quarterly (2005) Bulletin No. 7, 30 September.

Calcutt, A. (2008) 'Forcing The Market, Forging Community: Culture as Social Construction in the Thames Gateway', in Cohen, P. and Rustin, M. (eds) (2008) *London's Turning: The Making of Thames Gateway,* Aldershot: Ashgate.

Fincher, J.H. (1981) *Chinese Democracy: The Self-government Movement in Local, Provincial and National Politics 1905–1914*, London: Croom Helm.

GLA Economics (2007) *London's Economy Today* 53, January.

Hui, D. (ed.) (2006) *Study of the Relationship between Hong Kong's Cultural and Creative Industries and the Pearl River Delta*, Centre for Cultural Policy Research, University of Hong Kong, http://ccpr.hku.hk, last accessed 15 September 2006.

HM Treasury (2006) *Science and Innovation Investment Framework 2004–2014*, London: HM Treasury.

Hunt, T. (2006) 'How The Past Informs The Future', Thames Gateway Forum 23 November.

Hutton, W. (2007) *The Writing On The Wall: China and the West in the Twenty-First Century*, London: Little Brown.

International Financial Services (2006) *Economic Contribution of UK Financial Services 2006*, London: IFS.

Jin, Y. (2006) 'Beijing's Legacy to the World', paper to Host Cities conference at London Excel, convened by University of East London, http://www.uel.ac.uk, last accessed 15 September 2006.

Jowell, T. (2006) evidence to Parliamentary Select Committee, Culture, Media and Sport, broadcast on Parliament Channel, 28 December (author's notes).

Kroeber, A. (2006) *China Insight* 14, 23 March, *China Economic Quarterly.*

Livingstone, K. (2006) speech to Thames Gateway Forum, 23 November.

London 2012 (2004) 'Olympism', *Candidate File*, http://www.london2012.com/news/publications, last accessed 17 March 2008.

Lu, Y. (2005) *Environmental Civil Society and Governance*, Chatham House Asia Programme, Reference No. ASP BP 05/04, August.

Marx, K. (1983 [1867/1887]) *Capital: A Critique of Political Economy*, Vol. 1, London: Lawrence and Wishart.

Metcalf, D. and Li, J. (2006) 'Trade Unions in China', *Centrepiece*, Summer, London School of Economics.

OECD (2005) *Economic Surveys: China*, issued 16 September, http://www. oecd.org/document21, last accessed 15 September 2006.

Office of the Mayor of London (2006) 'We are Londoners, We are One', publicity campaign devised and coordinated by the Office of the Mayor of London, http://www.london.gov.uk/onelondon, last accessed 17 March 2008.

Pei, M. (2006) *China's Trapped Transition: The Limits of Developmental autocracy*, Cambridge, MA: Harvard University Press.

PSC (2007) *London 2012 Olympic and Paralympic Games, Funding and Legacy*, report of the Parliamentary Select Committee for Culture, Media and Sport, January.

Poynter, G. (2006) Corporate Capital and State Dependency.

Putnam, R.D. (2000) *Bowling Alone: The Collapse and Revival of American Community*, New York: Simon and Schuster.

Ren, H. (2005) 'Humanistic Olympics: Where Will it Lead To?', Beijing Sport University, http://www.playthegame.org, last accessed 23 January 2007.

Smith, C. (2000) Remarks at the inaugural symposium of the Pavis Centre for the study of culture, Open University, Milton Keynes (author's notes).

Taylor, C. (1979) *Hegel and Modern Society*, Cambridge: Cambridge University Press.

Wales, R. (2006) 'The Spirit of Newham', *Rising East Online* May, http://www. risingeast.org, last accessed 23 January 2007.

Williams, R. (1965) *The Long Revolution*, Harmondsworth: Penguin.

Woodall, P. (2006) 'The New Titans', the *Economist* survey of the world economy, 16/9/2006.

WTO (2006) *World Trade Report 2006*, Geneva: WTO.

Yeh, A. (2004) 'Killer App', *China Economic Quarterly*, Q2.

Young, M. and Willmott, P. (1957) *Family and Kinship in East London*, London: Institute of Community Studies/Routledge and Kegan Paul.

Zemin, J. (2002) Report to 16th National Congress of Communist Party of China, http://www.china.org.cn/english, last accessed 18 March 2008.

PART 4
Olympic Legacies

Chapter 18

Olympic Cities and Social Change

Iain MacRury and Gavin Poynter

Introduction

The concluding chapter focuses on three themes raised in this book. First, the characteristics of the Games as the world's premiere 'mega event' are examined, picking up discussions found in Part 1. In particular, we focus on the necessity for the Olympic movement to sustain its adaptive capacities if the Games is to continue as the leading global sporting event. Second, the Games as 'legacy' is conceptualised and analysed with reference to the experiences of those cities discussed in earlier chapters in Part 2. Finally, the possible trajectories of the legacy for East London are briefly discussed in the light of earlier contributions and with reference to the aspirations of government, 2012 'stakeholders' and the area's communities. In particular, the discussion of East London examines the challenges facing all of us who are concerned with social change and the reshaping of East London in the twenty-first century.

The Premiere Mega-Event

Whereas earlier phenomena of popular culture such as the Expo were used in the nineteenth century to demonstrate the material achievements of industrial production and empire, global sporting events have assumed a different role in the contemporary world. Hosting the Olympics in the twenty-first century provides an opportunity to celebrate the creation and consumption of the products and services of post-industrialism, with the event affirming a new kind of global status to the city that proves it can be a successful host. The mega event has become a fashionable tool by which cities and governments seek to utilise the Olympic brand to enhance regional and global status and catalyse social and economic change. The Olympic and Paralympic Games is the most prestigious event or international prize for an aspirant host city – its scale, global audience, concentration in one major city and embrace of the ancient and modern conceptions of festival lend it a unique quality in a world in which the staging and transmission of regional and international sporting events has become a regular affair.

A brief comparison with another international sporting event, the FIFA World Cup, gives some appreciation of the global significance attributed to the Olympics in terms of its audience and popular appeal. The 2006 FIFA World Cup took place in Germany with 232 countries providing television coverage; the Athens Olympics (2004) was transmitted to 220 countries. The tv audience worldwide for the world cup in Germany was 26.3 billion, while for the Athens Games the estimate is 34.4 billion. Whilst care is required in comparing and interpreting the figures – the estimates for Germany were based on cumulative viewing hours (the numbers of viewers tuning into coverage) and for Athens, total viewing hours (the sum of all viewer hours per programme) – the summer Olympics achieves an audience comparable to the most popular soccer event televised in the world (IOC 2008; FIFA 2007). With the Beijing Games, the worldwide television audience will be boosted massively by the viewing figures achieved by the host nation's population. Equally, by 2012 it is likely that the first 'mobile' summer Games will take place, with audiences tuning in via a diversity of mobile telecommunication technologies to receive transmissions from accredited broadcasters, bloggers and spectators. The Games' concentration in one city magnifies the impact of the event on that city, while soccer world cup venues are distributed around several towns and cities in the host nation. Finally, the Olympic and Paralympic Games carries with it an ethos (Olympism) that aspires to confer social and cultural meanings and values not shared by other sporting events. In this sense, the modern Games, unlike soccer events, are defined by their character as 'festival' and 'commodity'; as MacRury explains in Chapter 3, an often contradictory combination reflected in the IOCs embrace of the sponsorship of international enterprises within its conception of the Olympic family and its commitment to expanding the socially responsible dimensions of the Games to incorporate environmental, cultural, economic and social legacies.

As Michael Rustin indicates in the first chapter of this book, as an international agency, the IOC has adeptly managed a transition over the past decade from an international sporting organisation tainted by allegations of corruption and bribery to one that promotes socially responsible agendas that seek to legitimise or justify the vast sums of money required to put on the Games. These chameleon-like qualities have ensured that the IOC has re-invented the event in a manner apparently suited to the contemporary global era, mobilising the competitive instincts of cities and nations to bid for the Games while also seeking to put in place structures designed to manage or modify the excesses of commercialism that naturally arise around such market-oriented competitions. The Olympic Games Global Impact Study (OGGI) agreed by the IOC in 2001 and implemented for the first time by a host city by the Beijing Olympic Games Organising Committee (BOCOG) may be seen in this light. The study is designed to evaluate the Games' legacy for the host nation and city against a raft of social, economic, cultural and environmental indicators, hence providing an 'evidence base' for measuring the positive societal consequences of the Games for its hosts.

In brief, the revival of the appeal to host the Games has several dimensions in addition to the ways in which the IOC has repositioned itself and its primary global event over recent years. It offers a capacity for the host nation and city to affirm or reinvent itself as a site for investment in consumption based service industries such as tourism, financial and business services and event and conference management. It legitimates, in the domestic sphere, the coming together of private and public partnerships to stimulate infrastructure investment and development consistent with this economic vision. It acts as a catalyst for the expansion of the service industries – leisure, cultural and creative – associated with this post-industrial economy; especially through the Cultural Olympiad; a festival that is focused upon the host city and lasts for the four years that precedes the Games. Finally, it enables the host city and nation to appropriate the Olympics to affirm or announce its distinctive role and presence in the contemporary world. Such prizes are it seems greatly valued by cities in the twenty-first century. The competition for hosting the 2016 Games is already underway, with seven cities in the frame – Baku, Chicago, Doha, Madrid, Prague, Rio de Janeiro and Tokyo.

Maintaining the appeal of the Games is not, however, a straightforward affair. The reasons for its current popularity may rapidly become causes of its potential decline as the world's premiere mega event. The recent reinvention of the Games rests upon some unspoken assumptions about the stability and direction of the global economy in the twenty-first century. The international turmoil in financial markets in early 2008 and the underlying shift in the dynamics of growth in the world economy (as indicated in Chapter 2) from the 'western' developed nations to the east, and especially China, East Asia and India, alters the economic and political environment and perceptions of the economic and political 'models' upon which the viability of the Games rests. There is, in short, a greater diversity lent to the motivations and aspirations of bidding cities and nations as the process of capital accumulation and wealth creation expands to encompass newly developed parts of the world (Arrighi 2007).

For example, whilst for London hosting the Games is designed to unlock the future potential of urban regeneration, for China, the Beijing Games represents an expression, in economic terms, of what it has already achieved – a sustained period of economic growth that has propelled the nation into the world's top five economies. For London, and especially East London, regeneration relies heavily upon the promotion of consumption-based service industries, particularly financial and business services and the creative industries – all of which are under significant pressures arising from recent financial crises. By contrast, the Beijing Games reflects the confidence of a nation whose economy has rapidly expanded but for whom its relatively new prominence in the international 'community' is politically problematic – as the social unrest in Tibet in early 2008 and the protests surrounding the Beijing bound flame relay in cities like London, Paris and San Francisco reveal. The significant shifts in the dynamics of the international economy and international affairs that are surfacing in the latter part of this decade, create important challenges to the Olympic movement's capacities to continue to adapt to this new environment especially, as Rustin suggests in Chapter 1, when it comes to reconciling vast expenditure by the host city and nation with programmes designed to achieve positive social legacies in the host city and nations.

Legacy Effects

Here the discussion of legacy divides into two parts. First, a brief review of the case studies of past host cities discussed in Part 2 of this book is undertaken. The review addresses key themes that were formative in shaping the legacies achieved by recent host cities. Second, the concept of legacy is unpacked in order to provide some insights into what might constitute a more rigorous framework for analysing the social impact of mega events such as the Olympic Games.

In his chapter on Olympic driven urban development (Chapter 4), Dean Baim deploys Preuss's categorisation of the sectors of a city that may be affected by hosting the Games – transportation, telecommunications, sports venues, housing, urban culture and ecological investment (Preuss 2004: 91–2). Setting aside telecommunications since all hosts have sought to improve this infrastructure, Baim helpfully demonstrates how over the history of the modern Games, host cities have undertaken investment in a growing number of these sectors, especially since the Seoul Games (1988). The subsequent chapters in Part 2 of the book provide some more detailed insights into the successes and failures of the host cities in turning this investment into a sustained longer term advantage. How such 'advantage' is defined and quantified, however, is a complex affair.

One approach to evaluating advantage may arise from a longitudinal study of the host city encompassing the pre-event, event and post-event phases. Such a study may provide insights into the relationship between the published objectives of the host city, contained in the initial tender document or 'bid book' presented to the IOC, and the actual outcomes achieved at the end of a period of, say, three to five years after the Games has taken place. Only recently have such longitudinal studies been seriously considered, with the IOCs OGGI being the prime example. Such approaches have real merit in evaluating the success or otherwise of public investment in relation to clearly identified policy commitments and performance outcomes (and have been adopted by UK government departments, as early as 2008, as an important component of their evaluation of the 2012 Games) but they may not capture the full picture of the impacts of the Games on the host city and nation. The Games has intended and unintended consequences and intangible advantages and disadvantages for host cities that may not be easy to capture in 'data driven' studies.[1] The discussion of legacy outcomes here attempts to illustrate these issues in the light of the experience of the host cities discussed in Part 2, particularly in relation to questions of governance and 'city-building'.

Governance

The concept of governance has arisen in policy circles from a recognition of the potential of 'market failure' and an unwillingness of policy makers at least in 'western' nations, such as the UK, to return to forms of direct state intervention that typically occurred in the 1960s (Bacon and Eltis 1976). Governance refers to ways of bringing institutions representing the state and market into forms of public/private partnership to deliver infrastructure development and major projects. The concepts of governance and partnership are fluid, contested terms in the academic literature (Jones and Evans 2006). Partnerships between the state and private sector may vary according to the levels of cooperation and interdependence of the public and private institutions engaged in specific projects (Davies 2001) and vary with the trajectory of capitalist development pursued by different nations, especially in the non-western context of development that has occurred in countries such as Japan, South Korea and China. Here, academic authors have characterized state/market relations in a variety of ways, typically highlighting the importance of the state in creating 'the governed market' or 'capitalist developmental state' which, according to Chalmers Johnson, is characterized by the state giving priority to economic development, committing to private property and enterprise, establishing extensive consultative processes with the private sector and managing the economic system via an extensive bureaucracy whilst typically a single party runs political affairs (Wade 1990: 26–7).

Whilst it is important not to ignore or underestimate the significant differences of governance structures between nations, and indeed cities, it is possible to suggest that all the cities that host the Games establish a network of institutional relations that encompass the city's Olympic Organising Committee and other city-wide and national institutions. The network of institutional relations – national, local, public, private – may assume the character of 'self-organisation' in implementing mutually agreed goals, be dominated by private or corporate interests or, lastly, remain largely 'state centred' with control firmly in the hands of national government. The self-organised form involves institutions engaging directly with the communities in which renewal takes place; corporate dominance places the Games firmly within the nexus of commercial or market relations while the state-centred approach, particularly in the 'western' democracies tends to focus upon using quasi-state agencies

---

1   For a discussion of various approaches to measuring the Olympic effect, see Poynter (2006) and Theodoraki et al. (2005).

in partnership with the private sector to develop and deliver regeneration programmes, with community involvement often confined to tokenistic forms of consultation (Raco and Henderson 2005: 2–3). The governance structure for a host city/nation may facilitate or impede the processes by which the Games achieves its proposed legacy outcomes. As Baum suggests, the recent adoption of a wider range of 'social' as well as 'commercial' legacy indicators are likely to generate an increased potential for conflicts to arise between the institutions brought together to deliver the Games and its legacies.

A review of the governance structures for past host cities is not a simple matter. The capacities of Olympic Organising Committees to raise finance and sponsorship for the Games are subject to local as well as IOC 'conditions'. Nations have their own legal and political structures that may preclude direct national or federal governmental support for cities (the USA being one example), with the consequence that federal aid is channelled by other means. Equally, political interventions by citizens groups at city level may stop local taxation schemes being used to support the hosting of the event, or, the specific influence of the different actors may not be fully revealed by published accounts. In summary, governance structures for the Games are subject to wider societal developments and the interactions of the state, market and civil society; interactions which can only be briefly referenced in the following discussion.

The 'state-centred', indeed state directed, mode of governance is evident in the case of Beijing. National and municipal state agencies established detailed plans for infrastructural and event related investment and clearly located these within the framework of national policies designed to use the Games to affirm China's international status and the trajectory of the capital city's own economic and social development. As Brunet and Zuo Xinwen clearly identify in their chapter, however, the primary purpose of the state and municipal authorities was to utilise the Games to promote and develop China's market economy, with the Olympics offering opportunities to strengthen or develop the high technology sector and 'new' service industries in areas like finance, business services and the media and creative sectors. Whilst corporate interests are broadly the most significant beneficiaries of such policies they perform a relatively minor part in the governance process itself; it is the central state that provides leadership with municipal authorities performing a subordinate role.

Seoul manifested the 'state-centred' mode of governance but in modified forms by comparison with Beijing. As Yoon explains in her chapter, Seoul's mode of governance was 'state-centred' but within a wider political setting that was witness to a significant transition from military dictatorship toward a more democratic form of government achieved through presidential elections in December 1987 and parliamentary elections in April 1988. The Games, while not the catalyst of democratisation, influenced the pace and peaceful nature of the process, with democratic opposition to the military regime using the lead up to the Games to effectively mobilise public support for regime change. The Games had absorbed considerable public investment but was used, by the military regime and subsequently the civilian government, to promote national policies designed to announce South Korea's emergence as a developed rather than developing economy.

In their chapters on Barcelona and Sydney, Brunet and Cashman present a picture of two cities for whom the governance structures broadly assumed the character of a multi-level partnership between federal, regional and city authorities and the private sector. While public institutions dominated, governance was characterised by what Brunet has called in the Barcelona case a high degree of 'inter-institutional consensus', approximating a model of self-organisation that involved dialogue with community interests and, at least in part, some responsiveness to community-based concerns. For Cashman, the period since the Games has witnessed the harnessing of this capacity for partnership working around legacy issues to accrue to a level of expertise, via management consultancy and project management, that has enabled Australia to develop a profitable Games-related export industry. For Athens, however, an apparently similar model of multi-level partnership achieved rather different outcomes. Athens, as Panagiotopoulou has revealed in her chapter, experienced difficulties in coordinating effectively the mainly state-centred agencies involved in the governance of the Games, though the legacy achieved ultimately provided some significant improvements to the infrastructure of Athens and its surrounding region.

By contrast to Barcelona and Sydney, Atlanta may be characterised as a Games dominated by commercial interests with its governance structures reflecting that dominance to the relative exclusion of wider social goals. The result was divided aspirations and an unclear vision for the legacy to be achieved by the Games; the regeneration objectives designed to address inner-city poverty that were set down in the city's bid to the IOC were not achieved. While the Atlanta Organising Committee (ACOG) espoused primarily commercial goals as the outcome of the Games, the Corporation for Olympic Development in Atlanta (CODA) sought to improve fifteen impoverished districts. As Poynter and Roberts indicate in their chapter, the ACOG perspective prevailed and, notably, commercial interests have continued to dominate new infrastructure projects for the decade following the Games.

Of all the cities reviewed in this book, London 2012 has perhaps the most complex governance structure involving several tiers of government, quasi-state agencies, national sports bodies, regional authorities and local boroughs (including the designated five Olympic boroughs of Tower Hamlets, Hackney, Newham, Greenwich and Waltham Forest). The unfolding of the Olympics project and its location within the wider Thames Gateway scheme, involve complex networks of institutions operating within tightly determined temporal and spatial conditions. Under such conditions it is not possible to fulfil the expectations of all stakeholders, nor is it possible to effectively integrate or embed these institutions in the local community. The achievement of a 'successful' Games appears to rest upon the capacity to sustain the public rhetoric of partnership while local interests are increasingly dominated by national government supported by the City's Mayor and the London Development Agency – an institution funded by central government but under the political guidance of the Mayor. Inevitably, a 'state centred' mode of governance defines the regeneration legacy. Weak local or civic voices may well result in a local legacy that primarily favours commercial viability (especially given the public outcry over costs discussed in Chapter 11) rather than addressing the deep-seated and long term social, housing, employment and education issues facing East London.

A brief review of governance structures suggests that the mode of partnership working – between the state, market and wider society – is critical to the success or otherwise of the Games and the type of balance achieved between the 'public good' and 'commercial' legacies or outcomes that result from hosting the event. Perhaps inevitably, several host city experiences have illustrated the tendency toward a state-centred approach, which arises from the tight temporal and spatial constraints imposed by the event and the requirements of the IOC for the public purse to underwrite the costs of the Games. The capacities of cities to manage these constraints have, however, varied considerably. The IOCs commitment to requiring cities to achieve a wider range of social, environmental and cultural objectives as a result of winning the right to host the Games places an increased burden on these cities and their governance structures; governing institutions have not only to deliver the most complex of global sporting events but also engage with the wider project of city building.

City Building

The attractiveness of the mega event as a vehicle for city-building has increased significantly over recent years. In the aftermath of de-industrialisation many western cities have sought to use major sporting events, such as the Games, to catalyse a form of post-industrial economic expansion mainly based on the growth of the service sector and the production industries that serve it. This catalyst model emerged primarily from city planners in the USA as a response to declining federal government aid and the de-industrialisation experienced by urban centres following the protracted period of economic restructuring that commenced in the 1970s. The hosting of the Olympics, or other large scale events, was a highly visible example of the type of regeneration strategy that more often spawned new convention centres, cultural facilities, sports centres, theme parks and shopping malls in many US cities in the 1980s and 1990s. The strategy encompassed new ways of financing and accelerating urban renewal and development while also combining elements of political change and social re-engineering aimed at reducing inner-city social tensions and the potential for civic unrest (Poynter 2006: 4). The catalytic model has gained popularity in non-western cities and states over recent years as newly industrialized nations have sought to use the Games or other major regional and international events to announce their appearance on the global economic stage and, domestically, address some of the pressing issues that arise from rapid urbanization, the rise of mass consumption and the emergence of post-industrial modes of economic growth.

The mega event is a fashionable tool of urban development for several reasons – it may create or confirm the regional or global status of the city; it provides opportunities for the construction of iconic buildings and parks; it attracts visitors and industries that are synonymous with the expansion of the new consumer-driven service economy and it legitimizes a rapid programme of infrastructural development that typically would not be achieved at a similar speed within the host city if the event had not taken place. The efficacy of such a strategy for 'city building' is, however, a contested affair, often attracting support from politicians, business leaders and commercial consultancies and criticism from academic sources and local community-based activists, with critics tending to focus upon the mega event as the mechanism that often achieves the removal or dilution of local democratic controls over development (Andranovich et al.), the displacement of vulnerable or poorer communities (COHRE 2007) and an increase in social polarization in the host city (Roche 2000: 232–4).

Two important aspects of the Games driven process of city building relate to the symbolic status accorded the Olympic Park after the event has finished and, what might be called, the social trajectory of urban development that the Games project catalyses or contributes to. In all the cities reviewed in Part 3, the Park 'after the Games' has been the subject of close public attention, especially in relation to its post-Games usage; host cities seek to avoid the label of 'white elephant' being attached to the permanent structures that remain after the Games. As Cashman has identified, Sydney's Olympic Park was planned and constructed to provide a legacy that addressed three dimensions of Olympism – sport, culture and the environment. A 'super sports' precinct was constructed, environmentally sensitive parkland developed and areas for cultural and leisure events were established. In the two years following the Games, however, the Park's venues were underutilised and it was frequently empty, prompting widespread media criticism and public debate over the rising costs of maintaining the area. By May 2002 a new master plan for the Park was prepared, modifying the original vision, and including a major development of commercial and residential facilities. By 2006, the Park began to achieve its integration into the commercial and social life of the city. Sydney exemplifies, initially negatively and subsequently positively, the importance of planning the relationship between the new Olympic development and the existing life of the city (Millet 1996: 123–9), a lesson that, according to Pangiotopoulou, Athens has yet to learn. Olympic venues, such as the athletes village may be utilized to enhance housing stock and realize the potential for urban renewal, as Barcelona demonstrated when locating the new residential area, bequeathed by the athletes village, close to its renovated coastal area.

Integration into the existing life of the city, is but one dimension of the determinants that effect the successful utilization of the Olympic Park after the Games. A further dimension relates to how the Park may be used as a signifier by city authorities of their political will to address problems of inner city decline, social inequality or, in the case of Beijing and Seoul, the consequences of rapid urbanization and economic development. The evidence from recent host cities suggests that the Olympic Park development tends to impact on housing markets and catalyse patterns of social renewal that favour commercial interests (especially Atlanta) and the gentrification of areas in and around the Park via rising land values, increased house prices and the displacement of poorer communities (Barcelona, Seoul and Beijing). London's responsibility to address such issues in relation to the Olympic park development rests, institutionally, with the LDA. In 2008, the LDA initiated, on behalf of all the London legacy partners, a legacy masterplanning team consisting of KCAP Architects and Planners, Allies and Morrison Architects and EDAW. Working with local agencies, the planning team is required to develop a Legacy Masterplan Framework (LMF) for the Olympic Park. The Framework will provide the basis for planning applications for the Park's development post-2012 (LDA 2008). The concluding part of this chapter conceptualizes legacy and discusses the possible trajectories of legacy for London 2012.

Conceptualising and Debating 'Legacy'

Like cultural artifacts, rituals and prized goods of other kinds, but on a far wider and larger scale, festival-mega-events provide spaces connected to, but also, in a sense, 'outside' everyday socio-cultural routines and exchanges. Such phenomena are continuous with and affirming of the everyday life lived in embedded cycles of planning and institutional and economic ordering. Traditionally, at home, Christmas enacts familial relations microcosmically. In UK domestic sport, the Football Association Cup Final affirms and unites the football community to bring the season to its close.

However, (paradoxically) such phenomena (and mega events are a case in point) provide a strong sense – and an emergent reality – that affirms a distinct order; another area of activity; something 'special'. Cup Final day and Christmas day are not 'normal' days. Thus it is with the Olympics. 2012 will be based upon, will enact and fulfill a number of institutions' internally coherent plans for 'ordinary' and 'in train' developments in East London; this continuous (in many ways) with broader regeneration agendas transforming London and Thames Gateway (Cohen and Rustin 2008) and including considerations for housing, jobs, transport, educational development and other social policy priorities.

However, the Games also stand as an intervention as if 'out of the blue'. They bring a spectacular not to say 'irrational' scheme to catalyze 'ordinary' redevelopment progress tangentially; cutting across but nevertheless stimulating renewal processes and drawing a new front line. The 2012 Olympics provide a new 'story'; new 'scripts' for communities, stakeholders, developers, private investors and government. The Olympics is conceived (in this sense) to leverage and legitimate activities and engagements 'above and beyond' the ordinary. The Olympics is a great and unexpected 'prize' (Jowell 2008: 2)

A good deal of current effort, aside from the considerable achievements in facilities building and infrastructure development, finds government and the Olympic institutional bodies working hard at making this second *extra-ordinary* Olympic story credible. The mystique-story of the Olympic intervention in London, as a (legitimate and legitimating) source of transformative power within the city and its communities is in some ways a compelling one. There is a will to believe on all sides[2]. East London after all continues to experience tensions and contradictions connected to recent rapid changes[3] and modernization. There is a hunger for good news about the city. The Games are seen (perhaps over-eagerly by governments and elites, as Calcutt has argued in Chapter 17) as a device able to forge connections between disparate and isolated communities, individuals and populations smarting daily from experiences of a variously fragmented and disorienting city.

However, given the popularization of a certain 'incredulity towards meta-narratives' in recent decades, especially those meta-narratives such as 'the Olympics-as-regeneration story' espoused by an unlikely alignment teaming governmental bodies, blazer-wearing sports officials with town planners, PR gurus and slick admen, the rush for regeneration by mystification has typically lead to raised eyebrows – and raised voices.

Thus, and as a critical and ongoing counterpoint, a good deal of work goes into *demystifying* the Olympic story. Poynter has highlighted the prominence of the cost debate in arguments raised from a variety of political perspectives. Cost-benefit driven critiques – with or without indignant flourishes or debunking cynicism – are substantial interventions asserting pragmatic conceptions of East London regeneration against the Olympic enthusiasts' visionary, if not 'fanciful' narratives. This is not just a London 2012 issue. Globally the Olympic movement – faced with concerted criticisms

---

2   Popular support remains high and positive enthusiasm in winning, as in backing the bid was widely reported.

3   These include de-industrialisation and its aftermaths, boom, bust and shortage in housing markets, anxieties about (youth) crime, increasing discrepancies (within tight geographic areas) in wealth and opportunity – notably in the regenerating East of London.

prompted by problems connected to drug-taking, sporting professionalism, commercialism, and various scandals – has had to find means to reaffirm the distinctive value and mystique of Olympism as a modern global movement. As MacRury argues in Chapter 3 this has been partly played out in ongoing defense, diffusion and development of the Olympic brand. But defending and legitimating Olympic mega events (in current terms of scale and city-based formats) against numerous critiques, of excess and 'White Elephant' waste, must offer more than brand-values (however sincerely and compellingly this is done). Bidding cities, OCOGs and the IOC itself have sought ways of justifying the expense and the perceived excesses of Games. Increasingly this is done by invoking and evoking 'Legacy'.

'Legacy' has come to prominence in Olympic discourse in recent decades because of the capacity the term offers in managing tensions between Olympic dreams (or promises) and municipal-financial realities. Olympic 'legacy' offers bridges between two potentially divergent narratives setting the practical accountancy (and financial and political accountability) of ordinary city planning, against the 'creative accounting' that underpins Olympic dreams and promises.

The negative financial aftermath of some Games, from Montreal on, has focused attention on the IOC and (in turn) upon OCOGS to better assure a positive future after the Games. 'Legacy' becomes prominent because it takes the emphasis away from the sporting mega event – and away from the conspicuous-consumer-like excessiveness of the global spectacular that invited (legitimate) questions. The legacy discourse attempts to give weight to the narrative and historical context of the Games and the (after-)life of the city (and/or host nation). As DCMS put it in their report title, 'before, during and after', are terms to affirm a narrative conception in the Olympic/city intervention. Games are no longer seen as ends in themselves. They become a means – a means for something good. That 'Good' is legacy. As Preuss (2007), Cashman (2005) and Moragas et al. (2003) all point out 'legacy' is a contested term in the mega event and Olympic literature. It is sometimes conflated with (much shorter term) ideas such as 'impact', when, in fact, it should be seen as counter to such temporary (macro or micro-) economic fluctuations. Nor is there consensus that 'legacy' is always to be positive (Preuss 2007). There are negative 'legacies' although these are often re-badged as unforeseen (and unforeseeable) consequences rather than 'legacies' as such.

Nor must legacy be confined either to the concrete and steel infrastructure of sports stadia. There are other infrastructure benefits to consider. Land remediation lacks profile, but such fundamental preparatory work is at the heart of urban transformation and underpins a lot of the 'hidden' gains attaching to Olympic projects and connected regeneration. But there are, in addition.' 'soft' legacies; civic pride, individuals' educational or skills gains as direct or indirect results of Olympic 'inspiration'. At the supra-individual level, it is common to talk of 'buzz' or 'can-do' attitudes emerging in cities around projects such as the Olympics. Such 'buzz' can be an index of more deep routed/rooted developmental transformation of global and, in particular, local social and cultural networks.

The definition of 'legacy' is partly constituted in the measurement of immaterial 'cultural' factors such as city image, but also in less readily auditable changes in morale and affect (however distributed and registered) . As 'legacy' works to legitimate the Games, 'legacy outcomes' become subject to accountability. The definition and assurance of 'legacy', alongside cost, is typically at the heart of stakeholders' agendas. As such the indices of legacy take on a certain prominence in the planning, management and governance of the event in the long and short term. The depth or superficiality of legacy measures, and the seriousness with which the measurement processes and the dissemination of findings is taken becomes itself a further index of the credibility of the 'good' Games. While macro and micro economies can be tracked, building and employment rates monitored, and approval ratings collated and compared, there are certain 'feel good/feel bad' factors around the Olympics city-brand which can be rendered in ways so reductive as to diminish the sought for legacy-credibility. As MacAloon (2008) shows, in rich detail, the 'legacy' discourse in some ways complements and in other ways supercedes the 'brand' discourse within the IOC.

Two Versions of the London 2012 Legacy: 'Top Down' and 'Bottom Up'

'Legacy' refers to a number of things – more or less precisely. Legacy is a structured and structuring set objectives and outcomes emerging from the Games events – roads, infrastructure and new (physical) networks. After 2012 we will see material changes to the look and feel of the city. There will be accountable changes in economic and other social activity, including new jobs and homes. These are sometimes called 'hard' legacies. 'Legacy' also refers to certain 'inspirational', moral or affective gains. It is hoped that improvements to the material and 'spiritual' well-being, of east Londoners and others will be registered post 2012 and in the longer term and that new and established personal, social and cultural, global and local networks will be created or affirmed as a consequence of the Games and its attendant festivals. This is sometimes corralled under the heading 'soft legacy'.

Finally, 'legacy' refers to a way of conceiving the Olympics. It is a discursive intervention focusing on the long term narrative structure of 'before, during and after'. 'Legacy' so understood better enables a narrative conception of Olympic planning. It is mobilized as a legitimating narrative to offset critiques of 'immediate Olympic gratifications' and waste, in favour of a vision of a 'good' deferred future city – to which the Olympic investment and experience will be (and will have been) a major contributory factor. It is useful to look at some indicative approaches to the 2012 legacy. This provides a substantive sense of what is happening and what is planned, but, also serves to demonstrate the contested, ongoing and various nature of legacy. The continuing work of debating, thinking and defining legacy becomes, in a sense, a legacy achievement of its own.

'Top Down' Legacy

In her foreword to the DCMS (2008) 'legacy plan', *Before, During and After: Making the Most of the London 2012 Games*, Tessa Jowell states:

> This is not the last word, or the ceiling of our ambitions. It is the minimum we pledge to do, and the start of four years work to give Britain and the world a reason to remember London 2012. I am accountable to parliament and the public for it, and will in turn hold to account all those who have pledged support. I am sure that much more will flow from this plan than is contained in these pages. The prize is the greatest in a generation – the chance to turn the rhetoric of Olympic legacy into fact. Faster progress towards a healthy nation. Higher aspirations for young people in their work and their play. A stronger community, bound by self-belief and the knowledge that Britain has hosted the greatest Games ever. (DCMS 2008: 2)

As Jowell eschews 'rhetoric' in favour of 'fact' ambitious commitments to public policy objectives are (nevertheless) integrated into a reworked version of Coubertin's three-part Latin Olympic motto (*Citius, Altius, Fortius* – Faster, Higher, Stronger). The DCMS document, it is claimed, will prove to be the basis for the promised move from fanciful promises to real sustained achievements. 'Legacy' is the watchword for such resolutions. The UK government offers its definition of legacy:

> The 'legacy' of the London 2012 Games refers to the imprint they will leave. It is therefore not just what happens after the Games, but what we do before and during them to inspire individuals and organizations to strive for their best, to try new activities, forge new links or develop new skills. The Olympic Games and Paralympic Games have a unique power to inspire all of us as individuals, to motivate everyone to set themselves a personal London 2012 challenge. (DCMS 2008: 8)

The largely inspirational and individualist emphasis on 'personal' Olympic legacy, a kind of 'get on yer (racing) bike'[4] approach seems to underplay a more broad based social approach that might (in some estimations) be required in the longer term to achieve the kind of regeneration ends entailed to promises such as the ambition to 'transform the heart[5] of East London'. This definition locates the Olympics as, amongst other things, a symbolic catalyst for individuals' self-help plans. Seemingly 'soft' legacy is to be writ large in the planning.

Overall the DCMS plan works up the government's 'five legacy promises'. These have been in circulation since 2007 and are the chosen articulation for a significant portion of UK Olympic policy. The 2012 Olympic and Paralympic Games aim:

- to make the UK a world-class sporting nation, in terms of elite success, mass participation and school sport;
- to transform the heart of East London;
- to inspire a new generation of young people to take part in local volunteering, cultural and physical activity;
- to make the Olympic Park a blueprint for sustainable living;
- to demonstrate that the UK is a creative, inclusive and welcoming place to live in, to visit and for business (DCMS 2008).

These promises serve as headlines to more detailed projects and aims and will constitute a major part of the UK government's legacy planning (DCMS 2008) between now and 2012.

The movement between 'rhetoric and fact' that Jowell hopes to deliver depends, heavily, on the idea of 'legacy' as a narrative which, over time, will see extra-ordinary dreams made concrete in the everyday lives of citizens in East London – and throughout the UK. Legacy then becomes the locus for a more or less likely, more or less possible fusion of Londoners' realities and the fantasy-utopian post-Olympic city envisioned in the bid book, by political leaders, by sponsors and other Olympics-as-regeneration advocates. Headline

---

4   'Get on yer bike' was the advice given by government minister Norman Tebbit in 1981 to the UK unemployed – an injunction that provoked a certain amount of dissent at the time. It has subsequently come into currency as a phrase suggesting a more general return to values of self-reliance. This is not to say however that an increase in cycle-based popular leisure would be incompatible with the broad legacy agenda.

5   The choice of 'heart' here is interesting. It is a somewhat vague term for such a significant policy. Does heart mean the 'spirit and morale' of East London, does it mean the geographical centre? Or, is there here, even, a hint at improving the cardiac health of East Enders? As with much attaching to legacy there is often a balance between the largeness of the initial promise and the vagueness of what, finally, is to be delivered up.

Olympic promises are shown alongside DCMS's listing of corresponding programs (Table 18.1). 'Legacy', it is assumed, will emerge somewhere at the cusp of the rhetorical promise and the 'fact' of the proposed and outlined program of activity.

Table 18.1   'The five legacy promises'

Legacy promise	DCMS legacy main programme
To make the UK a world-class sporting nation, in terms of elite success, mass participation and school sport	The PE and Sport Strategy; Sport England's strategy for quality community sport; £75 million healthy living marketing campaign; and UK Sport's World Class Performance Programme.
To transform the heart of East London	The ODA Delivery Plan for the Olympic Park; the Legacy Masterplan Framework and Regeneration Strategy for the area; and local jobs and skills training initiatives including the London Development Agency (LDA), London Employment and Skills Taskforce for 2012 (LEST) Action Plan.
To inspire a new generation of young people to take part in local volunteering, cultural and physical activity	The Cultural Olympiad and the work of Legacy Trust UK; the Personal Best programme; the London 2012 Education Programme; and The International Inspiration programme.
To make the Olympic Park a blueprint for sustainable living	The London 2012 Sustainability Plan; a new methodology for measuring carbon foot printing; and local sustainability initiatives.
To demonstrate that the UK is a creative, inclusive and welcoming place to live in, to visit and for business	The Business Network brokerage service for businesses across the UK, Train to Gain Compact for 2012, Personal Best, skills strategies in construction, hospitality and leisure, sport and media, the Government's Tourism Strategy, and the Cultural Olympiad.

Source: adapted from DCMS (2008: 3).

The commitment to a transition from rhetoric to fact on the part of government via plans outlined in the legacy plan document is, in itself, a significant gain. The document acknowledges risk of a 'gap' between Olympic intentions and real developments and achievements. The DCMS plan, which runs to 80 pages, outlines the detail and intentions of the legacy ambition quite comprehensively. Charges regarding the occasionally airy, and the 'usually easier said than done' quality of legacy promises are disarmed if not rebutted. Certainly there *are* substantive plans, both at headline level and 'in the detail'. However, quite a number of the main 'programs' (merely) refer to other Olympic bodies and their initiatives, in a way that hints that much within the programs remains undefined – not to mention under-funded in relation to the scale of the main 'legacy promises' (however the extent of ambition is judged[6]). This is certainly the case in relation to the Cultural Olympiad, which (on the evidence) here carries a good deal of the legacy 'burden' – notably in relation to promises Three and Five. The Cultural Olympiad has a limited budget – one which has not increased relative to increases across the rest of the Olympic costs. On the evidence of past cities, the Cultural Olympiad has not had the sustained 'legacy' impact hoped for in relation to London's cultural festival.

Nevertheless it is clear that governmental bodies, on paper to date, but also in blueprints, on the ground in the Olympic park, have grasped 'legacy' as a central organizing concept. The Games have, in conception at least, a clear narrative – a headline conception of 'before, during and after' which might readily feed a sense of developmental continuity across Olympic and other regeneration projects. The scale of the substantive projects indexed to the five promises may seem less grand than the ambitions to which they are entailed. On the one hand this avowedly 'minimum' approach to legacy qua 'fact' could be seen as a healthy dose of realism. The plan has not ditched the commitment to promises that imply greater scope and scale to 'legacy', but expectations are clearly being revised down. Controversies over cost are proportionately more likely to impact activities deemed to be peripheral, such as the Cultural Olympiad, and 'legacy', since much in the event costs and site preparation are relatively non-negotiable. The accounts and accountabilities attaching to non-delivery of an Olympic venue by 2012 are far more rigorous than those attaching to 'inspiring young people for the future' and other 'soft' (but crucial) ambitions. The cost-conscious realities appear, as the DCMS report acknowledges, to be diminishing the legacy plan. That said, there are measures in place (via a charitable trust) to garner support for the promised 'legacy'.

> Many of the benefits will come from enhancing existing programmes, and within existing Departmental budgets. There is therefore no addition to the total Games funding package of £9.3 billion. But we have jointly created a new, London 2012-inspired charity called Legacy Trust UK. The Trust's mission is to use sporting and cultural activities to ensure communities from across the UK have a chance to take part in London 2012, and to leave a sustainable legacy after the Games. Using money from existing sources, including the Lottery and the Arts Council, it is endowed with £40 million

---

6   For instance, from a certain perspective, the £75 million entailed to the PE and sport strategy is certainly a substantial amount. However, if we consider the transfer fees and wages of top level Premiership footballers – some of whom may be appearing during London 2012's football tournament, then the relative differences between elite and everyday sport are placed in clear relief. A fee of £80 million was recently mooted in relation to one young player – Cristiano Ronaldo – to move from Manchester United to Real Madrid.

of expendable funds, with a target to double the value of the fund by 2012. (DCMS 2008: 8)

It would be unfair to accuse the London government, LOCOG and other associated bodies of entirely ignoring legacy. A more legitimate critique might point to the deferred, indeterminate and unsubstantiated nature of some of the legacy projects. The legacy plan is heavily pre-occupied with the nomination, delegation and redistribution of 'legacy' responsibilities across the various stake holding bodies (LDA, LOCOG, ODA and other governmental agencies) while popular or local participation is accorded a marginal or merely 'consultative' status consistent with the 'state-centred' mode of governance outlined earlier in this chapter.

'Bottom Up' Legacy

'Legacy' has equally been mobilized as a major term in the critical discourse – questioning the Government approach. In a (2008) report, conducted in partnership with Community Links and entitled 'Fool's Gold: How the 2012 Olympics is Selling East London Short', the New Economics Foundation have outlined an account of legacy focusing on a local agendas. They structure their recommendations in two areas: 'procurement' and 'assets'. In terms of procurement the report makes six recommendations to try to ensure that local people and communities participate in a benefit from the Games.

The nef report also offers a detailed set of recommendations for the governance and disbursement of Olympic assets, understood as much here as a 'gift' to East London, as an 'asset' to be realised on the pseudo-open market of developer-led regeneration. The exclusive and specific reference to 'local' benefits can be set against, general, non-specific and corporate, individual-inspiration-based or market solutions that define their 'bottom up' approach to legacy. The focus is on real asset shifts, post -Games, so that local public goods are enhanced – this, even if there is a failure to maximise financial returns on the Olympic assets, e.g. by selling off Olympic properties to the highest bidder.

Legacy: Integrations, Narrative and Momentum

Legacy is about the relationship achieved between fact and promise, fantasy and reality, ambitions and resources. The two indicative statements on legacy examined above (DCMS 2008; nef 2008) are both, in their way and in context, substantial and relevant contributions to the legacy 'debate'. It is certain that the DCMS outline will guide policy and practice in regard to legacy planning in significant ways as 2012 approaches. The nef (2008) report is also highly

Table 18.2a   The nef procurement strategy suggestions to assure a string local input to the 2012 legacy

The nef suggests the following procurement strategies as the best way to assure a string local input to the 2012 legacy

Recommendation 1:
Make community benefit a key criterion for all new contracts: The Olympic Delivery Authority (ODA), and other Olympic bodies should incorporate community benefit and the regeneration objectives of the local authority as part of existing 'Balanced Scorecard' criteria in awarding all contracts. Olympic authorities should make sure that a core purpose of their contracts is the stimulation of SMEs, the voluntary sector or social enterprises, as a step towards their stated inclusion policy.

Recommendation 2:
Make contracts accessible to local SMEs and social enterprises: The ODA and other Olympic authorities – as well as the main contractors – should break down the size of future contracts so that local SMEs and social enterprises have a realistic opportunity to compete. Where this is not possible, the reason should be made explicit and be scrutinised by the Commission for a Sustainable London 2012. Second-tier contractors should also be asked to demonstrate how they work with SMEs.

Recommendation 3:
Establish and monitor targets for the proportion of locally based SMEs and social enterprises employed, and the number of local people employed, under all Olympic contracts. Potential suppliers should be asked to show how their organisation will create positive local economic impact and social and environmental outcomes in the delivery of their contracts.

Recommendation 4:
Set new private sector standards for incorporating community benefit into procurement contracts. As a private company not subject to European or UK Value for Money (VfM) requirements, The London Organising Committee of the Olympic Games (LOCOG) should set new standards for the commercial sector in terms of incorporating community benefit into its procurement criteria. LOCOG's procurement policy should incorporate measurable social impact clauses, specified throughout the commissioning process, so that it can measure the ability of bidding organisations to meet these criteria objectively.

Table 18.2b The nef procurement strategy suggestions to assure a string local input to the 2012 legacy

In relation to the subsequent (post 2012) disbursement and management of the Olympic assets The nef suggests strategies as the best way to assure a string local input to the 2012 legacy

Recommendation 5:
Appoint a new Board position on the Olympic and Lower Lea Valley planning boards for the local voluntary and community sector. This would give a genuine voice in the Olympic legacy Planning Master Framework to disadvantaged local residents.

Recommendation 6:
Establish an asset-holding organisation for the Olympic legacy. The Olympic bodies should establish an asset-holding organisation for the Olympic legacy, which has presence and credibility in the area. It should have the capacity to play a transitional 'caretaking' role to ensure ownership of assets devolves to the local community. This organisation should be guided by a cohort of community-led organisations and develop plans for long-term community ownership.

Recommendation 7:
Establish a community development trust to design and oversee the community facilities in the Athletes' Village. A shadow board of representatives from the community should be established to oversee the community facility which will form part of the Athletes' Village, and a community development trust created to help co-design, and then run the community facilities.

Recommendation 8:
Establish a community reinvestment fund to ensure ongoing community benefit from privately owned facilities on the site. Investment should be made on behalf of the community in any future privately owned facilities – including housing – that are developed from the assets on the Olympics site. This would mean a future revenue stream for the local community from the new developments in its midst.

Recommendation 9:
Build the foundations of future community sustainability by building into the development community-owned retail and work space, and land for growing food. Community ownership and management of assets should not be restricted to the community facility in the Athletes' Village, and the Olympic authorities should aim to develop a wide range of community-owned or managed facilities for the Athletes' Village zone of the Stratford City development, to include retail, workspace and land for growing food which would support an ongoing stream of benefits to the community.

Recommendation 10:
Ensure that community facilities are transferred directly to the community development trust. The Olympic authorities must negotiate with the developer to ensure that the proposed community development trust becomes the long term owner of the community facility, so that it can be used as collateral in future community developments.

Source: nef (2008: 6–7).

relevant as it will serve, alongside other analytic resources, to continue to place the Games and its promised legacies in question – especially in terms of a local East London orientation.

The approaches differ in the degree to which legacy is conceived as predominantly material or non material. The DCMS has highlighted the important potential of 'soft' gains, and resources (charitable, voluntary and personal motivational) in fulfilling aspects of the Olympic promises. The nef account of legacy focuses on local, social political-economic and institutional mechanisms to ensure that legacy is adequately grounded in the East London locale. The risk the nef perceive, rightly, that a too generalised 'soft-focus' version of legacy (on its own) brings, legacy promises that may only ever be realised in the abstract. Rhetoric does not transform, as Jowell hopes it will, into fact unless there is sufficient contact with the significant materiality of local life. To offset this risk more structural and localised systems are useful. The nef outlines a number of concrete – 'hard' – legacy-governance structures to better assist the long term and sustainable benefits that accrue locally.

Hard and Soft: Interaction

London must certainly pursue 'hard' legacy gains: infrastructure, the reorientation of city spaces, improved amenity, new types of land use and economic activity. It is important to ensure that the political-economic architecture – the governance structure – of the resultant assets is, as the nef argues, sufficiently oriented to local benefits in the long term. Important 'soft' gains in terms of confidence, buzz, reputation, tourist driven and commercially driven national and international status, and 'pride of place' are, as the DCMS hope, likely to be recorded.

Some passage of time is required for the successful emergence of soft social legacy to be realised. In the right conditions (where local pride of place is to the fore) hard legacy can become iconic and significant as monumental place-markers and tourist attractions. 'Soft' legacy becomes 'hard' as feel good factors, governance structures and 'can do' attitude evolve to form productive social networks. With sufficient attention to local needs, this is in prospect for London after 2012.

Legacy Momentum and Governance

The working definition of 'legacy' (across governments and communities) is in part constitutive of the legacy achievement itself. As it is formulated (as narrative and consensus) 'legacy' can become a functional term in the complex planning and evolving conceptions underpinning urban change in London in the longer term. As such 'legacy', and the controversies, activities and values entailed to it, can come to provide a catalytic 'site for debate' and a 'vocabulary of motives' forming (eventually and incrementally) a legitimating discourse enabling politicians, communities and their individual representatives to improvise, invent and justify 'extra-ordinary' investments, and evolve new strategies and activities connected to and connecting city-developmental Olympic gains.

However, radical variation in the meanings of 'legacy' as conceived by central Olympic-related bodies such as DCMS (but also TOP sponsors, LOCOG, ODA and local partner agencies) or between such high level and influential bodies and the communities they aim to serve: such disjuncture may destabilise and diminish beneficial legacy. Instead of a developmental process linking event planning to creative agendas for urban regeneration, the Games and legacy planning become a further arena for the enactment of displaced socio-cultural contradictions. The consequent inertia will diminish the success of the 2012 Games – as event and as a regenerative intervention.

However, as the debate and definition of legacy continues to emerge, there is a real opportunity for evolving integrations of perspective. This depends upon effective governance binding local, municipal and national agendas to the day to day management of the Games projects (ODA and LOCOG) – and to the overarching agendas set by the IOC. Legacy depends upon ensuring meaningful ongoing dialogue within and between communities of interest and engagement – and the various levels of delivery and governance. This is the best way to ensure that the 'narrative' developmental process implicit in 'legacy' promises and priorities corresponds with the explicit and felt mode of Olympic planning and delivery. As such a 'momentum' will develop, a momentum lasting long after the Games. Such legacy momentum is of value as an energising and integrative vector binding disparate agendas (public, private, national and local, ordinary and extra-ordinary) towards optimally capitalising on the Games as an urban-regenerative intervention. However, such socio-cultural legacy requires ongoing and vigilant planning, stewardship, flexibility and continuity of vision. Legacy is not a state achieved –an 'outcome'- but instead it describes an unfolding, multiform process of debate and action. Good legacy is driven by such momentum (born of soft and hard factors) continuous, but also, at points, sporadic. Such 'soft' factors require political-institutional innovation so that social and economic capital and evolving and engaged governance structures and networking capacities can engender genuine cooperative entrepreneurship; community buy in, openness; strong communications links, civic confidence, alertness to 'the next project' and 'buzz'. Positive socio-cultural legacy momentum will emerge to the extent that these factors are sufficiently evident. These soft legacy 'factors' sustain co-ordination, communication and consensus, before, during and after the Games. Local communities, municipal, Olympic governance and delivery bodies, national government; national, local and international media; sporting associations, national teams: all need to be acknowledged as active and productive stakeholders in the range of projects, large and small. 'Legacy' will emerge as a credible and extra-ordinary narrative of change as and where such conjunctions are made to work before, during and after 2012.

References

Andranovich, G., Burbank, M. and Heying, C. (2001) 'Olympic Cities: Lessons Learned from Mega-Event Politics', *Journal of Urban Affairs* 23(2): 113–31.

Arrighi, G. (2007) *Adam Smith in Beijing*, London: Verso.

Bacon, R. and Eltis, W. (1976) *Britain's Economic Problem: Too Few Producers*, London: Macmillan.

Cashman, R. (2005) *The Bitter-sweet Awakening. The Legacy of the Sydney 2000 Olympic Games*, Sydney: Walla Walla Press.

Centre on Housing Rights and Evictions (COHRE) (2007) 'Fair Play for Housing Rights', http://www.cohre.org/mega-events.

Cohen, P. and Rustin, M. (eds) (2008) *London's Turning: The Prospect of Thames Gateway*, Aldershot: Ashgate.

DCMS (2008) *Before, During and After: Making the Most of the London 2012 Games*, London: HMO, DCMS.

Davies, J. (2001) *Partnerships and Regimes: The Politics of Urban Regeneration in the UK*, Aldershot: Ashgate.

FIFA (2007) The FIFA World Cup Viewing Figures 1986–2006, InfoPlus, http://www.fifa.com/mm/document/fifafacts.

Jones, P. and Evans, J. (2006) 'Urban Regeneration, Governance and the State: Exploring Notions of Distance and Proximity', *Urban Studies* 43(9): 1491–509.

IOC (2008) Olympics Marketing Fact File, 2008 edition, http://www.olympics.org.

London Development Agency (2008) Annual Report 'Employment and Skills Activity Associated with the 2012 Games', London: LDA, January.

Jowell, T. (2008) 'Foreword' in *Before, During and After: Making the Most of the London 2012 Games*, London: HMO, DCMS.

MacAloon, J (2008) '"Legacy" and Managerial/Magical Discourse in Contemporary Olympic Affairs', paper presented at The International Journal of the History of Sport Conference *Olympic Legacies*, 29–30 March, St Antony's College, Oxford.

Millet, L. (1996) 'Olympic Villages after the Games', in Moragas, M, Llines, M. and Kidd, B. (eds) *Olympic Villages, International Symposium on Olympic Villages*, Lausanne: IOC.

Moragas, M., Kennett, C. and Puig, N. (eds) (2003) *The Legacy of the Olympic Games: 1984–2000*, proceedings of the International Symposium, 14–16 November 2002, Lausanne: International Olympic Committee.

nef (2008) 'Fool's Gold', New Economics Foundation, http://www.neweconomics.org/gen/z_sys_publicationdetail.aspx?pid=251.

Poynter, G. (2006) *From Beijing to Bow Bells: Measuring the Olympic Effect*, London East Research Papers in Urban Studies, London: University of East London.

Preuss, H (2004) *The Economics of Staging the Olympics – A Comparison of the Games 1972–2008*, Cheltenham: Edward Elgar.

Preuss, H.(2007) 'The Conceptualisation and Measurement of Mega Sport Event Legacies', *Journal of Sport and Tourism* 12(3–4) August–November: 207–27.

Raco, M. and Henderson, S. (2005) 'From Problem Places to Opportunity Spaces: The Practices of Sustainable Regeneration', paper presented to the SUBR:IM conference, 1 March.

Roche, M. (2000) *Mega-events and Modernity*, London: Routledge.
Theodoraki, E., Malfas, M. and Hoolihan, B. (2005) A Critical Evaluation of the 'Olympic Games Global Impact', programme of the International Olympic Committee, Loughborough University: Institute of Sport and Leisure Policy, mimeo.
Wade, R. (1990) *Governing the Market*, Oxford: Princeton University Press.

Index